From Medieval Frontiers to Early Modern Borders in Central and South-Eastern Europe

Eastern and Central European Studies I

Edited by Christian Gastgeber and Alexandru Simon

Vol. 6

PETER LANG

Florin Nicolae Ardelean / Liviu Cîmpeanu /
Romulus Gelu Fodor / Livia Magina (Eds.)

From Medieval Frontiers to Early Modern Borders in Central and South-Eastern Europe

PETER LANG

Bibliographic Information published by the Deutsche Nationalbibliothek
The Deutsche Nationalbibliothek lists this publicationin the Deutsche Nationalbibliografie; detailed bibliographic data is available in the internet at http://dnb.d-nb.de.

Library of Congress Cataloging-in-Publication Data
A CIP catalog record for this book has been applied for at the Library of Congress.

Cover image: Danubius, Fluvius Europae Maximus a Fontibus ad Ostia.../
The Danube, from its sources to the Black Sea
Willem Janszoon Blaeu, 1635, copper engraving
(Kultur- und Dokumentationszentrum der Landsmannschaft der Banater Schwaben, Ulm).

ISSN 2191-8864
ISBN 978-3-631-88011-1 (Print)
E-ISBN 978-3-631-88012-8 (E-PDF)
E-ISBN 978-3-631-88013-5(EPUB)
DOI 10.3726/b19870

Peter Lang – Berlin · Bruxelles · Lausanne · New York · Oxford

This publication has been peer reviewed.

www.peterlang.com

The publication of this volume was supported by a grant of the Romanian Ministry of Education and Research, CNCS – UEFISCDI, project number PN-III-P1-1.1-TE-2019-0457, within PNCDI III; From Medieval Frontiers to Early Modern Borders. The Military organization of the Western Parts of the Transylvanian Principality in the XVI-XVII centuries.

Content

List of Contributors

Florin Nicolae Ardelean

Academic Cultural Heritage Department,

Babeş-Bolyai University,

Cluj-Napoca, Romania

florin.ardelean@ubbcluj.ro

Zoltán Péter Bagi

Municipal Archive of Győr,

Győr, Hungary

zoliszeged@gmail.com

Liviu Cîmpeanu

Institute of Social Sciences and Humanities,

Romanian Academy,

Sibiu, Romania

Academic Cultural Heritage Department,

Babeş-Bolyai University,

Cluj-Napoca, Romania

liviucimpeanu@yahoo.com

Florina Ciure

Țării Crişurilor Museum,

Oradea, Romania

florinaciure@gmail.com

Ovidiu Cristea

„Nicolae Iorga" Institute of History,

Romanian Academy,

Bucharest, Romania

cristeao@gmail.com

Izsán Csaba

Babeş-Bolyai University,

Cluj-Napoca, Romania

izsan_csaba@yahoo.com

Julia Derzsi

Institute of Social Sciences and Humanities,

Romanian Academy,

Sibiu, Romania

jderzsi@yahoo.com

Gelu Fodor

Academic Cultural Heritage Department,

Babeş-Bolyai University,

Cluj-Napoca, Romania

fodorgelu2015@gmail.com

Csaba Horváth

Babeş-Bolyai University,
Cluj-Napoca, Romania
horvathcs93@gmail.com
Zoltan Iusztin
National Museum of Banat,
Timişoara, Romania
iusztin.z@gmail.com
Adrian Magina
Titu Maiorescu Institute for Banatian Studies,
Romanian Academy,
Timişoara, Romania
Museum of the Highland Banat,
Reşiţa, Romania
adimagina@gmail.com
Livia Magina
Museum of the Highland Banat,
Reşiţa, Romania
Academic Cultural Heritage Department,
Babeş-Bolyai University,
Cluj-Napoca, Romania
maginalivia@gmail.com
Jelena Ilić Mandić

Institute of History,

Belgrade, Serbia

j.ilic@yahoo.com

Gizella Nemeth

Centro Studi Adria-Danubia,

Duino Aurisina, Trieste, Italy

adriadanubia@gmail.com

Adriano Papo

Centro Studi Adria-Danubia,

Duino Aurisina, Trieste, Italy

adriadanubia@gmail.com

Ioan-Aurel Pop

Romanian Academy, Bucharest

Babeş-Bolyai University,

Cluj-Napoca, Romania

ioanleruapop@gmail.com

Alexandru Simon

Romanian Academy,

Centre for Transylvanian Studies,

Cluj-Napoca, Romania

alexandrusimon2003@gmail.com

Nándor Virovecz

Eötvös Loránd University,

Budapest, Hungary

virovecz@gmail.com

Introduction

This volume gathers a variety of essays and studies on the topic of territorial boundaries (frontiers/borders) in Central and South-East Europe, from the late middle ages (fifteenth century) until the end of the early modern period (eighteenth century). The initiative of collecting a series of scientific contributions on this broad subject was conceived as a fundamental activity within a research project entitled: *From Medieval Frontiers to Early Modern Borders. The Military Organization of the Western Parts of the Transylvanian Principality in the XVI-XVII centuries* (PN-III-P1-1.1-TE-2019-0457). Analysing the particular case of the Western frontier of Transylvania in a broader, regional context, was the main reason behind this initiative. A comparative perspective is fundamental for a better assessment of social, economic and military dynamic of borderlands.

The research of frontiers/borders has a long tradition in historiography. Understanding political, social and cultural boundaries, in the past of humanity, have been constant preoccupations in modern historical writing. Undoubtedly, the essay of Frederick Jackson Turner, *The Significance of Frontier in American History*,[1] had a fundamental role in establishing a new theoretical paradigm which inspired both similar approaches[2] and constructive criticism. Many scholars have made efforts to establish "clear borders" between the terms and concepts used when describing territorial delimitations in historical writing. Although unanimity is far from being achieved, there is a tendency to use the term frontier for the premodern world, while the term border has a clear connection with modern times and the development of modern cartography. Borders are usually

1 Frederick Jackson Turner, *The Frontier in American History* (New York: Henry Holt and Company, 1920), 1–39.

2 A very popular thesis, following a similar interpretative pattern, was developed by the Austrian historian, Paul Wittek, regarding the early expansion of the Ottoman Empire, Paul Wittek, *The Rise of the Ottoman Empire* (London: Royal Asiatic Society, 1938); on the influence and relevance of Wittek's theory see, Colin Heywood, "The Frontier in Ottoman History: Old Ideas and New Myths," in *Frontiers in Question: Eurasian Borderlands, 700–1700*, eds. Daniel Power and Naomi Standen (New York: St Martin's Press, 1999), 228–50.

characterized as static, precise and restrictive, while frontiers are often defined as contact zones, permeable and fluid.[3]

Recent research on the topic of late medieval and early modern boundaries has been focused on identifying and defining a process of transition from vague and entangled medieval frontiers to static and well-defined modern borders. This is also one of the major objectives of this collective volume of studies. Most scholars have emphasized the complex nature of this transition process and its long duration. Furthermore, the linearization of borders is viewed an even longer phenomenon, one which transcends the chronological limits of the early modern period.[4]

The study of boundaries (frontiers/borders) is relevant for understanding how people built their sense of identity and how political control was exercised.[5] Late medieval and early modern political boundaries indicated the physical limits of state authority in terms of jurisdiction and tax collection.[6] This is the reason why many scientific inquiries on the nature of political boundaries were influenced by two fundamental questions: Who exercised authority in the borderlands of medieval and early modern states? What was the relation between central authority and local elites on the matter of frontier management?

The medieval Kingdom of Hungary has an interesting dynamic of central vs. local authority in the borderlands. According to Nora Berend, the Hungarian

---

3 David Abulafia, "Introduction: Seven Types of Ambiguity, c. 1100–c. 1500," in *Medieval Frontiers: Concepts and Practices*, eds. David Abulafia and Nora Berend (London and New York: Routledge, 2016), 1–34; Daniel Power, "Frontiers: Terms, Concepts, and the Historians of Medieval and Early Modern Europe," in *Frontiers in Question: Eurasian Borderlands, 700- 1700*, eds. Daniel Power and Naomi Standen (New York: St Martin's Press, 1999), 1–13; Christian Langer, Manuel Fernández-Götz, "Boundaries, Borders and Frontiers: Contemporary and Past Perspectives," in *Political and Economic Interaction on the Edge of Early Empires*, ed. David A. Warburton, *eTopoi: Journal for Ancient Studies*, Special Volume 7 (2020): 33–47.

4 Kerry Goettlich, "The rise of linear borders in world politics," *European Journal of International Relations*, 25 /1 (2019): 203–28.

5 Power, "Frontiers: Terms, Concepts," 1.

6 Reingard Esser, Steven G. Ellis, "Introduction: Border Regions in early Modern Europe," in *Frontier and Border Regions in Early Modern Europe*, eds. Reingard Esser, Steven G. Ellis (Hanover: Wehrhahn Verlag, 2013), 7–17; A good example of political boundaries perceived as limits of juridical authority and taxation is provided by the article of Christopher Maginn, "Beyond the Pale: Regional Government and the Tudor conquest of Ireland," in *Frontier and Border Regions in Early Modern Europe*, eds. Reingard Esser, Steven G. Ellis (Hanover: Wehrhahn Verlag, 2013), 39–57.

kings exerted more political control over the borders than the hinterland of their realm, for as long as they sustained an active policy of expansion.[7] The Mongol Invasion of 1241 determined a transfer of responsibility regarding the frontier of the kingdom, from central authority to local structures. In the particular case of Transylvania, the frontier along the Carpathians was consolidated through military colonisations and by building a network of fortifications.[8]

In the Eastern half of Europe, in many cases, frontiers were vast and sparsely populated areas. From this point of view they can be defined as "frontiers of settlement", in analogy with the "North American model" of Frederick Jackson Turner.[9] Colonisation in the borderlands was always encouraged by central authorities and was perceived as an efficient way of exploiting local resources and consolidating military defence.[10]

The importance of local elites in managing the frontier has also been emphasized in the case of the Ottoman Empire. The European frontier in particular had a special status within the imperial administrative system. The rule of these regions was entrusted to "marcher lords" (*uc begleri*) descendants of prominent state-founding dynasties such as Evrenosoğlu, Mihaloğlu, Turahanğlu, Ishakoğlu, and Malkoçoğlu, who enjoyed a high degree of autonomy. Their authority was hereditary and they commanded large military retinues. Architectural patronage was another important feature of their authority.[11] The metaphor "ottoman wild

---

7 Nora Berend, "Hungary „the Gate of Christendom," in *Medieval Frontiers: Concepts and Practices*, eds. David Abulafia and Nora Berend (London and New York: Routledge, 2016), 200.

8 Adrian A. Rusu, *Castelarea carpatică: Fortificațiile și cetățile din Transilvania și teritoriile învecinate (sec. XIII-XIV)* (Cluj Napoca: Editura Mega, 2005), 295–312.

9 Power, "Frontiers: Terms, Concepts," 6–11.

10 An interesting case study which underlines these aspects is provided by Žemaitija, a region situated between Western Prussia (territory of the Teutonic Order until 1525) and the Grand Duchy of Lithuania, see Stephen C. Rowell, "The Lithuano-Prussian forest frontier, c. 1422–1600," in *Frontiers in Question: Eurasian Borderlands, 700–1700*, eds. Daniel Power and Naomi Standen (New York: St Martin's Press, 1999), 182–209.

11 Among the more recent contributions on this subject, see Mariya Kiprovska, "Shaping the Ottoman Borderland: The Architectural Patronage of the Frontier Lords from the Mihaloğlu Family," *Bordering Early Modern Europe*, eds. Maria Baramova, Grigor Boykov, Ivan Parvev (Wiesbaden: Harrassowitz Verlag, 2015), 185–220; Mariya Kiprovska, "Agents of Conquest: Frontier Lords' Extended Households as Actors in the Ottoman Conquest of the Balkans," Revue des études sud-est européennes, LIX (2021): 79–104.

west" used by Nikolay Antov to describe the Balkan frontier of the Ottoman Empire highlights a complex social and military situation. One of the most interesting issues raised by Antov in his recent monograph is the settlement of Muslim communities in Deliorman („Wild Forest") and Gerlovo areas. This colonization policy is fundamental in understanding the perception of central authority on the matter of frontier defence and management.[12]

Late medieval and early modern political boundaries in Central and South-East Europe were strongly influenced by Ottoman expansion and the subsequent confrontation with the other major political actors in the region. The topic has been treated at both macro- and micro-historical levels, from various perspectives. Although a thorough overview of this historiographical issue is beyond the scope of our short introductive study, we would like to underline, in a selective manner, some of the most relevant recent contributions on this subject. From the Ottoman perspective, Gábor Ágoston provides a survey of the wars waged by the sultans in Europe. Rethinking Paul Wittek's theory on the Holy War (*Gâza*) as a primary method of conquest, the author analyses the complicated mechanism of warfare, involving political, social, economic and technical factors (such as the wide use of gunpowder) that determined the (almost) constant shifting of the Ottoman frontiers towards Central Europe, between the fourteenth and the early eighteenth century.[13] In a mirror perspective, Tamás Pálosfalvi reveals how the medieval kingdom of Hungary struggled against the constant onslaught of the Ottoman Empire, from the battle of Nicopolis (1396) to the battle of Mohács (1526). One of his most interesting conclusions is that the almost constant state of "frontier warfare" eroded the human and material resources of the Realm of Saint Stephen, and determined the final outcome of the Ottoman-Hungarian confrontation.[14] This perspective is completed by the work of Géza Pálffy on the Hungarian Kingdom between the Habsburg Monarchy and the Ottoman Empire, from 1526 to 1711. After a complicated dynastic struggle with the Szapolyai Dynasty and the loss of the central parts of the realm to the Sublime Porte (1541), the Habsburgs strengthened their positions in Hungary by establishing a military frontier, delimited by fortresses with permanent garrisons, provided by the *hinterland* and divided in several military provinces

12 Nikolay Antov, *The Ottoman "Wild West": The Balkan Frontier in the Fifteenth and Sixteenth Centuries* (Cambridge, New York: Cambridge University Press, 2017).

13 Gábor Ágoston, *The Last Muslim Conquest. The Ottoman Empire and its Wars in Europe* (Princeton-Oxford: Princeton University Press, 2021), 664 p.

14 Tamás Pálosfalvi, *From Nicopolis to Mohács. A History od the Ottoman-Hungaria Warfare, 1389–1526* (Leiden-Bostol: Brill, 2018), 504 p.

or captaincies.[15] This early "military border" was constantly put to the test by the troops of the Crescent, as demonstrated by the example of the Ottoman siege of Szigetvár, in 1566. The proceedings of the conference that commemorated this important event in 2016, have been gathered into a volume edited by Pál Fodor, in which researchers from the United States, England, France, Spain, Austria, Croatia, Hungary and Turkey evoked not only the historical event, but also the main political actors who struggled for supremacy on the Christian-Ottoman border in Central Europe, in the mid-sixteenth century.[16] Another successful attempt to overcome the one-sided perspective on the Habsburg-Ottoman frontier in Hungary was made by David Geza and Pál Fodor with a volume of essays published in 2000. Motivated by the need to make "a more realistic assessment of the significance of the Habsburg-Hungarian-Ottoman frontier" this volume offers a comprehensive perspective on this vast borderland, stretching across Central and South East Europe. The frontier is described and defined as an area of contacts and disputes, a permeable space where two different civilizations interacted for a very long time. The studies emphasize the importance of border military organization and the defense systems on both sides of the frontier, and, of course, the variety of interactions between Christians and Muslims. The issues like Hungarian defense before the battle of Mohács or the „military revolution" created new research paths reconsidering the military frontier perspective.[17] Focusing on the more particular issue of ransom slavery, David Geza and Pál Fodor have edited another collective volume which sheds light on this dominant aspect of frontier life.[18] The monograph of Klára Hegyi on the military organization of the Ottoman frontier in Hungary represents another fundamental contribution to the overall understanding of political boundaries in Central and South East Europe. From a methodological point of view, the analysis of both Ottoman and Christian sources, offers an integrative approach to this complex subject.[19]

---

15 Géza Pálffy, *Hungary Between Two Empires 1526–1711* (Bloomington, Indiana: Indiana University Press, 2021), 284 p.

16 *The Battle for Central Europe. The Siege of Szigetvár and the Death of Süleyman the Magnificent and Nicholas Zrinyi (1566)*, ed. Pál Fodor (Leiden-Boston: Brill, 2018), 569 p.

17 *Ottomans, Hungarians, and Habsburgs in Central Europe. The Military Confines in the Era of Ottoman Conquest*, ed. Pál Fodor and Geza David (Leiden; Boston; Köln: Brill, 2000).

18 *Ransom Slavery along the Ottoman Borders (Early Fifteenth–Early Eighteenth Centuries)*, eds. Géza Dávid and Pál Fodor (Leiden; Boston; Köln: Brill, 2000).

19 Klára Hegy, *The Ottoman military organization in Hungary. Fortresses, fortress garrisons and finances* (Berlin: Klaus Schwarz Verlag, 2018).

A more eastern perspective is provided by the work of Ovidiu Cristea and Liviu Pilat on the Romanian Principalities, as border(land)s of Christendom in the context of the Late Crusade. Located on the eastern flank of Christian (i.e. Catholic) Europe, both Moldavia and Wallachia had to seek the political and military support of the neighbouring realms of Hungary, Poland, and even Venice, who had economic interests in the Black Sea, in order to face the ever growing Ottoman threat.[20] Later on, the same authors approached the issue of frontiers in the north-western Black Sea region, in a volume entitled *From Pax Mongolica to Pax Ottomanica*. Several researchers from Poland and Romania revealed the role of these borderland regions, especially of Moldavia and Wallachia, in politics, warfare and trade, between the thirteenth and the late sixteenth centuries.[21]

The problem of boundaries in history is strongly connected to the idea of cultural and technological transfer. Frontiers and borders were never able (or meant) to stop the circulation of people, goods and knowledge. On the contrary, medieval and early modern frontiers are often characterized as areas of contact and exchange between states, communities and civilizations. Form the conceptual perspective of "entangled history" (*histoire croisée*) borderlands can be seen as privileged areas of interconnectedness and trans-cultural exchange.[22] This methodological approach has inspired the first section of our volume, entitled: *Entangled Frontiers*. The first article, written by Ioan Aurel Pop and Alexandru Simon, analyses two diplomatic reports sent on 6 March 1476 by Giorgio Passelis and Carlo Visconti from Bologna to Galeazzo Maria Sforza, duke of Milan, describing the victory of Prince Stephen the Great of Moldavia over the Ottoman host at Vaslui, in early January. These sources reveal an extensive network of political and strategic interests which transcended the frontiers of Central and Eastern European states. Faced with the increasing Ottoman threat, European monarchs and statesmen adjusted their perception of political boundaries.

---

20 Liviu Pilat, Ovidiu Cristea, *The Ottoman Threat and Crusading on the Eastern Borders of Christendom during the 15th Century*, (Leiden-Boston: Brill, 2018), 337 p.

21 *From Pax Mongolica to Pax Ottomanica. War, Religion and Trade in the Northwestern Black Sea Region (14th–16th Centuries)*, eds. Ovidiu Cristea, Liviu Pilat (Leiden-Boston: Brill, 2020), 324 p.

22 Michael Werner, Bénédicte Zimmermann, "Beyond Comparison: Historie Croisée and the Challenge of Reflexivity," *History and Theory* 45 (February 2006): 30–50; for the relevance of this methodological approach to the research of early modern borders, see Esser, Ellis, "Introduction: Border Regions," 8–9.

The economic impact of warfare on the southern frontier of the Hungarian Kingdom during the last decades of the fifteenth century represents the subject of the article by Zoltan Iusztin. Focusing on the particular case of Ferenc Haraszti, ban of Bosnia, the author underlines the difficult task entrusted to the high ranking officials of the Hungarian borderlands. Despite receiving financial (yet, insufficient) support from the royal treasury, Haraszti asked King Wladislas II to dismiss him from the office, after only one year of service, because he lacked the means to defend his fortresses against the relentless attacks of the Turks. This case study reveals the critical situation of the Hungarian frontier, slowly collapsing under Ottoman pressure in spite of the efforts made by both royal authority and local elites.

The following article, signed by Adrian Magina, offers a vivid depiction of daily life in a frontier area constantly threatened by the devastating effects of war during the fifteenth century and the first half of the sixteenth century. The author of this paper focuses on a section of the southern frontier of the Hungarian Kingdom, delimited by the rivers Danube, Mureş and Tisza, later known as "the Banat". Both official and narrative sources reveal that raids were far more damaging than large scale campaigns and, as a consequence, many settlements were abandoned and entire areas were depopulated. To counterbalance these effects, Hungarian kings encouraged the settlement of newcomers, especially Serbs who decided to flee from the territories occupied by the Turks. Thus, the author argues that in some cases late medieval frontiers were areas dominated by violent contacts with a strong economic and demographic impact.

Starting from a similar social and demographic perspective, Livia Magina offers a thorough overview of cross-border mobility, in the second half of the seventeenth century. The new territorial gains of the Ottomans caused a significant migration, affecting nobles and commoners alike, towards the Transylvanian hinterland. The author identifies two main routes of refuge: from the Banat of Lugoj-Caransebeş (occupied by the Ottomans in 1658) towards Haţeg and Hunedoara, and from Oradea (conquered in 1660) towards the towns of Turda and Dej. The newcomers were greeted with mixed feelings by locals, sympathy being accompanied by fear and envy. Thus, the refugees anxiously awaited the liberation of their homelands, in order to recover their lost possessions, The author of this paper reveals not only the political and military context in which the inhabitants of the borderlands sought refuge in Transylvania, and their status in the new settlements, but also the actual hardships of such a difficult exodus. All these details reflect the immediate consequences of the Ottoman conquest of the Transylvanian borderlands, in the second half of the seventeenth century.

After the battle of Mohács (1526) and the conquest of Buda (1541), the Ottoman-Habsburg conflict in Central Europe entered into a new phase. The main focus of military and diplomatic efforts, on both sides, was the vast frontier stretching from the shores of the Adriatic Sea in the West to the Carpathian Mountains in the East. The Habsburgs adopted a predominantly defensive strategy by building a vast network of modern (bastioned) fortifications.[23] The preliminary phase of this ample process constitutes the subject of the essay written by Nándor Virovecz, focusing on the northern parts of the Hungarian Kingdom. The author underlines the importance of local elites and communities in managing a frontier where war became a part of everyday life. A militarized society developed on both sides of this disputed borderlands, with a significant proportion of its members engaged in violent contacts, plunder raids and ransom slavery.

An article dedicated to the issues of frontiers and border defence in eighteenth century Transylvania, by Gelu Fodor, concludes the first section of the volume. Analysing the relation between local and central institutions on the matter of frontier management, the author identifies a radical shift of authority in favour of the former. The overall process of centralization in the Habsburg Monarchy was felt particularly strong on the edges of the empire, accelerating the process of transition from "entangled frontiers" to modern, linear borders.

As several of the articles from the first section have demonstrated, late medieval and early modern boundaries in Central and South-East Europe were affected by prolonged military confrontations. Narrative and official sources offer an abundance of details regarding both conventional (campaigns, sieges, pitched battles) and irregular (raids, ambushes, skirmishes) forms of warfare in these areas. The "armed men", a dominant figure in the borderlands, represents the subject of the second section of our volume. Going beyond the traditional approach of military history, these articles bring under scrutiny various aspects like: the economic and social impact of military presence on the frontiers, the

23 On the importance of the Habsburg defensive policy in Hungary see, Géza Pálffy, "The Origins and Development of the Border Defence System against the Ottoman Empire in Hungary (Up to the Early Eighteenth Centrury)," in *Ottomans, Hungarians and Habsburgs in Central Europe. The Military Confines in the Era of Ottoman Conquest*, eds. Géza Dávid, Pál Fodor (Leiden; Boston: Brill, 2000), 3–71; Géza Pálffy, "The Habsburg Defense System in Hungary against the Ottomans in the Sixteenth Century: A Catalyst of Military Development in Central Europe," in *Warfare in Eastern Europe, 1500–1800*, ed. Brian J. Davies (Leiden; Boston: Brill, 2000), 35–61.

transfer of military knowledge and technology and the social background of those drafted into borderland armies.

The first essay of this section, signed by Liviu Cîmpeanu, presents in great detail the military obligations of the Transylvanian-Saxons. Colonized on the south-eastern frontiers of the Hungarian kingdom, beginning with the twelfth century, these communities were able to maintain their privileged status through military service. By building fortified settlements and by organizing local militias (sometimes replaced by hired mercenaries), the Transylvanian Saxons were able to defend the interests of the Hungarian Crown in this remote area of the kingdom and oppose, with a certain degree of efficiency, the Ottoman threat.

The slow transition from vague frontiers to well-defined borders was also reflected in the military organization of the borderlands. The speed and versatility of light cavalry units (akıncı and hussars alike), which dominated frontier warfare in late middle ages was of little use against well provisioned bastioned fortifications. The defence of political boundaries relied more and more on such strategic fortified points, which ensured an efficient control over local human and material resources. In this context and also connected with the wide spread of gunpowder weapons, a new type of soldier emerged in these parts of Europe, the guardsman (*trabant/ drabant/darabont*). The problematic origins, status a role played by these soldiers represent the subject of the following two essays by Florin Nicolae Ardelean and Csaba Izsán. As both authors argue, this widespread denomination stands for a large variety of soldiers, ranging from town guardsmen, hired mercenaries, royal guards to semi-privileged peasant-soldiers. This new type of infantry, with the above mentioned typological variations, was widely spread in Central and South-East Europe, from Bohemia and the Habsburg hereditary provinces to Hungary, Transylvania, Wallachia, Moldavia and Ragusa. This is a clear situation of cross-border transfer in the field of military knowledge and technology, one that was strongly connected to the new principles of frontier defence and management.

Csaba Horvath's research on the 45th Wallachian Border Guard dragoon regiment adds up to the efforts undertaken by the Romanian historiography to shed light on various aspects regarding the creation of the Transylvanian Military Border system in the Eighteenth century. By reconstructing the history of a less studied regiment and offering details about its staff composition, this study fills a gap in an otherwise researched area.

Jelena Ilić Mandić's study also explores aspects regarding the creation of the Habsburg military border in the Eighteenth century, but shifts the focus of analysis from the Transylvanian regiments to the process of militarization in the Banat area. The author thoroughly explores the impact that the militarization process had on the local population (i.e., resettlements, colonization of veterans, resistance to militarization and emigration in the neighboring areas), but also depicts the complex changes that came with a military administration.

Fortifications can be defined as frontier-based institutions,[24] with a complex material and human component. Fortresses, castles, outposts or fortified settlements were the most visible landmarks in the borderlands. Sieges, followed by the conquest or loss (depending on the perspective) of fortifications were the most remarkable events in the daily life of frontiers. These fundamental aspects represent the focus of the last section in our volume.

The multiple functions of a border fortification are presented in the essay of Julia Derzsi. Analysing the case of Turnu Roşu, a fort on the southern border of Transylvania, the author identifies the various roles fulfilled by such a fortification. In spite of its modest size, the tower defended one of the most important mountain passes into Wallachia and served, at the same time, as customs post and postal hub. The analysis of the background and careers of those who served in the tower represents another important contribution to understanding the social component of sixteenth century frontiers.

The last essays of the volume present four sieges from the sixteenth and seventeenth centuries, which offer a comprehensive perspective on the conduct of siege warfare in early modern Central Europe: the Ottoman siege of Eger from 1552 (Gizella Nemeth, Adriano Papo), the Ottoman conquest of Hegyesd and the subsequent Habsburg-Hungarian siege in 1562 (Zoltán Péter Bagi), the unsuccessful Ottoman siege of Oradea from 1598 (Ovidiu Cristea) and the conquest of Ottoman Oradea by the Habsburgs in 1691–1692 (Florina Ciure). In the sixteenth century bastioned fortifications were quite common in these parts of Europe and offered a significant tactical advantage to the defenders. Major fortifications were rarely taken by force. Besieging armies were usually able to achieve their objective when garrisons decided to surrender. Well provisioned fortresses were able to withstand the assault of considerably larger military forces. Eger and Oradea were major fortifications able to resist prolonged sieges (Eger 38 days, Oradea 40 days), while Hegysed was a smaller fortress on the shores of Lake Balaton, which was conquered after a surprise attack by the Turks. The new owners of the fortress were able to resist for 10 days before deciding to surrender. By the end of the seventeenth century, the military operations required for a

24 Naomi Standen, "Nine case studies of premodern frontiers," in *Frontiers in Question: Eurasian Borderlands, 700- 1700*, eds. Daniel Power and Naomi Standen (New York: St Martin's Press, 1999), 24.

successful siege were more complex and time consuming, as the Habsburg siege of Oradea from 1691 to 1692 clearly illustrates. The size of armies had increased considerably although the most commonly used siege techniques were roughly the same: blockades, sustained artillery fire, mining tunnels, local assaults etc. The Habsburg-Ottoman confrontation continued to be the dominant feature of Central and South-East European politics but the perception on boundaries was gradually changing. With each passing decade, the vast borderlands of previous centuries were being reduced to precise borders defended by armies with a higher degree of professionalism.

The Editors

Entangled Frontiers

Ioan-Aurel Pop and Alexandru Simon

March 1475:

The Italian Reception of Warfare on the Eastern Frontiers of Christendom

Abstract: In April 1475, the Venetian envoy, Geronimo Zorzi, on his way to Mehmed II, met with Mara Branković, the sultan's – favourite – stepmother. Mara had actively tried to bring – via talks on Mount Athos as well – an end to the Venetian-Ottoman war that had begun in 1463. According to her, the Turks had never suffered a greater defeat than the – recent – one in *Valachia*. There had never been a better time for negotiations between the *Serenissima* and the High Porte. Based on a series of reports issued the "Bologna station" of the Milanese duchy of Galeazzo Maria Sforza, the paper explores the reality, as well as the reception of assertions. Although the main objectives (targets) of the "station" were Italian, French and Burgundian, anti-Ottoman warfare in the East received much attention because its outcome was – justifiably – deemed as power shifter in the Italian Peninsula, foremost due to the prolonged involvement of the Papacy and of the Republic of Venice, who further did not hesitate to spread "fake-news" about Ottoman defeats in order to fortify her Italian stand and deflect attention from her real problems. The reports from March 1475 reveal that the Western reception of the unquestionably major victory at Vaslui was prepared in the East, not only by Matthias Corvinus of Hungary, but also – and already – by Stephen III of Moldavia, his vassal and the true victor over the Turks. Consequently, news then reached Rome that duke *Stephen voivode*, appointed king of Bosnia by Matthias, was on his way to the Holy City to be crowned by Pope Sixtus IV. A king of Bosnia appointed by Matthias in 1471 was indeed on his way to Rome, but he was Nicholas Újlaki (Iločki), the hostile ally of the Hunyadi family. He was later depicted in the *Corsia Sistina* as the *King of Bosnia and Wallachia*.

Keywords: Mehmed II, Galeazzo Maria Sforza, Matthias Corvinus, Stephen III of Moldavia, Nicholas Újlaki, Milan, Venice, Wallachia Bosnia, Crusading, Propaganda, Disinformation

Introduction

In April 1475, the Venetian envoy, Geronimo Zorzi, on his way to Mehmed II, met with Mara Branković, the sultan's – favourite – stepmother. Mara had actively tried to bring – via talks on Mount Athos as well[1] – an end to the

1 Mihailo Popović, "The Holy Mountain of Athos as Contact Zone between Venice and the Ottoman Empire in the 15th Century," in *Imperium Bulgariae. Studia in honorem*

Venetian-Ottoman war that had begun in 1463.[2] According to her, the Turks had never suffered a greater defeat than the – recent – one in *Valachia*. There had never been a better time for negotiations between the *Serenissima* and the High Porte.[3] The advice was taken and a truce was concluded between the warring empires.[4] Afterwards, among quite many others,[5] Giovanni Maria Filelfo,[6] the son of the significantly more famous humanist Francesco Filelfo,[7] convincingly argued – in his abruptly turned anti- from pro-Ottoman treatise *Amyris*[8] – that this truce allowed the Ottomans to take Genoese Caffa in the Crimea (June 1475) and to attack Stephen III of Moldavia, who had defeated them at Vaslui in January, that same year.[9] The Italian aftermath of the battle of Vaslui is – once more[10] – worth a closer inspection.

annorum LX Georgii N. Nikolov, ed. Angel N. Nikolov (Sofia: Университетско издателство „Св. Климент Охридски, 2018), 774–83.

2 Franz Babinger, *Mehmed the Conqueror and his Time*, ed. William C. Hickmann (Princeton, NJ: University Press, 1978), 221–32, 249–53.

3 [Domenico Malipiero,] *Annali veneti dall'anno 1457 al 1500 del Senatore Domenico Malipiero ordinati e abbreviati dal senatore Francesco Longo*, ed. Agostino Sagredo (Florence: Giovanni Pietro Vieusseux, 1843), 112. The report sent by Zorzi reached the Laguna before 9 May 1475.

4 An overview: Kenneth M. Setton, *The Papacy and Levant (1204–1571)*, II. *The Fifteenth Century* (Philadelphia, PA: The American Philosophical Society, 1978), 319–26.

5 For the (anti-Venetian) Italian "trend" (Ottoman matters included), see also Giustiniano Degli Azzi, "Un frammento inedito della Cronaca di Benedetto Dei," *Archivio Storico Italiano* 110, 1 (1952): 99–113 (111–113).

6 Still valuable Guillaume Favre, "Vie de Jean-Marius Philelfe," Guillaume Favre, *Mélanges d'histoire littéraire*, ed. Jacques Adert, I (Geneva: Ramboz et Schuchardt, 1856), 9–221, at 176–218 (177–178).

7 *Francesco Filelfo: Man of Letter*, ed. Jeroen De Keyser (Leiden-Boston: Brill, 2019).

8 *Amyris. De vita et gestis Mahometi Turcorum imperatoris*, ed. Aldo Manetti (Bologna: Pàtron, 1978), 196–97, 202.

9 See already Andrei Pippidi, "1475: atacul otoman asupra Cetății Albe," *Analele Putnei* 7, no. 1 (2011): 29–36.

10 Ovidiu Cristea, "The Aftermath of a Victory: An Episode of Stephen the Great's Diplomacy after the Battle of Vaslui (10 January 1475)," *Banatica* 28-II (2018): 453–63.

The "Milanese Station" in Bologna

On 6 March 1476, two reports were sent from Bologna to Galeazzo Maria Sforza, the duke of Milan, on the recent defeat of the Turks in *Valachia*.[11] The defeat had just been confirmed by 12 Wallachian and Hungarian knights. Some of them had even fought in the great battle in *Valachia*. The knights had passed that day through Bologna on their way to the Jubilee in Rome.[12]

The most elaborate report was authored by the Bolognese notary, Giorgio Pasellis,[13] former Milanese commissioner in Lugano, as well as former governor of Corsica.[14] The second *dispaccio* was signed by Carlo Visconti,[15] an experienced diplomat, who also controlled the Milanese print for his duke.[16] Pasellis and Visconti were the main figures of the "Milanese station" in Bologna,[17] ruled by Giovanni II Bentivoglio, married to Ginevra, the illegitimate daughter of Alessandro Sforza, the brother of the late Francesco (and thus the first degree cousin of Galeazzo Maria).[18] The main task of the "Milanese station" in Bologna

---

11 Ioan-Aurel Pop, Alexandru Simon, "Regii Bosniei și ai Valahiei la Jubileul de la Roma (1475)," *Analele Academiei Române. Memoriile Secțiunii Istorice*, 5th series, 35 (2015–2020): 9–28.

12 According to the Papal secretary Falvio Biondo as well (1452/1453), it was not unusual for Wallachians to travel to Rome, not only on the occasion of the Jubilee, *Ad Alphonsum Aragonensem serenissimum regem de expeditione in Thurcos Blondus Flavius Forliviensis*, in *Scritti inediti e rari di Flavio Biondo*, ed. Bartolomeo Nogara (Rome: Biblioteca Apostolica Vaticana, 1927), 45.

13 *La società dei notai di Bologna*, ed. Giorgio Tamba (Rome: Ministero per i beni culturali e ambientali, 1988), 219.

14 Paul Schaefer, *Il Sottoceneri nel Medioevo. Contributo alla storiadel Medioevoitaliano* (Lugano: GEP – Ex allievi della scuola politecnica federale, 1954), 361–62; Laura Balletto, "Sullefonti notarili per la storia della Corsica," *Archivio Storico Italiano* 136, no. 1 (1978): 89–112 (107–108).

15 Lydia Cerioni, *La Diplomazia sforzesca nella seconda metà del Quattrocento e i suoi cifrari segreti*, I (Rome: Il Centro di Ricerca Editore, 1970), 252–53.

16 Fabio Cusin, "Impero, Borgogna e politica italiana. L'incontro di Treveri del 1473," *Nuova Rivista Storica* 20 (1934): 34–57 (39); Giovanni Bonifati, *Dal libro manoscritto al libro stampato: Sistemi di mercato a Bologna e Firenze agli albori del capitalismo* (Turin: Rosenberg & Sellier, 2008), 165–66.

17 On these missions (and "stations"): Paolo Margaroli, *Diplomazia e stati rinascimentali. Le ambascerie sforzesche fino alla conclusione della Lega italica (1450–1455)* (Florence: Nuova Italia, 1992).

18 Cecilia M. Ady, *The Bentivoglio of Bologna: A Study in Despotism (Oxford: University Press, 1937); Gaspare de Caro, "Giovanni Bentivoglio," Dizionario Bibliografico degli Italiani 8 (1966), sub voce.*

was to procure mercenaries for Burgundy, Milan's old adversary and new ally through the treaty of Moncalieri, sealed in January 1475.[19]

Two years earlier, at the time of the first major invasion of Wallachia by Stephen III of Moldavia,[20] Carlo Visconti had played an important part in the failure of the talks conducted at the *Reichstag* of Trier between Charles the Bold, duke of Burgundy, and Emperor Frederick III of Habsburg (September-November 1473).[21] Charles failed to receive his desired royal crown from Frederick.[22] Visconti claimed that he had told the Portuguese physician of Frederick that Mary, Charles' daughter, was unhealthy.[23] Consequently, Frederick refused to marry his only son and heir, Maximilian, to Mary, and left Trier in haste, breaking off any ties to duke Charles.

The political (and matrimonial) context was however more complex. The Duchy of Milan was the traditional partner of Louis XI of France (the entente had a weak link: Savoy desired by both parties).[24] Louis was Charles' nemesis. Milan was an imperial fief. This issue was settled only through the marriage between Maximilian and Bianca Maria, Galeazzo Maria's daughter (1493) and the former wife – by proxy – of John, the illegitimate son of Matthias Corvinus

19 *Dépêches des ambassadeurs milanais sur les campagnes de Charles le Hardi, duc de Bourgogne, de 1474 à 1477*, ed. Frédéric Jean Charles de Gingins-La-Sarra, II [*1476–1477*] (Paris-Geneva: Joel Cherbuliez, 1858), 37–38, no. 159.

20 Ştefan S. Gorovei, Maria-Magdalena Székely, *Princeps omni laude maior. O istorie a lui Ştefan cel Mare* (Putna: Muşatinii, 2005), 100–101.

21 Richard J. Walsh, *Charles the Bold and Italy: Politics and Personnel*, ed. Cecil H. Clough (Liverpool: University Press, 2005²), 208–09, 227–28; Jane Black, *Absolutism in Renaissance Milan: Plenitude of Power under the Visconti and the Sforza. 1329–1535* (Oxford: University Press, 2009), 82.

22 Graeme Small, "Of Burgundian Dukes, Counts, Saints and Kings (14 C.E.-c. 1520)," in *The Ideology of Burgundy: The Promotion of National Consciousness. 1364–1565*, ed. D'Arcy Jonathan Dacre Boulton, Jan R. Veenstra (Leiden-Boston: Brill, 2006), 151–194 (174–175); Heribert Müller, "Warum nicht einmal die Herzöge von Burgund das Königtum erlangen wollten und konnten: um 1473," Heribert Müller, *Frankreich, Burgund und das Reich im späten Mittelalter. Ausgewählte Aufsätze* (Tübingen: Mohr Siebeck, 2011), 421–62, at 423, 453.

23 Robert Vaughan, *Charles the Bold: The Last Valois Duke of Burgundy* (Woodbridge: Boydell Press, 2002), 153–54.

24 Vincent Ilardi, "France and Milan, the Uneasy Alliance (1452–1466)," *Gli Sforza a Milano e in Lombardia e i loro rapporti con gli stati italiani ed europei (1450–1535)* (Milan: Cisalpino-Goliardica, 1982), 415–47.

(born precisely in April 1473).[25] Alike his father, Francesco, Galeazzo Maria was concerned to have his rule acknowledged by Frederick.[26] For this reason, the duke had to decline the matrimonial offer of Matthias, the emperor's enemy. In fact, Frederick himself had asked Charles for the meeting in Trier out of fear of potential Burgundian-Hungarian alliance against the emperor.[27]

East and West in Italian Politics and in Anti-Ottoman Warfare

Meanwhile in the East (November 1473), alike Casimir IV Jagiello of Poland,[28] Frederick (to whom Charles had promised that he was to leave on crusade, in exchange for a royal crown) still believed that Vienna held Wallachia against Matthias, through Frederick's *capitaneo*, *vanoida* [!] Stephen of Moldavia.[29] Earlier (in August 1473), Casimir had stated that he counted – again against Matthias – on the *der grosse Walache* (the same Stephen) and on *die hern und stet in Sibenburgen* (the lords and the estates of Transylvania).[30] Furthermore, Matthias was challenged at the time – from the Adriatic – by the Kingdom of Naples,[31] Milan's "strange ally".[32]

Within a year, Matthias escaped from encirclement. For this he had to thank – from East to West – to Stephen III, Venice and Sixtus IV.[33] The voivode stayed at

25 D. M. *Bueno de Mesquita,* Gian Galeazzo Visconti, Duke of Milan (1351–1402): A Study in the Political Career of an Italian Despo*t (Cambridge: University Press, 1941), 154–73.*

26 F. Cusin, "L'impero e la successione degli Sforza ai Visconti," *Archivio Storico Lombardo* 62 (1936): 1–116.

27 Attila Bárány, "Matthias Corvinus and Charles the Bold," *Chronica* 12 (2012): 69–88 (76–77).

28 Şerban Papacostea, "Politica externă a lui Ştefan cel Mare: opţiunea polonă (1459–1472)," *Studii şi Materiale de Istorie Medie* 15 (2007): 13–28 (21–22).

29 *Regesten Kaiser Friedrich III. (1440–1493). Nach Archiven und Bibliotheken geordnet* (= J. F. Böhmer, *Regesta Imperii*, XIII), eds. Heinrich Koller, Paul-Joachim Heinig, Alois Niederstätter, supl. II-1 *Das Taxregister der römischen Kanzlei 1471–1475* (Haus-, Hof- und Staatsarchiv Wien, Hss. weiss 529 und weiss 920), eds. P.-J. Heinig, Ines Grund (Vienna-Cologne-Graz: Böhlau, 2002), 523, no. 3539.

30 Felix Priebatsch, *Politische Correspondenz des Kurfürsten Albrecht Achilles, 1470–1486,* I. *1470–1474* (Leipzig: S. Hirzel, 1894), 556, no. 660.

31 Luka Spoljarić, "Nicholas of Modruš and his *De Bellis Gothorum*: Politics and National History in the Fifteenth-Century Adriatic," *Renaissance Quarterly* 72, 2 (2019): 457–491.

32 Paul M. Dover, "Royal Diplomacy in Renaissance Italy: Ferrante d'Aragona (1458–1494) and his Ambassadors," *Mediterranean Studies* 14 (2005): 57–94.

33 Norman Housley, *Crusading and the Ottoman Threat. 1453–1505* (Oxford: University Press, 2012), 32–34.

the king's side and went to war against Mehmed.[34] Overwhelmed by the Porte, the republic agreed to support and fund Matthias if he fought the sultan.[35] The pope mediated the marriage contract between the son of John Hunyadi and Beatrice, the daughter of Ferdinand of Aragon, king of Naples.[36]

These changes complicated Milan's stand. Sforza Milan had endorsed Sixtus' election in 1471[37] and feared any increase of the power of the Republic of St. Mark.[38] In the winter of 1474–1475, the attention of the duchy, forced to suspend its French relation and to turn to Burgundy, was more than ever focused on the borders between Hungary and the Ottoman Empire.[39]

It was in this context that, on March 6, 1475, Wallachians and Hungarians passed through Bologna on their way to Pope Sixtus IV to whom they brought part of the spoils of war taken after Stephen III of Moldavia's victory over the

---

34 Ovidiu Cristea, Nagy Pienaru, "Țara Românească, Moldova și Bătălia de la Bașkent," *Analele Putnei* 8, 1 (2012): 17–36; Alexandru Simon, "Habsburgs, Jagiellonians and Crusading: The Wallachian Case in the 1470s." *The Jagiellonians in Europe: Dynastic Diplomacy and Foreign Relations*, ed. A. Bárány (Debrecen: University Press, 2016), 53–68.

35 *I viaggi degli ambasciatori veneti Barbaro e Contarini*, eds. Laurence Lockhart, Raimondo Morozzo della Rocca, Maria-Francesca Tiepolo (Rome: Istituto poligrafico dello Stato, 1973), 12–13, 268–69, 299–300; Oliver-Jens Schmitt, *Das venezianische Albanien, 1392–1479* (Munich: Oldenbourg, 2001), 622–28.

36 Ferdinand, enthroned in the same year, 1458, as Matthias, was the illegitimate son of Alfonso V. His reign was constantly challenged by the French Angevines, see Francesco Storti, "*La più bella guerra del mundo*. La partecipazione delle popolazioni alla guerra di successione napoletana (1459–1464)," in *Medioevo, Mezzogiorno, Mediterraneo. Studi in onore di Mario Del Treppo*, eds. Gabriella Rosetti, Giovanni Vitolo, I (Naples; Liguori, 2000), 325–46.

37 Egmont Lee, *Sixtus IV and Men of Letters* (Rome: Edizioni di storia e letteratura, 1978), 31–32. We recall that Sixtus IV was Genoese. Genoa was Milan's vassal. The main harbours of Stephen III were former Genoese colonies (in part).

38 See, for instance, the fears and the innuendos from the days of Pius II and Francesco Sforza, edited by Ludwig von Pastor, *Acta inedita historiam pontificium romanorum praesertim saec. XV, XVI, XVII illustrantia*, I. *1376–1464* (Freiburg-in-Breisgau: Herder, 1904²), 162, no. 127; 170, no. 132.

39 The documents preserved in the Archivio di Stato di Milano, Milan, Archivio Ducale Sforzesco, Potenze Estere series (especially in the *Roma* and *Venezia* collections) reveal that between 1475 and 1476 basically not a single day passed without a news or a rumour related to Mehmed II or to the rulers in his vicinity.

Ottoman army at Vaslui (10 January 1475).[40] The Milanese representatives in Bologna hurried to inform their duke. Galeazzo Maria Sforza had rightfully doubted the veracity of the news on the Wallachian victory due to the practices of Venice,[41] whose main agent at the European border of the Porte Stephen had become.[42]

The Miraculous Battle and Its Unnamed Victor

Giorgio Pasellis' authority in Bologna was undermined by Carlo Visconti[43] and also by Roberto Sanseverino.[44] For Pasellis, the meeting with the Wallachian and Hungarian knights brought a breath of fresh air. He was able to confirm to his master the news that the duke otherwise much distrusted. Some of the information collected by Pasellis was perfectly credible and even true, for instance the ones related to the military operations (as much as the contemporary sources allow us to see).[45] Others were outright exaggerations,[46] above all the size of the attacking Ottoman army and the overall Ottoman casualties, including one major figure, called *Pasha*[47] by the pilgrims.

40 Jan Długosz, *Annales seu cronicae incliti Regni Poloniae* (=*Jan Dlugosii Senioris Canonici Cracoviensis Opera omnia*, XI–XIV), eds. Alexander Przezdziecki, IV (Krakow: [s.n.], 1887), 622.

41 Alexandru Simon, "Anti-Ottoman Warfare and Crusader Propaganda in 1474: New Evidences from the Archives of Milan," *Revue Roumaine d'Histoire* 46, 1–4 (2007): 25–39, (30–31).

42 Ioan-Aurel Pop, Alexandru Simon, "*Ungaria et Valachia*: promisiunile valahe ale Republicii Sfântului Marcu din anii 1470," *Revista Istorică*, NS, 25, 1–2 (2015 [2016]): 5–66.

43 See Annex I.

44 The known condottiere Roberto Sanseverino de Aragon (1418–1487), along whom Pasellis had served in Lugano immediately after the death of Francesco Sforza in March 1466 (Alessio Russo, "Roberto Sanseverino d'Aragona," *Dizionario Biografico degli Italiani* 90 (2017), *sub voce*).

45 See also Alexandru Simon, "În jurul bătăliei de la Vaslui (1474–1475). Considerații asupra relațiilor dintre Moldova, Țara Românească și Regatul Ungariei," *Studia Universitatis "Babeș Bolyai". Historia* 49, 2 (2004): 3–26 (8–11).

46 See in particular Cristea, "The Aftermath of a Victory," 453–63.

47 Possibly Ali Mihaloğlu, bey of Vidin and Smederevo. He had raided Oradea, in February 1474, in retaliation for the support rendered by Matthias to Stephen, who had invaded Wallachia, in November 1473 (Aurel Decei, "Incursiunea (*Akîn*) a lui Mihaloglu Ali Beg asupra Orăzii în anul 1474, pe temeiul istoriei lui Ibn Kemal," in *Sub semnul lui Clio. Omagiu Acad. Prof. Ștefan Pascu*, ed. Nicolae Edroiu (Cluj: Universitatea Babeș-Bolyai, 1974), 296–301).

Nevertheless, the Wallachians denied the capture or even the death of a son of Mehmed II.[48] This denial of a rumour that had rapidly spread came to the advantage of the victors. It lent credibility to their statements on the fallen Ottomans and on the value and on the quantity of the spoils. All in all, for the "servant and slave"[49] of the Milanese duke, the news received from "the said Wallachians, who were at the said defeat of the Turks", signified a triumphant blessing.

Carlo Visconti's report,[50] from the same day, was less exuberant. After briefly summarizing the same data as in Pasellis' message, Visconti, almost bored, concluded: [...] "From this, Your Excellency will make the judgement and the estimate that appears right" [...]. Visconti was more eager to inform the duke of his recent meeting with the brother of Cola Gaetano,[51] a famed *condottiere* who had fled from Milan[52] and now wanted to make amends to Galeazzo Maria.

Both Pasellis and Visconti recorded only the Wallachians as victors of the Turks, although the Wallachian knights, who passed through Bologna on their way to Rome, were accompanied by Hungarian knights and the subjects of Matthias had also fought at Vaslui.[53] The human losses announced by the "Wallachian pilgrims" are therefore even more astonishing. 107.000 Turks had perished and only 2.000 Christian had lost their lives. Obviously, the exaggerations concerning the victory were not the fruit of Matthias Corvinus' propaganda.[54] They originated in Suceava, the capital of Stephen III of Moldavia. Matthias then only added his – fair – royal share.

This was quite justified. For better or for worse, Matthias had supported Stephen since he had started fighting against Mehmed in late 1473. And, less than five days after the Milanese reports from Bologna, word was sent from

48 Since spring 1474, Mehmed had only two living sons: Bayezid (II) and Djem.

49 Federico Piseri, "*Filius et Servitor*. Evolution of Dynastic Consciousness in the Titles and Subscriptions of the Sforza Princes' Familiar Letters," *The Court Historian* 22, 2 (2017): 168–188.

50 See Annex II.

51 For the career of Nicola Gaetano/ Gaetani (Caetani) de Sermoneta: Lorenzo Giustiniani, *Dizionario geografico-ragionato del Regno di Napoli*, VI (Naples: Vincenzo Manfredi, 1803), 123; Jane Stevenson, *Women Latin Poets: Language, Gender, and Authority, from Antiquity to the Eighteenth Century (Oxford: University Press, 2005), 172.*

52 Giacomo/ Gaspare de Caro, future apostolic prothonotary (Guglielmo Caetani, „Gaspare de Caro," *Dizionario Bibliografico degli Italiani* 16 (1973), *sub voce*). Strangely, Visconti did not mention him by his name.

53 Gorovei-Székely, *Princeps omni laude maior*, 112.

54 As postulated for instance by Ștefan S. Gorovei, „Informație, propagandă, mistificare: scrisoarea din 25 ianuarie 1475," *Analele Putnei* 3, 2 (2007): 21–26.

Rome to Mantua that Matthias had regally rewarded Stephen, whose name had been conspicuously left out from the *dispacci* sent by Pasellis and Visconti.[55]

The Royal Coronation in Rome of "Duke Stephen Voivode"

On 11 March 1475, Giampietro Arrivabene, future bishop of Urbino, educated by the humanist Francesco Filelfo,[56] wrote from Rome to Ludovico III *il Turco* Gonzaga.[57] Arrivabene was the ambassador of the margrave of Mantua at the Papal curia,[58] and also served as the secretary of Ludovico's son, Cardinal Francesco Gonzaga.[59] In spring 1462, Francesco had been among the first to learn about the 21.660 victims of Vlad the Impaler, King Matthias' relative (by marriage).[60]

Arrivabene's missive, based on a wide network of informants, was a professional synthesis of the Adriatic *imbroglio* that connected the Balkan Peninsula to the Italian Peninsula.[61] He began by informing his lord of the death of the mistress of the prefect of Rome, Giovanni della Rovere, the nephew of Pope Sixtus IV.[62] The deceased was the illegitimate daughter (previously unknown)

55 It is highly unlikely that the Wallachians failed to mention their lord. Because both rivals did not recall Stephen, the explanation is that his name was disliked already in Milan because of his Venetian association (i.e. "affiliation").

56 Alessandro *Luzio*, Rodolfo Renier, "I *Filelfo* e *l'umanesimo* alla *corte* dei *Gonzaga,*" *Giornale Storico della Letteratura Italiana* 16 (1890): 119–27. Filefo affectionately named Arrivabene *Eutyches*, the happy/ blissful one, a name typical for Roman *liberti*, freed slaves. Filelfo also called Arrivabene *humanissimus* (*Francisci Philelfi Epistolarum Familiarum Libri XXXVII* (Venice: de Gregorijs, 1502), f. 195^{r}).

57 Isabella Lazzarini, "Ludovico III Gonzaga, marchese di Mantova," *Dizionario Bibliografico degli Italiani* 66, (2006), *sub voce.*

58 David S. Chambers, "Giovanni Pietro Arrivabene (1439–1504): Humanistic Secretary and Bishop," *Aevum* 58, 3 (1984), 3: 397–438.

59 I. Lazzarini, "Francesco Gonzaga," *Dizionario Bibliografico degli Italiani* 57 (2002) *sub voce.*

60 Alexandru Simon, „The Pope, the Hunyadis and the Wallachians: The Curious Case of Pius II," *Banatica* 30-II (2020): 59–108.

61 Norman Housley, "Christendom's Bulwark: Croatian Identity and the Response to the Ottoman Advance, Fifteenth to Sixteenth Centuries," *Transactions of the Royal Historical Society, 6th series, 24 (2014): 149–64;* Spoljarić, "Nicholas of Modruš," 476–81.

62 *La quercia dai frutti d'oro. Giovanni Della Rovere (1457–1501) e le origini del potere roveresco*, eds. Marinella Bonvini Mazzanti, Gilberto Piccinini (Ancona: Deputazione di storia patria per le Marche, 2004).

of Ferdinand of Aragon, who ruled over the Papal fief of Naples.[63] Plans were made in the Papal entourage to wed Giovanni[64] to one of the unmarried daughters of Ferdinand's brother-in-law, Giovanni Francesco Marzano, prince of Rossano (imprisoned by Ferdinand).[65] Two of the daughters of Marzano and of Ferdinand's sister, Eleonora Diana, had married in Italy: Maria had wed Antonio Todeschini-Piccolomini, duke of Amalfi and the nephew of Pope Pius II,[66] and Camilla had wed the lord of Pesaro, Costanzo Sforza, the first degree cousin of Galeazzo Maria.[67] A third daughter, Margareta, had wed in May 1474 the (co-) duke of St. Sava (Herzgovina), Vlatko Košaca, the brother of the widow-king of Bosnia, Catherine (Tomaš).[68]

"The leap" then made by Arrivabene in his report was in fact "a crossing" (he did not recall Francesca[69] among Marzano's married daughters). After reviewing the matrimonial arrangements, Arrivabene informed Ludovico III (who, since 1470, had mediated contacts between Catherine, Margareta, Vlatko and Mehmed)[70] about the arrival in Rome, in four days' time, of "duke Stephen

---

63 Ernesto Pontieri, *Per la storia del regno di* Ferrante I d'Aragona *re di Napoli* (Napoli: Edizioni scientifiche italiane, 1969²), 1–58.

64 Engaged, since summer 1474, to 11 year old, Giovanna, the daughter of Federico de Montefeltro, duke of Urbino (Benedetta Borello, "Giovanna di Montefeltro," *Dizionario Bibliografico degli Italiani* 76 (2012), *sub voce*).

65 Ernesto Pontieri, *La Calabria a metà del secolo XV e le rivolte di Antonio Centelles* (Naples: Fiorentino, 1963); Patrizia Sardina, "Marino Marzano," *Dizionario Bibliografico degli Italiani* 71 (2008): *sub voce.*

66 Maria, Antonio's wife since 1461, was deemed the daughter of Ferdinand and of his mistress Diana Guardato (Ilaria Puglia, *I Piccolomini d'Aragona duchi di Amalfi (1461–1610). Storia di un patrimonio nobiliare* (Naples: Editoriale Scientifica, 2005), 19–24). The hypothesis must be refuted.

67 The wedding was celebrated two months after the report of Arrivabene, see *A Renaissance Wedding: The Celebrations at Pesaro for the Marriage of Costanzo Sforza and Camilla Marzano D'Aragona, 26–30 May 1475*, eds. Jane Bridgeman, Alan Griffiths (London-Turnhout: Brepols, 2013).

68 *Szabolcs de Vajay*, "Un ambassadeur *bien choisi*: Bernardinus de Frangipanus et sa mission à Naples, en 1476," in *The man of many devices, who wandered full many ways: Festschrift in Honour of János M. Bak*, eds. Balazs Nagy, Márcell Sebők (Budapest-New York: CEU Press, 1999), 550–57.

69 Lajos Thallóczy, *Studien zur Geschichte Bosniens und Serbiens im Mittelalter* (Munich: Duncker & Humblot, 1914), 170, 181. According to others, Margareta married Vladislav, Vlatko's brother.

70 Hans Joachim Kissling, "Francesco II Gonzaga ed il sultano Bâyezîd II," *Archivio Storico Italiano* 125, 1 (1967): 34–68.

voivode", the future king of Bosnia. Because it is self-evident who this Stephen was, we recall the address of Sixtus IV from April 1476 (when Stephen was engaged in a full diplomatic conflict with Matthias): *dilectum filium nobilem virum Stephanum Wayvode Ducem Moldaviae.*[71]

Duke Stephen had been named king by Matthias, again the *de iure* suzerain of Bosnia since December 1463 (Catherine's adoptive stepson, King Stephen Tomašević, had been beheaded by Mehmed).[72] At the time of Arrivabene's report, following the intervention of Sixtus, Ferdinand had accepted Matthias as his son-in-law (September 1474),[73] closing the "Adriatic gap" between them. Additionally, Sigismund Tomašević, the son of Stephen Tomaš and Catherine, had recently converted to Islam. He became Isak Beg Kralević.[74] A new king of torn Bosnia was needed.

Bosnia and Wallachia in the "Corsia Sistina"

Rome expected to see Sixtus IV crown "duke Stephen voivode", Matthias' "nominee", as king of Bosnia. According to Arrivabene, Stephen, who – already – ruled over "beautiful state" (obviously different from Bosnia), should have felt honoured.[75] Arrivabene therefore concluded his report by promising the margrave of Mantua to write more about the future king after his arrival in Rome, when Arrivabene hoped to be better informed about the voivode's "deeds" (an eloquent clue that he was thinking of the victor of Vaslui). "Last but not least", Filelfo's disciple wrote to Ludovico III that the *carpioni*, the delicious fish from Mantua's Lake Garda, had arrived.[76]

---

71 Augustin Theiner, *Vetera monumenta historica Hungariam sacram illustrantia*, II. *Ab Innocentio PP. VI. usque ad Clementem PP. VII. 1352–1526* (Rome; Typis Vaticanis, 1859), 452–53, no. 636.

72 See also Veljan Atanasovski, *Pad Hercegovine* (Belgrade: Narodna knjiga. Istorijski institut, 1979), 100–101.

73 For an overview: Péter E. Kovács, "Magyarország és Nápoly politikai kapcsolatai a Mátyás korában," in *Tanulmányok Szakály Ferenc emlékére*, eds. Pál Fodor, Géza Pálffy, István György Toth (Budapest: MTA Társadalomkutató Központ, 2002), 229–47. The wedding was celebrated only in December 1476.

74 Hedda Reindl-Kiel, "*Some Notes on Hersekzade Ahmed* Pasha, his Family and his Books," *Journal of Turkish Studies* 40 (2013): 315–26.

75 The original text read: [...] *E par mi che costui habia un bel stato sera honorato come Re* [...] (Annex III).

76 Al. Luzio, R. Renier, *Mantova e Urbino*: *Isabella d'Este ed Elisabetta Gonzaga nelle relazioni famigliari e nelle vicende politiche (Turin-Rome: L. Roux, 1893), 57.*

In fact, not Stephen was on the road to Rome to be crowned king of Bosnia. The former (co-) voivode of Transylvania, the protector, ally and then adversary of John Hunyadi, Nicholas Újlaki (Iločki) was travelling to Rome, officially as a pilgrim.[77] Four years earlier, in September 1471, Matthias had appointed Újlaki king of Bosnia,[78] successfully detaching him from the new regional anti-Hunyadi conspiracy,[79] which Stephen of Moldavia halted from the East (his envoys had met with Matthias in his native city of Cluj in May, before the royal appointment of Újlaki).[80] Yet, similar to the Kingdom of Naples,[81] the Kingdom of Bosnia was one peculiar item within the *Patrimonium Sancti Petri*.[82] Papal approval of royal rule over Bosnia was naturally mandatory.

In 1477, Nicholas died.[83] His crown did not pass on to his son, Lawrence (Matthias kept it – eventually – for his own, illegitimate, son, John).[84] Nicholas was

77 Tamás Fedeles, "*Bosniae…rex…apostolorum limina visit:* die Romwallfahrt des Nicolaus Újlaki im Jahre 1475," *Ungarn-Jahrbuch* 31(2011–2013 [2014]) : 99–118.

78 A coronation did apparently take place in May 1472, in Buda, not in Jajce, Bosnia's capital (Davor Salihović, An Interesting Episode: *Nicholas of Ilok's Kingship in Bosnia, 1471–1477* [MA thesis] (Budapest: CEU, 2016), 59–60).

79 András Kubinyi, "Zur Frage des bosnischen Konigtums von N. Ujlaki," *Studia Slavica Academiae Scientiarum Hungaricae* 8 (1958): 373–84.

80 Eudoxiu de Hurmuzaki, *Documente privitoare la istoria românilor*, XV-1. *Acte și scrisori din arhivele orașelor ardelene Bistrița, Brașov, Sibiiu, 1358–1600*, ed. Nicolae Iorga (Bucharest: Socec, 1911), 77, no. 133 (August 1471); Ioan Bogdan *Documentele lui Ștefan cel Mare*, II (Bucharest: Socec, 1913), 313, no. 139 (July 1471); *Urkundenbuch zur Geschichte der Deutschen in Siebenbürgen*, VI. *1458–1473*, eds. Gustav Gündisch, Herta Gündisch, Gernot Nussbächer, Konrad Gündisch (Bucharest: Editura Academiei RSR, 1981), 496–99, 3867–870 (May 1471).

81 Girolamo Arnaldi, *Le origini dello Stato della Chiesa* (Turin: UTET Libreria, 1987), 105–09.

82 Emir O. Filipović, "The Key to the Gate of Christendom? The Strategic Importance of *Bosnia* in the Struggle against the Ottomans," in *The Crusade in the Fifteenth Century: Converging and Competing Cultures*, ed. Norman Housley (New York: Routledge, 2017), 151–168.

83 Ede Reiszig, "Az Újlaki-család (II)," *Turul* 56 (1942): 56–65. He died prior to Stephen's new Wallachian campaign of November 1477, meant – alike in 1473–1474 – to relive Ottoman pressure from besieged Venetian Scutari in Albania (Al. Simon, "The Costs and Benefits of Anti-Ottoman Warfare: Documents on the Case of Moldavia. 1475–1477," *Revue Roumained'Histoire* 48, 1–2 (2009): 37–53).

84 See also T. Fedeles, "Miklós király és Lőrinc herceg. Az utolsó két Újlaki vázlatos pályaképe," *Személyiség és történelem. A történelmi személyiség*, eds. József Vonyó, Enikő Csukovits, György Gyarmati (Budapest-Pécs: Magyar Történelmi Társulat-Kronosz, 2017), 135–168, at 148–151, 164.

then depicted in a fresco in the *Corsia Sistina* in Rome as *Bossinae quoque Rex ac Valachiae.*[85] In spite of his old age, he had come *ad limina Apostolorum*. The composition was completed, when relations between Sixtus IV and Matthias,[86]but also between Matthias and Stephen,[87]were very strained (1479–1480).[88]

After Queen Catherine too had died (1478),[89] the image and the text in the *Corsia Sistina* sent a message.[90] Both the thrones of Bosnia and of Wallachia (though Nicholas had been king only of the former) were vacant. Sixtus and not Matthias had the final say.[91] According to Arrivabene, this was true already in spring 1475.[92] The battle of Vaslui had been in fact only means to an end.

---

85 This was the original inscription, dictated by or written under the supervision of Bartolomeo Sacchi *Platina*, closely connected to the House of Gonzaga (Vincenzo Forcella, *Iscrizioni delle chiese e d'altri edificii di Roma*, VI (Rome: Tipografia delle Scienze Matematiche e Fisiche, 1875), 380; cf. already Florio Banfi, "Romei Ungheresi del Jubileo del 1475. Niccolo Ujlaki re di Bosnia in un affresco nell' Ospedale di Santo Spirito dell' urbe," *Archivio di Scienze, Lettere ed Arti della Società Italo-Ungherese* Mattia Corvino 3, no. 2 (1941): 499–512, see 509, 512, notes 25–26).

86 E.g. [Imre Kelcz,] *Epistolae Matthiae Corvini Regis Hungariae ad pontifices, imperatores, reges, principes, aliosque viros illustres* (Kosice: Typis Academicis Societatis Jesu, 1743), pars IV, 55, no. 27.

87 According to Queen Beatrice herself (Iván Nagy, Albert Nyáry, *Magyar diplomacziai emlékek. Mátyás király korából 1458–1490* (=*Monumenta Hungariae Historica*, IV, 1–4), II. [*1466–1480*] (Budapest: Magyar Tudományos Akadémia, 1876), 436–40, nos. 288–89).

88 Eunice Howe, *Art and Culture at the Sistine Court* (Vatican City: Biblioteca Apostolica Vaticana, 2005), 93; Carla Keyvanian, *Hospitals and Urbanism in Rome, 1200–1500* (Boston-Leiden: Brill, 2015), 351, 354, notes 21, 26.

89 See also E.O. Filipović, „Was Bosnian Queen Catherine a Member of the Third Order of St. Francis?" *Radovi Zavoda za Hrvatsku Povijest* 57, 1–2 (2015): 165–82 (165–69).

90 Alexandru Simon, "*Duca Stephano vaivoda intitulato re* <de Bosna>*dal Re de Hungaria* și <Nicolaus>*Bosniae et Valachiae Rex*:despre identitatea regală a *valahilor*," in *Sub semnul împlinirii și al datoriei. Studia in honorem Dorina N. Rusu*, eds. Ioan Bolovan, Ioan-Aurel Pop, Victor Spinei (Bucharest: Editura Academiei Române, 2021), 147–74.

91 The (Bosnian) problem had already emerged in the days of Pius II (Dubravko Lovrenović, *Na klizištu povijesti (sveta kruna ugarska i sveta kruna bosanska). 1387–1463* (Zagreb-Sarajevo: Synopsis, 2006), 341–50). Another issue "had arisen" at the same time, in 1461–1462 (Ioan-Aurel Pop, "Matthias Corvinus, *Re de Ungaria, de Dacia etc.*, in 1462," *Transylvanian Review*, 29, suppl. 1 (2020): 41–52).

92 His report from March 11, 1475, was deliberately omitted by Banfi in "Romei Ungheresi". Note 20 (at p. 512) read: *Archivio di Stato di Mantova, lettera di I. P. Arrivabeni, in data del 24 marzo 1475, ove è detto che il Re della Bosnia era venuto a Roma solo a motivo del Giubileo*. In the text (at p. 504), the note corresponds to the sentence: *Per soddisfare*

Annex I. Bologna, March 6, 1475

(Archivio di Stato di Milano, Archivio Ducale Sforzesco., Potenze Estere, *Romagna*, cart. 184. *1475*, fasc. 3. *Marzo*, not numbered)

Illustrissime Princeps et Excellentissime Domine, D[omine] mj Singularissime, humili semper servili recomendatione premissa etc.,/ Piu tempo fa, non ho scripto alla V[ostra] Excellentia per non essere achaduto la chasone, e anchora per che/ credo alle ocurencie que lo Magnifico Signore d[omino] Roberto, e anchora lo referendario de V[ostra] Illustrissima Signoria,/ alla zornata, screveno apieno aquella. Creda della rotha dellj Turchj in Valachia che V[ostra] Excellentia,/ per piu vie, ne sia stata avisata. Ma per che qui hozi ce sono passati circha dodexe chavalj tra/ Ungarj e Valachj, li quali vano a Roma al Iubileo, e dellj quali Valachj, parte de loro se sono/ ritrovati a dicta rotha, cum li quali io glio parlato, volendo io comparare da loro uno chavalo/ turcho conquistata a dicta rotha, m'e parso, per fare lo mio debito, avisare V[ostra] Illustrissima S[ignoria] de quanto ho/ sentito da loro. Dichano che zia sono piu de trj mixj pasati, che una grandissima mol/titudine de Turchi veneno in Valachia, e discorseno per uno mexe per una grande parte/ de Valachia, facendo grandissimij danj, e che in questo tempo dictj Valachi feno uno exer/cito de sexanta milia Valachj tra pede e achavalo, e andono a ritrovare dictj Turchj, e/ prima glie tolseno uno paso a dictj Turchj, azio non poteseno fugire, e ritornare in dreto, e/ da poi fono alle mane cum loro in bataglia, la quale duro trj dj e tre nocte continuamente,/ ch'a ma non feno altro ch'a combatere inseme, e finalmente dictj Turchj fono rothj e mortj circha/ cento sete milia Turchj, e circha doa milia Valachj, che da poi dicta rothura dictj Valachj/ persequiteno per dicta Valachia, per dj quindexe, de moltj Turchj, li qualj herano figitj e naschosi, li/ qualj tuttj hano mortj, salvo che quindexe capitani Turchi, li quali hano salvati per prisonj, tra/ li quali glie uno si chiama lo Basi, e dichano non havere preso ne morto alcuno/ figliolo del Turcho, e che per lo Danubio fugino circha dexemilia Turchi, e dichano che ma/ non se vide la mazore moltitudine de corpi mortj ch'a questa, e che lj Valachi hano facto/ uno grandissimo quadagno tra de robe, argentj, dinarj asay e cavallj. Questo he lo/ effecto de quello me hano dicto dictj Valachi se sono ritrovatj adicta rotha de Turchj. Lo/ altissimo Dio sempre sia laudato e rengraciato. Me ricomando quanto so e posso ex corde/ alla V[ostra] Illustrissima S[ignoria], della quale sono stato e sono schiavo e fidele servitore per li beneffitij ho/ receputo da quella,

---

all' indulgenza del Giubileo, come attesta l'agente romano dei duchi di Mantova[20] *egli [Niccolò] vi rimase tutto il mese di marzo <à Roma>.*

la quale s'e digne commandarme, che sempre sero presto cum fede ad obidire/ quella.// Ex Bononia, die XJ Martij 1475.

<Written below, by the same hand:> E[xcellentie] V[estre] Illustrissime D[ominationis] servitor et sclavus semper et merito/ fidelissimus Georgius de Paxellis etc.

<Written on the verso, by the same hand:> Illustrissimo principi et Excellentissimo domino,/ domino Duci Madiolanj etc.,/ d[omino] meo unico etc.

Annex II. Bologna, March 6, 1476

(Archivio di Stato di Milano, Archivio Ducale Sforzesco., Potenze Estere, *Romagna*, cart. 184. *1475*, fasc. 3. *Marzo*, not numbered)

Illustrissimo et Excellentissimo Signore mio, Sonno passati per qua alcuni Hungari et Vallachi, li quali (se a loro/ se po credere) dicono se ritrovarono alla rotta che hanno havuto Turchi in Vallachia. Narrano/ la cosa in questo modo: che essendo intrato una grande multitudine de Turchi in dicta/ provintia, quelli del paese se misero in sieme et chiuderono li passi che non potessero fugire,/ poi hebbeno ad fare in sieme et li rumperono, et ne amazarono piu de cento millia, et/ pochi de loro moritero, donde che Vallachi sonno rimasti assai piu richi che non erano./ Li agiongono che hanno preso quindeci capitanei Turchi, quali hanno servato vivi, et/ el principal de loro, che se dimanda el Bassi. Di questo ne fara la Vostra Excellentia quello/ iudicio et stima li parira.// Uno fratello de Misser Colla Gaietano, quale novamente e venuto qua ad studiare,/ dice che circa uno mese se parti da casa, lasso d[omino] Colla in firmo proposito et deliberatione/ de volere venire ad questo San Giorgio ad visitare la Vostra Signoria. Se questo e vero,/ credo che essa el sapij d'altrove, pur anche io li ho voluto scrivere quello ne ho/ inteso dal fratello proprio che, per rispecto de Vostra Excellentia, mi e venuto ad visitare. Humilmente/ mi ricommando alla V[ostra] S[ignoria].// Datum Bononie, die VJ Martij 1475.

<Written below, by the same hand:>Illustrissime Dominationi Vestre fidelissimus servus Karolus vicecomes.

<Written on the verso, by the same hand:> Illustrissimo Principi et Excellentissimo Domino/ meo singularissimo,/ duci Mediolani etc.

Annex III. Rome, March 11, 1475

(Archivio di Stato di Mantova, Mantova, Archivio Gonzaga, E. Affari esteri, XXV. *Roma*, busta 834. *1404–1499*, not numbered)

Ilustrissime Signore mio, questi di e venuta la nova de la morte de la figliola del re moglisse del prefecto.[93] Ragionano/-mo de darli una figliola del principe de Rossano. Doe ne sono gia maritate. Una al duca d'Amalfi e / l'altra al signore de Pesaro. Fra quatro di se aspecta qui lo Re de Bosna, el qual dicono essere un duca/ Stephano vaivoda intitulato re dal Re de Hungaria, al qual dicono spectar de far lo Re de Bosna/ perche quello regno vacava essendosi fatto Turco lo figliolo de la Regina qui. E par mi che costui habia un/ bel stato sera honorato come Re. Quando ne sia qui, parlavo piu informatamente de fatti suoi. Me raccomando/ a la gratia de la Vestra Signoria. Roma, XI Martii 1475. Heri sera arrivavono li carpioni.

<Written below, by the same hand>Illu[strissime]. D[ominationis] V[estre] Servitor Io[annes]. P[etrus] Arrivabenus.

<Written on the verso, by the same hand> Illustri Principi et Excellentissimo Domino, domino meo/ singularissimo L[udovico], Domino Marchioni Mantue,/ …ducali Locumtenenti Generali etc.

93 *Moglisse* meaning mistress or "test wife", because her former "husband", the recently appointed prefect of Rome, Giovanni della Rovere, was engaged to Giovanna de Montefeltro.

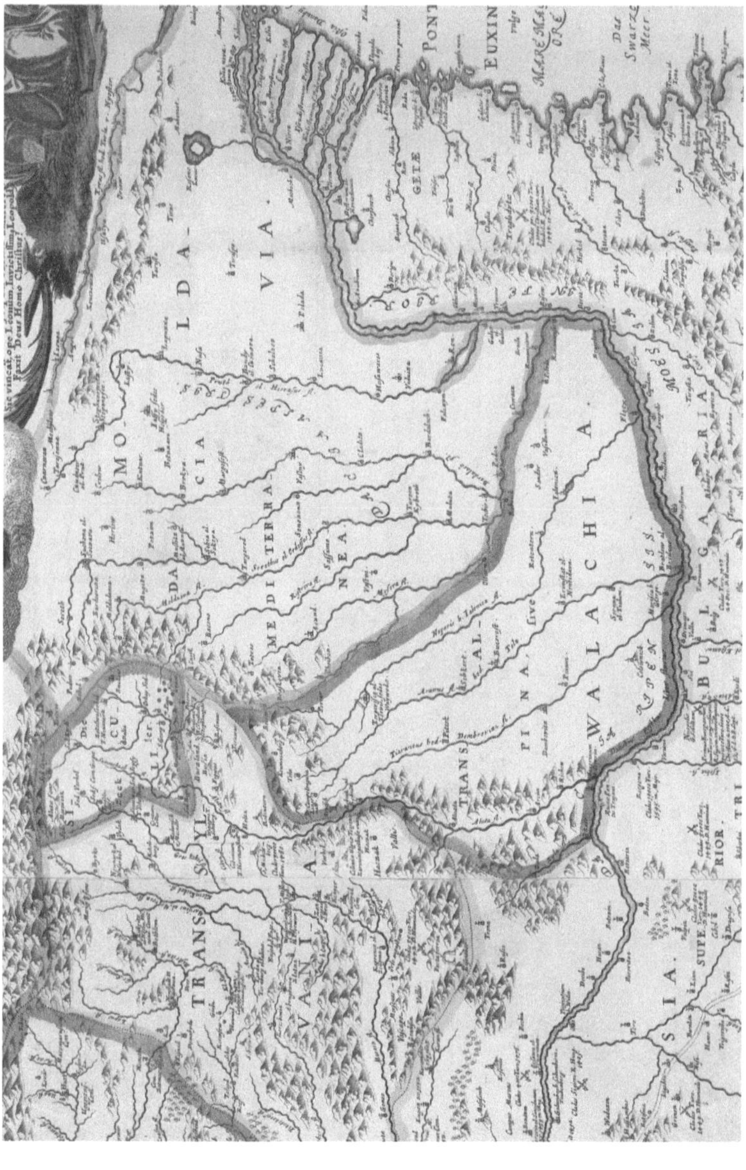

Moldavia, Walachia and Transylvania, detail from *Danubius Fluviorum Europae Princeps…*/The Danube, Monarch of European Rivers, Sigmund von Birken/Jacob von Sandrart, 1683, cooper engraving, (Badische Landesbibliothek, Karlsruhe)

Zoltan Iusztin

Ratio Oeconomicam – War Economy at the South-Western Frontiers of the Hungarian Kingdom at the End of the Fifteenth Century

Abstract: The last decade of the fifteenth century found the Hungarian kingdom in a difficult situation. Matthias Corvinus' conquered territories in Austria and Bohemia were lost during the conflicts between the pretenders to the Holy Crown of the kingdom. Among them was the duke John Corvinus, who relinquished the Crown after the defeat of Csontmező. In exchange for the recognition of the new king, the prince was appointed ban of Dalmatia, Croatia and Slavonia and received also the fortresses of Bosnia. The latter represented the south-western military frontiers of the realm, next to the Ottoman Empire. As captain of the Bosnian fortresses, the duke appointed one of his familiaris, Francis Haraszti. After one year during which he defended and administrated this first line of the front, Haraszti unexpectedly resigned, accusing financial problems. He wrote desperately to the king, claiming that he can't defend anymore the assigened fortifications against the Turkish assaults, asking to be replaced from his dignity as ban of Bosnia. He also accounted the expenses of his service, asking the prince to pay them. The king reelased him from the dignity of ban, and thus Haraszti left the prince's service. Despite the claimed difficulties, his financial activity was not affected, as proved by the pawn contracts which he further concluded.

Keywords: Ban of Bosnia, War Economy, Borders, Dominions, Pawn Contracts

Introduction

In the last decade of his reign, King Matthias I (1458–1490) expanded the territories and the authority of the Hungarian kingdom. The north-western frontiers were settled beyond Vienna, which became the new royal seat. Thus, the Holy Roman emperor, Frederick III (1452–1493) was defeated and also humiliated. At the same time the southern frontiers were avoided by Ottoman raids, which led to rumors about a secret agreement with the Sublime Porte. But this situation changed radically after the king's death.

One by one, the Austrian and Bohemian territories were lost and the kingdom was affected by the civil war between the pretenders to the crown. One of them, John Corvinus was King Matthias' illegitimate son. His political and military power was not negligible because half of the counts in the realm were his familiares, as well as the royal fortresses and castles, especially those on the southern frontiers, which were under his direct control.[1] Many of the king`s knights remained in his service, unlike the barons. Even though the latter owed their political career to the same king, they rebelled and fought against the prince at Csontmező. The defeat, followed then by the recognition of the new king, turned the prince into a dignitary of the kingdom. He was named ban of Dalmtia, Croatia and Slavonia and became responsible for the defense of the south-western frontiers.[2] As a result, Duke John Corvinus commissioned the fortresses of this area to his familiares. One of the duke`s most powerful subjects was Francis Haraszti, who was assigned as ban of Bosnia, receiving the administration of the castles located on this frontline,[3] because, in the new political context, the Ottomans resumed the offensive.

Simultaneously, John Corvin supported Wladislas II (1490–1516) with his own army against the Austrian and Polish attacks from the northern frontiers. This effort of the duke was only possible with the economical commitment of his familiares. This is confirmed by the new king himself, who states that, in addition to the defense of the Bosnian fortresses, John Corvinus provided him military aid, ensured by his own resources.[4] The financial and human effort had long-term consequences that the prince did not anticipate. However, his lack of tact cannot by blame because, as emphasized by some historians, several of his familiares were compensated by King Wladislas from his own patrimony.[5] As for Francis Haraszti, the king granted him a castle in Moravia, with the special permission to sell it.[6] This privilege is unusual for the Hungarian customs inasmuch as the beneficiary din not receive a real estate but only a pawn or pledge, without the possibility of bequeathing it to his heirs as a possession.

---

1 Pál Engel, Gyula Kristó, András Kubinyi, *Magyarórszág története 1301–1526* (Budapest: Osiris, 2005), 327.

2 Gyula Schönherr, *Hunyadi Korvin János* (Budapest: A magyar töténelmi társulat kiadása, 1894), 156–67.

3 Zoltan Iusztin, "În serviciul Corvinilor: Francisc de Harazth, Banus Zewreniensi. Cursus Honorum (II)," *Banatica* 30-II (2020): 116–23.

4 Iusztin, "În serviciul Corvinilor," 118.

5 András Kubinyi, "A megyésispánságok 1490-ben és Corvin János trónörökösödésének problémái. Adatok a veszprémi püspök örökös főispánsági joga felfüggesztéséhez," *A Veszprémi Múzeumok Közleményei* 16 (1982): 174–76.

6 Zoltan Iusztin, "In the Corvin's Service. Francis of Haraszth, Banus Zewreniensis (I)," in *Politics and Society in the Central and South-Eastern Europe (13th–16th centuries)*, I, ed. Zoltan Iusztin (Cluj-Napoca: Editura Mega, 2019), 148; see also Magyar Nemzeti Levéltár Országos Levéltára Diplomatikai Levéltár ((further MNL OL DL) 59796.

Pawn and War Economy

Descendend of a noble family in the service of the Court, Haraszti acquired from King Matthias the dignity of ban of Severin.[7] Thus, he was not a courtier, but a knight who commanded a troop of light cavalry, better known as hussars.[8] With this task, he served the Crown faithfully, fighting both on the Austrian and Bohemian front and against the Ottoman Turks.[9] From this point of view, he was a hard-fought soldier as attested not only by the official documents, but also his contemporaries, especially the court chronicler Antonio Bonfini, who describes him as a brave knight, hardened in various campaigns.[10]

Other official sources prove that Francis Haraszti also carried out economic activities. He offered money loans in exchange for various real estates. The pledge or the pawn custom was widespread in the late Middle Ages, being almost a daily activity. In the absence of specialized institutions, anyone could offer a loan which was guaranteed with various goods, especially real estates.

During his career, Francis Haraszti also practiced this kind of loan, but for the present paper we will focus only on those from the last decade of the fifteenth century. Up to this period of time, the largest amount lent by him rises to 3.100 gold florins. In exchange, he received the town of *Nagy Tapolchan* (Nagytapolcsány/Topoľčany, in Slovakia), 23 villages and two tax customs, one of which was the fair custom.[11] The amount is not small as demonstrated by the numerous possessions received as pawns.

His financial power is attested by the agreement with one of his own familiares. Francis Haraszti, the ban of Severin, lent 100 gold florins to Nicholas Danch of Macedonia without any guarantee for the first few months, receiving a village as pledge, only after 29 September.[12] The agreement was concluded little before the death of King Matthias. Afterwards, Haraszti had to support his liege lord both military and financial.

John Corvinus himself stated that, during the times of trouble in 1490, he had the chance to rely on his *familiarius*.[13] The latter lent him 2.000 gold

7 *Magyarország világi archontológiája 1458–1526*, I *Főpapok és bárók*, eds. Norbert C. Tóth, Richárd Horváth, Tibor Neumann, Tamás Pálosfalvi (Budapest: MTA Bölcsészettudományi Kutatóközpont - Történettudományi Intézet, 2016), 150–51.

8 Iusztin, "În serviciul Corvinilor," 109–27.

9 Iusztin, "În serviciul Corvinilor," 109–27.

10 Iusztin, "În serviciul Corvinilor," 109–27.

11 MNL OL DL 59759.

12 MNL OL, DL 59789.

13 Iusztin, "In the Corvin's Service," 149–150; MNL OL, DL59807; MNL OL, DL59819.

florins.[14] It is hard to asses the whole finnancial effort invested by Francis Haraszti in supporting the prince for the battle of Csontmező. It is certain though that after the recognition of the new king and the end of hostilities the ban returned to his financial affairs. In September, he offered 100 gold florins to Sebastian Abramfy of *Gerla*, receiving in exchange a part of the *Gerendas* estate, as a pawn.[15] After one month, the bishop of Eger, Urban of *Naghluche* (Nagylucsei), and his brothers pledged three estates from Pest County to Francis Haraszti, for the sum of 1.000 gold florins.[16]

These testimonies prove the financial wealth of Haraszti who, in a single year, was able to lend a few thousand gold florins. Simultaneously, he invested in the new acquisitions as mentioned by Duke John Corvinus, at the beginning of 1491.[17] He also bought the *Almaszeg* possession from his brother-in-law, for 500 gold florins.[18]

Politically, the duties performed to his liege lord brought him new honors. In the summer of 1491, he was appointed ban of Bosnia[19] and got involved in the takeover of the fortresses located on the south-western border of the realm. John Corvinus already stated on 20 June, that he sent Haraszti to occupy Jajce,[20] the most important castle of the Bosnian front. The ban did not hesitated to perform his duty, as the duke proved in late summer, when he commissioned him again with the occupation of a few castles from Slavonia.[21] In addition to these, he received a new task, to defend the castles against the Turkish attacks.

This time, the effort proved to be particularly difficult. In the autumn of 1491, the Ottomans conquered Koszorúvár (Vinac, Bosnia-Herzegovina) and besieged Jajce,[22] causing him to ask the duke for help. Paul Derencsenyi was sent to his aid with some soldiers and a sum of 1.500 gold florins. Unable to deal with the situation by himself, John Corvinus asked the king for help.[23] Other barons, like Peter

14 Iusztin, "In the Corvin's Service"; MNL OL, DL 59807.

15 MNL OL, DL 59794.

16 MNL OL, DL 59796.

17 Iusztin, "In the Corvin's Service," 149–150; MNL OL, DL 59807.

18 MNL OL, DL 59807.

19 *Magyarország világi archontológiája 1458–1526*, I, 140.

20 Lajos Thallóczy, *Jajca (bánság, vár és város) története. Oklevelek (és egyes történtirókból vett részek) 1450–1527* (Budapest: Kiadja a Magyar Tudományos Akadémia, 1915), 79, LIV.

21 MNL OL, DF 233598.

22 Thallóczy, *Jajca története*, 80–81, LV.

23 Schönherr, *Hunyadi*, 184.

Varadi, also warned King Wladislas about the desperate situation of Jajce castle.[24] However, the situation did not change in the following year either and the duke was forced to send material aid to the citizens and soldiers of Jajce.[25]

Haraszti defended the fortress with his own resources by granting a loan of 2.000 florins to the prince. The loan was officialy concluded at the end of 1492, with the guarantee of the palatine.[26] A day later, Francis issued a document containing his financial contributions to the defense of the Bosnian castles, with a total cost of 3.800 golden florins. According to his own testimonies, the prince had to grant him as pledge the castles of Şoimoş and Lipova along with all their pertinences.[27] Both documents attest that John Corvinus promised to pledge him the fortress of Arva, if he would fail to return the entire loan in time.[28]

The financial efforts led Haraszti to relinquish the administration of the Bosnian frontier and to vehemently ask the king to release him from this dignity. As a result, a new ban was appointed, in the person of Baltazar Battyanyi, who was ordered, beginning with March 1493, to take over the leadership of the province.[29] Probably, the calculations Francis Haraszti made in the previous year, convinced him that he did not have the means to hold this important office. His attitude displeased John Corvinus, who was not impressed by the justifications of his *familiaris*. Of course, the duke was aware of Haraszti's fortune, but we do not know if he overestimated it or if he noticed the lack of sacrifice in his favor. It is certain that he did not believe in the existence of the deficiencies accused by his ban and did not conceive the fact that his financial resources would not suffice for the defense of the province.

The new ban took over the leadership of Jajce fortress only on 7 June, when one of Haraszti's *familiaris* handed him the ammunition inventory.[30] His replacement came later than hoped, but instead some promises were obtained from the king. A hint is provided by the register of royal accounts from 1494 to 1495, which attests the sums that Haraszti collected from the donations in Pest County.[31] The

24 Thallóczy, *Jajca története*, 81–83, LVI.
25 Thallóczy, *Jajca története*, 94, LIX.
26 MNL OL, DL 59819.
27 MNL OL, DL 37676.
28 MNL OL, DL 59819; MNL OL, DL 37676.
29 Thallóczy, *Jajca története*, 95, LXI.
30 Thallóczy, *Jajca története*, 97–99, LXIII.
31 Johann Christian Engel, *Geschichte des ungarischen Reichs und seiner Nebenländer*, I (Halle: bey Johann Jacob Gebauer, 1797), 42, 47. XXX; Tibor Neumann, *Registrum proventum regni Hungariae. A Magyar Királyság kincstartójának*

source states that Francis was allowed to collect the gate tax on his estates on account of the expenses for the maintenance of the Bosnian cities. At that time Haraszti no longer provided for the defense of this province, so the ex-ban had been compensated for the expenses he had made during the first part of 1493.

Following the agreement concluded with John Corvinus, Francisc took over the administration of Arva fortress, after 24 April of the same year. Some evidence suggests that he did not actually take possession of this castle,[32] but one can observe the constant intentions of the duke to recover it. An unsuccessful attempt took place in April 1494, when his envoys and those of Haraszti met in the presence of the Arad Chapter. Although he was presented with a sealed chest, Haraszti's delegate found inside only half of the amount.[33] Therefore, the transaction was postponed.

Francis Haraszti insisted to recover the sum, but at the same time he managed his own affairs, thus the situation on the frontier no longer interested him, even though he received the castle of *Segowyna* (Šagovina Cernička, Croatia), along with a few villages.[34] This castle was located in southern Slavonia, at a distance of 140 km north of Jajce, so it was close to the Ottoman front. The earliest testimony, albeit from an indirect witness, which attests the castle in his propriety dates from 1497.[35] Thus, its acquisition must be related to his ban offices.

Maybe this was the main reason why the duke didn't accept the resignment of his *familiaris* from the defense of the Bosnian castles and frontier. Corvinus hurried to recover all the assigned pledges, offering them to other creditors. Consequently, the Şoimoş fortress was pledged to Peter Derecsenyi, who, in return, paid his debt.[36] The Lipova market town was also recovered, by similar means.[37] The desire to break all connections with Haraszti as soon as possible and to immediately cancel his usufruct rights resulting from the pledge contracts

---

számadáskönyve (1494–1495) (Budapest: MTA Bölcsészettudományi Kutatóközpont – Történettudományi Intézet, 2019), 138, 139, 172,

32 *Magyarország világi archontológiája 1458–1526*, II. *Megyék*, eds. Tibor Neumann, Tamás Pálosfalvi, András W. Kovács (Budapest: MTA Bölcsészettudományi Kutatóközpont – Történettudományi Intézet, 2017), 35, note 10–11.

33 MNL OL, DL 37686.

34 Iusztin, "In the Corvin's Service," 142.

35 MNL OL, DL 59870.

36 MNL OL, DL 59860.

37 Adrian Magina, *Acte şi documente privitoare la părţile de jos ale Regatului Ungar 1500–1552* (Cluj-Napoca: Editura Mega, 2020), 31, IV.

highlights even more clearly the duke's attitude towards his ungrateful and traitorous *familiaris*.

The Military Debt behind the Financial Interest

The duke's memorandum, submitted to the Estates of the realm on the occasion of the general congregation of 1498, was directed against those who were at odds with him after the death of his father, or who tried to take possession of his ancestral domains. Archbishop Thomas Bakocz and some of the barons stood out among the accused, but Haraszti was not forgotten either.[38]

John Corvinus accused Francis of refusing to hand him over Arva fortress, even though he already sent 2.000 florins to the Arad Chapter. Moreover, Haraszti appropriated sums of money from the expenses provided for the maintenance of some fortresses and asked the king for more money, on account of his salary as a *familiaris* of the duke. He also unjustly took goods from the Şoimoş castle.[39] As one can see, the duke's reproaches were mainly related to the administration of the Bosnian Banat. His accusations, insofar as we do not know all their effects, betray rather the desire to punish the unfaithfull *familiaris*. For the duke, resigning Bosnia was tantamount to treason. Harasztis withdrawal from the mentioned office directly affected his political position. Thereby, the duke became unable to defend the south-western frontiers of the realm, for which he was responsible.

Interestingly, his accusations did not go unheeded. Haraszti was mentioned in Article 42 of the laws passed by the Estates, which recorded those who were responsible for the loss of some borderforts of the Hungarian Crown, in order to receive their punishment.[40] Francis was accused of losing the Koszorúvár fortress in Bosnia. According to some opinions, this article was included in the document by the Estates following the intrigues at Court, especially since all the mentioned lost fortresses were located in the Banat of Bosnia. Obviously, only the former governor of the province could be behind these intrigues.

But Haraszti was not punished. After leaving the duke's service, he became a direct familiaris of the Crown, as in the time of King Matthias. Through this

38 Iván Nagy, András Stummer, Károly Ráth, Dezső Véghely, *Hazai Ókmánytár*, IV (Gőr: Typis Victoris Sauervein, 1867), 442.

39 *Hazai Ókmánytár*, 442.

40 Ferenc Döry, *Decreta Regni Maedievalis Hungariae*, IV, ed. Péter Banyó, Martyn Rady, János M. Bak (Idyllwild CA: Charles Schlacks, Jr. – Budapest: Department of Medieval Studies, Central European University, 2010), 116–17.

political act, he became immune to all the accusations and reproaches. From this point of view he gained a more important political position and his military career was not affected.[41] However, in his case, the financial activities acquired the foreground, as the documentary sources are suggesting.[42]

However, a few more questions regarding his office as a ban of Bosnia remaine open. As ban of Severin, Haraszti did not encounter any difficulties in fulfilling his duties. Despite frequent interruptions, he succesfully led the defense of the south-eastern frontiers for approximately 10 years.[43] In this area, he also confronted the Ottoman army as a hard-fought soldier and brave hussar captain,[44] contrasting his attitude manifested on the south-western frontier of the realm. The intensity of the enemy attacks can explain this latter situation and also his advanced age. Some of his own testimonies reveal him as an old soldier, tired of battles, but these confessions were made over a decade and half later, after the resignment from the Bosnian frontier.[45]

Probably the intensity of the attacks required more expense than he could afford. On the other hand, for a hussar captain the fixed position warfare was unpleasant and for him, maybe, new, since during King Matthias' reign the south-eastern frontier and it's castles were not besieged. Unlike direct combat, the defence of a fortress requires ammunition and provisions, besides the wages of the hussars. Then, the castle repair requires more expenses and efforts. From this point of view, fortress war was more expensive than light cavalry incursions, which apparently suited Haraszti much better. Of course, the reasons are multiple but the financial aspects weighed a lot.

41 Iusztin, "În serviciul Corvinilor," 109–27.

42 MNL OL, DL 59881.

43 Iusztin, "În serviciul Corvinilor," 116.

44 Iusztin, "În serviciul Corvinilor," 113.

45 Zoltan Iusztin, "Domeniul nobiliar Târgoviște (jud. Timiș)," *Banatica* 31-II (2021): 45, V.

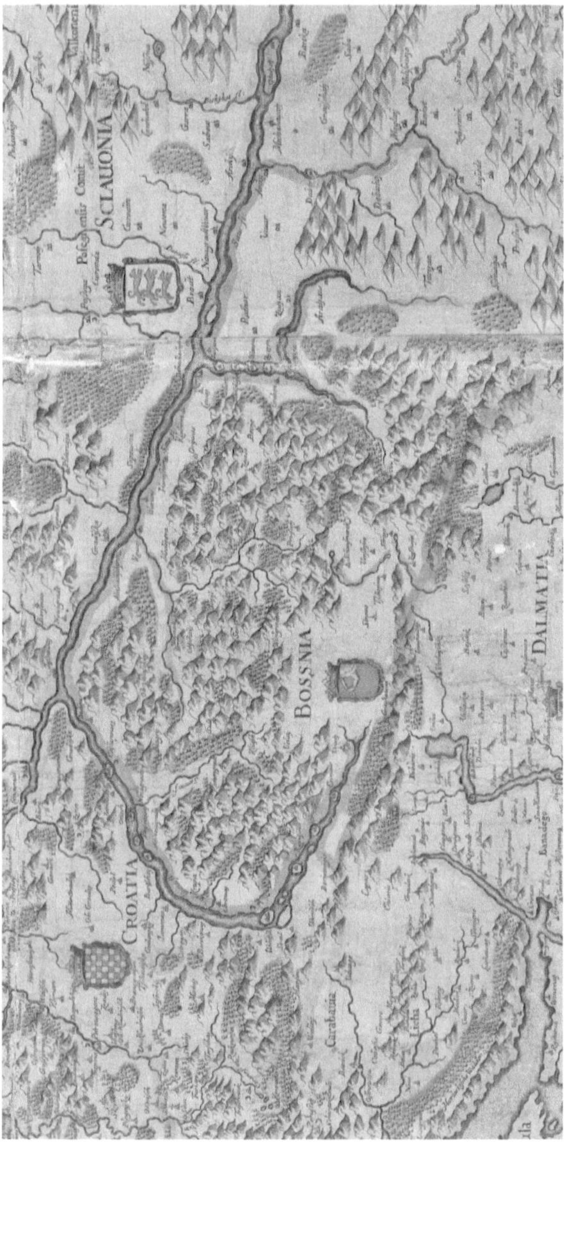

Croatia, Bosnia, Slavonia, detail from *Landkarten des Königreichs Ungarn*…Martin Stier/Moritz Lang, 1664, cooper engraving (Landesarchiv Baden-Württemberg Abt. Generallandesarchiv Karlsruhe)

Adrian Magina

Living in Fear. Life at the Southern Frontier of the Hungarian Kingdom

(in the Fourteenth–Sixteenth Centuries)

Abstract: The southern parts of the medieval kingdom of Hungary, known today as the Banat, have always been a frontier territory. In the fourteenth century, after the conquest of the Balkan Peninsula, the Ottoman Empire reached the vicinity of Hungary. Most raids of the Ottoman army aimed precisely this borderland. In order to stop Turkish invasions, the Hungarian court built up a system of fortifications on the Danube that proved only partially effective. These strongholds managed to hold major invasions but left the way open for many raids, which induced great insecurity for those living in the region between Danube, Mureş and Tisza rivers. Documents from fifteenth and early sixteenth centuries indicate that relatively large areas have suffered human and material losses, the inhabitants being under constant threat. Following the destruction of a dozen settlements, the region was partially depopulated. To compensate for the loss of population, Hungarian kings encouraged the settlement of southern Slavs (especially Serbs), who were fleeing the Turkish rule. Despite various measures taken by the Hungarian court, insecurity was a permanent state, especially at the beginning of the sixteenth century. In mid-20` of the same century, the defensive system of the southern frontier finally collapsed. The fall of fortresses left the southern parts of the kingdom defenceless and in the end, following two violent campaigns in 1551–1552, the Ottoman Empire conquered the area.

Keywords: Medieval Hungary, The Lower Parts, Ottomans, Raids, Insecurity

> *...quod cum hiis diebus proxime transactis auditis adventu sevissimorum Turcorum partes inferiores regni nostri devastantium...*[1]
> *"...I heard that in the past few days the arrival of the frightening Turks*
> *laid the Lower Parts of our kingdom to waste"*

The words quoted above are found in a royal decree of 1439 and express a specific situation for the southern borderlands of medieval Hungary, increasingly threaten

1 *Decreta Regni Hungariae. Gesetze und Verordnungen Ungarns 1301–1457*, eds. F. Döry, G. Bónis, V. Bácskai (Magyar Országos Levéltár kiadványai, II. Forráskiadványok 11) (Budapest: Akadémiai Kiadó, 1976), 305.

by the Ottomans. Beyond the typical exaggerations of the age, the source indicates a common phenomenon which can be found in many other documents of that time, namely the pressure and destruction that the people living at the southern frontier of the medieval Kingdom of Hungarian had to face. In this article I will analyse how the Ottoman threat was perceived by the inhabitants of the territory bordered by the Mureş, Tisza, Danube, and the Carpathians, how strong their feeling of insecurity was, to what degree they were affected, and what was the impact on their daily lives? The military confrontations that took place at the southern border of the kingdom have been identified by the Hungarian, Romanian and South-Slav historiographies, but the analyse was focused on the defensive system and the direct confrontation with Ottoman troops, while the impact of those military confrontation on the local population received less attention.[2]

---

2 Bodóg Milleker, *A töröknek első betörései Dél-Magyarországba Zsigmond és Albert királyok idejében és Keve és Krassó vármegyék megszűnése 1393–1439* (Temesvár: A csanád-egyházmegyei sajtó nyomasa, 1914); Ferenc Szakály, "Phases of Turco-Hungarian warfare before the battle of Mohács (1365–1526)," *Acta orientalia Academiae Scientiarum Hungaricae* 33 (1979): 65–111; Ferenc Szakály, "The Hungarian-Croatian border defense system and its collapse," in *From Hunyadi to Rákóczi. War and Society in Late Medieval and Early Modern Hungary*, eds. Béla K. Király, János M. Bak (Boulder-Colorado: Columbia University Press, 1982), 141–158; András Kubinyi, "Magyarország déli határvárai a középkor végén," *Várak a későközépkorban. Die Burgen im Spätmittelalter. Castrum Bene* 2 (1990): 65–76; Pál Engel, "A török-magyar háborúk első évei 1389–1392," *Hadtörténelmi közlemények* 2 (1997) (special issue: *Memoria rerum Sigismundis regis*): 12–28; Tamás Pálosfalvi, *From Nicopolis to Mohács: A History of Ottoman-Hungarian Warfare, 1389–1526* (Boston-Leiden: Brill, 2018); István Petrovis, "Dél-Magyarország és a török veszély a 14. század vége és a 15. század dereka között," in *„…úgy Írhassak mint volt. " Ünnepi tanulmányok a 65 esztendős Tóth Sándor László tiszteletére*, ed. Bagi Zoltán Péter (Szeged: Kiadja a Szegedi Tudományegyetem Középkori és Kora Újkori Történeti Tanszéke, 2019), 104–119; Ioan Haţegan, *Pavel Chinezu* (Timişoara: Helicon, 1994); Adrian Magina, "Border and Periphery. The southern frontier of medieval kingdom of Hungary between Belgrade and Severin (14th–16th centuries)," *Иницијал. Часопис за средњовековне студије*, књига 4/ *Initial. A review of medieval studies*, 4, Centre for advanced medieval studies (Belgrade, 2016), 141–164; Adrian Magina, "In the hands of the Turks. Captives from southern Hungary in the Ottoman Empire (14th–16th centuries)," in *State and society in the Balkans before and after establishment of ottoman rule*, eds. Srđan Rudić, Selim Aslantaş, (Belgrade: Institute of History, 2017), 65–78; Davor Salihović, "The Process of Bordering at the Late Fifteenth-Century Hungarian-Ottoman Frontier," *History in Flux* 1 (2019): 93–120; Davor Salihović, "*Pro sustentatione castrorum*: the role of the Hospitaller priory of Hungary in King Matthias Corvinus' anti-Ottoman defensive policies, *c.*1464–90," *Journal of Medieval History* 47, no. 1 (2021): 89–11.

The southern parts of the medieval kingdom of Hungary were throughout their history both a borderland and a contact zone between the civilization of Western influence and the one of Eastern, Byzantine structure. We might speak about a large territory, from Croatia through Bosnia and Serbia to the frontier of Wallachia. For the present issue I will limit my approach to the area bordered by the Mureş River on the north, the Danube on the south, the Tisza on the west and the Carpathians on the East, a territory of about 30.000 square kilometres, known today as the Banat, with 60 % of its surface belonging to Romania, 39 % to Serbia, and 1 % to Hungary. During the Middle Ages and the Early Modern Age (up to 1718) that area was administratively divided in the counties of Timiş (Temes), Caraş (Krassó), Torontal (Torontál), Arad and Cenad (Csanád), and the Banate of Severin (Szörényi bánság, *banatus Zoriniensis*).[3] The latter administrative structure was specific to the borderland of the kingdom. The Hungarian banates stretched from Croatia to the frontier of Wallachia, with an obvious role in the defence of the frontier.[4] The balance of power in the Balkans changed dramatically because of the presence of the Ottoman Empire that reached a common frontier with Hungary, after the conquest of Bulgaria and a part of Serbia.[5]

3 There is no unique perception of the territory of the present day Banat, as the national historiographies (Romanian, Hungarian, Serbian and German) are interested in the past of the area bordered by the Mureş-Danube-Tisza, and the Carpathians. For the different opinions on the medieval territory of today's Banat, see: Bálint Varga, "In the middle of the nation, on the margins of the academia: historiography in Banat in the long 19th century," *New Europe College Yearbook* (2012–2013): 307–31; István Petrovics, *A középkori Temesvár. Fejezetek a Begaparti város 1552 előtti történetéből* (Szeged: JatePress, 2008); Vasile Docea, "History, Ideology and Collective Memory. Reconstructing the Identities of Timişoara by Means of Monographies and Street Names during the Communist Regime (1947–1989)," *Acta Universitatis Sapientiae. European and Regional Studies*, 1, no. 1 (2010): 83–102; Vasile Docea, "The Historical Monographs of Banat Germans as Identity Discourse," in *Paths to Belonging. Constructing Local Identity in Banat by Means of Monuments, Cultural Heritage and Historiography*, ed. Vasile Docea (Baden-Baden: Nomos, 2016), 189–200; Aleksandar Krstić, "Banat u srednjem veku,"Миодраг Матицки, Видојко Јовић, eds. *Банат кроз векове, слојеви култура Баната* (Београд: Вукова задужбина, 2010); Johann Heinrich Schwiker, *Geschichte des Temeser Banats* (Grosz-Becskerek: Verlag von r. P. Bettelheim, 1861).

4 Viorel Achim, *Politica sud- estică a regatului ungar sub ultimii Arpadieni* (Bucureşti: Editura Enciclopedică, 2008); Szakály, "The Hungarian-Croatian border," *passim*.

5 Pál Engel, *Regatul Sântului Ştefan. Istoria Ungariei medievale 895–1526* (Cluj-Napoca: Mega, 2006), 256–62.

The term "frontier" had several meanings in the medieval and early modern times: it could refer to a political limit, could indicate a geographical area, could mark the limits of an ecclesiastical or noble landholding (diocese, estate), or just a natural or anthropic landmark. This was also the case for Hungary. In a restrictive sense, the Danube from Belgrade to Severin was considered a line of division between the Hungarian kingdom and the territories south of the river.[6] The southern parts of the kingdom (to which I henceforth refer to as Banat), identified as *confinia* in contemporary sources, were considered as borderlands along the line of the Danube. This region that stretched from the Mureş River in the north to the Danube in the south was about 150 kilometres wide.

Thus, one of the attacks coming from the south reached the *confinia et districtus comitatum Themesiensis et de Crassow*, by the end of the fourteenth century; the noblemen who had contributed to repel the attack in those *confinibus regni nostri*, were awarded with various possessions by the king. It is clear that not only the area next to the Danube was perceived as *confinium/confinia*, but also the territory of other counties: Timiş, Torontal or Caraş, located in a larger area, covered the meanings of the term "frontier". Even more, the source produces evidence on the invaders' nature, an aspect of great importance in drawing another meaning of the notion of frontier. The attackers are none other than the *paganorum Turcorum scilicet at aliarum cismaticarum nationum*, wreaking havoc and damages, and increasing the feeling of an exposed, unsafe area. At the beginning of the fifteenth century (1418), in a similar context of an attack of the *perfidissimos Turcos Crucis Christi inimicos et alias nationis barbaricas et schismaticas versus parts inferiors Themesienses*, that feeling is once again indicated by the sources. Thus, we might note that the frontier on the Danube had also other meanings, the political line being doubled by a confessional one: the Christians north of the river, the pagans and schismatic south of it (of course, they referred to the Serbs and Bulgarians, allies of the Ottomans).[7]

The need for a fortified line at the southern border of the realm occurred during Sigismund of Luxembourg's rule, as an answer to the catastrophic defeat at Nicopolis and the increasingly frequent Ottoman forays in the territories north of the Danube. Up to the beginning of the fifteenth century, only a few fortresses were built on the river side of the Banate, far from forming a well-structured

---

6 Neven Isailović, Miloš Ivanović, "The Danube in the Serbian Hungarian relations in the 14th and 15th centuries," *Tibiscum* 5 (2015): 377–394; Magina, "Border and Periphery," 142.

7 Magina, "Border and Periphery," 144–45.

defensive system. Initiated by Sigismund, with the support of the Florentine *condottiere* Pippo Spano, count of Timiş, a fortified line along the Danube was erected in a few decades, in order to hold the Ottoman advance north of the river. The system consisted of about 20 forts, on a length of 200 km, between Belgrade and Severin. Those were considered border forts – *castra finitima*, or fortresses of the Lower Parts, by the Danube – *castra inferior cis Danubiana*, thus on the outskirts of the kingdom, being at the same time a defensive bulwark against the Ottoman threat. The fortresses of Severin and St. Ladislas (today Coronini, Caraş-Severin County) were the main pillars of the mentioned defensive line; in addition, there were a series of smaller fortifications, or rather fortified positions for watching and controlling the above mentioned border section of the Danube.[8] The maintenance of this fortified system and of the troops stationed at the borders was a heavy burden for the royal treasury, that couldn't support the exorbitant expenses, by the end of the fifteenth century. Thus, local and neighbouring communities were also involved in the support of the defensive system, contributing with money and troops in order to keep the southern frontier functional.[9] The organization of a new administrative structure, the so called Lower or Inferior Parts, was a further step in managing the border area. Since the fourteenth century the expresion *partes inferiores* was usual in naming the southern area of the Hungarian kingdom. In 1418, it was also used for Timiş County. Some years later, in 1436, King Sigismund ordered that a lawsuit should be postponed, for one of the involved parts was at the time involved in a military campaign in the borderlands (*ad partes inferiores more exercituantium*). We find a similar situation at the beginning of the next year, when another lawsuit of a nobleman was postponed, because he was *in partibus nostris inferioribus in confinnis Themesiensibus foret occupatus*. Thus, one can note that the usage of that term is definitive in the first decades of the fifteenth

8 Mark Whelan, "Catastrophe or Consolidation? Sigismund's Response to Defeat after the Crusade of Nicopolis," in *Between Worlds: The Age of the Jagiellonians*, eds. Florin Ardelean, Christopher Nicholson and Johannes Preiser-Kapeller (Frankfurt am Main: Peter Lang, 2013), 215–27; Jason Michael Snider, *A military analysis of key river fortifications given to the Theutonic order in the Banat of Severin* (MA Thesis, Budapest: CEU, 2019); Erik Fügedi, "Medieval Hungarian castles in existence at the start of the Ottoman advance," in *From Hunyadi to Rákóczi. War and Society in Late Medieval and Early Modern Hungary*, eds. Béla K. Király, János M. Bak (Boulder-Colorado: Columbia University Press, 1982), 61–62.

9 Szakály, "The Hungarian-Croatian border," 147–49; Engel, *Regatul*, 373–74; Magina, "Border and Periphery," 147–51.

century, naming only the marginal area, the southern border of the kingdom, largely corresponding to the territory known today as the Banat. In the context of the increased Ottoman attacks, the older ideology regarding Hungary as the defender of Christendom received new meanings and valences, since its territories, located on the periphery of the Christian world, were under constant pressure from the "barbarians", coming from the Ottoman world.[10]

Was that defensive system efficient in stopping the Ottoman forays? Yes and no. Yes, if we take into account that not many large-scale Ottoman expeditions advanced deep into the territory of the kingdom. Every major Ottoman army avoided that fortified section when attacking Hungary. The efficiency of system may be also correlated to the state efficiency, especially in finance. The most prosperous era of the kingdom was registered during Matthias Corvinus' reign (1458–1490), when there as a good financial support for the border, from Bosnia to the frontier of Wallachia. It also was a period of active policy, with attacks of the Hungarian troops south of the Danube, a war of attrition interrupted by truces and agreements. But the mentioned defensive system wasn't very efficient when speaking about the impact of those minor expeditions of destroying and plundering enemy territories, just like the ones that affected the local population. The territories situated along the Danube were the most affected as small Turkish raiding parties were able to bypass the defensive system and attack local settlements.

From the last decade of the fourteenth century onwards, the charters periodically record such raids at the southern frontier of the Hungarian kingdom. Despite the traditional interpretation of the historiography, that the first Ottoman invasions occurred as early as 1375,[11] regular attacks began in 1390, being recorded quite frequently by the end of that century and during the beginning of the next one. This was the factor that affected the administrative structure of the region, bringing the dissolution of some counties.[12] Two Catholic monasteries were destroyed in the county of Caraş[13] during those first

10 István Petrovics, "John Hunyadi, defender of the southern borders of the medieval kingdom of Hungary," *Banatica* 20, 2 (2010): 63–75; Magina, "Border and Periphery," 144–45.

11 Bernát Kumurovitz, "I Lajos királyunk 1375. évi Havasföldi hadjárata (és török) háborúja," *Szazadok*, 117 (1983): 942–45.

12 Petrovis, "Dél-Magyarország és a török veszély," 110–113; Engel, "A török-magyar háborúk," 16–26; Milleker, *A törököknek első betörései Dél-Magyarországba*, 7–40.

13 *Diabolus...per saevissimos Turcos quamplura ordinis nostri monasteria videlicet Dobycza quod erat de primis in Dalmatia et S. Petri in Zlatkagora, item ultra fluvium Themes duo claustra Boldoghew et Gatal ac monasterium S. Petri juxta Zalonkemen fecit desolari et*

attacks; both of them were placed at a considerable distance from the Danube (about 70 km). The first one was Gatal (today Gătaia, in the Timiş County), the second one was located close to the administrative center of Caraş County, Mezősomlyó (today Şemlacu Mare, in the Timis County) and to the domain of the powerful nobles Himfi of Remetea. The latter deeply felt the impact of the Ottoman raids. A few years after the first Turkish incursions, in 1396, King Sigismund of Luxemburg donated Stephen of Remetea (a member of the Himfis) the estate Halas in Csongrád County, because „during those eventful times all the possessions he had inherited from his parents were attacked and integrally laid to waste by the miserable Turks".[14] Undoubtedly, there were in question the possessions in the Caraş County, partly lost today, around the village of Berzovia, located at the boundary between today's counties of Caraş-Severin and Timiş, in the lowlands of the Bârzava River. Likewise in 1396, Sigismund congratulated, Nicholas Marczali, count of Timiş, who, brave as a lion, succeeded holding of the Ottoman attackers at Ciacova (Csák, near Timisoara), after they pillaged and burned the countryside and capturing many inhabitants.[15]

The Ottoman raids generated more insecurity than their attacks on monasteries or estates. Thus, the local population had to take refuge from the plundering troops of the Crescent, because they were regarded as "precious goods" and their capturing brought fair ransoms. The inhabitants of the frontier areas had no other possibility than to flee towards more secure regions, but such demographic movements affected in a certain measure the social order. That's why King Sigismund ordered the officials of the kingdom, in 1399, especially the ones on the southern borderland, in the vicinity of the Sublime Porte, to return the serfs who fled in fear from the area between the two rivers of Timiş (Temesköz),

---

exterminari, see *Documenta Artis Paulinorum*, I, ed. Béla Gyéressy (Budapest: MTA Művészettörténeti Kutató Csoportja, 1975), 20, quoted also by Engel, "A török-magyar háborúk," 20, footnote 86.

14 Magyar Nemzeti Levéltár Országos Levéltára (MNL OL), Diplomatikai Levéltár (DL), no. 52950: *Universe eiusdem hereditarie possessiones his temporibus inpacatis per nephandorum Turkorum insultus prorsus et omnino existunt devastate.*

15 Frigyes Pesty, *Oklevelek Temesvármegye és Temesvárváros történetéhez*, I. 1183–1430, ed. Tivadar Ortvay, (Pozsony: Eder István Könyvnyomdáya, 1896): *hostiliter subintrasset et eadem devastando et conburrendo, ac quamplurimos nostros regnicolas captivando, penes possessionem Chak appellatam hys crudeliter peractis descendisset, tunc prefatus magister Nicolaus Comes, leonina audacia suffultus, unacum suis asseclis, et ceteris nostris fidelibus, noctis ín silencio post eos properans et cum eisdem sevissimis paganis bellica certamina uti atleta Dei ibidem conmittens, et in area ipsius certaminis, contra eosdem, celico opitulamine victoriam optinens.*

along with their goods.[16] To the success of the first Ottoman attacks north of the Danube could have also contributed the way in which the attackers took advantage of the cooperation of some nobles from the borderland. Such was the case of a nobleman named Paul, who betrayed the Christian faith and supported the Turks in entering the kingdom. As a consequence, he lost his possessions in the Cuvin (Keve) county to Nicholas of Gara, during the same year, 1396.[17] The charter also came with an important statement: the Ottomans (Turks) became arch-enemies (*capitales inimicos*), the main threat of the Hungarian frontiers, a status they maintained during late Middle Ages and in the Early Modern Age.

The Ottoman raiding incursions were still in their early phase, but they had already inspired feelings of fear and insecurity. Throughout the entire fifteenth century, this situation was repeated many times, affecting areas farther north from the Danube, reaching over 100 km beyond Ottoman territories. By the mid-fifteenth century, the nobles of the counties located between the Mureş and the Danube, complained about the Turks who had lain to waste the Lower Parts of the realm, reaching the Mureş Valley, where they attacked the noble residences and destroyed the documents of property.[18] It is clear that the swift Ottoman troops performed devastating attacks in the proximity of important urban centres, where the most estates were concentrated in the region south of the Mureş River. But such raids were still rare during the age of Matthias Corvinus. By the end of the fifteenth century, they became more frequent in context of the major political, financial and military crisis of the Hungarian kingdom. Lack of funds created problems in defending the territories located near the Turks. The commanders of the border fortresses were always complaining about the lack of money and provisions or the insufficiency of their troops.[19] In theory, at the

---

16 MNL OL, DL 92112: *iobagiones de ipsa terra nostra Temeskus propter metum Turkorum evasos, eosdem unacum rebus suis universis restituat.*

17 MNL OL, DL 8512: *Paulus tamquam armiductor sceleris et perfidie ac infidelitatis sectator et invitator perversus non verens in sacram orthodoxam fidem zyzaniam seminare sevissimos Turcos, nostros et regni nostri capitales inimicos, sub cuiusdam false excusationis velamine in regnum nostrum introducere non expavit.*

18 Magina, "In the hands of the Turks," 67–68.

19 The bans of Severin for instance, permanently asked the king and the Saxon towns in Transylvania for support. The king seldom tried to involve various actors in supporting the southern frontier (Saxon University, Roman-Catholic bishopric of Transylvania, voivode of Transylvania), but only with a partly success; see: Adrian Magina, "*As the Turks moved on them*…New documents on Severin and the Lower parts of the Hungarian kingdom before the battle of Mohács," in *Politics and Society in the Central*

beginning of the sixteenth century, almost 5.100 soldiers were available along the Danube frontier, and more than twice as many troops in Croatia, from which 1.300–1.400 hussars, covering a territory of about 30.000 km.[20] The hussars, mainly of South-Slavic origin, represented the light cavalry, settling mostly in the north of the province, on the royal domains and on those of the Serbian nobles, near Timişoara. The inefficiency of money allocation was another problem. For instance, the military high officials (counts of Timiş or bans of Severin) were given thousands of florins, theoretically enough to maintain a certain number of troops, but the money never came in due time or in sufficient amount. The Royal Court allocated only 400 florins in cash and 100 florins in salt[21] to restore four forts on the Danube, but the sum was not enough for a thorough restoration. In 1509, Emeric Perényi, palatine of the Hungarian kingdom, ordered the noble community of Caransebeş to send, as usual, the necessary workers (*rusticos et iobagiones*) for the repairs at the fortress of Severin.[22]

The people living in the southern parts of the kingdom were the ones who suffered the most because of the Ottoman attacks. As we have already seen, in 1396, such a raiding party reached Ciacova (Csák), only 30 km away from Timisoara. Another example of such an attack comes from the beginning of the sixteenth century, when Stephen Werbőczy (author of the famous *Tripartitum*, the most notorious law-book of medieval Hungary) was given an estate near the same city of Timişoara. The donation charter, dating from 1507, reveals how affected the areas around the largest urban centre between the Mureş and the Danube were. It is noted there that the estate granted to Werbőczy had only 20 populated settlements, all the others (62) being totally desolated by the Turks.[23] A raid of the swift Ottoman troops reached the town of Oradea in 1491, the

---

and South-Eastern Europe (13th–16th centuries), II, ed. Zsuzsana Kopeczny (Cluj-Napoca: Editura Mega, 2021), 93–100.

20 András Kubinyi, "A Szavaszentdemeter-nagyolaszi győzelem 1523-ban. Adatok Mohács előzményéhez," *Hadtörténelmi Közlemények* 25 (1978): 196.

21 Thallóczy Lajos, *Jajca (bánság, vár és város) története* (Magyarország melléktartományainak oklevéltára. Codex diplomaticus partium regno Hungariae adnexarum 4) (Budapest: Kiadja a Magyar Tudományos Akadémia, 1915), 180: *Civitatibus Zewren, Orswa et Petyz et civitati Sebes, que de novo muratur in pecuniis dantur pro subsidio.......400, in salibus.....100.*

22 *Acta et Documenta partes regni Hungariae inferiores concernentia 1500–1552* (*Acta et Documenta*), collegit et edidit Hadrianus Magina (Cluj-Napoca: Editura Mega, 2020), 64.

23 *Acta et Documenta*, 59–61, especially page 61: *maxima in earum parte premissum Turcorum ob insultum, iam in predia conversarunt.*

unfortified suburbs of Timişoara were attacked and burnt to the ground, while its hinterland was gravelly affected.[24] The low ground around Timişoara, suitable for such fast raids, ended with the destruction of some settlements and the enslaving of the local people. Ottoman incursions also affected the eastern, highland areas, the Banat of Severin namely, located at the frontier with Wallachia. Members of some noble families in Caransebeş (at a distance of about 100 km from the Danube) were captured during Turkish raids, considerable amounts of money being requested for their ransom.[25] Most likely the Ottomans penetrated the Timiş Valley, avoiding the fortifications on the Danube, and the inner fortresses like Mehadia. They were probably small raiding parties (a few hundred soldiers) mostly light cavalry (*akingi*) who set out for plunder, producing as much damage as possible. In 1509, the town of Caransebeş was attacked again by the Ottomans, who wreaked havoc there. As a consequence the inhabitants asked the Transylvanian Saxon towns for help in holding at bay future Turkish invasions.[26]

The documents of the first half of the sixteenth century increasingly record destroyed settlements, burnt dwellings and depopulated areas as the Turkish threat increased. Belgrade was occupied in 1521 and several fortresses and market towns (*oppida*) on the Danube, like Peth or Orşova, were burnt down. The fortress of Severin was occupied and destroyed in 1524. After the fall of Severin, the whole defensive line on the Danube collapsed and the borderlands were left defenceless. The attacks of the Crescent went on, culminating with the defeat of the Hungarian army at Mohács (1526), where the king and many members of the noble and ecclesiastical elites of the kingdom, died on the battlefield.[27] The destruction of the frontier regions was continuous and evident for

---

24 Antonii Bonfini, *Rerum Ungaricarum Decades* (Posonii: Typis Royerianis, 1744), 547, quoted also by Katona István, *Historia regvm stirpis mixtae*, Tom. X, Ord. XVII 1490–1495 (1793): *Omnis aetatis et sexus hominibus in servitutem abstractis divorumque fanis incensis, quum 20 millibus passuum ad Varadinum accessissent; coortum in provincia tumultum veriti, primo in fines suos incolumes fe cum praeda retulerant; deinde auctis ex prospero rerum successu animis, ultra Themesuarum excursionem fecerunt: et oppidum, quod Stephani Bathorei in potestate erat, concremarant: totique provinciae, quam milite vacuam esse cognoverant, vulnera gravissima inflixerant.*

25 Magina, "In the hands of the Turks," 72–73.

26 Costin Feneşan, *Diplomatarium Banaticum*, I (Cluj-Napoca: Editura Mega, 2016), 264.

27 The impact of the battle of Mohácas, August 29, 1526, in János B. Szabó, *A mohácsi csata* (Budapest: Corvina Kiadó, 2011); *Több mint egy csata: Mohács az 1526. évi ütközet a magyar tudományos és kulturális emlékezetben*, eds. Pál Fodor, Szabolcs Varga (Budapest: Oszkár, 2019); Pálosfalvi, *From Nicopolis to Mohács*.

the contemporaries, including the king who lamented: "the Lower Parts of the kingdom are continuously depopulated (laid to waste)".[28]

Several measures were taken in order to increase the efficiency of the defensive system and contain the Ottoman scourge at the southern frontier. In the second half of the fifteenth century, a captain general (*capitaneus generalis partium inferiorum*) was appointed to coordinate the defence of the "Lower Parts" (*partes inferiores*) of the kingdom. Paul Kinizsi was the most representative figure who held this office for two decades and managed to maintain the defence of the southern frontier operational and even initiated offensive actions in the Ottoman territories.[29] The documents of that time mention two officials (captains) in the case of Severin, a key position on the southern frontier, for a better management of the dangerous situation generated by the Ottoman expansion.[30] The Habsburgs continued the course set in the second half of the fifteenth century, and during the short time they controlled the kingdom after Mohács (1526), they tried to keep two officials at the defensive structures of the border areas.[31] On the other hand, the noble and ecclesiastical elite found a way to withstand the Ottoman impact by building some fortifications which offered limited protection, at least against Turkish raids. Dozens of such fortified residences or castles were built in the southern parts of the Hungarian kingdom, from the late fourteenth century up to the early sixteen century.[32] This is the case of the castle at Galad, built by the family Hagymási of Beregsău (Beregszó) in 1461, a fortification of 32×32 m, with 1.5 m thick walls, probably built of bricks on a stone

28 Jenő Házi, *Sopron szabad királyi város története*, part I, 7. *Oklevelek, levelek és iratok 1521-től 1531-ig* (Sopron: Székely és Társa Könyvnyomdája, 1929), 22: *partes inferiores regni continue depopulantur.*

29 His activity and countless fights with the Ottomans, in Haţegan, *Pavel Chinezu, passim.*

30 Bans in Severin in an update list, in Norbert Tóth, Richárd Horváth, Tibor Neumann, Tamás Pálosfalvi, *Magyarország világi archontológiája, 1458–1526*, I. *Főpapok és bárók* (Budapest: MTA Bölcsészettudományi Kutatóközpont, Történettudományi Intézet, 2016), 149–53.

31 Haus-, Hof- und Staatsarchiv (HHStA), Ungarische Akten (UA). Allgemeine Akten (AA), fasc. 8, konv. A, f. 5v: *In confinibus et ad confinia regni tales officiales locare et tenere dignetur et personaliter residentiam illic habere debeant vel causam in quibus potissimum necesarium fuerit duos officiales tenere.*

32 A list of the fortifications located in the southern territory of Mureş River, even incomplete, in Dumitru Ţeicu, *Cetăţi medievale din Banat. Medieval fortifications in Banat* (Timişoara: Cosmopolitan Art, 2009).

foundation.[33] This structure succeeded in playing the role it had been built for during the first decades of the sixteenth century, and thus two noblemen were granted some possessions in 1528, for their part in the defence of the Hagymási fortification against the Ottoman attacks.[34] At Opatiţa, not far from Timisoara, the church was surrounded by wooden walls, in order to protect it from the Turks, since the late fourteenth century. After the wooden walls were ruined by the passing of time, in 1432 two noblemen asked for a permission to rebuild the fortification.[35]

It wasn't just the lowland nobles who tried to protect themselves this way, but also those in the highland of the Banat of Severin. A hearing from 1539 in a lawsuit between two noblemen from the Banat of Caransebeş and Lugoj records the testimony of a noble lady that remembered how she took refuge during her childhood (probably in the early sixteenth century), for fear of the Turkish attacks, in a castle built for this purpose by a nobleman, in the Cerna Valley, near Mehadia.[36] Clearly, such small forts could have offered protection only for a few people and only for a short time, as hideouts for refugees from the swift Ottoman riders.

The measures mentioned above (defensive reorganization, castle building) were not always efficient in protecting the population, especially during the times of crisis in the kingdom. Most of the inhabitants had no other option but to flee or to lose their goods, and sometimes their life, because the attacks had

---

33 Livia Magina, *La periferia Europei centrale: studii privind Banatul medieval şi premodern* (Cluj-Napoca: Academia Română – Centrul de Studii Transilvane, 2015), 33–35.

34 *Acta et Documenta*, 142, no. 77: *in conservatione castrorum ipsorum interiorum que periculosissimis temporibus strenue animositer defenderunt ab hostibus, sed et etiam in multis conflictibus cum sevissimis Turcis habitis.*

35 Koloman Juhász, *Die Stifte der Temeswarer Diozese im Mittelalter* (Münster: Aschendorf Verlag und Buchhandlung,1927), 263–265: *Supplicatio nobilis Simonis Stamsie et nobilis Dean Ratico pro licentia aedificandi sive restaurandi muros in villa Opatiza, Cenadiensis diocesis. In qua quidem villa est quoddan casale, in quo quaedam ecclesia parochialis sub vocabulo Virginis gloriose fundata, habetque dicta ecclesia a superiore parte in angulis duas sacristias, super quibus olim ad tuendam ecclesiam contra incursiones Turcorum muri de lignaminibus aedificati sunt. Qui muri autem iam vetustate consumpti sunt, quam ob rem praefati nobiles viri eos lapidibus reparare desiderant.*

36 A. Magina, L. Magina, "O ascultare de martori şi realităţi bănăţene într-un document din 1539," *Analele Banatului, S.N., Arheologie-Istorie*, XXII (2014): 271: *relicta condam Ioannis Therewk de Zwpan, iurata et examinata fassa fuisset, scire veraciter, quod Michael Fodor, avus Francisci Fodor, castellum erexisset prope Kys Themes et ipsa tunc puella existens dum fama Thurcarum audita fuisset, tunc in illud castellum confugissent.*

become more frequent in the first decades of the sixteenth century. A series of reports from the late 1520s mention the frequency and impact of the Ottoman raids that affected the settlements in the Mureş Valley and even further within the kingdom.[37] The Turkish expeditions at that moment must be understood in the context of the civil conflict for the throne, between Ferdinand of Habsburg and John Szapolyai, a dispute with major consequences for the safety of the Hungarian frontiers.[38] The Ottomans were on Szapolyai's side, an opportunity to intervene in the southern borderlands of the realm controlled by Ferdinand's loyalists, who were sending alarming news about the presence of the Turkish armies which acted at will and unhindered in the region.[39] A year later, in 1528, a Turkish fleet and cavalry troops went up the Tisza River and pillaged the territories they crossed.[40] The Ottoman troops destroyed the countryside by Nădlac (Nagylak) and Timişoara, towards Gyula; they burned and destroyed the goods and estates of George marques of Brandenburg and Lossonczi family.[41] From there the Ottomans went north, up to Satu Mare (Szatmár), where they brutalized the locals (*Turcis ipsi crudeliter tractavit*), men, women, maidens or men of church alike.[42] Nevertheless, John Szapolyai relied on the support of the Turkish troops to impose his own authority in the Lower Parts, still loyal to Ferdinand. Szapolyai's soldiers met the Ottomans at Cenad, and went together towards Timisoara in order to besiege it.[43] With Turkish support, John Szapolyai

37 HHStA, UA, AA, fasc. 11, konv. C, f. 99: *desolatis iam fuga colonorum omnibus fere locis inferiorum partium regni, usque ad duas has civitates Budensis et Pesthiensis.*

38 Gábor Barta's work, *La route qui mène à Istanbul: 1526–1528* (Budapest: Akadémiai Kiadó, 1994), *passim*. Well observed the dispute for the throne in Hungary.

39 Thus, John Vitez of Kalló wrote at the end of 1527: *venit quidam famulus noster de partibus inferioribus, quod retulit gentem Turcarum nolle discedere, quoad voluntati eorum placuerit*. HHStA, UA, AA, fasc. 7, konv. A, f. 28.

40 HHStA, UA, AA, fasc. 9, konv. A, f. 21: *duas et centum Thurcarum naves per Tibiscum ascensisse et validum equestrem exercitum ad Naghlak castra metatum…multis locis diruptis ac igni ferroque vastatis, magnaque preda abacta.*

41 HHStA, UA, AA, fasc. 9, konv. A, f. 13 (August 1528): *validum Thurcarum exercitum ad Naghlak, qui locus non longe a Themeswar abest castra posuisse ac aliquot millibus ad populandum missis, usque ad Gywla cuncta igni ferroque vastare incepisse, bona dominorum marchionis palatini et Lossonczy aliorumque nobilium combusta, utrum hic exercitus cum preda retrocessent nondum accepimus.*

42 HHStA, UA, AA, fasc. 9, konv. A, f. 25.

43 Eudoxiu de Hurmuzaki, *Documente privitoare la istoria Românilor*, XV/1. *Acte şi scrisori din arhivele oraşelor ardelene Bistriţa, Braşov, Sibiu 1358–1600*, ed. Nicolae Iorga (Bucureşti: Socec, 1911), 308: *Ioannem vidisse in Chanadino cum Mehmetbek et iuniore fratre Ymbraym Bassa, essentque Thurce in magna copia, ita ut Thurce et Rasciani cum*

succeeded by the late 1520s and in the first years of the next decade to impose his authority in the southern territories of the kingdom.

Which were the consequences of these Turkish raids? How did they affect the local population?

Firstly, as noted above, we may speak about devastations, loss of goods and human lives, facts on which all the sources agree. Some of the inhabitants were enslaved, although there are only a few documented cases, coming exclusively from the noble milieu.[44] How many of the local inhabitants were captured, especially from the unprivileged social categories? We will never know, but their number must have been quite high if taking into account the frequency of the raids and the value of human resource. Given the insecurity of the southern frontier, there were also other consequences. I consider the change of the local habitat and the population movements as most significant, leading to depopulation and, partly, to the change of the ethnic structure of the province.

For the first case, I rely on the quite recent archaeological investigations, albeit mostly unpublished until today, which show that, despite the marshy lowland terrain, most of the settlements were located in areas surrounded by water. Many small settlements were concentrated in the narrow marshy valleys. The farmland was not located in the areas threatened by water. The hypothesis of the archaeologists is that the inhabitants chose the most adequate variant to be protected from Turkish invasions and destructions, and the floodable valleys and areas offered a relative protection. This is not a final conclusion as the investigations are still ongoing and the collected material was only partially published.[45] The archaeological data is consistent with the written sources of the

Polonis aliisque copiis facerent XI millia hominum preter certa millia ianiczarorum, quos Ioannes omni die expectaret. This piece of information, dating from December 1528, circulated among the Saxons of Transylvania that arrived in Vienna at the beginning of 1529, where they had not known yet that John Szapolyai was waitng for the help of the Ottoman cavalry – *Thurcos equites expectat* – HHStA, UA, AA, fasc. 11, konv. A, f. 98; in another sources the number is categorically exaggerated, 40.000 Ottomans had have to come so (*expectant ad XL*[ta] *millia Turcarum*) – HHStA, UA, AA, fasc. 10, konv. B, f. 105.

44 Magina, "In the hands of the Turks," *passim*.

45 Investigations of a team lead by Dorel Micle and late Liviu Maruia (West University Timisoara), who kindly provided me the data they had, after their research in situ. Part of those investigations were published in an archeological study on Moşniţa [Liviu Măruia, Cristian Floca, Alexandru Berzovan, Oana Bordea, Dorel Micle, Andrei Stavilă, Lavinia Bolcu, *Geografia istorică a zonei Moşniţa Veche. Rezultatul cercetărilor arheologice de teren* (Cluj-Napoca: BioFlux, 2012)] or in Liviu Maruia's PH Disertation,

time, since, in the fifteenth century, the settlements located on noble estates were concentrated in narrow areas, being small- or middle-sized and very close to each other.[46] Such an organization protected only partially the local population from the devastating effects of the Ottoman raids, as we can see in the reports on the destructions occurred at the beginning of the sixteenth century, but it imposed a specific habitat which would be modified only in the eighteenth century, with the arrival of the Habsburgs.

There are more generous sources for the second case. It is, first of all, a matter of regional migration – the inhabitants fleeing towards areas they considered more secure. Such a phenomenon might be noticed from the late fourteenth century onwards, but it became more frequent by the end of the fifteenth century and the beginning of the next one, in circumstances of increased insecurity. The nobles of the highland in the Banat of Severin are the most representative case. Since the first half of the fifteenth century, the local noble elite took refuge in the city of Caransebeş, a larger fortified settlement that offered a better protection compared to their small fortified residences in the countryside. It was a long process lasting for more than 100 years, but already in the first decades of the sixteenth century these nobles were completely integrated into the urban milieu. The town was changed into a genuine noble residence (*rezidenza di nobili*) where nobles took over the town magistrate and thus the entire administration.[47] The nobility had yet another way of escape: the relocation to a remote estate, located far enough from the risk factors, where they could resume their lives far from the Turkish threat. After losing all their fortune due to the Ottoman invasions, the less favoured social categories had to start over again even relocated. Fleeing from the invaders was the simplest way of escape. However, this led to the depopulation of certain areas on the southern borders, where the density of population was the lowest in the whole kingdom. Both the noble and royal estates

---

Cercetări interdisciplinare vizând reconstituirea geografiei istorice a Dealurilor Lipovei (Timişoara: Excelsior Art, 2011).

46 For instance, on the estate of *Chery*, located on a narrow landstrip, the charters of the age record tens of rural settlements, which must have been of small size, very close to each other – Adrian Magina, "Estate and fort Chery," in *Interethnic Relations in Transylvania. Militaria Mediaevalia in Central and South Eastern Europe*, eds. Zeno Karl Pinter, Anca Niţoi (Sibiu: Editura Astra Museum, 2015), 63–71. For an identical situation on the domain of the family of Danffy of Duboz, see Livia Magina, "La famille Danffy de Duboz," *Banatica* 20, 2 (2010): 21–47.

47 Bálint Lakatos, "Városi nemesek Karánsebesen a 15–16. század fordulóján," *Urbs. Magyar Varostorteneti Evkonyv* 3 (2008): 71–94.

were affected, but since no one wanted to lose their work force, the recovery of human capital was regulated to a certain degree. The loss of human resource was compensated by external migration, mostly from the South-Slavic territories.[48]

Up to the death of Despot George Branković (1456), we might speak only about a scars presence of the Serbs in Hungary, as familiars or servants on the huge domains the South-Slavic potentates owned all over the kingdom; thus, the migration was a reduced one, with a couple of exceptions represented by the communities located on the Danube, like Kovin and Haram. The medieval Serbian state collapsed in 1459, after the fall of the of Smederevo fortress, the political centre of the Despotate. The fall of the fortress to the Ottomans determined several waves of migration, both of elites and a part of the Serbian population, to the kingdom of Hungary where they could find the much-needed protection. It was only in the age of King Matthias, when the borders were stable and the Ottoman impact on the southern areas the kingdom has not yet been felt so strongly. The nobles were the first refugees, among whom the Jakšić family was the most important. The continuous warfare at the borders and the raids of the Hungarian troops in Serbia generated the opportunity for a part of the South-Slavic population to leave the Ottoman rule. Paul Kinizsi, count of Timiş and captain general of the Hungarian troops at the southern borders of the realm, was directly interested in populating the areas under his jurisdiction, previously devastated by the Turks. 200.000 individuals came or were brought to the kingdom between 1480 and 1483, originating from the areas of Smederevo and Kruševac, located between the rivers Mureş, Danube and Tisza. These massive groups of population settled near their places of origin, mainly in the southern parts of the present day Banat, the most depopulated areas because of the geographic environment and the previous Ottoman invasion. Others settled near Timişoara or on the Mureş Valley, both regions devastated by the Ottomans and thus prone to demographic movements. Due to the military role of the nobles and South-Slavic population, King Matthias and, later, the Jagiellonians encouraged their settlement, in order to fortify the southern border of the kingdom against the Ottoman threat. For instance, on the estates of the Jakšić family at Nădlac and on those of Voivode Miloš Belmužević near Timişoara, the charters of the early sixteenth century record more often South-Slavic names instead of the Hungarian

48 For the South-Slavic population of medieval and early modern Hungary, see Aleksa Ivić, *Istorija Srba u Ugarskoj: od pada Smedereva do seobe pod Čarnojevićem, 1459–1690* (Zagreb: Privrednikova knijižara, 1914) and Ferenc Szakály, "Délszlávok a középkori Magyarországon," *Napjaink* 5, 2 (1991): 11–18.

names recorded in the second half of the fifteenth century. In the mid-sixteenth century, a tithe register recorded that 25 % of the total population was of Serbian origin. The Serbs were registered as *Rasciani sunt, decimis non tenentur* or simply *non dant decimas*, because they didn't pay taxes to the CatholicChurch.[49]

The Ottoman expansion could not be contained in spite the efforts of Hungarian kings to minimize the effects of the invasions from the south. The Turkish raids on the borderlands between the Danube and the Mureş, although never ceased, lost their intensity after King John Szapolyai consolidated his position on the throne of Hungary and appointed his loyalists as officials of the southern parts of the kingdom. After the collapse of the fortresses on the Danube, the Lower Parts of the kingdom (the territory of the present day Banat) became an open space for Ottoman expansions, the troops of the Crescent being able to cross the Danube unhindered. The political context following Szapolyai's alliance with the Sublime Porte temporarily diminished the Turkish threat.[50] After King John Szapolyai death (1540) the plan of the Habsburgs for the recovery of the Hungarian kingdom resumed. The reaction of the Sublime Porte was swift: in 1541, Buda was occupied while the central part of the Hungarian kingdom was transformed into an Ottoman *eyalet*. A new attempt of the Hapsburgs to impose their authority, this time in Transylvania, by removing Isabella Jagiellon, Szapolyai's widow (1551), determined a new Ottoman offensive. Following two violent campaigns, the lowlands of the present day Banat (including the cities of Timişoara and Lipova) were occupied and integrated in the Ottoman administrative system (1552), for more than one and a half century. It was the conclusion

49 Adrian Magina, "Le long voyage vers la terre promise: les migrations serbes en Banat (XVe–XVIe siècles)," in *Between Worlds: The age of Jagellonians*, eds. Florin Nicolae Ardelean, Christopher Nicholson, Johannes Preiser-Kapeller, (Frankfurt am Main: Peter Lang GmbH, 2013), 129–140.

50 A rumour of 1538 mentioned an Turkish invasion in the areas around Timişoara and Caransebeş, despite the fact that Peter Petrović was by that time count of the Timiş County, and a loyalist of King Szapolyai, an intimate of the Ottomans: *Thurcae… regnum intra Tibiscum et Transylvaniam circa Themeswar invadant; …magnam iam predam circa Karansebes factam et locum illum interceptum esse per Thurcas…* Országos Széchényi Könyvtár, Budapest, Kézirattár, fond 432/32, *Pesty Frigyes kivonatai a bécsi állami levéltárból 1532–1602*, f. 98v (the original document in HHStA, UA, AA, fasc. 36, konv. B, f. 63–65). The Ottoman intervention in the Lower Parts of the kingdom may be understood in this case in the context of the political events of the year, the concluding of the treaty of alliance between Szapolyai and the Habsburgs (the Treaty of Oradea), correlated with the Turkish attack against Moldavia ruled by Petru Rareş.

of a war of attrition that began 150 years before, a conflict won in the end by the Ottomans. Once integrated into the Ottoman world, the political, ethnic and religious structures of the southern territories of the kingdom were permanently changed.

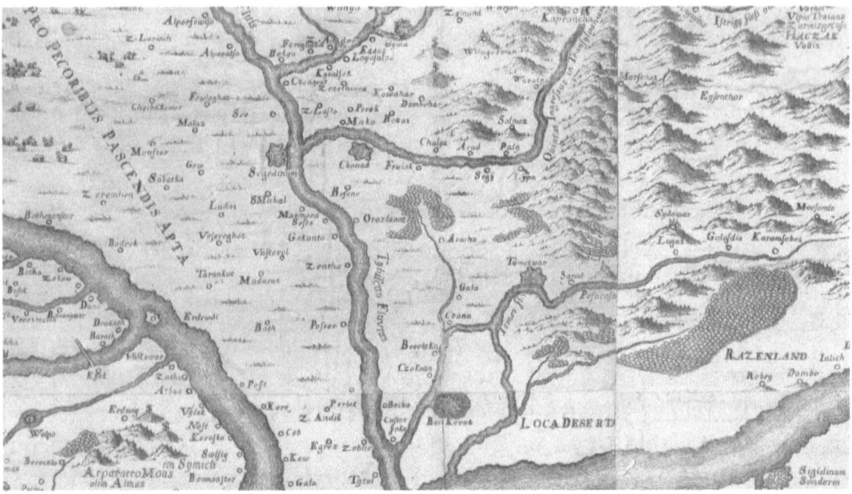

The Lower Parts of the Hungarian Kingdom bordered by the Carpathians and the Danube, Tisa and Mureș rivers, detail from *Ungaria cum finitimiis provinciis...*/Hungary and its frontier provinces, Georg Matthäus Vischer/Matthias Greischer, 1682, cooper engraving (Landesarchiv Baden-Württemberg Abt. Generallandesarchiv Karlsruhe)

Nándor Virovecz

Ottoman Advancement into the Northern Parts of the Hungarian Kingdom between the Conquest of Buda and the Evolution of the Border Fortress Line, 1543–1549

Abstract: Though the Battle of Mohács (1526) may be the most widely known event of the Ottoman conquest of the Kingdom of Hungary, the permanent military presence of the Turks was not established until after the Capture of Buda in 1541. A few years following that, the Ottomans launched an attack to establish a defensive zone around their northernmost garrison. In answer to this new threat, King Ferdinand I and some of the noble Hungarian orders tried to organise the construction of a line of fortresses. By 1549 Ferdinand managed to solidify his hold on the northern part of the kingdom, with the main strongholds reorganised under a new form of management; however, from 1543 to 1549, due to frequent Ottoman raids, the region north of Buda (especially Bars and Hont counties) became a permanent war zone. This paper aims at presenting the most important events of this period that took place in this contested region before the creation of the border guard fortress-line, focusing on the changing reactions of the local society. Most of the sources cited are yet unpublished letters from the Archives of Banská Štiavnica (Schemnitz/Selmecbánya).

Keywords: Ottomans, Buda, Fortifications, Border, Balassa Menyhárt

This study focuses on the Ottoman conquest of Hungary in the second-third of the sixteenth century. The territory primarily affected by the Ottoman advancement in the given period was the co-called Lower Hungarian region (Alsó-Magyarország), particularly the North Central parts of the Hungarian Kingdom, stretching from Buda northwards to the area of the mining towns. The time frame of this study is set between the conquest of Esztergom (Strigonium/Gran) in 1543 and the strengthening of King Ferdinand I's power in the region in 1549 marked by the construction of a border fortress line in the area.

Although, the Battle of Mohács (29 August 1526) is associated with the beginning of the Ottoman era in Hungary, the conquest of Hungary spanned over decades of Suleiman I's reign, and the Ottoman expansion commenced gradually in several phases. In reality, Ottoman presence in Hungary began with the fall of Belgrade (Beograd) and the occupation of Srem (Szerémség) in 1521, while the lasting conquest of the central parts of Hungary happened only in 1541, the first time when the Ottomans stationed army units permanently in the area. Stopping the Ottoman advancement was hindered by domestic political factors in Hungary primarily because the kingdom had two elected monarchs – Ferdinand I of the Habsburg dynasty and János I of the Szapolyai dynasty – since 1526/1527: While the latter was a vassal to the Ottomans, the former, King Ferdinand was supported by his elder brother, Emperor Charles V of the Holy Roman Empire, who relied on a significantly larger budget than Ferdinand. Ferdinand's dependency on Charles materialized in financial aspects and determined or limited the former's policies and opportunities in Hungary. Notably, Emperor Charles V was not indifferent towards the events of Central Europe: influenced by *Universitas Christiana*, the Emperor sent Spanish troops to aid his younger brother's positions in Hungary during the 1540s, which proved to be a decisive contribution to successfully halt the Ottoman advancement.

The Ottoman conquest of Buda and the establishment of Ottoman Hungary in 1541 fostered cooperation and consensus between the Hungarian high nobility and King Ferdinand to establish new effective and lasting defence lines. Although the joint armies of the Hungarian high nobility and the Holy Roman Empire made an attempt to liberate Buda in 1542, their failure led to the realization that the Ottoman presence would be lasting. Consequently, the new situation required new forms and lines of defence. Although plans for a new border fortress line were soon devised, they could not be put in practice,[1] as in effect, Ferdinand's reign in Hungary was strictly limited to few Western counties and towns. However, in the 1540s Ferdinand gradually expanded his territory of rule with the help of the pro-Habsburg Hungarian high nobility and the financial and military aid of Charles V.[2] In essence, the future of the Hungarian Kingdom depended on the imperial and great power politics of the Habsburgs, especially on the military positions of the dynasty in Western Europe.[3] Ferdinand's lasting rule in Hungary was eventually reinforced by Capitan General Niklas graf zu Salm's campaign, which resulted in recapturing a number of strategically

---

1 Concerning these early plans, Géza Pálffy, *A császárváros védelmében* (Győr: Győr-Moson-Sopron Megye Győri Levéltára, 1999), 45–56.

2 Further details, Zoltán Korpás, *V. Károly és Magyarország* (Budapest: Századvég, 2008); Zoltán Korpás, "Álvaro de Sande hadjárata Trencsén vármegyében – 1545," in *Redite ad cor. Tanulmányok Sahin – Tóth Péter emlékére*, ed. Lilla Krász, and Teréz Oborni (Budapest: ELTE Eötvös Kiadó, 2008), 199–210.

3 Barnabás Guitman, Zoltán Korpás, Ferenc Tóth, and János B. Szabó, "A magyarországi török várháborúk nemzetközi háttere, 1547–1556," *Világtörténet* 9 (41), no. 2. (2019): 253–93.

important fortifications with a mixed Spanish-Germany-Hungarian army of 5.000 soldiers.[4] The success of this military campaign enabled King Ferdinand to create an administration capable of collecting taxes and governing the region, which also enabled the plans devised on a new border fortress line to be realized.

A Double Buffer Zone: Habsburg-Szapolyai Clashes and the First Ottoman Raids

Due to the internal power struggle of the two royal families, the Habsburgs and the Szapolyais, and the renewed Ottoman military activities since the spring of 1544 aiming at expansion or plunder, the North Central regions of the Hungarian Kingdom transformed into a buffer zone in the 1540s. The region was politically divided between King Ferdinand and King János, and their ever-changing rule was indeed determined by allegiance of the local land-owing nobility. Subsequently, local hostilities and land disputes often influenced and changed loyalties. Besides the Church, András Báthory of Ecsed, the Podmaniczky and Kosztka families, in the Central regions Balassa and Nyáry families, while in the Eastern regions Ferenc Bebek, István Losonczy and the *homo novus* Mátyás Basó possessed the largest estates in the Northeast region. Antagonism among these land-owners frequently culminated in prolonged local feudal wars like in the case of the Balassa and Nyáry brothers' decade-long clashes.

Competition for the *comes* position was the main reason for the above-mentioned hostility. Although King Ferdinand nominated Menyhárt Balassa as the *comes* of Hont county on 23 April 1533,[5] he did not take the oath. Eventually Menyhárt Balassa and his brothers switched sides and subjected themselves to the rule of King János, therefore King Ferdinand gave the position to Ferenc Nyáry on 6 January 1535.[6] Similarly to his "predecessor", Nyáry did not take the oath, however, both Balassa and Nyáry considered themselves as the official *comes* of Hont. Soon their conflict was channelled into the internal struggle between the two royals of Hungary. On 28 October 1537, Zsigmond Balassa,

4 On the campaign, Zoltán Korpás, "Egy spanyol zsoldosvezér levelei a XVI. század közepén vívott magyarországi háborúkról. Adalékok Bernardo de Aldana magyarországi tevékenységéhez (1548–1552)," *Fons* 6, no. 1–2 (1999): 3–129; Nándor Virovecz, "Száműzetéstől főkapitányságig. Balassa Menyhárt és az erdélyi hatalomváltás (1549–1552)," *Hadtörténelmi Közlemények* 128, no. 1. (2015): 31–54.

5 Magyar Nemzeti Levéltár Országos Levéltára, Budapest (MNL OL), A 57 Magyar kancelláriai levéltár, Libri Regii, Vol. 1, 208.

6 Appointment of Ferenc Nyáry Ferenc as *comes*, MNL OL, A 57, Vol. 1, 311.

the older brother of Menyhárt, married Barbara Fánchy (Fáncsi), the widow of István Pemfflinger, the former Castellan of Diósgyőr, who passed away in May. Following the marriage, the Balassas took the fortification of Diósgyőr, and Nyáry was tasked to recapture it.[7] Although both royals called for maintaining peace, by the end of the year Nyáry plundered the territories of Zsigmond Balassa,[8] prompting the Balassa brothers to take revenge, thus the hostility developed into a genuine local war between the two sides.

Zsigmond and Menyhárt plundered the territories under Nyáry in Hont County with the final aim to conquer those.[9] Meanwhile the son of Tamás Soós, a *familiaris* of Zsigmond Balassa, was beaten half to death by Nyáry when the former paid an official visit to the Forgách brothers.[10] A few years later the clashes ceased, the Balassa family recognized the rule of King Ferdinand. Nevertheless, their relationship with Ferenc Nyáry did not significantly improve. In the end, the dispute over the *comes* position of Hont was discussed by the Diet of Pozsony (Bratislava/Pressburg) in November 1542: the Diet requested the nobles to take the oath and reunify the county. Should they fail to suit this request, the Diet asked King Ferdinand to demote both nobles from their position.[11] By the second half of the 1540s, Menyhárt Balassa became the largest land-owner in the area

7 [...] *ex Wiennae audivi quod domina Barbara Fanchÿ relicta Stephani Peniflinger cum Sigismundo Balassa contraxit matrimonium, dominica die ventura solemnitatem nuptiae celebrari determinaverunt,* [...] *forsan jam castrum GÿosGÿewr obsiderunt et Franciscus Nÿarÿ cum equitibus armatis et peditibus lanczkneht ac servitoribus suis pro defensione huius terrae et montanarum civitatum advenire debebit contra illos Balassa* [...]. Letter of Tamás Dalmady to the judge, community and senate of Schemnitz (*judici et dominis civibus totique senatui Sempnicziensis*), Dalmad, 25 October 1537, MNL OL, R 314 Mohács utáni gyűjtemény, Városi iratgyűjtemény 142/2 tétel, no. 26.

8 Letter of Tamás Dalmady to Tadeus Valkó Bartphensis/Bartfelder, Dalmad, 16 December 1537, Ministerstvo vnútra Slovenskej Republiky, Štátny archív v Banskej Bystrici, pobočka Archív Banská Štiavnica (MMBŠ), fond Magistrát Mesta Banská Štiavnica, Litterae missiles, Box 1537.

9 Letter of Elek Thurzó to King Ferdinand, Sempte, 4 April 1538, József Bessenyei, *Enyingi Török Bálint* (Budapest: Magyar Történelmi Társulat, 1994), 157–58.

10 Letter of György Fráter to Pál Várday, Buda, 30 March 1538, Árpád Károlyi, "Fráter György levelezése s egyéb őt illető iratok a bécsi cs. és kir. államlevéltárból. I. közlemény," *Magyar Történelmi Tár* no. 2, (1878) 218.

11 Acts 37–38 passed by the Diet of 1542 in Pozsony, Vilmos Fraknói, ed., *Magyar országgyűlési emlékek,* 2. (1537–1545) (Budapest: Ráth Mór, 1875), 416–47; Further requests were made in this regard for Balassa later in time, Fraknói, *Országgyűlési emlékek,* 548.

around the mining towns. Marrying Anna Thurzó, he came into the possession of Léva (Levice) in Bars county, also becoming the *comes* of the county in late 1542 through the guardianship of the under-aged János Lévai. In August 1543, Balassa occupied and built a fortification at the Mountain Szitnya (Sitno) next to Schemnitz.[12] In 1546, he managed to purchase the fortification and estates in Csábrág (Hrad Čabraď) from Péter Pálffy.[13] Meanwhile, Zsigmond, his brother, occupied the neighbouring area, and fortified the Premonstratensian monastery at Bozók (Bzovík).

Ottoman military activities in 1543–1544 aimed to make the route leading to Buda protected and safe by strengthening defence positions in the northernmost guard stations. Following a successful siege, Esztergom was captured in August 1543, but no further advancements were made as the Danube and the Mountain Börzsöny proved to be crucial natural obstructions. Consequently, Bars and Hont counties were untouched by Ottoman forces for the time being. However, after capturing Vác, Nógrád, Visegrád and Hatvan in the spring of 1544, it seemed that the Ottoman forces in Buda and Pest would make an attempt against these two counties. Contradicting this assumption, there had been sporadic rumours spreading from Ottoman Buda since 1543 that the target of a new Ottoman attack would be the fortress of Eger.[14] As a consequence, the area of the River Ipoly became a buffer zone affecting primarily the lands owned by István Losonczy and the Balassa and Nyáry families. Besides soldiers of the Archdiocese of Esztergom stationed at Ság (Šahy/Ipolyság) and Drégely, these families had private armies – consisting of a few hundred soldiers – in the region. Soon Ottoman raids became frequent, which forced the local nobility to take action.

On 19 May, Menyhárt Balassa, his younger brother, János, István Losonczy and several other nobles unified their armies at Szécsény to move towards Eger and clash with the Ottoman troops.[15] Demand for a pro-active initiative against

12 Letter of Zsófia Dersffy of Szerdahely (Pálffy Péterné) to Schlacher Quirinus the judge of Schemnitz, Castle of Csábrág, 1 September 1543, MMBŠ Missiles, Box 1543.

13 Two letters of Menyhárt Balassa Menyhárt to Péter Pálffy, Kékkő, 8 June 1546 and Léva, 13 July 1546, Országos Széchényi Könyvtár, Kézirattár, Magyar Nyelvemlékek, 41–42.

14 Letter of Benedek Serédy to Gáspár Serédy, Szikszó, 23 February 1543, Österreichisches Staatsarchiv, Haus-, Hof- und Staatsarchiv, Viena (ÖStA HHStA), Ungarische Akten, Allgemeine Akten (UA, AA), Fasc. 50, Konv. B, f. 73.

15 Originally, Losonc would have been the meeting place of the units, however, as news reached Kékkő concerning the Ottomans, plans were revised: [...] *et dicunt, quod Thurcae die hesterno sese cum copiis suis versus Agriam movissent et jam in itinere essent. Copiarum numerus non est satis exploratus. Hodie hora ferme quinta ante meridiem domini Melchior et Johannes Ballassa versus Zechen cum gentibus suis armis instructi*

Ottoman attacks led to a meeting held on 6 July in Sajószentpéter with the participation of most nobles from the Central and Northeast. The convening nobles discussed the possibilities of involving the locals in the defence, decided to strengthen the fortress of Eger and asked King Ferdinand for assistance.[16] Their efforts proved to be late, as in the same month the Ottoman troops reached Eger. Although they were unable to take Eger, they pillaged the surrounding area and then moved towards Miskolc (Miškovec/Mischkolz), where they caused signification damages and kidnapped local inhabitants. Based on contemporary reports, it can be assumed that the Ottoman army numbered 5000 soldiers. The same documents testified that the high nobles of the North Eastern region who had clashed with each other before – like the Balassa brothers, István Losonczy, Ferenc Bebek and Mátyás Basó – were on the same page and cooperated with each other.[17]

At the time of the Eger-Miskolc attacks news spread of a possible Ottoman attack against the mining towns. Following an ambush on the Ottoman camp at Pest, Balassa's units learnt that the Ottomans had devised plans to plunder the mining towns besides Eger, therefore they alarmed the town council of Selmecbánya in late May.[18] During the summer, „Perwana" (Pferdana), the ottoman Vojvoda of Esztergom, and Mehmed, the Pasha of Buda sent several letters to the town council.[19] The former offered news concerning Ottoman plans in exchange for a silver cup in his letter written on 24 June in Esztergom.[20] The

descenderunt, ibi dominus Steffanus Lossonchi et alii domini copias gentium suarum cum illis conjugent, illic tandem contra Thurcas versus Agriam descendent […], letter of Ferenc Rácz to Tadeus Valkó Bartphensis/Bartfelder, judge of Schemnitz, Kékkő, 19 May 1544, MMBŠ, Missiles, Box 1544.

16 Fraknói, *Országgyűlési emlékek*, 597–98. 602–05.

17 Letter from the judge and councilors of Pukantz to the judge and councilors of Schemnitz, Pukantz (Bakabánya/Pukanec), 22 July 1544, MMBŠ, Missiles, Box 1544.

18 […] *ut servitores nostri iverant versus Pesth et illinc ex castris Turcarum abripuerunt equos et Turcos aliquos necaverunt et dicunt magnam copiam turcarum esse in promptu in campo Pesthiensi, qui istis diebus faciunt eruptionem et depraedationem. Ipsi quidem Thurci promulgare velle ire ad obsidendam arcem Agriensem* […] *ut volunt ad montanas civitates irrumpere*." Letter of Menyhárt Balassa to the judge of Schemnitz, Léva, 29 May 1544, MMBŠ, Missiles, Box 1544, no. 53.

19 Letter of Perwana, Vojvoda of Esztergom to Tadeus Valkó Bartphensis/Bartfelder, judge of Schemnitz, Esztergom, 18 May 1544, MMBŠ, Missiles, Box 1544; to Kremnica and Nová Baňa, Esztergom, 17 June 1544. MMBŠ, file copy of original correspondence f. 32v.

20 MMBŠ, file copy of original correspondence f. 33r.

latter complained in his letter written on 20 June in Buda for the lack of communication experienced on the behalf of the mining towns since the Ottoman conquest of Buda, also informing them the arrival of his envoy, Péter Kis.[21] A month later, the Pasha of Buda informed the town council of Kremnitz (Kremnica/Körmöcbánya) and other mining towns in a letter written on 16 July that he had been expecting their envoys to negotiate their yielding.[22]

As besides making demands, the Ottoman forces had not moved into the area, the nobility was convinced that the Ottomans would launch an attack eastwards instead of northwards. Previous experience with the Ottomans seemed to support their belief in this regard, which was further strengthened by the fact that the already mentioned natural obstructions had significantly minimalized the chance of an attack northwards.

The Battle of Szalka

From the night of 8–9 September 1544, the Ottoman guard at Esztergom – numbering almost 1.500 soldiers – attacked Léva. Their advancement was halted at the gates of the Léva castle, and was pushed out to the Lower Ipoly region in the course of almost a day-long clash. The withdrawing Ottomans took the river crossing between Ipolypásztó (Pastovce) and Ipolyszalka (Salka) to find that their path had been blocked by the unified Moravian and Hungarian armies. These units decimated the enemy, leaving half of the Ottomans dead on the battlefield.

One of the most detailed and redundant accounts on the Battle of Szalka is attributed to Sebestyén Tinódi, a contemporary epic poet, who presented the events in his poem *About the Encounter on the Plain of Szalka* (*Az szalkai mezőn való viadalról*), composed in Nagyszombat (Trnava), three months after the battle.[23] Besides the poet, a nobleman from Hont county, Tamás Dalmady, the future *vicecomes* of Hont gave a contemporary account on the battle, which he had partially witnessed of. Two days after the battle, he wrote about the events in a letter sent to Tadeus Valkó Bartphensis or Bartfelder, the judge of Schemnitz.[24]

---

21 MMBŠ, file copy of original correspondence f. 32r.

22 MMBŠ, Missiles, Box 1543.

23 "XIX. Az szalkai mezőn való viadalról," István Sugár, ed., *Tinódi Sebestyén: Krónika* (Budapest: Európa Könyvkiadó, 1984), 467–76.

24 Letter of Dalmady to Tadeus Valkó Bartphensis/Bartfelder, Dalmad, 11 September 1544, MNL OL, R 314 142/2 tétel, no. 52.

These two accounts enable the reconstruction of events commencing for several days in the region of Esztergom-Léva-Ipolypásztó-Ipolyszalka.[25]

Despite the sources, the exact launching point of the Ottoman units has still remained unclear. While Dalmady did not mention any launching places, Tinódi believed it to be Esztergom. The former only noted that two days prior the battle, on the Sunday of 7 September some Ottoman soldiers had crossed the mountains at Drégely. It may be assumed that this unit might have joined the Ottoman units marching against Léva during the night on the Monday of 9 September. Based on the direction of the Ottoman retreat and Dalmady's addition that soldiers had also arrived from "other places" on Monday, the most likely launching point is the Esztergom and Kakat (later known as Párkány, Štúrovo) area.[26]

In this case, the Ottoman troops' route would have led next to the River Garam. Provided they moved upstream on the right bank of Garam, taking the route of Zselíz (Želiezovce), they had to cross the river to march towards Léva.[27] Between the left bank of the river and the Garamkövesd–Léva North-South road line (laying 1–2 kilometres eastwards of the river), the area was swampy, covered with woods and groves. Overall, it made a more suitable place for hiding than the road on the right bank, which cut through villages. Moving during the night also supports the idea that the Ottomans had wished to remain undetected. Although, the exact crossing point on the River Garam is unknown, nonetheless, they reached Léva by moving upstream on the left river bank and avoiding inhabited areas. The gathering Hungarian-Moravian units later indeed retrieved information from an Ottoman captive, who remained stuck in the swamp during the night march. A few weeks later, Balassa informed others that 400 Ottoman

---

25 Although Tinódi mixed contemporary and past events in his poem, his lines fit the accounts of Dalmady. On the similarities and dissimilarities of the two sources, Virovecz Nándor, "Tinódi történeti hitelességéhez: kortárs beszámoló a „szalkai viadalról", *Történelmi Szemle* 62, no. 2 (2020): 223–44.

26 Another possible launching point could have been the castle of Nógrád as units had been dispatched from Esztergom to Nógrád between the spring and summer of 1544. Moreover, these units might have joined the attack launched from Esztergom, Klára Hegyi, *A török hódoltság várai és katonasága. II. A budai vilájet várainak adattára* (Budapest: MTA Történettudományi Intézete, 2007), 698, 751.

27 More than 100 years later, Kálna (Kalná nad Hronom, Slovakia) became the alternative river crossing point on those parts of the Garam where the campaign had commenced in the 1540s. Balázs Sudár, "A zsarnócai csata (1664) – török szemmel," *Történelmi Szemle* 58, no. 3 (2016): 475–81.

marauders had hidden in the marshy flood area at Sáró (Šarovce), located south to Léva.[28]

Only estimates can be made concerning the number and composition of Ottoman units: overall almost 1.500 soldiers marched against Léva, probably consisting of 1.000 riders and 500 janissaries, and no artillery. Based on the accounts, the janissaries stayed behind to protect the route. When it comes to the goals of the campaign, once again we rely on guesses. As the Ottomans ambushed and burnt the town at dawn, and then marched immediately against the castle, it can be assumed that capturing Menyhárt Balassa had been among their objectives. Undoubtedly, the Ottomans regarded Balassa as the prime trouble-maker hindering the submission of the area to Ottoman rule. Additionally, any schemes devised against the mining towns would have been in vain without the elimination of Léva, conclusively making the occupation of the fortification an imperative. In essence, the decrees made by the Sublime Porte (Imperial Council) pertaining to Hungary had already included plans on taking Léva. Based on the letter the Pasha of Buda received from the Porte on 12 January 1545, it can be assumed that the pasha had reported before that Balassa's raids had caused issues in regard to the food management of the Buda and Pest garrisons. According to the Pasha, some of Balassa's soldiers had been captured and areas and town belonging to him had been burnt in retaliation. Likely, these vague claims on the counteractions served to hide the fact that Balassa had managed to score victories over Ottoman soldiers on different occasions.[29]

The attack on Léva, however, caused as much surprise for the ambushing Ottomans as for Balassa: at the night of the attack, Balassa resided in Balassagyarmat, and was therefore absent from Léva.[30] Nonetheless, it cannot

---

28 Tinódi's poem recalled the events as Ottomans having stuck in the mud, while the letter of the judge and councilors of Pukantz sent to the judge and councilors of Schemnitz accounted 400 Ottoman units in the flood area, Pukantz, 17 September 1544, MMBŠ Missiles, Box 1544.

29 Géza Dávid and Pál Fodor, "*Az ország ügye mindenek előtt való.*" *A szultáni tanács Magyarországra vonatkozó rendeletei (1544–1545, 1552)* (Budapest: MTA Történettudományi Intézete, 2005), 25–28.

30 [...] *castrum Lewa et oppidum Lewa invaserunt et incineraverunt et anteriores portas castri deseccaverant, nisi Deus avertit, si ingenia habuissent in absentia domini Melchioris Balassa, qui eo tunc in Gÿarmath fuit, sed noctis tempore festinantissime superadvenit et comitabatur Turcas castrum obtinuissent*. This is the most significant contradiction between Tinódi's poem and Dalamdy's accounts. However, other primary sources also verify Balassa's initial absence like the letter of Andreas Noldel, a merchant-entrepreneur in Schemnitz, who summarized the events for the town council of Schemnitz. Letter

be dismissed that the Ottomans might have been aware of this, and had indeed tried to take advantage of his absence. After burning the town, the Ottomans attacked the castle and managed to crack its outer gates. Before the arrival of the Ottomans to Léva, Balassa had already been informed about enemy movement. As a result, by that time the attack on the castle began, Balassa and his soldiers had returned hastily to Léva. Besides relieving the town, they freed the captives and killed those who had partaken in the burning of the town. Under the new circumstance, the Ottomans could not take the castle, and chose to retreat with their loot. At dawn, following a rapid reinforcement, Balassa made the decision to pursue the Ottomans with 50–100 soldiers.[31] To take a strategic advantage of the janissaries left behind, the Ottomans tried to engage the enemy at Ludány (Mýtne Ludany), a few kilometres southeast to Léva to cover the withdrawal of the cavalry packed with plundered goods. Being outnumbered, Balassa avoided any clashes, and patiently waited for the hussars of Ság to arrive.[32] With these reinforcements, Balassa's units numbered 400 soldiers, which started pursuing the retreating enemy. They only reached the Ottomans in late afternoon or early evening at Ipolypásztó. Provided, the launching point of the Ottoman expedition was Esztergom, the direction of Ottoman withdrawal towards Ipolypásztó raises several questions, which can be answered by investigating the geography of the region, and by revealing the events commenced at the same time as the attack on Léva.

In effect, the Ottoman campaign was immediately uncovered, and by the night even the westernmost guard stations were informed on the enemy intrusion. Bertalan Horvát (Horvátinovity) and Lőrinc Zolthay from Komárom (Komárno), Ferenc Nyáry from Nagysurány (Šurany) all mobilized their units, and Karl von Zierotin, a Moravian high noble from the far away Vágsellye (Šaľa)

---

of Andreas Noldel to the judge and councilors of Schemnitz, 1544 (without an exact date, however, most probably written a few days following the events), MMBŠ, Missiles, Box 1544.

31 Tamás Dalmady was an eye-witness, *extra possessionem Ludan oculis intuentibus vidi, quomodo oppidum Lewa et Olewa possessio cremabat, etiam vidi gestas et factas Turcarum depredationes et depopulationes eorundem et etiam iidem Turci cum preda et spoliis quomodo recedebant et dominus Melchior Balassa quasi cum equitibus quinquaginta citra vel ultra quomodo insequebatur vel comitabatur easdem*. See footnote 24.

32 *Tandem domini commilitones de Sagh huzarones et dominus Balassa cum gentibus suis in numero ut puta equites quadringenti festinaverunt prope Pazthoh et ibi Turcas invaserunt et dum cum Turcis pugnare incepissent* (…) See footnote 24.

also left with a 1.000 riders to provide aid. His soldiers had been dispatched to Hungary a few months before in the spring of 1544 to assist the defence in border region. As attested by a letter of Tamás Dalmady, he had learnt the presence of the Moravian cavalry before, as their captain had visited Nagyszombat on Palm Sunday, on 6 April 1544. On the following day, the captain had paid the soldiers and had allegedly managed to attract 3.000 (!) hussars/light cavalry soldiers to join him.[33] The arrival of the Moravian units could not have happened without the approval of the Bohemian and Moravian nobility, the extra taxes approved by the Imperial Diet, and last, but not least the consent of Emperor Charles V. Overall, the Moravian-Hungarian units had not been entirely unprepared for the attack, as most of them had already learnt the news on enemy movement by the time the Ottomans crossed the Danube. Following rapid mobilization, the troops arriving from three different directions met and unified in the course of the afternoon somewhere near the village called Kürt (Strekov). Altogether they numbered 1.300 soldiers with the Moravian horsemen constituting the majority. Besides Nyáry, Horvát and Zolthay, Imre Werbőczy and Péter Pálffy were present among the high nobles along with their soldiers negligible in number. The unified army marched to River Garam and blocked the Danubian pathway which the Ottoman units, pursued by Balassa, were using for retreat. Provided the Ottoman units had no intention to withdraw to Ottoman territories located in Nógrád, Vác or Pest by crossing the River Ipoly, it can be concluded that the blocked Danubian route had been the reason for their crossing at Ipolypásztó.

The first attack on the Ottomans at Ipolypásztó was launched by Balassa and the units from Ság. Their attack failed as the janissaries' gunfire halted the cavalry charge. Moreover, the trumpeter was shot, while Ambrus Nagy, the bailiff of Pásztó was beheaded in the course of the first charge.[34] To avoid further loses, the Hungarian soldiers retreated to the village, enabling the Ottomans to resume their withdrawal South-Westwards, anticipating they could eventually reach the Danubian crossing through Ipolyszalka. Nevertheless, this had never happened as reinforcement of von Zierotin and others caught up with the Ottomans and

---

33 *Carolus parvus capitaneus gentium Moraviensium dominica palmarum venit cum pecuniis ad Tirnaviam, feria secunda sequenti distribuit stipendiariis pecunias. Ipse conduxit et habebit ad rationem Moraviensium huzaronum levis armaturae equites tria milia*. Letter of Tamás Dalmady to Tadeus Valkó Bartphensis/Bartfelder, the judge of Schemnitz, Dalmad, 10 April 1544, MMBŠ, Missiles, Box 1544.

34 *Illi jancharones Turci pixidarii tubicinatorem ex pixide desagittaverunt et ille statim de equo cecidit, Ambrosium Nagh officialem de Paztoh iidem Turci in primo congressu capite privaverunt*. See footnote 24.

blocked the Danubian withdrawal route. Due to this development, the Ottomans opted to cross the Ipoly eastwards through the flood area, while the janissaries were trying to cover their movement. At that point, first, the leaders divided the Moravian-Hungarian army into three units, and then crossed the river with two of them to outflank the Ottomans from two sides. Meanwhile, Balassa and his units in Ipolypásztó were contacted and asked to join the attack. The joint offensive of the Hungarian-Moravian army concluded in a decisive victory, leaving at least 700 Ottomans dead.[35]

A Militarized Society in the Border Region: Cases of Szabács, the Ottoman Captive and Makray, the Renegade

Regardless of the Battle of Szalka, it must be stated that the Ottoman offensive on Léva had not been the only attempts made against North Central Hungary at the given time. Almost simultaneously Ottoman raids occurred in the region of Losonc (Lučenec), Rimaszombat (Rimavská Sobota) and Rimaszécs (Rimavská Seč), and later, on 10 September 300 riders appeared at Drégely. Overall, the victory at Szalka was significant, nonetheless, it did not prevent Ottoman intrusion to the region and even in the case of Léva, new Ottoman attempts were made against the town at the end of the month. At the end of the year, Dalmady reported that 8–10 villages were put to ashes and entirely depopulated in the Ság and Szécsény regions on 1 and 2 December.[36]

---

35 *Quare et dominationes vestrae citissime festinanter illuc veniant et eisdem commilitonibus huzaronibus Morawiensibus auxilio sint et sic unanimiter illuc festinantissime properarunt et jam Turci fugiebant. Dicitur quod ex equitibus et peditibus janchÿar sunt prostrati et infra secati plusquam septingenti Turci, alii per montes et silvas fugerunt fugaeque praesidio evaserunt. Ut audio de exercitu Morawiensi interfuerunt magnificus dominus Franciscus Nÿarÿ, magnificus dominus Emericus Werbewczÿ et Petrus Palffÿ, et de Komaron Bartholomeus Horwath et Laurentius Zolthaÿ, Moraviensi cum equitibus mille et trecentis, illi de Sagh et dominus Balassa cum equis quadringentis affuerunt.* See footnote 24.

36 Letter of Tamás Dalmady to Tadeus Valkó Bartphensis/Bartfelder, the judge of Schemnitz, Dalmad, 8 December 1544, MMBŠ, Missiles, Box 1544; Concerning the role of the Balassa family in the defense of the border fortress line in the following decades, Géza Pálffy, "A Balassi család szerepe a törökellenes határvédelemben az Ipoly és a Garam folyók mentén a 16. században," in *Zborník z medzinárodnej konferencie Modrý Kameň, jún 2012 – Rod Balašovcov v 13. až 19. storočí*, ed. Helena Ferencová and Erika Antolová (Modrý Kameň, 2013), 135–46.; in Slovakian: „Účasť rodiny Balašovcov na protitureckej obrane hraníc podlíž riek Ipeľ a Hron v 16. storočí," in *Zborník z*

Meanwhile, the Ottomans managed to capture a number of castles, and gradually took over control in the different areas by establishing guarding posts in them. In essence, these castles and garrisons built in the "Middle Ages" were obsolete. Due to the lack of space for defenders, munitions and supplies, their defence was next to impossible. Often these old fortifications were taken by the Ottomans without any clashes, as the local guards were either non-existent or left voluntarily due to being outnumbered. In such a case was Nógrád in the spring of 1544 and Szanda in July 1546.[37] In some instances, like in the case of Hasznos, located next to Pásztó in Nógrád County, these small and useless fortifications had been dismantled before the arrival of Ottoman troops.[38]

Eventually, due to frequent local clashes and raids, war became a part of everyday life in the region. Representing Pál Várday the Archbishop of Esztergom and Royal Governor —Zsigmond Pozsgay and János Dessewffy engaged in negotiations with the Pasha of Buda in 1545–1546. Their reports gave accounts on the contemporary "grievances" of the Ottomans, which included one of the raids executed by Balassa in Cegléd, and an ambush of the Hajduks at Visegrád resulting in the kidnapping of seven janissaries to Ság.[39] Later reports of Pozsgay and Erasmus Scheurer emphasized that the actions of Balassa and István Losonczy had caused significant issues to the Ottomans. Hajduks serving Balassa launched a raid from Léva, killing five Ottomans in Garamkövesd on 1 February. Additionally, the Ottomans voiced complaints against most fortifications of Balassa – Balassagyarmat, Léva and (Ipoly?)Pásztó –, while the Danubian river crossing at Kakat/Párkány had become a regular place of ambush for Nyáry and his units from Nagysurány.[40] Half a year later, János Dessewffy reported that besides the raids launched from Komárom, Balassa's units were blamed for causing grave shortages of food supplies for Ottomans in Esztergom.[41]

The prolonged war had a lasting effect on society as well. As usually there were no clearly defined and maintained borders between the Habsburg and Ottoman

---

medzinárodnej konferencie Modrý Kameň, jún 2012 – Rod Balašovcov v 13. až 19. storočí, Zost. Helena Ferencová and Erika Antolová (Modrý Kameň, 2013), 147–58.

37 Letter of Menyhárt Balassa to the judge and councilors of Schemnitz, Balassagyarmat, 21 July 1546, MMBŠ, Missiles 1546. d. (copy).

38 Letter of Zsigmond Balassa to the judge and councilors of Schemnitz, Diósgyőr, 19 October 1546, MNL OL R 314 142/2 tétel, no. 59.

39 ÖStA, HHStA, Staatenabteilungen, Türkei (Turcica) I, Kt. 6, Konv. 2. fol. 49–52(1545.05.24.).

40 ÖStA, HHStA, Turcica Kt. 6. Konv. 3. f. 31–37. (1546. 02. 02–09.)

41 ÖStA, HHStA, Turcica Kt. 6. Konv. 4. f. 94–97. (1546. 09. 25.)

Empires in Hungary, border regions could exercise a degree of freedom in action, and their society and everyday life became vastly different from that of the hinterland. Ottoman advancement in Hont and Bars counties not only resulted in the yielding of Southern villages to Ottoman rule, but it changed the composition of the local population likewise. The presence of armies and the perpetual raids in these regions militarized communities, making the dispossessed or often outlawed members of society the main actors in the borderlands. To explain the atypical composition of such border zone societies, two cases should be revealed as examples.

A significant source is credited to Bernardo de Aldana, the *maestre de campo* of Spanish troops deployed to Hungary to besiege and occupy the fortifications of Menyhárt Balassa. Besides Aldana's diary, his correspondence with King Ferdinand helps to uncover the details of the campaign, and to extract information regarding the border zone communities, contemporary key individuals, besieged fortifications and their defenders.[42] Concerning Balassa, Aldana noted the nobleman's qualities and traits, while also mentioning his bright-minded Ottoman captive called Szabács, whom he kidnapped during one of his raids.[43] Later Balassa sent Szabács to the Pasha of Buda as an envoy, and asked Szabács to pay 2 horses and 2000 talers as an exchange for being liberated, which the envoy fulfilled. The first source giving account on Szabács, however, was not attributed to Bernardo de Aldana, but to Gerhard Veltwyck. Veltwyck, the imperial envoy of Charles V, took time en route to Istanbul in 1546 to negotiate prisoners exchange with Pasha Rustan. The latter promised the former the release of three Christian prisoners – Joannes Theiiss/Hans Teys, Thomas Hopfner/Hoffner and Henrich Satler –, who were held in captivity with Bálint Török and István Mayládin the same tower. According to their deal, three Ottoman prisoners would have been set free in return. Among the three Ottoman captives the Pasha asked in exchange through his envoy, we find a prisoner named Szabács, who had been held in captivity by Balassa, and who was expected to be exchange for Joannes Theiss.[44] Despite the agreement, the exchange of prisoners had been postponed for years, when in 1549 it seemed that Szabács would be freed, Balassa

42 Ferenc Szakály, ed., *Bernardo de Aldana magyarországi hadjárata (1548–1552)*, trans. Scholz László (Budapest: Európa Könyvkiadó, 1986), 59–106.

43 Xabaz in the original Spanish version of Aldana's diary, Szakály, *Bernardo de Aldana*, 73.

44 *„Sabacz beym Balassa". Memoriale de quibusdam captivis liberandis*, ÖStA, HHStA, Turcica Kt. 6. Konv. 3. 1546. I-VI. f. 4.

intervened, and preliminary released Szabács – along with another prisoner – in February under the conditions described above.[45]

Surprisingly, despite these developments, the "captivity story" of Szabács did not end here. During the fall of Temesvár (Timişoara/Temeschwar), besieged by the Ottomans in 1552, Simon Forgách, a defender fighting alongside István Losonczy, was wounded and taken prisoner by the Ottomans during the retreat. Based on the claims made by the humanist historiographer Miklós Istvánffy in his work, Forgách was exchanged for the cavalry officer of Esztergom, named Szabács (!).[46] Although the historiographer's account causes confusion in regard to Szabács, other primary sources help to solve the puzzle. Among these, we find the plea sent by Zsigmond, the father of Simon Forgách to King Ferdinand, asking him to assist the release of his son. Accordingly, the king ordered János Balassa, the younger brother of Menyhárt to exchange Forgách for Szabács, the latter being kept prisoner in Csábrág.[47] Although we have no information on how and when Szabács was taken prisoner for the second time by the Balassa family, it can be assumed that some sort of mutually beneficial arrangement might have been brokered between the Balassas and Szabács, which had been in effect during the latter's six year of "captivity."

The diary of Aldana reveals another typical character of the border zone. Among the three castles of Balassa, the royal army first marched against Szitnya located next to Schemnitz, where the Hungarian noble had constructed a fortification in 1543. The siege of Szitnya took place in the spring of 1549, when Aldana's Spanish units – numbering a few hundred soldiers and assisted by artillery – managed to occupy the fortification after two days on 26 March. As it became clear for the defenders of the castles, they would not have been able to

45 Report of Zsigmond Pozsgay from the Pasha of Buda to Pál Várday and Niklas Graf zu Salm, Februrary 1549, Martinus Georgius Kovachich, ed., *Scriptores Rerum Hungaricarum Minores* (Buda: Typis Regiae Universitatis, 1798), 88; Further accounts from 1544 on the prisoners and their ransom in the letter of Tojgun, Pasha of Buda to Eck von Salm written in Rákosmező, on 6 August 1554. According to this source Eck's father promised Nikolas "Dely Sabacz" 4.750 talers for three prisoners. See also the letter of Dely Sabacz to Eck, Buda, 26 August 1544, Ernst Dieter Petritsch, *Regesten der Osmanischen dokumente im Österreichischen Staatsarchiv I. (1480–1574)* (Wien: Generaldirektion des Österreichischen Staatsarchivs, 1991), 296.

46 Péter Benits, ed., *Istvánffy Miklós magyarok dolgairól írt históriája, Tállyai Pál XVII. századi fordításában,* I/2. 13–24. books (Budapest: Balassi Kiadó, 2003), 194.

47 The letter of King Ferdinand to János Balassa, 3 September 1552, Hadtörténelmi Levéltár, Budapest, Törökkori Gyűjtemény, 1552/22.

hold the fortification for long therefore the castellan started negotiating terms of surrender with Aldana. Aldana's description of the castellan contains valuable details: he wrote about a man of slender-built posture with tan skin, who had a Turkish-style beard and was Turkish by origin. Furthermore, he had served as a janissary in Rhodes, converted to Christianity in Transylvania, where he later joined the service of Balassa.[48] Upon the fall of Szitnya, he had switched sides and served King Ferdinand until his demise three months later. Unfortunately, besides accounts in the diary, few pieces of information could be retrieved concerning him. Interestingly, his given name survived in three different forms: Aldana's diary recalled him as János Makray, the epic poet Sebestyén Tinódi referred to him as Lukács Makri in his poem commemorating the campaign.[49] Bertalan Horvát (Horvátinovith), the former Captain of Komárom, who had also been present at the siege of Szitnya, undertook the task to clarify the fate of Makray's legacy with the town council of Schemnitz via correspondence. Horvát asked them to send him the legacy of Makray along with two other persons. Eventually, he received these legacies in a camp on 29 May during the siege of Csábrág. In his letters, Horvát referred to Makray in several different given names: in the letter written on 6 April and sent from Németi, he used "Nicolanus Makray," during the siege of Csábrág, on 24 May, first he called him "Georgii Makraÿ," then on 29 May, he referred to him as „Mackhry Jurg."[50]

The examples and fate of these two individuals attest that the border zone provided a unique opportunity for social mobility as the lasting local war blurred the lines and differences between social strata. Without clearly defined borders and lack of such institutionalized control of the region as the future Captaincies of the Kingdom of Hungary, such phenomena were intense and frequent.

48 Szakály, *Bernardo de Aldana*, 71. Description of his weapons also bore Ottoman characteristics. Besides him, Balassa had several others from Transylvania in his service. For instance, Tamás Daczó, the castellan of Léva was a Sekler from Sepsiszentgyörgy.

49 X. Szitnya, Léva, Csábrág, Murán váraknak megvevése, Sugár, *Tinódi*, 356; Benits, *Istvánffy*, 126.

50 Correspondence with the judge and councilors of Schemnitz, MMBŠ, Missiles, Box 1549.

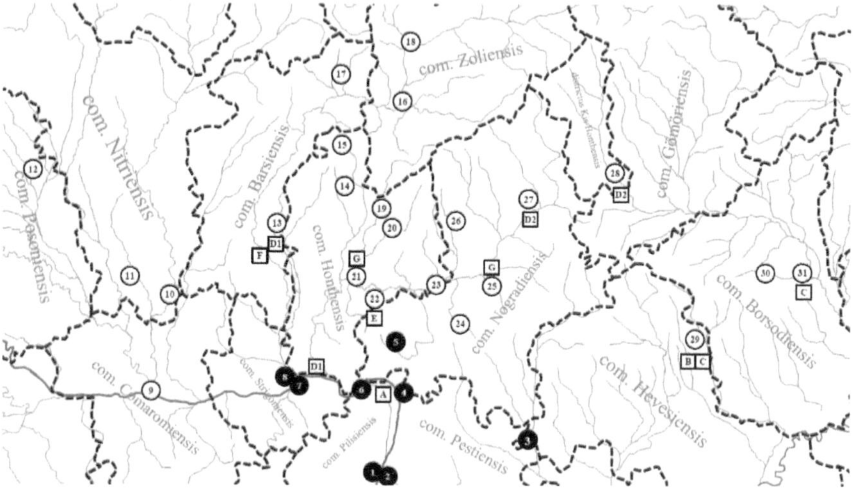

After the Spring of 1544.

Numbers in circles indicate towns; capital letters in rectangles indicate Ottoman raids.

Full circle: Ottoman guard post

Empty circle: Guard posts, castles or town under Christian control

Rectangle: Ottoman raids committed by larger units

1. Buda
2. Pest
3. Hatvan
4. Vác
5. Nógrád
6. Visegrád
7. Esztergom
8. Kakat (Párkány, Štúrovo)
9. Komárom
10. Nagysurány (Šurany)
11. Vágsellye (Šaľa)
12. Nagyszombat (Trnava)
13. Léva (Levice)
14. Szitnya (hegy és erősség, Sitno)
15. Selmecbánya (Banská Stiavnica)
16. Zólyom (Zvolen)
17. Körmöcbánya (Kremnica)

18. Besztercebánya (Banská Bystrica)
19. Bozók (Bzovík)
20. Csábrág (Hrad Čabraď)
21. Ipolyság (Šahy)
22. Drégely
23. Balassagyarmat
24. Szanda
25. Szécsény
26. Kékkő (Modrý Kameň
27. Losonc (Lucenec)
28. Rimaszombat (Rimavská Sobota)
29. Eger
30. Diósgyőr
31. Miskolc

Ottoman raids to the Northern Parts of the Hungarian Kingdom in 1544

A: Before 20 January: Oroszfalu/Kisoroszi 2000 soldiers
B: Around 19 May: towards Eger, unknown number
C: Before 22 July: raids of Eger and Miskolc, 4000 soldiers
D1: 8–9 September: Léva (the Battle of Szalka), 1500 soldiers
D2: 8–9 September: Rimaszombat, Rimaszécs, Losonc, unknown number
E: 10 September: Around Drégely, 300 horsemen
F: 27 September: Nearby Sáró, 400 marauders
G: 1–2 December: the raid of the region close to Ság and Szécsény, population of 8 or 10 villages kidnapped

Livia Magina

Cross-Border Mobility: War Refugees in Early Modern Transylvania*

Abstract: When the Banat of Lugoj-Caransebeş was ceded by Prince Acatius Barcsay to the Sublime Porte in 1658, a considerable number of townsfolk from the two urban centers and beyond chose the path of exile. One can observe that their main place of settlement, both in the seventeenth century and in the previous one, was the market town of Hunedoara, located north of the mountains, beyond the border, as well as the market towns of Haţeg and Orăştie, and the city of Alba Iulia. What were the conditions of their settlement and what were the political and economic promises that determined them to leave their homes? Answering these questions is the aim of the present paper.

Keywords: Refugees, Frontier, Principality of Transylvania, Banat of Lugoj-Caransebeş, Ottoman Conquest

Introduction

Historical research on borderlands and social mobility of a narrow geographical sector might be unjustly taken for micro-history or even local history. The struggles at the frontier could be often considered as exceptional, specific only to these areas but, concomitantly, they might be taken for miniature replicas of the major events. The question of refugees became more acute with the appearance of stable frontiers, the linear borders, towards the end of the nineteenth century, and the decline of the right of asylum. The two terms are directly connected as taking refuge means also passing borders.

I aim by the present study to highlight the immediate effects of the Ottoman impact on the population at the south-western frontier of the Transylvanian Principality, in the sixteenth and seventeenth centuries, a phenomenon of taking refuge to areas that were considered safer. My study is based on several fiscal-administrative records, some of them still unpublished, dating immediately after the Ottoman conquest; they refer to the area settled by the refugees: the

* This work was supported by a grant of the Romanian Ministry of Education and Research, CNCS – UEFISCDI, project number PN-III-P1-1.1-TE-2019-0457, within PNCDI III; *From Medieval Frontiers to Early Modern Borders. The Military organization of the Western Parts of the Transylvanian Principality in the XVI-XVII centuries.*

Urbarium of Hunedoara domain, elaborated in the spring of 1674,[1] the *tax register* of Orăştie (Szászváros/ Broos), dating from 1687,[2] the protocol of Alba County,[3] and the register of the rural gentry in the district of Haţeg (Hátszeg/ Hötzing), written in1687.[4]

Century of the Empires

After the Battle of Mohács – 1526, up to 1658, the Lower Parts of the Hungarian Kingdom, namely the territory known today as the Banat, was gradually integrated in the superpower of the south, the Ottoman Empire. The lowland of this geographical area, corresponding administratively to the counties of Arad, Timiş, and Torontal, was conquered by the Ottoman in 1552, while the highland around the towns of Caransebeş (Karánsebes/ Karansebesch) and Lugoj (Lugos/Lugosh) was integrated in the autonomous Principality of Transylvania. It was only after the Peace of Speyer in 1570, when the political situation established 20 years earlier was recognized: Transylvania kept the Banat of Lugoj-Caransebeş and a part of Zarand County not occupied by the Turks, as well as some counties in the *Partium Hungariae*: Bihor, Middle Solnoc, Crasna and Maramureş, along with several border forts: Ineu (Borosjenő), Cehul-Silvaniei (Szilágycseh/Bömischdorf), Tăşnad (Tasnád/Trestenburg), Oradea (Nagyvárad/ Großwardein) and Hust (Huszt/Хуст/ Hust) whilst the northern counties of Bereg, Ugocsa, Satu-Mare, and Szabolcs entered the administration of the Habsburg Monarchy.

While the Banat of Lugoj-Caransebeş was integrated in the recent established autonomous Principality of Transylvania for more than 100 years, up to 1658, Timişoara (Temesvár/Temeschwar) and its *hinterland* remained part of the Ottoman Empire until the early eighteenth century. The destiny of the population living in these settlements, predominantly Romanian, developed in the framework imposed by the Ottomans, until the Peace of Passarovitz (1718).

---

1 Biblioteca Academiei Române Cluj-Napoca (BAR CJ), Urbariul domeniului Hunedoara, nr. 124, the original document is preserved in Magyar Nemzeti Levéltár Országos Levéltárának (MNL OL), Erdélyi fiscalis levéltár, X szekrény., fasc, 1J, f. 1–78.

2 Serviciul Judeţean al Arhivelor Naţionale Cluj, fond 325 Primăria oraşului Orăştie (SJAN CJ Primăria Orăştie).

3 MNL OL, Gyulafehérvári Káptalan Levéltára, F 12 Lymbus, fasc. 24, Fejér megye jegyzőkönyv.

4 Koncz Jozsef, "Anno 1687. Haczog vidéki nemesseg regestruma," *A Hunyadmegyei Történelmi és Régészeti Társulat Évkönyve*, 3 (1907), 125–32.

Confronted with a new reality, the population at the frontier tried to adapt or to flee over the mountains.

It was only in 1658, when the Ottoman Empire managed to incorporate the Banat of Lugoj-Caransebeş in the *eyalet* of Timişoara, in the context of the insubordination of Prince George Rákóczi II. Yielded by Acatius Barcsay in exchange for the princely title of Transylvania, both Caransebeş and Lugoj, just like the fortress of Oradea, were to be "dedicated" to the sacred cities of Islam, Mecca and Medina.

The Phenomenon of Permeable Frontiers

It is self-evident that the term "frontier" is directly connected to political and military expansion. The frontier, as a dividing line between two administrative units, has been a topic of historiographical debate for a long time. Recent research defines it rather as a permeable area of meeting and interaction, so to say, a common space on both sides of the "dividing line". The debate on frontiers has theoretically developed and changed, from the most popular thesis of Frederick Jackson Turner,[5] who connects the idea of democracy itself to that of frontier and the expansion towards uninhabited territories, to the ones of Christian Langer and Manuel Fernández – Götz who describe the frontiers as a space, not as a precise demarcation; they clearly distinguish between the static and restrictive border, and the frontier which develops as a permeable, fluid, and diffuse area.[6] One must also consider the theoretical debate over frontier terminology and the "inquest" of Lucien Febvre in "Limites et frontièrs", published in 1947,[7] that distinguished the diversity of frontiers and, of course, the importance of the natural one and, maybe, even the geographic influence over the development of settlements.

For the geographic area I analyse in this paper, a useful interpretation is that borderlands overlap with certain communities, stretching on both sides of the line of their theoretical delimitation. This aspect has been emphasized

---

5 Frederick Jackson Turner, *The Frontier in American History* (New York: Henry Holt and Company, 1920), 1–39.

6 Christian Langer, Manuel Fernández-Götz, "Boundaries, Borders and Frontiers: Contemporary and Past Perspectives," *Journal for ancient studies*, 7 (2020), Introduction: a myriad of terms, 35–47.

7 Lucien Febvre, "Limites et frontières," *Annales. Économies, Sociétés, Civilisations*, 2 (1947), 201–07.

by research on the everyday life of the population of early modern frontiers.[8] A good example is the relation between the Romanian Calvinist communities in the Banat and Hunedoara, between which there was already a social mobility due to Calvinist preachers who brought with them not only the ideas of their confession, but also a certain type of culture and social attitudes. A notorious case is that of the preacher Péter of Orăştie, *alias* "Pop of Lugoj", Calvinist parish priest of Haţeg who was ennobled in 11 January 1644. He is explicitly attested as "the priest of the Calvinist Romanians of Haţeg", in the letter of tax exemption for his house and garden in Lugoj.[9] Most likely, Peter served as a Romanian-Calvinist priest both in Lugoj and in Haţeg. The source highlights the identity of language and culture of the two communities, which will remain in contact also in the future. One can find the same aim in the donation charter issued in 1665 for the Calvinist College of Aiud (Nagyenyed/Straßburg am Mieresch), by several noble families, among them Balthazar and Michael Măcicaş, nobles from the Banat, who took refuge to Transylvania, already having a strong bound with the Calvinist community from the region.[10]

Another argument for the existence of frontier communities is the visible tendency of the nobles in the Banat of Lugoj-Caransebeş to set "bridgeheads" north-east of the mountains, in the neighbouring counties of Transylvania (Hunedoara, especially), by buying properties or arranging marriage alliances. This was a common situation in the seventeenth century, dating back to the previous one, by building up an area of "kinship" south and north of the mountains. A permeable social and religious frontier offered the opportunity to adapt more quickly to dangers and offered a certain degree of security.

The everyday life at the frontier is another clue to the fact that the common boundary supported several types of activities: passing of livestock from one side to the other, or illegal activities as, for instance, the escape of thieves across the border.[11] Another example of common frontiers comes from the correspondence

---

8 Suraiya Faroqhi, *The Ottoman Empire and the World Around it* (London – New York: LB. Tauris), 2004, 1–25.

9 Ana Dumitran, "Petrus Szászvárosi alias Pap de Lugoj. Consideraţii asupra statutului socio-economic al preotului român calvin în secolul al XVII-lea," *Annales Universitatis Apulensis, Series Historica*, 4–5 (2000–2001), 67–72.

10 *Erdélyi Országgyűlési Emlékek / Monumenta comitialia regni Transylvaniae* (MCRT), XIV (1664–1669), ed. Szilagyi Sandor, (Budapest: A Magyar Tudomany Akadémia Könyvkiadó Hivatala, 1889) 425: May 10, 1665.

11 Costin Feneşan, "Viaţa cotidiană la hotarul osmano-transilvănean," *Banatica* 12/II (1993), 75–88.

of Ismail, *alaybey* of Timişoara, with Sigismund Fiat of Armeniş (Örményes/Armönisch), the *tricessimator* of Caransebeş, on the tax for pig feeding on acorns, amounting 21 florins.[12]

Refugee and Outsider

Wars, territorial division, religious persecutions or calamities were the main reasons why entire communities chose the path of exile. War refugees, climate refugees and especially religious refugees are present all over the world and during all times. From the departure of the Israelites from Egypt to the refugees of 2021, the image of those who left their homes behind and the attitude of locals towards their presence in new regions seem to be the same: marching convoys, on the one hand, and the hostility of the resident population, on the other. European historical research was focused on the religious exile, but for the eastern parts of Europe, the Ottoman conquest had particular effects.

The refugees enjoyed some tax exemptions from their new homeland, for a certain period of time, precisely for the start of a new life. Recent historiography also demonstrated that the population left behind in the territories of the Ottoman Empire found itself in the unfortunate position of a condominium, being forced to pay taxes both to the new rule and to the nobles.[13] Besides, the nobles of Severin County gathered north of the mountains in a genuine assembly of the exiled county of Severin County, if we consider the documents researched by Costin Feneşan and Cristina Feneşan.[14]

In the sixteenth century, the Ottomans managed to consolidate their positions north of the Danube, as a preliminary step in their effort to reach Vienna. After the Battle of Mohács (1526), the seats of the Hungarian kingdom became an eyalet, and soon after the territories east of the Tisza River were also conquered. Thus, a new Ottoman province emerged, the *eyalet* of Timişoara, under the authority of a *beylerbeyi*.[15] In the context of the conquest, there were inhabitants

---

12 Costin Feneşan, "Viaţa cotidiană," 75–88.

13 Cristina Feneşan, "Quelques aspects du condominium osmano-transylvain au XVII siècle," *The journal of ottoman studies* (1991), 111–21.

14 Costin Feneşan used the plastic expression „Caransebeş after Caransebeş" in his article "Caransebeşul după Caransebeş – note cu privire la destinul nobilimii şi orăşenimii din Banatul Caransebeşului şi Lugojului după anexarea de către poartă (1658)," *Patrimonium Banaticum* 3 (2004), 85–101.

15 Cristina Feneşan, *Vilayetul Timisoara 1552–1716* (Timişoara: Ed. Ariergarda), 2014, passim.

from each market town and fortress who left for inner Transylvania (the noble elite, clergymen, urban officials, etc.). A well-known case is that of the refugees from Timişoara and Lipova (Lippa) who settled in Alba Iulia (Gyulafehérvár/ Weißenburg), after 1552, probably at the request of Queen Isabella but also attracted by the opportunity to integrate in the main city of the Principality and gain access to Court; their neighborhood received the name Lipova, after their place of origin.[16] The imperial general, Castaldo, wrote to King Ferdinand in August 1552, about the exodus of those who fled the occupied areas: there were one hundred thousand, along with their women and children, in 13.000 wagons,[17] who had left for Transylvania. Many of them settled nearby, in the episcopal city of Alba Iulia. Their number was large enough to have a representative in the council,[18] playing thus an active role in the decision making of the city. I consider that crossing the frontier was not specific only for the period immediately after the Ottoman conquest, but also for the entire sixteenth century and for the next one. Scattered documentary evidence attests this situation. In 1597, Stephen Josika, the chancellor of Transylvania, requested István Toldi of Salonta, deputy captain of Lipova, to return a plot of farmland and two house plots in Breazova (Brázova), the district of Margina, to a noble family who, afraid of the Turks, took refuge and lived for a while in Lipova, whilst the commander of the fortress took over their goods.[19] In the protocols of the county assembly of Alba, gathered in 1693–1694 at Sânbenedic (Magyarszentbenedek/ Benedikt) and Alba Iulia, one can still find persons bearing the name "Lipovanul", like Mihály Szabo *alias* Lippai, or István Lippai.[20] Other inhabitants who once left Lipova were present at the military conscription of the Turda county, in 1670, possibly settled in or around Turda (Torda/ Thorenburg), like János Lippai, Martin Lippai, István Kadar "Lipovanul", and Endre "Lipovanul".[21]

---

16 Gálfi Emőke, "A gyulafehérvári Lippa fertály és a lippai menekültek a 16. század közepén," *Testimonio Litterarum. Tanulmányok Jakó Zsigmond tiszteletére* (Kolozsvár: Erdélyi Múzeum-Egyesület, 2016), 143–49.

17 András Veress, "Déva és környéke Castaldo idejében," *A Hunyadmegyei Történelmi és Régészeti Társulat Évkönyve* 9 (1896–1898), 38.

18 Gálfi, "A gyulafehérvári Lippa fertály," 145.

19 Costin Feneşan, *Diplomatarium Banaticum*, II (Cluj-Napoca: Editura Mega, 2017), 187–88, no. 60.

20 MNL OL, Gyulafehérvári Káptalan Levéltára, Lymbus, F 12, fasc. 24, f. 672–73.

21 Biás István, ifj., "Torda vármegye lustrája 1670-ből.," *Genealógiai Füzetek* 2 (1908), 51, 53, 54.

Constant warfare at the Turkish frontier determined similar evolutions in the seventeenth century. After the fall of Oradea (1660), the defensive system of the Transylvanian Principality was reorganized beyond the mountains of Piatra Craiului and Meseş, having as landmarks the fortresses: Şimleul Silvaniei (Szilágysomlyó/ Schomlenmarkt), Cehu Silvaniei, Hoďod (Hadad/ Kriegsdorf), Valcău (Valkó vára/ Burgfeld), and Bologa (Sebesvár), all subordinated to the new captaincy of Cluj, established in the place of Oradea. The refugees from the *Partium Hungariae* had to cross this new defence line.

The case of the refugees from Oradea, dating after the Ottoman conquest of the fortress in August 1660, developed almost parallel with the one of the refugees coming from the Banat of Lugoj-Caransebeş, except for fact that the former were called *nobiles hungarici*. The chronicler Szalárdi records that Ali Pasha gathered over 50.000 inhabitants from the villages between the fortresses of Ineu and Oradea, and brought them to the latter city. The survivors were escorted by the host of Seidi Ahmed Pasha towards Debrecen, and not to Cluj, as they had formerly agreed.[22] Through the resolutions of the Diet in Alba Iulia, from May 1665,[23] the refugees from Oradea were assigned three distinct areas of settlement in Transylvania: Dej (Dés/ Desch), Turda Veche (Ótorda), Turda Nouă (Neu-Thorda/Újtorda) and the village of *Egyhaz* (disappeared), belonging to the fiscal authority. Four articles issued by the assembly of the Principality refer to this matter: 1. The refugees were considered noblemen, with the same obligations towards the county as the rest of the nobility; 2. They were exempt from paying the tithe; 3. They were allowed to trade salt and to keep inns and butcheries in Turda Veche, Turda Nouă, and Dej; 4. In order to increase safety in Dej, the inhabitants were allowed to raise a palisade wall around the settlement, the inhabitants of the neighbouring counties (Inner Solnoc and Dăbâca) being obliged to assist them. The inhabitants of these market towns did not like the situation of the newcomers and many grievances have arisen. As a consequence, in 1668, Prince Michael Apafi ennobled the other inhabitants of Dej, too, in order to eliminate inequality.[24] One year later, in 1669, the refugees from Oradea settled in Turda Veche also requested the prince for military exemption, excepting the general levy of the country, but their request was unsuccessful. However, it

22 Liviu Borcea, "Contribuţii la istoria oraşului Oradea în timpul stăpânirii otomane (1660–1692)," *Crisia*, (1981), 113.

23 MCRT, XIV, 124–126: May, 1664, Art. 36–40.

24 Miklós K. Papp, "Dees város levéltára," *Történeti Lapok* (17 of January 1875), 665: concerning the resolutions of Bistriţa, 25 January 1668.

seems that at least a part of the nobles from Oradea reached also the city of Cluj, like Janos Polyk, a member of a family, ennobled in the early seventeenth century, originating from Egyek (Hajdú-Bihar County).[25] Another case, but a century ago, is that of Miklos Bethlen's grandfather, Istvan Varadi, who left Oradea in the late sixteenth century.[26]

The case of those who left the Banat for Transylvania in the sixteenth and seventeenth centuries, known in the historiography, has been studied less. Located at the frontier of Wallachia and also of the Ottoman Empire, the Banat of Lugoj-Caransebeş remained in 1552 a part of the Transylvanian Principality. It must be said that this territory was for a long time a borderland, even before the sixteenth century, being exposed to the pressure and threat of the Ottoman colossus, at the peak of its might. Despite having the unfortunate fate of a borderland, the area also had opportunities, especially for trade, being linked to the Principality by the road that still passes today through the Iron Gate of Transylvania, and to the north, by the road known as "drumul Făgetului".

Already in the late sixteenth century, the noble and urban elite at the Ottoman border found it more prudent to take refuge to Transylvania, buying thus estates and manors across the mountains. In this situation we find notorious noble families like Josika of Brăniste, Fiáth, Macskasi or Gámán, but also some members of the middle nobility from the urban centres of Caransebeş and Lugoj: Duma, Mikanda, Bobik, Ivul or Csako. If the members of these families and their relatives could take refuge from their "beloved homeland", what became of the commoners, not well to do inhabitants, townsfolk or merchants?

The matter of the refugees from Lugoj and Caransebeş in the year 1658 is quite a story. In September 1658, Acatius Barcsay[27] accepted the unconditional cession of the Banat of Lugoj-Caransebeş to the Grand Vezier Küprülü-Mehmet Pasha, in the military camp at Ineu, in exchange for his appointment as Prince of Transylvania.[28] The chronicler János Szalárdi from Oradea recorded

25 Livia Magina, Claudiu Călin, "O familie armalistă la frontiera de vest a Principatului Transilvaniei: Polyk de Oradea," *Banatica* 30/2 (2020), 191–212.

26 Nicolae Bethlen, *Descrierea vieții sale de către el însuși*, (Cluj-Napoca: Casa Cărții de Ştiință, 2007), 52.

27 Acatius Barcsai of Bârcea Mare, ban of Lugoj and Caransebeş since 1644, and the count of Hunedoara County.

28 The episode of the negotiations in the tent of the great vizier of Buda, described by Johannes Lutsch, the royal judge of Sibiu, eyewitness of the events of early September 1658, Johannes Lutsch, *Jurnal de captivitate la Istanbul (1658–1661)/Johannes Lutsch-Tagebuch seiner Gefangenschaft in Istanbul (1658–1661)*, ed. Cristina Feneşan, Costin Feneşan (Timişoara: Editura de Vest, 2006), 213.

metaphorically the prince's words on that occasion: "better cut off a finger than hurt the whole body".[29] On the same September day, Barcsay, who knew the situation south of the mountains very well, as former ban of the region, wrote to the administration of the two urban centres a motivation for letting them in the hands of the Turks. In the letter, he promised the inhabitants of Caransebeş and Lugoj that, if they were going to relocate, they will receive land "at least as good or even better" in their new settlements, ordering them not to oppose the new rule.[30] They actually did this, without waiting for support from the authorities, which only came almost a year later. The endless pressure on the population and its disappointment for being left in the hands of the Turks, then for being abandoned in the places of refuge, were cried out at Diet of Sebeş (Szászsebes/ Mühlbach) held in May-June.[31] Thus, the general assembly of the Principality considered discussing their situation after almost one year after their immigration. In this assembly, the representatives of Caransebeş and Lugoj accused Acatius Barcsay of paying for his throne with their lands and homes. During the same meeting[32] it became clear that the city authorities of Lugoj and Caransebeş have not been entirely loyal, being accused by the Estates of the Principality, who stated that, in fact, they left their homes not because of a promise made by the prince, but as a consequence of their treason, considering thus that the Transylvanians owed nothing to the refugees of the latter city: *Arcem enim Karansebes non ad ammonitionem legatorum, sed ob motum Turcarum in manus Turcicas tradiderunt*; *His dimissis causa Karansebessiensium resumitur examinanda, ubi iustificatur ill. princeps Barcsaj quod Karansebessienses non ad interpositionem Barczaj dereliquerunt suam civitatem verum sua sponte perterriti a Turca*

29 Szalárdi János, *Siralmas Magyar krónikaja*, ed. Kemény Zsigmond (Pest: Emich Gusztáv könyvnyomdája, 1853), 422: *Lugasi, karánsehesi bán voltam, vagyok most bán itt is, ott is, hála istennek. Expedit, unus pro populo moriatur. Inkáb ujomnak egy ize, mint épen testem elvesszen az ország lakosival együtt.*

30 Feneşan, "Caransebeşul după Caransebeş", 88:"Jószága helyet ha szintén nem egyenlőt is de hasonlót adni el nem mulattyuk"; Pesty Frigyes, *Krassó vármegye története*. 4. kötet. (Budapest: Athenaeu, 1883), 353.

31 *Erdélyi Országgyűlési Emlékek / Monumenta comitialia regni Transylvaniae* (MCRT), XII (1658–1661), ed. Szilagyi Sandor (Budapest: A Magyar Tudomany Akadémia Könyvkiadó Hivatala, 1887), 284: June 6, 1659: *Demum legitur supplicatio Karansebessiensium et Lugossiensium quibus mediantibus rogatur terra habitationis secundum assecurationem dominorum legatorum apud supremum wezerium tum temporis commorantes scilicet generosi Achatii Barczai, Francisci Daniel, Matthei Balogh, Johannis Lutsch regii iudicis Cibiniensis, tamen nihil hac vice obtinent.*

32 MCRT, XII, 299–301, Art. 10.

aufugerunt.[33] For the refugees from the south, Turda was assigned as their new settling place: *cum confluxissemus Karansebessiensium causa finienda proponitur igitur ab universis regnicolis Thorda libertatur dictis Karansebessiensibus, ut illic resideant cum nobili praerogativa permanere volentes. Collatio enim haec illis ita est tam per principem, quam per regnicolas exhibita, ut nullo tempore revocari possit.*[34] From the same resolutions read out to the Estates it appears that the citizens of Caransebeş and Lugoj might have wanted to put up armed resistance, but Barcsay capitulated.

This complicated and complex episode reveals the special situation of the inhabitants at the borderlands. They had little time to think, being obliged to adapt to the new context, for there could be no question of resistance without the support of the Transylvanian central authority. According to previous research, after the battle of Mohács (1526), many refugees from Hungary to Transylvania were the younger sons of families with a stable situation at home,[35] which is not the case here. The ones who took refuge lost their homes and the grace of the prince, while the fate of those who were left behind is barely known. Fiscally, the refugees enjoyed tax exemption for three years, in order to build houses for themselves.[36] Fifteen years later, both in Hunedoara and Haţeg one can still find families who enjoyed tax exemptions, like Gabriel Macskasi or Balthasar Barcsai, as well as Péter Szebessiyan or János Szakacs.[37] On the other hand, for some of the refugees one can observe a preferential fiscal regime, even two decades after their arrival, by paying only the tax "of the ones from Caransebeş", in value of 4 florins.[38] Many of them pretended to be noble and were exempted from tax paying, but they could show no written evidence: *nobilitatio pretendal.*

In the general picture of the Ottoman-Transylvanian frontier in the mid seventeenth century, one can conclude that the refugees coming from *Partium* settled the area of Dej-Turda, while the ones from the Banat of Lugoj-Caransebeş,

33 MCRT, XII, 299–301.

34 MCRT, XII, 301.

35 Ildikó Horn, "Together or separately - family strategies and resilience in divided Hungary," *Studies in honour of prof. Géza Dávid on his seventieth birthday*, eds. Pál Fodor, Nándor E. Kovács and Benedek Péri (Budapest: Research Centre for the Humanities,Hungarian Academy of Sciences, 2019), 128.

36 *Erdélyi Országgyűlési Emlékek / Monumenta comitialia regni Transylvaniae*, XVI (1675–1679), ed. Szilagyi Sandor (Budapest: A Magyar Tudomany Akadémia Könyvkiadó Hivatala, 1893), 228: December, 1675, Art. 19.

37 BAR CJ, Urbariul domeniului Hunedoara, f. 1–78.

38 BAR CJ, Urbariul domeniului Hunedoara, f. 1–78.

were assigned to Turda. Despite these legal provisions, the research indicates a more complex reality. Like other provisions of the Diet, the ones regarding the refugees were only partially implemented. The analysis of sources reveals that the road travelled by the refugees was not so long after all (from Caransebeş and Lugoj to Turda). Many of them settled much closer to their initial homes, a few dozen kilometres away, in the counties of Hunedoara or Alba. In order to reach their new homeland, from Caransebeş and the neighbouring villages to the settlements of the Transylvanian counties, they had to pass the Iron Gate of Transylvania. The excitement that accompanies a journey in such dire times must have been doubled by the difficulties of the road. Departed with all their goods, in ox- or horse-drawn wagons, with cattle and mules, on paths known only by spies or on the road of the merchants, through the Iron Gate, they could pass the mountains in one day, on good weather conditions. But during the winter, things could turn bad. The difficulties of this journey are vividly illustrated by the passage of the Ottoman army through the Iron Gate in 1661, on its way back to their winter camp: "we passed with great difficulty in three days and nights…five thousand prisoners perished of starvation and because of the harshness of the winter."[39]

The sources certify that the refugees from the Banat settled in the nearby market towns, across the mountains, in Transylvania: Hunedoara, Orăştie, Haţeg, but also in more remote locations of Alba County, like Bărăbanţ (Borbánd/Weindorf), Aiud or even Alba Iulia. One can distinguish between the settlements of the nobles and those of the commoners: while some of the well to do nobles settled on their own lands (manors, estates, etc.), the townsfolk and even some peasants, who left their villages, settled mainly in market towns, establishing genuine enclaves, neighbourhoods or distinct streets.

In 1674, several streets of Hunedoara were inhabited by refugees from the southern slopes of the mountains, the former being named after the latter's places of origin: "Surducului" street (*Szurduk ucza*, after Surducu Mare today, in Caraş-Severin County), where six refugee families lived. A whole street, named "Severinului", was inhabited by people coming from the so-called Turkish area (i.e. conquered by the Turks). Here was the house of Jacob Fiat's wife, who was exempt from taxes, enjoying guaranteed immunity (*magaj oletoig immunitas vagyon*). In 1674, the cottage held in Hunedoara by István Lippai, one of Dionysius Banfy's serfs, was also exempted from tax paying.[40] In the same year,

---

39 *Călători străini despre Ţările Române,* VI, eds. M.M. Alexandrescu-Dersca Bulgaru, Mustafa Ali Mehmet (Bucureşti: Editura Ştiinţifică şi Enciclopedică: 1976), 620.

40 BAR CJ, Urbariul domeniului Hunedoara, f. 1–78.

Péter Păduran was registered among the citizens of Hunedoara, as a newcomer from Wallachia: *havassal foldi Paduran Peter*.[41]

On the mill street lived István Nyergess from Caransebes, paying a tax of 6 florins. On the Greek street, by the Romanian (Orthodox) church, lived János Sebessian who pretended to be a nobleman, in order to avoid taxes. Jacob Fiat's wife also had a house on *Toth Szeri* Street (where the Orthodox Church was located), that was also exempted from taxes. On the Market Street, as well as on the Greek Street, one can find other two refugees from Caransebeş, owning ½ of a plot, respectively a whole plot.

In the market town Haţeg, very close to Caransebeş and Lugoj, found their new home some poorer families. Whole families left not only the latter market towns, but also the nearby villages. In 1674, on the "Zăvoiului" street in Haţeg (Zăvoi is a village from the Banat, 50 km form Haţeg), were 35 cottages of *jeleri* [lat. *inquilini*], most probably not incidentally, because many of them left the homonymous village.[42] On the street called "Futeşti" (*Futtjesti ucza*) 5 refugees from Caransebeş are registered as paying taxes of 4 florin each: Peter Cojocaru from Caransebeş (*Karansebessi Szocs Peter*), the widow of Dan from Caransebeş, Crăciun and Mathew from Caransebeş, but also Péter Bokan, coming from the same town. On the "Iazului" street (the village Iazul lies about 7 km from Caransebeş) and on the "Boilor" street (*Eokor ucza*; derived probably from the village Valea Boului), other four refugees were registered. In the Market Street, Gabor Cojocaru (*Szocs Gabor*) was paying a tax of 4 florins because he came from Caransebeş, and the cottage of Janos from Lugoj was entirely exempted from tax-payment. Popa Mihai, the priest of the Romanians, also paid a tax of 4 florins, same as the other refugees.

In the register of the nobles of the Haţeg District, dating from 1683,[43] other families originating from south of the mountains were conscripted, other than the ones attested in 1674: two members of the Bucoşniţa family, István and Isaac, each owning a horse, and two members of the Lăţug family, Miklos and Gábor. Many refugee families participated in the administrative life of their new communities, some of them having experience from home. Thus, besides Sigismund Ciula, there were other three members of refugee families who were judges of the nobility in the district: Mihály Luncaviţa, János Nyakazo and Mihály Fodor. At

41 BAR CJ, Urbariul domeniului Hunedoara, f. 1–78.
42 BAR CJ, Urbariul domeniului Hunedoara, f. 1–78.
43 Koncz, "Anno 1683. Haczogh vidéki nemesseg regestruma," 125.

the same time, a member of the Ivul family,[44] Mihály, held the office of *rationista*, continuing probably the tradition of his family.

Other nearby settlements where the refugees found shelter were Densuş (Demsus/Demsdorf), for the family Bucoşniţa, Ciula Mare (Nagycsula/Gross-Schullendorf), for the family Luncaviţa, and Peşteana Mare (Nagypestény) for the families Ivul and Bucosniţa.[45]

In 1687, at Orăştie (located 115 km away from Caransebeş, in the county of Hunedoara) the newcomers coming from across the mountains were still registered separately in the account books of the city. One cannot know if they were the descendants of those who came in 1658, or the population that arrived in the meantime. However, there are some names indicating their origin: the widow of János Sebessi, Miklós Sebessi, the widow of Mihály Szigarto from Lipova, the widow of György from Lipova, János of Cenad, János of Caransebeş, the widow of Péter from Cenad; Péter Lugojan and Martin Lugojan but there is also registered the cottage of János from Oradea, a less common case in this area because, albeit many inhabitants left this city after 1660, it would be surprising if he ended up in such a remote place like Orăştie.[46]

Other settlement where one can find refugees are Silvaşu de Jos and Peştişul Mic (Felsőpestes) in the county of Hunedoara. Some of the better known noble families, who already owned properties here, were Giurma, Macskási, Iosika,[47] and Pobora of Caransebeş Fiat and Gámán families also had properties in the district of Deva, at least towards the end of the eighteenth century.[48]

Several charters of ennoblement issued in the seventeenth century reveal the origins of their beneficiaries. George Duma of Silvasu de Jos, originating from Caransebeş, was a vice-judge of the nobles in Hunedoara County, in 1666. Most likely he had a manor at Silvaşu, bought before 1658.[49] Despite being a refuge from Caransebeş, as a representative of the nobles from Hunedoara County, he

---

44 Gabriel Ivul was the most famous member of the Ivul family: Philosophy PH (University of Trnava), Theology PH (Vienna University); he taught philosophy at the University of Košice, and theology at Vienna University, see Doru Radosav, *Cultură şi umanism în Banat – Sec. XVII* (Timişoara: Editura de Vest, 2003), 160–61.

45 Benkö, "Hunyádmegyeröl," *A Hunyadmegyei Történelmi és Régészeti Társulat Évkönyve* 12 (1901), 67–70.

46 SJAN CJ, Primăria Orăştie, 1687, 20 of April, f. 1v.-9.

47 Benkö, "Hunyadmegyerol," 67–70.

48 Benkö, "Hunyadmegyerol," 67.

49 MNL OL, R 391, Hunyad megyei gyűjtemény (former: P 102) August 17, 1666, 22 tetél, 2 csomó, f. 30.

managed to integrate in the social and administrative structures of the region he settled in.

Refugees from the Ottoman administration reached also the county of Alba where they contributed to the development of a Romanian Calvinist community. In the village Bărăbanţi, near Alba Iulia, a certain Ioan Duma, along with a few other nobles, seem to originate from Caransebeş.[50] This Ioan Duma is the one who reviewed the text of the catechism *Pâinea pruncilor* ["The infants' bread"], according to the subtitle: "it was turned into Romanian language by Duma Ianăşu of Borbanţi", around the year 1702. The fact that in Bărăbanţ settled Romanians is also visible in the conscription of the Alba County, dating from the following decades.[51]

The members of the Halics family were also known in intellectual circles as refugees who found shelter in Aiud, in the County of Alba. The motivation for choosing this location as a place of refuge is self-evident, since the father of the family, Mihail Halics, was a preacher. Father and son, representatives of the Humanism in the Banat,[52] became known for the promotion of the Church Reformation and their translations into the Romanian language. The older Halics kept his place of origin alive. As an adult, in 1658, he lamented over the fate of his home town and its inhabitants, through the translation of David's Psalms.[53] His son, known as Mihail Halics the Younger, studied at the Academic College of Aiud in 1664, and between 1666 and 1669 was rector of the Reformed College in Orăştie.[54]

Those who escaped the Turkish occupation were not exclusively members of the privileged class. The situation of the serfs at the frontier was a special one. Most of them have chosen to remain and to keep on serving the new rule of the Ottomans, but others fled to the Principality. The flight of the serfs on both sides of the frontier was not an unusual phenomenon, being actually a common reality of the seventeenth century. An example is also the flight of the serfs from the Turkish territories, several decades after the conquest. In 1621, following a

---

50 Pavel Binder, "Contribuţii la studierea factorilor interni în problema dezvoltării scrisului in limba română (secolele XVI–XVII) (Monumente din istoria culturală a satului Bărăbanţ)," *Apulum*, 20, 1982, 175–83.

51 Biás István, ifj., "Fejérmegye lustrája 1682-ből," *Genealógiai Füzetek*, 6, 1908, 148.

52 Radosav, *Cultură şi umanism în Banat*, 178–79.

53 Nicolae Drăganu, "Mihail Halici (Contribuţie la istoria culturală românească din sec. XVII)," *Dacoromania*, IV, 1924–1926, 78–9.

54 Radosav, *Cultură şi umanism*, chapter"*Respublica litteraria*". *Mihail Halici-fiul (1643–1712)*, 178–82.

period when a significant number of serfs from Timişoara and Vršac had fled towards the Banat of Lugoj-Caransebeş, causing for the treasury of the sultan an annual loss of 20.000 florins, Iusuf Pasha threatened with severe consequences if runaway serfs would be allowed on the territory of Transylvania.[55] Another phenomenon is that of the forced migration of the serfs in opposite direction, from the Christian frontier to the deserted villages of the Ottomans. The abuse committed by Abdullah, bey of Lipova, is maybe the most relevant. Around 1626, he managed to take by force serfs from the frontier estates of the Transylvanian noblemen, and to settle them in villages around Lipova.[56]

In the spring of 1673, Kasîm Pasha, beylerbey of Timişoara, requested Prince Michael Apafi to order the authorities of Haţeg to send back to Caransebeş the 30–40 serfs who had settled around the market town of Haţeg: "that being so [we complain] that more, namely thirty-forty serfs who belong to that town have fled over the years and went into the country of Your Grace, in the market town of Haţeg and its surroundings, settling and living there".[57] The Prince refused the request of the Ottoman official, claiming that "the inhabitants of Caransebeş surrendered their town, according to the order issued in the name of the almighty emperor. As a consequence, they were left alone, each to go where he pleases",[58] which, in the opinion of the Transylvanians, was equivalent with the right to cross the frontier in the Principality. Both situations are representative because they trace the phenomenon of entire groups of population crossing over the frontier that separated the territories of Transylvania from those of the Crescent. On the same note, Sultan Mehmed IV issued an order sent to Şahin Mehmed, pasha of Ineu, and to the *kadis* of Ineu and Lipova, forbidding any abuse against the peasants of the Transylvanian villages, located at the boundaries of the Ottoman territory, or on those crossing the frontier from one side to the other.[59] It was, in fact, an implicit recognition of the phenomenon of mobility across the imaginary line of the frontier and, at the same time, of the incapacity to stop human migration between territories arbitrarily separated by a demarcation line.

---

55 Feneşan, *Diplomatarium*, II, 417, no. 169: "when the serfs in the territories of Timişoara and Vârşeţ were counted, it became clear that several thousand household serfs were in Transylvania."

56 Feneşan, *Diplomatarium*, II, 419. no. 170.

57 Feneşan, *Diplomatarium*, II, 482, no. 196.

58 Feneşan, *Diplomatarium*, II, 484, no. 197.

59 Feneşan, *Diplomatarium*, II, 495, no. 202.

The Right to Return

The fugitives continued to consider the properties they left behind as their own. The lands and goods from their previous homes are mentioned in various testamentary decisions, although their descendants could not yet claim them. This attitude generated a situation of *condominium*, widespread along the entire Ottoman-Hungarian frontier, in which certain territories from the borderlands had two rightful owners.

In 1688, the Habsburg troops managed to push the Ottomans out of the highland area of the Banat and to recover, among others, the town of Caransebeş. A glimmer of hope for the possibility of returning home came on the occasion of the restoration that followed these events. Sources attest 167 former owners who claimed their proprieties within the walls of Caransebeş. They were members of noble and burgher families alike, notorious names like: Josika, Fodor, Fiáth, Macskási, Bobic, Halics, Lăţug, Mărgan (Márgai), Turnea, Groza, Kolovic, Oboroc, Giurma, Tivadar, Gârlişteanu (Gerlistyei), Peica, Vaida, Gámán, Ivul, Floca, and Micşa, but also other lesser known, who were involved in the urban life before 1658. All of them rushed to recover the inheritances left by their parents, to return to a homeland recovered from the hands of heathens.

What were the feelings of these runaways who were forced to leave their places of origin behind? How did they adapt to the status of refugee? Sources are not very generous in information regarding these aspects but some clues can be found in the words of Barbara Lăţug,[60] wife of Nicholas Gârlişteanu from Bolvaşniţa, who went with her entire family over the mountains, in 1658, to settle in Pestişul Mic, near Hunedoara. The Lăţug family already owned, from the end of the previous century, several estates in the county of Hunedoara: Lonka (disappeared today), Rapolt (Nagyrápolt/Großrapolt), and Binţinţi (Bencenc/Benzendorf).[61]

One can observe that Barbara's family wasn't the only one to settle in this village. On 6 September 1662, all the refugees from Caransebeş gathered in the house of George Vaida, located in Peştişul Mic: Jacob Fiat, István Kun, János Deak, and Péter Makrai, as well as the priest Danciu from Giosani, to assist to Barbara's last will. Less than four years after her refuge over the mountains, Barbara was still affected by the fact that: "the heathen Turks droved us out of

60 For the monograph on the Lăţug family, see Ligia Boldea, "Date asupra patrimoniului funciar al familiei Lăţug de Delineşti (secolele XVI–XVII)," *Vocaţia istoriei. Studii în memoria profesorului Nicolae Bocşan*, eds. Ligia Boldea, Rudolf Gräf (Cluj-Napoca: Editura Mega, 2017), 69–80.

61 Boldea, "Date asupra patrimoniului funciar al familiei Lăţug " 74.

our town and from our goods in Caransebeş." "Helpless in this foreign land," but still supported "in my old age, in my weakness at dangerous times of war," by her daughter Anuţa and the latter's husband, Mihail Giurma of Caransebeş, as well as by her younger, unmarried daughter Tinca, "without having anything to offer them for their miserable everyday life," she divides between them the goods she inherited from her parents near Caransebeş. Mihail Giurma, her son-in-law, was designated to inherit the village Ruieni, while he was also meant to inherit the village Zorlenţ, if his wife, Anuţa, would die before him; he would also inherit the mill and the garden by the fortified town of Caransebeş, all amounting a sum of 1.000 Hungarian florins, "if God would eventually grant us Caransebeş and our estate back."[62] Obviously, the noble lady wouldn't live to see the places of "the sweet fatherland"[63] again, a common situation for many of those who were already old when they left home, losing their lives in foreign places. The descendants of these families, who lived up to 1718, knew about their parents or grand-parents' places of origin only from the latter's memories.

Those Who Remained Behind

The situation of the town, which after the conquest was still inhabited by those who were left behind, is described by the famous Ottoman traveller, Evlia Celebi, in 1661: "(the fortified town of Caransebeş) was conquered by Vizier Küprülü and by Seidi Ahmed Pasha at Sultan Mehmed's order. It is a sancakbey's residence in the *eyalet* of Timişoara. The income of the bey amounts 300.000 *akçes*. It comprises 15 *zeamets* and 105 *timars*; it has an *alaybey* and other office holders; its army consists of one thousand men. It is a recent organized *kaza* at the range of 150 *akçes*. It has three units of janissaries, *subaşi*, *topci* and *gebegi* (commanders of artillerymen and heavy cavalry), *muhtesib* (police captain) and tax collector, a town *kehaia* (administrator) and an *aga* for the *harac* (officer for the tribute). All the *raya* (subjects) here are Romanians."[64] In the western area, the county of Zărand was only partly taken over by the Turks, thus the reactions of the population were different. In February 1663, the noblemen of Zărand County (from the areas that remained to the Principality) addressed Prince Michael Apafi regarding a delicate and undoubtedly pestering matter. Some inhabitants of the county pledged allegiance to the Turks and gained offices from the local pasha.

62 Feneşan, *Diplomatarium*, II, 466, no. 186.

63 Adrian Magina, "Mirajul patriei pierdute. Ocuparea Caransebeşului de către otomani în memoria locuitorilor săi," *Studii şi Materiale de Istorie Medie*, 37, 2019, 185–94.

64 *Călători străini*, VI, 534.

Thus, the noblemen requested the prince to negotiate with the pasha of Ineu on the matter of the *paraszt oláhok* ("Romanian peasants", pejoratively referred to as such), in order to call them to trial in Deva.[65] This wasn't an unusual behaviour. In the conscription of the village of Berzeus (disappeared today), near Jdioara (Zsidovár), drawn up in 1588, the finding of the officials is categorical: "the people are poor and, living in the proximity of the Turkish territory, they will flee at once to the Turks, if they are not allowed to pay only half of the taxes, as they demand."[66] This is another hint to the fact that the frontier wasn't an obstacle at all, being crossed by the local population for various reasons. The ones who remained behind were obliged, perhaps much more than the refugees, to adapt in order to survive in a new social and political order.

Final Reasons

The frontier was like a patch of "quicksand", an area of changing loyalties, and a flexible territory of a community that knew both sides of the demarcation line between the two polities. The local population wavered between the two options, to take refuge or to stay. There was one single goal: to survive and, in the case of the nobles, to keep their proprieties, establishing thus the peculiar situation of *condominium*. Although refugees have been given a specific place to settle, they preferred to remain close to their homelands. The common population chose to settle in market towns, while the serfs often fled without having the slightest hope for the future.

65 SJAN Cluj, Colecţia Kemény József, cutia 27 (not inventoried), February 23, 1663, Baia de Criş. I hereby thank Professor Susana Andea for this information.

66 Feneşan, *Diplomatarium*, II, 169, no. 51.

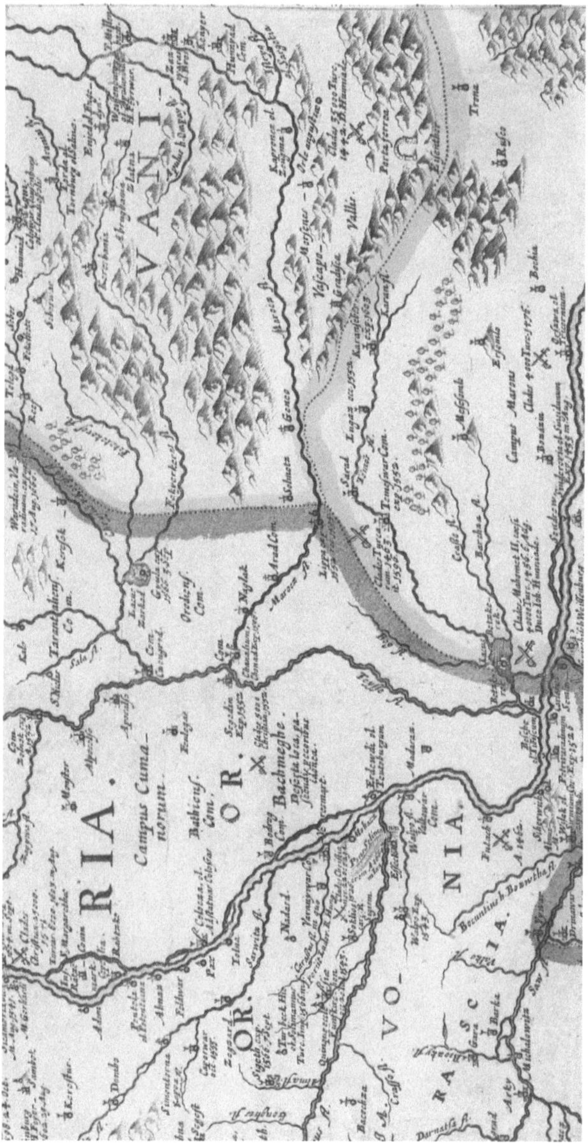

The south-western frontier of Transylvania in the second half of the seventeenth century, detail from *Danubius Fluviorum Europae Princeps*…/The Danube, Monarch of European Rivers, Sigmund von Birken/Jacob von Sandrart, 1683, cooper engraving, (Badische Landesbibliothek, Karlsruhe)

Gelu Fodor

An Eighteenth Century Constitutional Struggle: Institutions, Defence and Border Legislative Matters between the Imperial Court and the Transylvanian Diet*

Abstract: The current study aims to provide an integrative overview of the constitutional role of the Transylvanian Diet regarding institutions, defence and border legislative matters, while covering a period starting from 1691 (i.e. the issue of the Leopoldine Diploma) till the beginning of the 1760s (i.e., the first initiatives for the establishment of the military border). The study starts by examining the political and legal aspects that had a decisive contribution in shaping the constitutional realities of the Transylvanian Principality at the end of the seventeenth century and the beginning of the eighteenth. Next, the focus shifts to the arguments that supported the necessity of organizing the border defence system of the Transylvanian Principality in the early 1760s as depicted in the State Council debates. Finally, the study explores the institutional and legislative role of the Diet as a representative authority of the nobility in its relationship with the new Habsburg sovereigns. The Diet remained the main forum whereby the estates defended their interests in their struggle for power with the new authorities from Vienna. As such, the debates that took place within this institution were often very harsh and with unforeseen results and the study intends to provide an accurate depiction of this dynamics.

Key words: constitution, military border, Diet, Estates, Transylvanian Diet.

Transylvania under the Habsburg Rule: The Leopoldine Diploma (1691)

The failure in capturing Vienna by the Ottomans in 1683 marked a turning point in the central and south-eastern history of Europe, thus giving the Habsburgs the opportunity to expand their authority to the former lands of the Kingdom of Hungary. The advance of the Habsburg imperial armies in Hungary first and, starting with 1686, in Transylvania as well, whereby general Scherffenberg occupied the cities of Dej and Cluj, marching next to Sibiu, forced the Transylvanian

* This work was supported by a grant of the Romanian Ministry of Education and Research, CNCS – UEFISCDI, project number PN-III-P1-1.1-TE-2019-0457, within PNCDI III; *From Medieval Frontiers to Early Modern Borders. The Military organization of the Western Parts of the Transylvanian Principality in the XVI-XVII centuries.*

political factors to start a series of negotiations with the Habsburgs.[1] The content of the negotiations among the Transylvanian statesmen and the imperial representatives and their underlying power dynamics fluctuated depending on the course of the war between the imperials and the Ottomans up till 1690.[2] Although emperor Leopold's intentions regarding Transylvania were clearly in favour of subordinating all its institutions and thus including the Principality within a centralised monarchy, the outgoing war with the Ottomans forced him to a compromise. Therefore, on 4 December 1691, the emperor ratified the *Leopoldine Diploma.* Including 18 articles, it was considered to be a genuine Constitution of Transylvania for more than 150 years.

From a legal point of view, The Diploma highlighted the Principality's place within the Habsburg Monarchy and established the core principles by which it was to be governed. It also acknowledged all privileges of the four recognized confessions (i.e., Lutheran, Calvin, Unitarian, and Catholic) and forbade any change of status such as introducing new confessions. The Diploma explicitly stated that *no changes will be made to officially recognized confessions*, and it granted an advantage to the Catholics such that they could build churches even in communities in which they had very few parishioners.[3]

Other articles in the Diploma strengthened all privileges, donations, dignities, and lands granted successively by the kings of Hungary and princes of Transylvania,[4] which had been previously established by the ancient laws of the country. In particular, the Diploma relied on and confirmed the privileges established by the Werböczy Tripartitum (1517) but without the 9th article of King Andrew which had granted the nobility the right to oppose the sovereign, the Approbate Constitutiones (1653), the Compilatae Constitutiones (1669), and the local constitutions and the different laws of the Saxons.[5] It also recognized all the ancient administrative and judicial institutions basically maintaining the legal system intact.[6] No change was made to the right of the three privileged

1 Anton E. Dörner, *Reformismul Austriac şi administraţia din Transilvania în secolul al XVIII-lea* (Cluj-Napoca: Ed. Napoca Star, 2009), 111.
2 For details concerning negotiations between Habsburg and Transylvanian reprezentatives see Dörner, *Reformismul Austriac,* 111–19.
3 Art. 1 of the Leoplodine Diploma, for a Romanian translation of the Leopoldine Diploma see, Romulus Gelu Fodor, *Sistemul Legislativ al Transilvaniei în secolul al XVIII-lea* (Cluj-Napoca: PhD thesis, Babeş-Bolyai University, 2014), 296.
4 Art. 2, in Fodor, *Sistemul Legislativ*, 296–97.
5 Fodor, *Sistemul Legislativ*, 297.
6 Fodor, *Sistemul Legislativ*, 297.

nations (i.e., Hungarian, Saxons, and Szeklers), regardless their confession, to occupy all dignities. The Diploma thus prevented foreigners from accessing such privileges.[7]

The most important office of the country was the *Supremum Status Directorem* or the *Governor*, an equivalent of the ancient Voivode of Transylvania. The person occupying this position had to fulfil several key requirements such as to hold the political power, to obey the laws, and stay in the country at all time. In theory, the Estates had the power to change annually the governor, but this procedure had to be approved by the sovereign,[8] thus making it difficult to apply in practice.

In order to maintain a balance between the central and the local authority, all candidates for high-level offices in the country, including that of the Governor, had to be confirmed by the emperor.[9] A special attention was granted to the catholic confession and its representation in the Government also known as *Consilio Intimo*. As stipulated by article 9, at least 3 of the 12 members had to be Catholics.[10] According to chancellor Nicholas Bethlen, the original proposal submitted for approval to the emperor was for the Government to include *tantum* or *at most* three catholic counsellors, but this stipulation was modified in *saltem* or *at least*.[11] The change of an adverb gave a considerable movement space for the emperor in imposing loyal candidates in the office, thus overturning the religious balance of forces.

The legislative dialogue between the sovereign and the Estates had to be carried out through the Diet, the representative political institution of the Principality, reconfirmed by article 10. The task of summoning an annual Diet rested with the governor, but decisions could not become laws until they received the emperor's approval.[12] This last provision created a very complicated situation for the Estates, because as long as the bills were not promulgated by the sovereign, they were called historical documents and had no legal power. The monarch had the right to approve them in full or in part, to postpone the promulgation, which happened quite often, or simply to refuse to sign them.[13] Until 1744, even though

7 Fodor, *Sistemul Legislativ*, 297.
8 Fodor, *Sistemul Legislativ*, 298.
9 Fodor, *Sistemul Legislativ*, 298.
10 Fodor, *Sistemul Legislativ*, 298.
11 Nicolae Bethlen, *Descrierea vieții sale de către el însuși*, (Cluj-Napoca: Ed. Casa Cărții de Știință, 2004), 222.
12 Art. 10, Fodor, *Sistemul Legislativ*, 298.
13 Rolf Kutschera, *Landtag und Gubernium in Siebenbürgen 1688–1869* (Köln-Viena: Böhlau Verlag, 1985), 79.

the Diet was summoned almost every year, very few initiatives had received the imperial ratification, transforming the institution to a highly sterile and inefficient forum of debates.

Articles 12, 13, and 15 referred to the contributions that the Principality had to pay to the Habsburgs; 50,000 talers were due in times of peace, whereas 400,000 Rhenish florins[14] were due in time of war. The articles also stipulated that no fees and unusual taxes were to be introduced[15] and that the noblemen's rights and privileges concerning commerce were guaranteed.[16]

The Diploma also included a set of stipulations regarding the military organization of the Principality of Transylvania, which had a crucial role in Vienna's strategy to exercise control over this region. According to article 17, the Transylvanian armies were only partially composed of native soldiers and the troops were under the authority of a German general,[17] an asset that allowed the commander to exercise a considerable political influence in the following decades. The measure was justified by the border position that Transylvania had, which required the presence of a permanent and professional army. The article also stated that the commander had to work with the governor and other decision-makers in the Principality, but without the right to intervene in matters related to political decisions of the Government.[18] This commitment was not always respected by the Viennese authorities in the Eighteenth century, when different commanders were appointed as governors, thus violating the provisions of the Diploma.[19] Although expressly mentioned in the Diploma, the indigenous militia[20] was mustered only on exceptional occasions.

Negotiated in an extremely complicated political context, the Leopoldine Diploma represented a temporary compromise between the Viennese Court and the political factors in Transylvania, thus theoretically guaranteeing a certain balance of power between central and local authorities. Nonetheless, the ambiguities of some articles concerning the proportion of Catholics in certain fundamental institutions or regarding state leadership had given way to subsequent intrusions by the Viennese Court inside the political affairs of the Principality,

14 Art. 12, in Fodor, *Sistemul Legislativ*, 299.
15 Fodor, *Sistemul Legislativ*, 299.
16 Fodor, *Sistemul Legislativ*, 299.
17 Fodor, *Sistemul Legislativ*, 299.
18 Fodor, *Sistemul Legislativ*, 299.
19 Rolf Kutschera, "Guvernatorii Transilvaniei, 1691–1774," *Anuarul Institutului de Istorie Națională* IX (1944): 131–222.
20 Art. 17, in Fodor, *Sistemul Legislativ*, 299.

eventually leading to a reversal in the balance of power in favour of the central authorities, especially in the second half of the eighteenth century.

Between the Diet and the Imperial Court: Transylvania's Key Political Institutions (1692–1742): The Transylvanian Aulic Chancellery and the Government

As far as the Viennese Court was concerned the issue of controlling the key institutions of the Principality was far from being settled. Leopold and his descendants had no intention in leaving the initiative with the Estates and insisted that Transylvania's affairs must be submitted to him for resolution.[21] The negotiations between the central and local authorities continued and, during the 1692 Diet it was decided to create the Transylvanian Aulic Chancellery. This new institution initially had only a partially outlined administrative structure. It was based in Vienna and was independent of the other similar Chancellery's in the capital of the Empire.[22] The institution became operational only in 1695, when the hierarchical and organizational framework was finalized. At the head of the Aulic Chancellery in Vienna was the vice-chancellor, whose role was to mediate between the local Principality's institutions and the sovereign.

Legally, the Aulic Chancellery was only a representation of the Transylvanian Chancellery (the proof is that its leader bore only the title of vice-chancellor), and, according to the instructions of the Cluj Diet, its members were accountable to the Government, the Diet and the Transylvanian Chancellery.[23] In order to consolidate the effective control over the institution it was legally stipulated that when the provincial chancellor, Nicholas Bethlen, was present in Vienna, he was granted the legal leadership of the Aulic Chancellery.[24] This is precisely the reason why he spent several years in the capital of the Empire, at the end of the seventeenth century. His presence there represented a good opportunity to remind the officials of the Aulic Chancellery of their duty to respect the laws

21 Dörner, *Reformismul austriac*, 61.

22 Zsolt Trócsányi, *Habsburg-politika és Habsburg Kormányzat Erdélyben. 1690–1740* (Budapesta, 1988), 223.

23 Anton E. Dörner, "Instituțiile centrale ale Transilvaniei în epoca reformismului iosefin," in *Studii de istorie medievală și premodernă. Omagiu profesorului Nicolae Edroiu, membru corespondent al Academiei Române*, ed. Avram Andea (Cluj-Napoca, 2003), 254.

24 Anton E. Dörner, "Administrația Transilvaniei în prima jumătate a secolului al XVIII-lea," *Revista Bistriței*, no. IX (1995), 181.

of the country and not to prejudice the interests of the Government and the Chancellery, the true governing bodies of Transylvania.[25]

Conceived by the Estates as an unimportant institution in the constitutional life of the Principality, with no other purpose than to ensure the connection between the Transylvanian authorities and those in Vienna,[26] over time, the Aulic Chancellery became one of the most important decision-making forums of the Principality. The possibility of subordinating the institution to the interests of the Court arose during the Rákóczi's War of Independence (1703–1711), when Chancellor Bethlen was arrested on suspicion of collaborating with anti-Habsburg insurgents. The Peace of Satu Mare (Szatmár) (1711) not only did not solve the successor problem, but also decided to delay the appointment of a successor for more than 30 years, thus favouring the interests of the Court in Vienna. The vacancy of the Chancellor position meant the final shift of the decision-making power from Transylvania to Vienna. One of the most effective means by which the Court managed to control the Aulic Chancellery had been to promote Catholics in almost all key positions. It is estimated that the process of subordinating the institution to the central power ended somewhere in the early 1730s.[27] The delay of the appointment of a chancellor continued until 1742, when Maria Theresia appointed Ladislau Gyulaffy (1699–1754) in the position, a Catholic and a pro-Habsburg.[28] With Gyulaffy's appointment the Empress also settled the issue of the chancellor's headquarters which was definitively moved to Vienna. Throughout Maria Theresia's reign, the decision-making influence of the Viennese Court over the Transylvanian Aulic Chancellery increased so much that the Empress authorized it to give direct orders to the Principality's Government.[29]

Along with the Chancellery, both for the Court in Vienna as well as the Estates gathered in the Diet had a key interest in controlling the Principality's Government. The origins of the institution date back to 1692, and it was led by a governor assisted by a 12-member council.[30] The institution was initially

25 Dörner, "Administrația Transilvaniei," 181.

26 Kutschera, "Guvernatorii," 6.

27 Trócsányi, *Habsburg-politika*, 315–27.

28 Dörner, *Reformismul austriac*, 253.

29 Vladimir Hanga și Ioan Ceterchi (eds.), *Istoria dreptului românesc*, I (București: Editura Academiei Republicii Socialiste România, 1980), 288.

30 Jozsef Benkő, *Transsilvania, sive magnus Transsilvaniae principatus, olim Dacia. Mediterranea dictus orbi mondum satis cognitus*, II, (Claudiopolis: Typis Lycei regii, 1833), 16.

devised as a temporary instrument for governing the Principality meant to provide the *interim* until the elected crown prince of Transylvania, Michael Apafi II, would come to legal age. The Government's oath of allegiance was held in Sibiu, on 15 March 1693, with the occasion of the General Congregation of the Principality.[31] The first governor of Transylvania was Count György Bánffy (1693–1708), who *de jure* administered the country along with the elected prince Michael Apafi II, until the latter resigned in 1696.[32]

During the anti-Habsburg uprising led by Francisc Rákóczi II (1703–1711), the Government was relocated from Alba Iulia (Gyulafehérvár) to Sibiu (Hermannstdt/Nagyszeben), which was considered a safer and better protected location, where it operated under military authority. In this tense context, more precisely in 1709, the Government was restructured and changed its name to the Country Deputation. The Deputation was an enlarged Governing Council now composed of 16 members, whereby the office of president reverted consecutively to István Haller (August 10, 1709–May 2, 1710) and István Wesselényi (2 May 1710–31 March 1713).[33] Once Rákóczi's uprising was defeated, the issue of the government restoration was brought back on the Transylvanian Diet's agenda. When convened in session in 1712, the Diet nominated István Wesselényi as a candidate for the Governor's position and submitted the proposal to Emperor Charles VI.[34] By appointing the catholic Zsigmond Kornis, a devotee of the ruling House, the Emperor's decision overturned, however, the plan of the Estates,[35] thus creating a dangerous constitutional precedent. The Diet's reaction was firm, and, in a long memorandum submitted to the sovereign, it demanded explanations for the decision, as well as clarifications on the appointment of a new provincial chancellor.[36] The answer came on 31 March 1713. The Court justified Kornis's appointment as Governor via the exceptional qualities he displayed and his vast administrative experience.[37] The question regarding the appointment of a new chancellor also received a very diplomatic response. It was argued that his

31 Benkő, *Transsilvania*, 16.

32 Avram Andea, "Instituțiile centrale ale Principatului Transilvaniei," in *Istoria romanilor* VI. Românii între Europa Clasică și Europa Luminilor 1711–1821, eds. Paul Cernovodeanu, Nicolae Edroiu (Bucuresti, 2002), 357.

33 Andea, "Instituțiile centrale," 352.

34 Andea, "Instituțiile centrale," 368.

35 Andea, "Instituțiile centrale," 358.

36 Biblioteca Academiei Române, Filiala Cluj-Napoca, (BAR CJ), Mss. R. 1027–1028, *Alpha et Omega als der…und das ende alter Göttlich*, 334–39.

37 BAR CJ, Mss. R. 1027–1028, 347.

situation was still unclear due to the pending trial of Miklós Bethlen, and that the position is suspended until the case is resolved.[38]

By disregarding the opinions of the Estates, the Viennese Court clarified its attitude and plans regarding Transylvania, namely confirming the political tendencies of isolation and subordination of Transylvania's key institutions. The Court's desire was to link the Principality as closely as possible to the Empire by exercising direct leadership or by close supervision of all of its governing bodies.[39] The appointment of the governor was far too an important issue to leave it to the discretion of the Diet, which, by an inspired move, could dominate the political and administrative life of the province. On the other hand, appointing a governor close and loyal to the Court was equivalent to imposing central authority and marginalizing the Diet in the constitutional life of the Principality. The Court's intrusions aimed to reduce the role of the governmental institution in the Principality, by transforming it into an executive centre, independent of the will and influence of the Estates and under direct Habsburg rule.

The situation of 1712 repeated with the same outcome in 1734, when the Diet gathered in Sebeş (Szászsebes/Mühlbach) voted the same István Wesselényi as governor, yet this time the emperor preferred appointing Johann Haller.[40] Once the precedent was set, the practice of not validating the will of the Estates concerning the office of the governor acquired a permanent character throughout the century.

The strengthening of Vienna's position within the Government was achieved gradually during the eighteenth century, as the institution was gradually submitted to the imperial authority. Once the issue of appointing governors was resolved by ignoring the proposals of the Diet, an attempt was made to introduce as many Catholic counsellors as possible into its structures. The year of 1721 marked an important success in this regard, when the newly established bishop of the Roman Catholic Episcopate appeared on the lists of the institution. Moreover, he occupied the second place in the hierarchy of the Government

---

38 […] *Propositio seu commendatio sollummodo (sic) fidelium notis Statuum petenda, quam sic quandam a prefatis Consiliaryis Nostris eam voto et opinione eorum clementer exspectabimus, Sed quia Cancelary Comitis Nicolai de Bethlen captivi sententia nondum est pronuntiata, Vacantia Cancellary nondum datum legitimi Candidatos aliorum ejus loco pro nunc Suspendenda.* […], BAR CJ, Mss. R. 1027–1028, 349.

39 Constantin Daicoviciu et al., *Din Istoria Transilvaniei,* I, (Bucureşti, 1961), 248.

40 László Gál, *Az erdélyi diaeták végzéseinek nyomdokái és a compilata constitutio után költ articulusok kivonatja.* (*Kolozsvár:* Tilsch és Fia, 1837–1838), 3, 219; Kutschera, "Guvernatorii Transilvaniei," 164.

after the governor[41] and consecutively a particularly important role in the institutional gear.

After Charles VI ascension to the Viennese throne in 1711, the pressure on Transylvanian institutions continued, yet they experienced a less accelerated rhythm as compared with the previous period. First, as he lacked direct male heirs, Charles knew that in order to solve this constitutional problem he had to resort to provincial diets. Second, Rákóczi's uprising determined the emperor to resort to a pacifying policy with the Estates. In his attempt to get them to vote the Pragmatic Sanction (the law on direct succession to the throne both in male and female line), Charles had to reduce the centralizing pressure and, given the general situation of the Empire, no strong action was recommended. The ratification of the Pragmatic Sanction by the Transylvanian Diet represented the last major victory of the central court until Maria Theresia's reign. By relinquishing the prerogative that allowed them to elect the prince, the Estates ceded one of the most important political attributes, and hence the advantage they had over the central authority, thus legitimizing the Habsburg rule over Transylvania.

State Council's Debates Regarding Transylvania's Border Regiments

The difficult situation of the Habsburg Monarchy during The War of the Austrian Succession (1740–1748) and then in the Seven Year's War (1756–1763) generated a series of discussions in Vienna about the need to reform the army. Maria Theresia's main collaborators and especially the State Chancellor Kaunitz presented several initiatives through which they tried to solve this pressing issue within a reasonable time. The main problem that triggered the debate was that of the traditional recruitment system, proven to be outdated and unable to guarantee the ever increasing need of soldiers in the context of longer and more intense confrontations. At the same time, the presence of an aggressive neighbour, as Frederick's Prussia proved to be, determined the Habsburgs to maintain a large permanent army even in peacetime. However, this aspect had major implications for the general welfare of society, subjected to an extremely high economic pressure. In order not to burden the subjects with exorbitant taxes, Kaunitz promoted the idea that the army must be proportional to the state's

41 Anton E. Dörner, "Structuri birocratice în Transilvania epocii prereformiste în contextul administrației habsburgice," in *În pragul Europei. Instituțiile Transilvaniei în epoca prereformistă*, eds. Remus Câmpeanu, Varga Attila, Anton Dörner (Cluj-Napoca: Presa Universitară Clujeană, 2008), 261–62.

income. Any overcoming of this balance would inevitably lead to the subjects' ruin and implicitly of the state.[42] In order to achieve this, the working options included an initiative aimed to settle and recruit Prussian prisoners, a project that was also submitted for debate within the Transylvanian Diet of 1761,[43] or to incorporate active citizens. The last initiative was disliked by Kaunitz due to profound economic losses. The agreed approach was, however, the one proposed by the state chancellor himself, which aimed at expanding the military border. The existing military frontier was broadly a territorial cordon stretching along the southern border of the Empire, from the Adriatic Sea to the Drava River, placed under the authority of the Aulic War Council or *Hofkriegsrat*. Its main purpose was to defend the south-eastern part of the empire against the Ottoman Empire but also to have active and well prepared troops ready to be mobilized and sent to other conflict zones if the situation required it. Originally inhabited by mercenary soldiers, the military frontier gradually evolved into communities of peasant soldiers who enjoyed land and religious rights in exchange for military service.[44]

Once Transylvania and then the Banat region in 1718 came under Habsburg rule, the possibility of extending the border regiments system in those areas was debated by the Aulic authorities. In Kaunitz's view, the expansion of the military frontier made it possible to maintain a sizeable army even in peacetime at minimal cost.[45] Among the benefits of expanding the military border, Kaunitz also listed the increase in the economic prosperity of the border guards, which would later attract immigrants from the Ottoman Empire and the Romanian Countries,[46] and at the same time prevent emigration across the mountains.[47] Border disputes with Moldavia were also a cause for concern in Vienna. In order to precisely delimit the border regiments attributions, the controversial border issue with Moldova had to be resolved first. During the eighteenth century, the

---

42 Franz A. J. Szabo, *Kaunitz and Enlightened absolutism 1753–1780* (New York: Cambridge Univeristy Press, 2004), 287.

43 Art. 7 of the 1761 Diet: *A' burkus foglyok's invalidus katonáknak béfogadása megtelepittése parancsoltatott*, Gál, *Az erdélyi diaeták*, 244.

44 Szabo, *Kaunitz and Enlightened absolutism*, 281.

45 Szabo, *Kaunitz and Enlightened absolutism*, 281.

46 Szabo, *Kaunitz and Enlightened absolutism*, 281.

47 The issue of Romanian emigrants fleeing from Transylvania to the extra-Carpathian Romanian countries was also debated by the State Council officials. See Österreichisches Staatsarchiv, Haus-, Hof- und Staatsarchiv, Viena (ÖStA HHStA) Staatsrat, Akten abschriften (St.K.),1761–1770, Akt. 1579/1761.

Viennese Court pursued a constant policy for the precise delimitation of the border with the neighbouring Principality, in terms as favourable as possible for the Habsburgs.[48] The issue of the frontier was particularly intense in the period between 1753 and 1765, when various commissions attempted to design a clear borderline and thus establish a more efficient control of it.[49] An intense moment in this border dispute is known from a report of the general commander of Transylvania submitted to the Aulic Chancellery in Vienna on 7 April 1763. The General informs the chancellor that Effendy [the Turkish ambassador] and the agent of the Moldavian prince in Constantinople intervened next to Baron von Benczei/Bencklei [incomprehensible name] in order not to report to the High Gate the abuse of the Moldavian voivode who raised a border post at Tatarhagos, thus violating the territory of Transylvania. The voivode of Moldavia feared that this complaint would bring him the same fate as that of the voivode of Wallachia who was removed from office, deprived of his possessions and sent into exile.[50]

Alongside military reasons, the expansion of the military frontier had profound political and social ones. In Kaunitz's vision, Hungary and implicitly Transylvania's problem required special attention because, properly and rationally exploited, the resources of these regions could increase the Monarchy's power.[51] Since the nobility was the main opposition factor to the implementation of reforms in the Principality, a solution had to be found to limit its power and thus force a reforming agenda. First, extracting the peasants and other social categories targeted for enlistment from the nobles' authority would weaken their economic strength, thus forcing it to be more compliant in accepting

48 Silviu Stoian, "Dispute de frontieră între Transilvania şi Moldova: Raportul Luchsenstein (prima jumătate a secolului al XVIII-lea), " *Studii şi Materiale de Istorie Medie*, XXXII (2014): 212.

49 Such is the case of a letter from 3 December 1753, written by the governor of Transylvania to the Voivode of Moldavia, asking the latter to respect the peace and with it the security of the border between the two Principalities, in ÖStA HHStA, St.K. Noten a.d. Siebenburg Hofkzl. 1751–1814,Alt. Fsz.1, f. 16 to 17 v; also an *Insinuatum,* from the 5 May 1760 adressed to Transylvanias Court Chancellary from Vienna, stating that: "circa componendas inter Transylvania ac Moldavia Principatus vigentes limitum controversias"; an *Insinuatum* addressed to the same Aulic Chancellery of Transylvania on 1 March, 1765, finds that: "amicabilem controversiarum circa limites inter Transylvanos et Moldavos subristentium compositionem concernans", in ÖStA HHStA,St.K. Noten a.d. Siebenburg Hofkzl. 1751–1814,Alt. Fsz.1, f. 45–45v.

50 ÖStA HHStA, St.K. Noten a.d. Siebenburg Hofkzl. 1753–1801, 80, Fsz.1, f. 30–30v.

51 Szabo, *Kaunitz and Enlightened absolutism*, 313.

innovations.[52] Second, by pulling out the peasants from the nobility's jurisdiction and thus guaranteeing them effective means of juridical protection, the simple man was won for the crown.[53] And third, creating a permanent military cordon in the vicinity of the nobility's estates populated with loyal peasant-soldiers would ensure the central authorities that any possible noble uprising would be quickly overcome. Basically, the larger the military frontier was, the smaller and more isolated the area under the Estates control. The border-guards could thus become not only an element of social stability due to their position as free men, but also an example for other serfs and, at the same time, a permanent threat for nobles.[54]

But for this strategy to be effective, reforms had to be imposed directly from Vienna, and this could only be achieved by not convening the Diet, which was seen as the main opposing factor to an enlightened government. The opportunity for the Austrians to force the implementation of reforms came precisely from Transylvania's political system that relied on the system of three equal nations. By speculating the differences between the Hungarian nobility, the Szeklers and the Saxons (the latter supported the border militarization project), the Empress Maria Theresia could avoid their opposition and thus create the desired border system. Once brought under the authority of the Aulic War Council, the reformation initiatives could first be implemented in the border territory, thus creating wealth and prosperity, while later on, relying on its success, the measure was to be implemented in the rest of the Principality.[55]

The fourth major advantage pursued by the Habsburgs through the creation of border regiments was to expand the Catholic confessional base within them. In order to consolidate their control over Transylvania, a very important component of the Central Court's policy carried out throughout the eighteenth century was to promote Catholicism, which was seen as an instrument of loyalty and

52 Andea, "Instituțiile centrale," 538; Vlad Popovici, "Establishment of the Austrian Military Border in Transylvania and Its Short and Medium-term Effects," *Povjesni prilozi* 54 (2018), 295–296.

53 Szabo, *Kaunitz and Enlightened absolutism*, 314; David Prodan also examines the struggle of the central authorities to win the serfs loyalty and eventually use it against the nobility. By transforming the peasant problem into a political one in which the absolutist and enlightened state is perceived as an entity situated above the social classes, the peasants must become the foundation of the monarchy, David Prodan, *Răscoala lui Horea* (București: Editura Științifică și Enciclopedică, 1984), 48–51.

54 Andea, "Instituțiile centrale," 539.

55 Szabo, *Kaunitz and Enlightened absolutism*, 334; Popovici, "Establishment," 296.

stability that further granted a certain legitimacy to the regime. Since the political nations of Transylvania were overwhelmingly Protestant, Vienna's attention turned to the Romanians, who were divided between the Orthodox Church and the Church United with Rome. The latter was established at the end of the seventeenth century, and played a very important role in the political, social, and religious emancipation movement of the Transylvanian Romanians. However, the union suffered a major blow and lost many parishioners after the confessional movements of the Orthodox monks Visarion Sarai and Sofronie from Cioara in the 1740s and 1750s. From a national point of view, until their inclusion in the military border, the Romanians were deprived of all political rights and, from a legal standpoint, they were only tolerated as population and religion, without the right to own land. By including them in the border system regiments, the Romanians were offered the opportunity to own land and the perspective of social equality with the other inhabitants of the country.[56] The prospect of creating a military border in areas mostly inhabited by Romanian Orthodox offered the Viennese Court on the one hand the possibility of expanding the religious union with Rome, one of its fundamental objectives in Transylvania, and, on the other hand, to create a gap between Transylvanian Orthodox Romanians and those from Trans Carpathian Romanian countries. The conversion of Romanians in militarized areas could thus become a barrier to emigration across the Carpathians and implicitly the solution of social, economic, and even sanitary[57] problems that the authorities had long faced in previous years.[58] The special importance that the court forums gave to the religious phenomenon also emerges from the large number of reports analysed by Viennese officials, both before the establishment of the military border and after its creation.

The empress's desire to combine the establishment of the military frontier with the expansion of the church's union was followed strictly by the Transylvanian

56 Mathias Bernath, *Habsburgii și începuturile formării Națiunii Române* (Cluj-Napoca: Editura Dacia, 1994), 173–74.

57 On the problem of plague epidemics and the transmission of this disease from Moldova to Transylvania, as well as its devastating effects on a Transylvanian community see the letter of Baron Wimpffen, colonel of the Szekler hussar regiment, in ÖStA HHStA, Hungarica Specialia, Transilvania separata, 1761–1825, Konv. A, Fasz. 362, 108–109; Popovici, "Establishment," 296.

58 Documents related to Wallachians emigrations across the Carpathians to the Romanian Lands, Russia, the Ottoman Empire or Poland can be found in numerous documents of the time, ÖStA HHStA, Staatsrat, Aktenabschriften,1761–1770, Akt. 1579/1761. Akt 2053, 2618, 3309, 89, 2575, 2686, 3309.

imperial army commander, general Buccow. As early as July 1761, the Aulic War Council granted him the mission to prepare and advance a project for the establishment of Transylvania's border units.[59] Apparently Buccow had been successful in promoting the union. In response to a speech given by the Transylvanian court chancellor Bethlen, from 22 September 1761, State councillor Borie considered that, after the final report will be presented by Baron Buccow, the general deserves to be complimented for the effort to attract to the Union the entire Bistrița (Beszterce/Nösen) district, with 4.508 families, an action of great importance for both the Church, as well as for the State, given that the Bistrița district represented the border with Moldavia.[60]

Although important progress had been made in the conversion of Orthodox believers to Catholicism, certain impediments occurred as well and were due to the refusal of the *Schismatic* priests to accept the union in the territories subject to militarization. A report submitted to the State Council by General Buccow in October 1761 synthesized the proposals of the United and Latin bishops regarding the religious union situation. The rejection of the Union by the Orthodox Romanians, says the report, represented a consequence of the "gross ignorance", both of the clergy as well as the common people.[61] However, the failure in converting Romanian Orthodox to Catholicism attracts a number of demographic problems due to mass emigration to Russia of the non-united, and with it the concern that this "evil" may spread to Hungary.[62] In order to break ties and prevent the non-united from making pacts with their Moldavian brethren, Borie recommends that "the most capable and skilful garrison must be placed on this border".[63]

Confessional issues in the area subjected to Romanian militarization continued in the years that followed. A report debated inside the State Council also included the petition brought by the Wallachian deputy in Sibiu, which stated that, despite the promise made, the Romanians refused to recognize the Union. Councilor Stupan appealed to a decision taken at the last State Council, which stipulated that the non-united bishop and his popes should not interfere in this matter and, above all, should not obstruct the Union by militating against it to the people. Stupan considered that the opposition of the Romanians did

59 Vasile Tutula, *Organizarea militară a Principatului Transilvaniei în perioada 1691–1774* (Cluj-Napoca: Ed. Nereamia Napocae, 2003), 169.
60 ÖStA HHStA,Staatsrat, Aktenabschriften,1761–1770, Akt. 1579/1761, Akt . 2295.
61 ÖStA HHStA, Staatsrat, Aktenabschriften, Akt 2675.
62 ÖStA HHStA, Staatsrat, Aktenabschriften, Akt 2675.
63 ÖStA HHStA, Staatsrat, Aktenabschriften, Akt 2675.

not start with the people, but it was rather provoked by the "wisest of all non-united popes"[64] [probably the Orthodox Bishop]. The council's resolution was harsh: "To be investigated, punished and dismissed!"[65]

Interesting aspects related to the confessional problems in the areas subject to militarization emerge from a document issued by the Aulic War Council from the 23 July 1763. The case involves the investigation of 10 Wallachian's arrested and imprisoned for alleged crimes. State Councillor Stupan stated that this document showed that the problem of the Wallachian's who came to Sibiu [from the Bistriţa area], 10 of whom were arrested, is of a confessional nature and it concerns the military aspect only indirectly. The document talks about "the ignorance" of the captives regarding the issues related to both the Orthodox and the United faith and that it was very probable that they had been urged to renounce the Union by the schismatic bishop and his priests. Councillor Borie considered that the Wallachians from Bistriţa were denying the Union in order to "free themselves from military service", as only the United could gain the "military status". Thus, the issue takes both a military and a confessional turn. As a punitive measure, the Aulic Council and the Aulic Chancellor of Transylvania reported: "this evil can be eradicated by exemplary punishments". However, baron Borie noted that the problems of the 9.000 families, almost 100.000 people in the Bistriţa district, were related to: the lack of catechesis, their complete ignorance regarding aspects related to the united or non-united confession, the impossibility of determining how many of them received the sacrament of baptism and even how many of them know how to make the sign of the cross. Therefore, he recommended that the Empress and the court chancellor should be notified of this problem, in order to find effective solutions. As a working option, Borie suggested the appointment of parish priests whose simple activity would lead to a basic catechesis of the people. Regarding the costs of this measure, he considered that they should not exceed 5.000 florins, easily supported by the very population of 100.000 people in that district, who paid 10.000 florins annually. Thus, they would redeem their souls for only 30 kreutzers. From a political point of view, the lack of catechesis was considered to be the main cause of the Wallachian nation instability while from a confessional point of view, Borie considered that this was not about eradicating a confession that was once tolerated, but about the conversion of some "real pagans". Blümegen, Daun, and Haugwitz entirely agreed with baron Borie's exposition, for the Wallachian's have "no notion of any confession", which is

64 ÖStA HHStA, Staatsrat, Aktenabschriften, Akt 2154.
65 ÖStA HHStA, Staatsrat, Aktenabschriften, Akt 2154.

also evident from the fact that neither the popes nor their clergy are united or schismatic.[66]

The opposition to the military border creation was also shared by the elite of the Roman Church in Transylvania, which also disavowed the new institution through the voice of the influential Bishop Baytay out of envy of favouring the militarized united Romanians.[67] A note from 28 June 1764 coming from Transylvania's court chancellor and addressed to the State Council called for the investigation and trial of Catholic clerics who became suspicious or guilty of opposition to the establishment of the border regiments. Councillors Stupan and Borie believed that although the issue of religion was concerned it should be resolved without him. [probably the Roman Bishop].[68]

The same zeal with which the Court promoted the Catholic confession within the border regiments area in Transylvania was also preserved in the process of militarization of the neighbouring territories. The resolution issued by the State Council following a note of the Aulic War Council, from 21 June 1767 recommended that extra attention should be paid to the request that only Catholics and United people should be accepted in the military district which is in the process of delimitation [unspecified]. In addition, as it has been already successfully processed in Transylvania, the "pure faith" should be kept in the already delimited district[69] [also unspecified].

Of all the reform measures initiated by the Habsburgs during the eighteenth century, none had such a complex impact on the political, social, and religious system of Transylvania as the project to create the military border. Coordinated and orchestrated by Chancellor Kaunitz, the proposals for the establishment of border regiments in Transylvania severely disrupted the principality's constitutional system. Through the measures that the central authority sought to introduce, the political system based on the privileges of the three nations received a severe blow. First of all, by diminishing the financial power of the nobility, it was forced to cede important estates to the state. Second, due to the military cordon created around such a large area, the emigrations over the mountains were carefully supervised by the border guards, and, to some extent, they exercised a certain control over the potential movements of the nobility. Third, the reforms initiated in the militarized territory increased the payment capacity of the

---

66 ÖStA HHStA, Akt 2325.

67 Apud Bernath, *Habsburgii*, footnote no. 1, 172.

68 ÖStA HHStA, Staatsrat, Aktenabschriften,1761–1770, Akt. 1796.

69 ÖStA HHStA, Staatsrat, Aktenabschriften, Akt. 1431.

subjects and at the same time created a certain well-being among the border guards. Fourth, through the promoted religious and social policies, a strong dynastic feeling was outlined, at least among the Romanian population, since the end of Maria Theresia's reign, but especially during the reign of Josef II, her son. Taken as a whole, the decisions that had a positive impact for the welfare of the people especially for the disadvantaged and oppressed classes have long remained in their memory. Popular legends about the Good Emperors spread rapidly throughout the era and remained vivid in the collective imagination of peasant communities even in the early Twentieth century.

The Constitutional Role of the Transylvanian Diet during Maria Theresia's Reign Regarding Military, Defence, and Border Legislative Matters

"La Transylvanie est placée depuis un temps immémorial sous un régime constitutionnel lequel differe sous plussieurs rapporte de tous les régimes constitutionnels anciene et modernes qui existent dans d'autres Etates. [...] Il serait difficile de se dissimuler que la véritable cause de l'obstination des Etats dait être principalement attribueé au mauvais jeu d'un parti qui influencé pas ce qu'an apris genéralemént l'habitude d'appeler l'esprit du temp s'est constitué en opposition ouverte contré le gouvernement. L'une des particularités propre à celui de ce pays, c'est que ce sont les Etats réunir en une seule chambre, mais subdivisér dans certaines occasions par nations et par religions[...]."[70]

[...]"L'empereur est le gardien fidèle des lois qui régissent ses etats, et moind il se permet d'enfreindre le privilegèr dous jouissent les corps constituér, plus il est bien déterminé, d'un autre côté, à ne pas tolérer que le droite de la couronne puissent jamais être violer par l'une ou l'autre de ces corporation. Ce qui vient de se passer pendant de huit mois en Transylvanie offre cependant un phénomène tout particulier; car ler attaquer del opposition virulente à la Diète ont été dirigéer bien plus positivement contre la constitution que contre le pouvoir royal. Il parait que les meneurs de la faction anarchique ne se sentent par assez forts pour attaquer directement l'autorité souveraine, ont cru devoir commencer par saper dans les fondement les lois en vigueur, et ila n'ont dèslors point tardé à se trouver engagér dans voyes qui n'aboutissent qu'à l'absurde."[71]

70 ÖStA HHStA, StK Provinzen Siebenbürgen 1–1 Korrespondenz der Staatskanzlei und des Ministeriums des Äußern mit dem siebenbürgischen Generalkommando und mit der siebenbürgischen Statthalterei, 1751–1860, 1–2 Varia (1786–1847), 24–24 v.

71 ÖStA HHStA, StK Provinzen Siebenbürgen, 28–28 v.

The above paragraphs are extracted from a letter written in 1835, which depicts the arguments that sustained emperor Ferdinand I's decision to dissolve the Diet of Transylvania during the same year. In just a few pages, the letter comprises the entire constitutional dynamics carried out for over 150 years between the Transylvanian Estates grouped within the Diet and the central power in Vienna. Ever since the incorporation of Transylvania in the Habsburg Empire at the end of the seventeenth century, there were two different political concepts promoted and supported either by the authorities from Vienna or by the local Estates gathered within the Diet. On one hand, the central authorities insisted on the development of a centralized state according to sixteenth and seventeenth century political theories, and, on the other, the local authorities who promoted a federal system with a strict balance of power between centre and periphery.[72]

The incorporation of the Principality of Transylvania in the Habsburg Empire also meant the beginning of an extensive process of administrative centralization through the energetic and insistent intervention of the Viennese Court in its internal affairs. The structural integration of the Principality in the institutional gear of the Empire started in full force under the reign of Emperor Leopold I but it slowed down later on under his successors, Joseph I and Charles VI, only to be resurrected during Maria Theresia's reign. The reason for such an approach was given by the desire to standardize all the institutional-administrative structures of the Empire but also by the aspiration to annihilate the provincial particularisms that endangered the unity of the monarchy.[73] The decision-makers in Vienna were convinced that the success of the program lay primarily in removing the opposition of the Estates grouped around the Diet. In doing so, they exploited the main Transylvanian constitutional problem which consisted of a system based on 3 privileged equal nations, each with their own political agenda. The political strategy recommended by Chancellor Kaunitz was *divide et impera*.[74] By favoring the Saxons, the Court hoped that they would represent a counterweight to the Hungarian nobility, and thus break the Diet's political monolith.[75]

---

72 Hans-Christian Maner, "Security, stability and Imperial self assurance. On the function of East and Southeast European Border regions of the Habsburg Monarchy in the Eighteenth and Nineteenth centuries: The cases of Galicia and Bosnia-Hertegovina and arousing awareness for history," *Medieval and Early Modern Studies for Central and Eastern Europe*, I, no. 1–4 (2009): 142.

73 Andea, "Instituțiile centrale," 392.

74 Szabo, *Kaunitz and Enlightened absolutism*, 333.

75 Robert J.W. Evans, *Austria, Hungary, and the Habsburgs Central Europe c. 1683–1867* (Oxford; New York: Oxford University Press, 2006), 28.

Until Maria Theresia's reign, the main purpose as shown above was to eliminate the influence that the privileged Estates could have in the appointment of the governor or the chancellor, considered to be key factors in the institutional and decisional gear of the country. Once this goal achieved, Vienna's plans focused on implementing fundamental reforms directed at increasing the tax base of the Principality but also its defensive capacity as a border province of the Empire. The almost permanent state of war in which the monarchy found itself during the eighteenth century entailed an increased need for money and soldiers. In Transylvania, the prerogative of increasing the amount of the annual tax belonged to the Diet, as stated in the Leopoldine Diploma of 1691 and, thus, the tendency of the Viennese authorities, in constant need of money, to ask for more frequently met their opposition. Imperial claims in this regard were fought with arguments by the Diet, which replied to the emperor invoking the country's ruin[76] due to the exaggerated and excessive financial demands.[77] In order to put an end to these issues, Vienna gradually imposed a system of taxation which circumvented the decision of the Diet, starting with *Systhema Bethlenianum* (1754), subsequently improved by *Systhema Buccowianum* (1763).[78] By depriving the Diet of its fiscal attribution, its authority was considerably reduced, as well as its role as a constitutional factor of the Principality.

Although military issues have been pursued since the establishment of Habsburg rule in Transylvania,[79] they received an increased attention during Maria Theresia's reign (1740–1780). The external context was extremely complicated, as the Monarchy was successively involved in the War for the Austrian

---

76 A long complaint (*gravamina*) sent to the emperor by means of a deputation, in which all the misfortunes of Transylvania are invoked, caused by the exaggerated requests of Vienna, in BAR CJ Mss. R. 1027–1028, 177–89.

77 The prospect of an imminent taxation of the nobility was outlined by the project of a land record, planned for April 1703. In addition to the substantial increase in the annual tax, which sometimes tripled compared to the amount specified in the Leopoldine Diploma, the possibility of taxing the nobility irritated the Estates who joined the insurrectionary movement led by Francis Rákóczi II, Trócsányi, *Habsburg-politika*, 194–304.

78 Avram Andea, "Absolutismul luminat. Reformismul terezian şi iosefin," in *Istoria Românilor*, VI. *Românii între Europa Clasică şi Europa Luminilor 1711–1821*, eds. Paul Cernovodeanu, Nicolae Edroiu (Bucuresti, 2002) 537.

79 The diets held during the reign of Charles VI sought to establish a military regulation for Transylvania, as follows: Art. 2 of the Sibiu Diet from 1717, Art. 2 of the Cluj Diet from 1719, Art. 3 of the Cluj Diet from 1720 and Art. 6 of the Sibiu Diet from 1728, in Gál, *Az erdélyi diaeták*, 210–14.

Succession (1740–1748) and later on in the Seven Years' War (1756–1763). As such, the focus of the central authorities was directed especially towards increasing the capacity of recruiting new soldiers and, starting with the 1760s, towards the extension of the military border in the marginal lands of Transylvania. Given the challenging external conditions with which the monarchy was confronted, during the first half of her reign, the Empress attempted to govern with the support of local Diets, and especially those of Hungary and Transylvania. By convening the Diets and appealing to their help, the Empress hoped to create a certain dynastic feeling that would eventually lead to the integration of the eastern provinces and thus consolidate the Empire under the Habsburg family. However, this strategy failed and an important cause was the obstinacy of the Hungarian and Transylvanian Estates to cooperate with the sovereign in matters that the Empress considered to be vital for the Monarchy's survival. These matters concerned the peasant problem, the reformation of the tax system, and, later on, the creation of the military border system in Transylvania. Interpreted by the Estates as an attack led by the central authorities on their ancient prerogatives, they tried to block the reform initiatives coming from Vienna through the Diet, thus creating a state of conflict which ultimately led to the Diet not being convened for a long time.

In short, the first half of Maria Theresia's reign represented a permanent attempt to cooperate with the Estates and the local Diets, making efforts to maintain as much as possible a constitutional rule. Since all decisions regarding public matters, the common good, the issue of the country's borders and fiscal assets, resolving border conflicts, the provisions regarding property rights[80] came in as topics for analysis and discussion of the Diet, the Empress tried to resolve some of the military problems concerning Transylvania by appealing to it. The ever-increasing need of soldiers determined the sovereign to demand either financial contributions over those established by the Leopoldine Diploma or, in extremely complicated situations for the monarchy, the incorporation of new soldiers at the

80 *Objecta Diaetae in genere sunt omnia illa, quae ad publica commoda et Legislationem pertinent, penes propositiones Regias, et Postulata Statuum assummenda […] aut communitatem aliquam, et respective privatas etiam Personas, in quantum scilicet in Objecta Diaetalia influunt, tangentium medela, determinatio quanti contributionalis, ejusque Repartitionis, et Exactionis modalitas, Electio, et Praesentatio Statuum ad Officia Diplomatica, Receptio in Indigenatum, Metarum Regni, et purarum Fiscalitatum Negotium, controversiarumque eatenus subversantium determinatio, et Jus Proprietatis* […] Art. XI of 1791 Diet, in Kolosváry S., Óváry K. eds., *Corpus Juris Hungarici, Magyar törvénytár, 1540–1848 évi Erdélyi törvények*, (*CJH*), (Budapest, 1900), 506.

expense of the Estates. Such was the case in 1741 and 1742, when the Diet voted for a tax increase of 257.806[81] respectively 157.806 florins, and for the incorporation of 1.000 de cavalry and 2.000 infantrymen.[82]

Apart from the permanent tax increases, the only notable military achievement obtained through the Diet was the adoption of the legislation regarding the deserters, which was debated and voted in 1751. The law articles established the way the deserters or new recruits who did not show up at the assigned garrison were to be handed over to the competent authorities, it clarifies aspects regarding the punishments that were to be applied to those found guilty of receiving and hiding these criminals, but also certain rules concerning persons who did not know that they were hosting deserters. The law differentiated the penalty according to the social status of the perpetrator, imposing a fine for a nobleman or a free person and 40 blows with a stick if the perpetrator was a peasant. It also prohibited forced conscription, by forbidding the incorporation of the family father and of the only son without whom the parental house would become empty and would no longer serve as a taxpayer house. The law also forbade recruiting servants, artisans, serfs of landlords, debtors or those accused of any wrongdoing. Finally, it forbade recruiters from breaking into the prisons managed by authorities or landlords in order to recruit detainees from there. The legal remedy by which those harmed in their rights could seek for justice was to file a complaint either to the supreme military commander of Transylvania or to his deputy, and, eventually, they had the opportunity to appeal to the emperor.[83] Other military issues were debated in subsequent diets,[84] but no such bill was ratified by the Empress and consequently they had no legal value. Nevertheless, the real test of trust between the central and the local power occurred at the beginning of 1760' and it concerned dealing with Chancellor Kaunitz's proposal to initiate the militarization of the Transylvanian borders.

The Viennese Court assigned the task of creating the border regiments to General Adolf Nikolaus von Buccow, who was sent to Transylvania and endowed with broad prerogatives first as general-commander, and from 1762 as the president of the government.[85] The project stipulated that the military border stretched on the mountain segment of Transylvania, from Banat to the border

81 Art. 4 of the Sibiu Diet from 1741 and art. 4, Gál, *Az erdélyi diaeták*, 224.

82 Art. 4 and *2* of the Sibiu Diet from 1742, Gál, *Az erdélyi diaeták*, 224–25.

83 Art. 2, 3, 4 and *5* of the 1751 Diet, in *CJH*, 420–24.

84 Art. 4, letters *c, d* and *e* of the 1753 Sibiu Diet; Art. 6 of the Sibiu Diet from 1757; Article 2 of the 1761 Sibiu Diet, in Gál, *Az erdélyi diaeták*, 238–43.

85 Bernath, *Habsburgii*, 170.

with Bukovina. The border regiments included Romanian infantry regiments totalling 3.000 soldiers, two Szekler infantry regiments, a Romanian dragon regiment and a Szekler hussar regiment of 1.000 horsemen each.[86] Buccow's plan, approved by the imperial resolution of 13 October 1761, foresaw the establishment of a Transylvanian border militia consisting of 17.000 soldiers.[87]

Because the militarization project also included measures that violated the constitutional rights of the Transylvanian nobility, Buccow proposed the Viennese authorities not to summon the Diet to debate the document. As a preventive measure, the Court instructed the Transylvanian governor, count Ladislau Kemény to pave the way for such a bold undertaking and thus to prepare the nobility. He replied that he could not work on the implementation of such a plan, as the approval and vote of the Diet were required.[88] In order to legally justify her decision to create border regiments, the Empress consulted Samuel von Bruckental and Nemes, the state jurist. Their resolution was favourable to the start of the project, stating that the country's laws will not be violated and that "Romanians themselves want to submit to military discipline."[89] Based on this favourable opinion, the Empress decided to remove the governor from office by forcing him to retire in 1762. To put an end to any possible delays, the Empress appointed General Buccow as President of the Government in the same year thus avoiding the constitutional debate in the Diet.[90] In fact, to completely cancel the Diet's opposition in terms of reform policy, the Empress conveyed to Buccow that the Diet should no longer be summoned: "The hostile position of the nobles towards any reforms upset the Empress so much that after 1761 she had not allowed the convocation of other Diets."[91]

---

86 Carol Göllner, *Regimentele românești din Transilvania 1764–1851* (București: Ed. Militară, 1973), 29.

87 Bernath, *Habsburgii*, 171.

88 Emil Micu, *Contribuțiuni la Istoricul Regimentului Grăniceresc Întâi Valah* (București: Impr. națională, 1943), 6.

89 Apud Micu, *Contribuțiuni*, 6. See also Ioan Bolovan, Sorina Bolovan, "Granița militară austriacă și românii din Transilvania în sec. XVIII-XIX (studiu de caz: zona Năsăud)," in *Pe urmele trecutului. Profesorului Nicolae Edroiu la 70 de ani*, ed. by Ioan-Aurel Pop and Susana Andea (Cluj-Napoca: Academia Română, Centrul de Studii Transilvane, 2010), 438–39.

90 Tutula, *Organizarea militară*, 169.

91 Apud Tutula, *Organizarea militară*, 169.

Started in 1761, the process of militarization of the Transylvanian border ended in 1783 when, at the initiative of Emperor Joseph II, the communes in the Bârgăului valley were expropriated from the Bethlen noble family.[92]

Conclusions

The subordination of the Chancellery and the Government to the Habsburgs' interests allowed them to gradually introduce the modern principles of government in Transylvania, thus gradually replacing the medieval legislation. By controlling the two key institutions, the Viennese authorities were able to force the Diet, the representative institution of the Transylvanian Estates to accept certain intrusions into the political life of the Principality. Such was the case in the 1740s and the 1750s when a series of laws granted the central power the possibility and legitimacy to intervene in certain matters concerning economic, social and juridical components.[93] Once the legal framework was created, removing the Diet from the constitutional gear was only a matter of time. The opportunity arose during the difficult economic, political and military context of Maria Theresia's reign, when the situation imposed radical and urgent reform measures. One measure that had a very strong impact on the Transylvanian constitutional system was undoubtedly the one on the creation of the military border system. Kaunitz's idea of extending the military border in Transylvania brought political, social, economic and religious benefits, in addition to the indisputable military advantages. By creating a very long military cordon in areas mostly under the authority of the nobility, Vienna tried to reduce and contain its power and the key role of this strategy was undoubtedly the religious one. Followed consistently by the Imperial Court, the confessional aspect took the form of converting Orthodox Romanians to Catholicism and therefore transforming Romanians into devoted agents of Vienna. By creating a strong dynastic feeling among the united Romanian border guards, the Viennese authorities hoped to isolate and then gradually eliminate the political influence of the nobility in the Principality.

By not convening the Diet after 1761 and practically eliminating it from the institutional equation of the Principality, Vienna's decision-makers were able to impose modernizing Enlightenment ideas through a much simpler and at the same time direct legal mechanism: edicts and patents. The abundance of these types of normative acts issued in a relatively short period of almost

---

92 Valeriu Șotropa, *Districtul grăniceresc năsăudean* (Cluj-Napoca: Ed. Dacia, 1975), 72.
93 Fodor, *Sistemul Legislativ.*

30 years highlighted the Habsburg's desire to reform and place the Principality's institutions in modern Enlightened patterns. Structural changes in the economic, social, juridical, educational, administrative fields brought a new, refreshing change of paradigm, based on principles of performance and administrative efficiency.

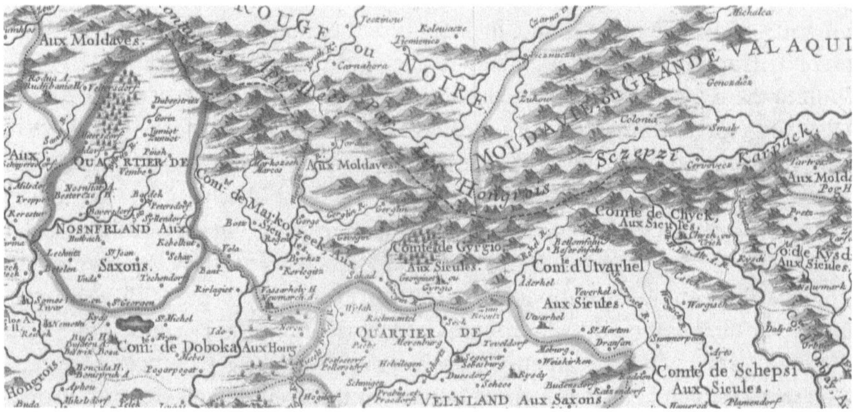

The border between Transylvania and Moldavia at the beginning of the eighteenth century, detail from *Principauté de Transilvanie divissée en Cinq Nations…*/The Principality of Transylvania divided in Five Nations, Nicolas de Fer, Herman van Loon, 1704, cooper engraving (Institut für donauschwäbische Geschichte und Landeskunde, Tübingen)

Borderland Armies

Liviu Cîmpeanu

Ad Retinendam Coronam. Military Organization At the Transylvanian Border in the Late Middle Ages

The Transylvanian-Saxon Militias*

Abstract: On the great seal of the Sibiu (Hermannstadt) County, the main province of the Transylvanian-Saxons, one could read around the coat of arms, representing two crossed swords, with their tips down and holding a crown above, the following legend: *Ad retinendam coronam*. It was a clear statement of the military obligations of the Transylvanian-Saxons towards the Hungarian kingship, in the late Middle Ages. According to their privilege charters, they had to take up arms and form militias, in order to join the royal army, especially in the defence of the realm. Since there in no comprehensive study on this topic, the aim of the present paper is to reveal the social background of the Transylvanian-Saxon militias, their recruitment, weapons and equipment, as well as other economic aspects implied by the war effort, up to the Battle of Mohacs (1526).

Keywords: Border Defence, Militia, Military Organization, Transylvanian Saxon, Late Middle Ages

Introduction

On the legend around the coat of arms of the great seal of the Transylvanian-Saxon province of Sibiu, also known as the Seven Seats, one could read *† S[IGILLIUM]. CIBINENSIS. PROVINCIE. AD RETINENDAM. CORONAM,*[1] which was a clear statement of its priviledged status and might. On the one hand, the legend expressed the direct connection of the Transylvanian Saxons to the Hungarian kingship and, on the other hand, their active role in the support of the Crown in the newly settled territories on the south-eastern border of the realm.

---

* This work was supported by a grant of the Romanian Ministry of Education and Research, CNCS – UEFISCDI, project number PN-III-P1-1.1-TE-2019-0457, within PNCDI III; *From Medieval Frontiers to Early Modern Borders. The Military organization of the Western Parts of the Transylvanian Principality in the XVI-XVII centuries.*

1 *Urkundenbuch zur Geschichte der Deutschen in Siebenbürgen*, II, 1342–1390 ed. Franz Zimmermann, Carl Werner and Georg Müller (Hermannstadt: In Kommission bei Franz Michaelis, 1897), 658.

This support has materialized, first of all, in manpower which generated economic wealth and, thus, a political influence. The latter was imposed by military means which they themselves assured, by taking up arms and organizing militias who joined the royal armies, according to their privilegial charters. Although the great majority of late medieval documents regarding the Transylvanian Saxons were published since the late nineteenth century, in the great collection *Urkundenbuch zu Geschichte der Deutschen in Siebenbürgen*, volumes I-VIII, the military aspects of their history were always treated by the historiography as marginal issues. For instance, in the classical works of Georg Eduard Müller on the Transylvanian-Saxon University, the military organization is treated only on a few pages for the whole period between 1141 and 1876.[2] Later historiography, especially in the communist era of the second half of the twentieth century, focused with predilection on social and economic history, as well as political history. In this trend falls also the study of Gustav Gündisch about Transylvania´s role in the anti-Ottoman defence, between 1395 and 1526 (published in 1974).[3] Consequently, there is virtually nothing known about the military organization of the Transylvanian Saxons in the late Middle Ages, thus the aim of my paper is to analyze all aspects of this issue, which can be extracted from the preserved sources: beginning with an overview of their military obligations towards the Hungarian kingship, I try to trace the information regarding the social componence, inner organization and weaponry of their militias, as well as the latter's defensive and offensive duties. For a better understanding of these aspects, I considered it necessary first to sketch the juridic-administrativ and territorial organization of the Transylvanian Saxons in the late Middle Ages.

The Transylvanian Saxons and their Local Authonomies

By the late Middle Ages, the Transylvanian-Saxons were considered one of the three priviledged nations (i.e. Estates) of the province, along with the nobles and Szeklers. The German-speaking free communities, under the direct authority of the Hungarian kingship, were organised in four different local authonomies,

2 Georg Eduard Müller, "Die Sächsische Nationsuniversität in Siebenbürgen. Ihre verfassungs- und verwaltungsrechtliche Entwicklung. 1224–1876," *Archiv des Vereins für siebenbürgische Landeskunde* 44, 2–3 (1928): 382–402; Georg Eduard Müller, *Stühle und Distrikte als Unterteilingen der Siebenbürgisch-Deutschen Nationsuniversität 1141–1876* (Hermannstadt: Krafft & Drotleff Verlag, 1941), 27–28.

3 Gustav Gündisch, "Siebenbürgen in der Türkenabwehr, 1395–1526", *Revue Roumaine d´Histoire* 13 (1974): 415–43.

along the Transylvanian borders and in the center of the province: on the central southern border, around the modern city of Sibiu (Hermannstadt/Nagyszeben), in the central region, around Mediaş (Mediasch, Medwisch, Medgyes), in the south-eastern corner of the province, around Braşov (Kronstadt/Brassó), and on the north-eastern border, around the city of Bistriţa (Bistritz/Nösen/ Beszterce). In the mid twelfth century, the first *hospites Theutonici* settled in Transylvania, founding several communities under the authority of local *comites*, called in German *gräven*, in and around the future city of Sibiu. The area of the first settlement grew into a royal county, stretching from Orăştie (Broos/Szászváros) in the west, to Drăuşeni (Draas) by the river Olt, in the east. The new county of Sibiu was organized in 1224, being under the authority of a count, appointed by the king, and thus it was cotrolled directly by the Hungarian kingship. After a rebellion of the Transylvanian-Saxons in 1325, they received the right to freely elect their royal judge, who had to be only confirmed by the central authority, a situation which leasted up until the nineteenth century. Furthermore, seven local *comites*, originating from the most influential *gräven*-families, who initially had the inferior jurisdiction over their fellow German-speaking settlers, received by the early fourteenth century the right to exercise penal jurisdiction over several neighboring communities, establishing thus at their residences seats of judgement. These would become the future Seven Seats of the Transylvania-Saxons, as territorial, administrative and juridic subdivisions of the main royal seat of Sibiu: Orăştie, Sebeş (Mühlbach/Szászsebes), Miercurea Sibiului (Reußmarkt/ Szerdahely), Nocrich (Leschkirch/Újegyház), Cincu Mare (Großschenk/ Nagysink), Sighişoara (Schäßburg/ Segesvár) and Rupea (Reps/Kőhalom). Already in the same century, some of these communities redeemed themselves from the jurisdiction of the *gräven* and received special privileges, becoming free market towns and even cities, like Sighişoara, Sebeş, Orăştie. By the mid sixteenth century, all villages, market towns and cities gained the rank of royal free communities. The Seven Transylvanian-Saxon Seats of Transylvania under the jurisdiction of the main seat of Sibiu kept their special status up to the second half of the nineteenth century.

The region located to the north of the Seven Transylvanian-Saxon Seats, up to the middle and inferior cours of the Târnava Mare (Großkokel/Nagy-Küküllő) river, was settled by German-speaking population only later, in the second half of the thirteenth century. The main settlements of this region were Mediaş and Şeica Mare (Marktschelken, Nagyselyk), which became first the seats of judgement of some influential *gräven* and later, after their liberation from the latters authority and the receiving of royal priviledges, free market-towns. Despite enjoing the same rights and privileges as the Transylvanian-Saxons of Sibiu (received 1315 and 1318), the Two Seats were placed under the authority of the Szekler count up to 1402, when they gained their authonomy from the Hungarian kingship. The Two Seats recognized the juridic authority of Sibiu in 1485, when they became part of the Transylvanian-Saxon University (= juridic and politic community), although they kept their political, administrative, fiscal and military authonomy. The Two Seats merged in 1552 becoming the Seat of Mediaş, as the latter received the rank of a free royal city.

Recent studies revealed that outposts of the first settlement of the Sibiu region, in the second half of the twelfth century, reached as far as the south-eastern corner of Transylvania, known as Ţara Bârsei (Burzenland/Barcaság). This region came for a brief period of time under the authority of the Teutonic Order (1211–1225), called by the Hungarian kingship to secure the south-eastern borders of the realm from the raids of the neighboring Cumans. The Teutonic Knights manifested tendencies of autonomy and attracted settlers on their lands from the county of Sibiu, thus coming at odds with the Hungarian king who banned them, despite the repeated protests of the Papacy. The Transylvanian-Saxon communities of Ţara Bârsei were set under the authority of the Szekely count, up to the early 1420s. In the meantime, the main settlement of Braşov became an important city of traders and craftsmen, whose status was secured by a set o royal privleges. Besides Braşov, in the region emerged other four great market towns: Prejmer (Tartlau/Prázsmár), Hărman (Honigberg/Szászhermány), Codlea (Zeiden/Feketehalom) and Râşnov (Rosenau/Barcarozsnyó), as well as other nine villages. All these settlements were under the direct jurisdiction of the city Braşov. In 1422, the homonymous district received from the Hungarian kingship the same rights and privileges of the Sibiu province, becoming in 1485 a part of the Transylvanian-Saxon University. Despite the recognition of the juridical authority of Sibiu, the city and province of Braşov kept its political, administrative, fiscal and military autonomy.

The first German-speaking settlers arived at the north-eastern border of Transylvania around 1200. They were called by the Hungarian kingship as miners in the silvermines of the Rodna (Rodenau, Radna) valley. Thus, their homonymous settlement quickly developed into a city, but it was destroyed by the Mongols, in 1241. After this catastrophic event, mining in the region went on, though the city of Rodna never recovered, and further German settlers came into the area, establishing new settlements. Out of these, Bistriţa evolved into a city of traders and craftsmen, during the fourteenth century. Since the mining region in north-eastern Transylvania was an appanage of the Hungarian queens, Bistriţa received a series of privileges from the kingship (1330, 1366), becoming a royal-free city. It was at the head of the homonymous district, which, unlike the district of Braşov, did not include other market towns, but only villages. In the fifteenth century, the whole district came under the possession of the Hunyadi family (1453–1463), but its Transylvanian-Saxon inhabitants spared neither blood nor gold in order to receive their former status. They succeeded not only by redeeming their former freedom, liberties and privileges from Matthias Corvinus (1463), but also received from the king the neighboring mining district of Rodna (1475). The city and district of Bistriţa received the same rights and privileges as the province of Sibiu only in 1485, when it became part of the Transylvanian-Saxon University. As well as the Two Seats and the district of Braşov, Bistriţa recognised only the juridic authority of Sibiu, keeping its political, administrative, fiscal and military autonomy.

The juridic uniformization of the four Transylvanian-Saxon authonomies, as well as the *fraterna unui trium gencium*, the establishing of the three priviledged nations of Transylvania (1437, 1438, 1459, 1467), prepared the road for the Transylvanian-Saxon University, established by Matthias Corvinus, in 1485. According to the royal charter, the German community of the four authonomies enjoyed the same rights and privileges (one customary law, self determination, free trade), recognizing the town magistrate (council) of Sibiu as the highest juridic instance. On the other hand, the University was the supreme political institution of the Transylvanian-Saxons and their highest fiscal authority and a dialogue partner of the Hungarian kingship. Thus, through a smart policy of gaining juridic privileges, they also gained economic advantages and political power, becoming thus one of the main military factors of Transylvania.[4]

In addition to the listed local authonomies of the Transylvanian Saxons, the city of Cluj (Klausenburg/ Kolozsvár) was also founded by *hospites Theutonici* in the early thirteenth century. Albeit it was a German-speaking settlement up to the second half of the sixteenth century, when it was gradually taken over by a Hungarian population. Cluj never became part of the Transylvanian-Saxon University, having from an early age the special status of a free royal city and thus a separate historical evolution.[5] Because of its special status, I will only reffer tangentially to the Transylvanian-Saxon city of Cluj.

4 The present *Introduction* summarizes the main results of my phd thesis, Liviu Cîmpeanu, *Universitatea Saxonă şi districtele româneşti aflate sub jurisdicţia ei în Evul Mediu şi Epoca Modernă* (Târgu Mureş: NICO, 2014), 31–140.

5 Dirk Moldt, *Deutsche Stadtrechte im mittelalterlichen Siebenbürgen. Korporationsrechte – Sachsenspiegelrecht – Bergrecht* (Köln-Weimar-Wien: Böhlau, 2009), 100–18.

Military Obligations and Social Componence of the Transylvanian-Saxon Militias

Since the four local autonomies of the Transylvanian-Saxons were established by different groups of settlers at different times and in different historical circumstances, it is self-evident that they enjoyed different sets of rights, privileges and obligations towards the Hungarian kingship, up to the establishment of the Transylvanian-Saxon University, in 1485. Relevant for the present paper are mainly the military obligations, thus I will analyze them chronologically, with a special emphasis on the social componence of the formers military might, their militias.[6]

The first preserved set of privileges received by the Transylvanian-Saxons from King Andrew II, dates from the year 1224. Actually, the royal charter called *Andreanum* is the cornerstone of the Transylvanian-Saxon University, as it conferred to the inhabitants of Sibiu county (and latter, to all the Transylvanian-Saxons) the free exercise of their own customary law, self determination, free trade and the special protection of the king(ship). In exchange, they had to pay consistent annual taxes and to perform military service. King Andrew II stipulated that the *hospites Theutonici* of the newly established county of Sibiu, should send 500 *milites* in the royal army, if the king would led his host within the borders of the realm, 100 *milites* for the offensive campaigns of the king, outside the borders, and only 50 *milites* if the royal army was led by one of the king's captains outside the borders of the realm.[7] Now, for the early period of the Hungarian Kingdom, in the age of the Arpadians, the term *miles-itis* did not ment *knight*, as it did in the late Middle Ages, but it reffered broadly to a warrior, belonging to the class of freemen, owing military service only to the king and/or his deputies.[8] This fits perfectly with the situation of the Transylvanian-Saxons of Sibiu, who were freemen with military obligations. Because of the great number of armed

6 I drew up a "cataloge" of the military obligations of the Transylvanian-Saxons, without insisting on the social componence of their militias, in Liviu Cîmpeanu, "Obligații militare și ordine de mobilizare a orașelor săsești din Transilvania la sfârșitul Evului Mediu," *Historia Urbana*, XXVII (2019): 125–30.

7 *Urkundenbuch zur Geschichte der Deutschen in Siebenbürgen*, I, 1191–1342, ed. Franz Zimmermann, Carl Werner, (Hermannstadt: In Kommission bei Franz Michaelis, 1892), 34.

8 *The Laws of the Medieval Kingdom of Hungary/Decreta Regni Medievalis Hugariae*, I, 1000–1301, ed. János M. Bak, Görgy Bónis, and/et James Ross Sweeney (Idyllwild CA: Charles Schlacks, Jr., Publisher, 1999), 80, 148. I hereby express my gratitude to Ladó Árpád-Gellért, for the clarification of the term *miles* in the Arpadian Age.

men they had to send in the royal army at such an early age, one can conclude that the king expected them all, or at least all valid men capable of bearing arms, to join his host. Since they were not professional soldiers, but conscripted townsfolk and peasents at arms, it appears clear that they formed only a militia and not a regular army. This statement is also confirmed by the orders of mobilization received by the central authorities of Sibiu from the Hungarian king and/or his military deputies, several of them being preserved from the second half of the fifteenth century. Through their central authorities, the Transylvanian-Saxons of the Seven Seats were called to arms *per singula capita*, i.e. all valid men, on several occasions: 1453, 1456, 1461 (together with the militiamen of the Two Seats), 1466, 1467, 1468, 1471.[9]

The *Andreanum* was confirmed by all the Hungarian kings, from Charles Robert (1317), to Wladislas II (1492),[10] and even later, by the Habsburg monarchs of Hungary and by the Transylvanian princes,[11] thus it is clear that the military obligations of Tranylvanian-Saxon province of Sibiu remained unchanged during the late Middle Ages, despite the juridical, administrative and teritorial developments, such as the establishment of the Seven Seats, in the early fourteenth century. As shown above, the early counts (*comites*) of Sibiu had under their command the militiamen from all the free communities of their county. After the establishsment of the Seven Seats under the authority of the main seat of Sibiu, one can observe that each seat had its separate contingent of armed men under the command of its judge royal or of an appointed captain, as I will discuss in detail below. Thus, the conscripted burghers and peasents from each of the Seven Seats of the Transylvanian-Saxons gathered under the banner of the judge royal of Sibiu and/or the mayor of the city (still bearing the title *comex Saxonum*). The first mention of this militia, as a whole, dates from the late second decade of the fifteenth century: sometime, between 1415 and 1419, the voivode and the bishop of Transylvania, along with the Szekler *comes*, requested the Transylvanian-Saxons of the Seven Seats to send a tenth of their armed men

---

9 *Urkundenbuch zur Geschichte der Deutschen in Siebenbürgen*, V 1438–1457, ed. Gustav Gündisch *et alii*, (Bucureşti: Editura Academiei, 1975), 399–400, 534–35; *Urkundenbuch zur Geschichte der Deutschen in Siebenbürgen*, VI, 1458–1473, ed. Gustav Gündisch *et alii* (Bucureşti: Editura Academiei, 1981), 108, 259–60, 283–84, 285, 340–41, 479

10 Cîmpeanu, *Universitatea Saxonă*, 103–19.

11 *Urkundenbuch*, I, 33.

in the royal host.[12] The militia of the main seat of Sibiu is literaly attested only in 1563,[13] albeit there is no doubt that it was the oldest military unit in the province of Sibiu.

The first attested contigent of a Transylvanian-Saxon seat is the one of Sighişoara, in 1431. The Wallachian throne pretender Vlad Dracul urged the Transylvanian-Saxons of Braşov to join his campaign against his rival, Alexandru Aldea, motivating that the inhabitants of Sighişoara were also joining him.[14] Besides this indirect refference, the military contingent of Sighişoara is attested on 1467 (militiamen) and 1493 (mercenaries).[15]

The town militia of Sebeş is also indirectly attested in 1438, in its desperate and hopless attempt to defend the city from an Ottoman siege.[16] The contingents of the seats Sebeş, Orăştie and Miercurea Sibiului are attested for the first time together, on 30 April 1481, when István Báthory, voivode of Transylvania, asked Thomas Altenberger, mayor of Sibiu and *comes Saxonum*, to call the three mentioned seats to arms, in order to prevent an Wallachian-Ottoman attack.[17] The militiamen, both cavalry and infantry, of Sebeş are attested again on 21 June 1491.[18]

The militiamen of Cincu are first attested on1 January 1471, when the authorities of Sibiu orderd the general mobilization of the seat (*per singula capita*

12 *Urkundenbuch zur Geschichte der Deutschen in Siebenbürgen*, III 1391–1415, ed. Franz Zimmermann, Carl Werner and Georg Müller (Hermannstadt: In Kommission bei Franz Michaelis, 1902), 651.

13 Mária Pakucs, *„zu urkundt in das Stadtbuch lassen einschreiben". Die ältesten Protokolle von Hermannstadt und der Sächsischen Nationsuniversität (1522–1565)* (Hermannstadt-Bonn: Schiller Verlag 2016), 254–55.

14 *Documeta Romaniae Historica*, Seria D. *Relaţii între Ţările Române*, I, 1222–1456, ed. Ştefan Pascu *et alii* (Bucureşti: Editura Academiei, 1977), 283–84.

15 *Urkundenbuch* VI, 287–289; *Urkundenbuch* VIII, no. 5302 (regest, available on following link: http://siebenbuergenurkundenbuch.uni-trier.de/catalog/4947; see the original on following link: https://archives.hungaricana.hu/en/charters/231770/?list=eyJmaWx0ZXJzIjogeyJEQVRBQkFTRSI6IFsiRExERiJdfSwgInF1ZXJ5IjogIjE0OTMtMDEtMDgifQ).

16 Georgius de Hungaria, *Tractatus de moribus, condictionibus et nequitia Turcorum*, ed. Reinhard Klockow (Köln-Weimar-Viena: Böhlau Verlag, 1993), 148–55.

17 *Urkundenbuch zur Geschichte der Deutschen in Siebenbürgen*, VII, ed. Gutav Gündisch, Herta Gündisch, Konrad G. Gündisch and Gernot Nussbächer (Bucureşti: Editura Academiei Române, 1991), 273.

18 *Urkundenbuch* VIII, no. 5124 (regest, available on following link: http://siebenbuergenurkundenbuch.uni-trier.de/catalog/5085).

exercitualiter [...] *parati esse debeatis*) for an anti-Ottoman campaign.[19] The preserved sources mentioned separately the contingents of the market towns Agnita (Agnetheln/Szentágota) - 1466 and Cincu - 1474 and 1492, as well as the armed men of the village Noiştat (Neustadt/Újváros) - 1494,[20] all three located in the seat of Cincu. For the social componence of the militia of Cincu we also have a late but interesting information from the year 1600: during the military turmoils of that year, marauding mercenaries routed 800 conscripted peasents of the mentioned seat.[21] This information confirms that by the Early Modern Age the militiamen of Cincu were still peasants at arms, and not hired mercenaries.

Finally, the militia of Rupea is attested in 1472, when it lost its banner in a skirmish with the armed forces of Braşov, in otherwise unknown circumstances.[22]

In 1315, the Two Seats, Mediaş and Şeica Mare received the rights and privileges of Sibiu County from King Charles Robert, who even tried to unite the two Transylvanian-Saxon auhtonomies.[23] This "royal experiment" did not succeed, thus Charles Robert granted to the Transylvanian-Saxons of the Two Seats the rights and privileges of Sibiu again, in 1318, when he established them in a separate local authonomy, under the jurisdiction of the Szekler count. Through the royal charter from 20 January 1318, the inhabitants of the Two Seats were exempted from all military obligations towards the Hungarian kingship.[24] It was only on 29 July 1369, that King Louis I reintroduced the military obligations of the Transylvanian-Saxons of the Two Seats, with the confirmation of the rights and privileges of Sibiu, they received from his father, Charles Robert. King Louis stipulated that the inhabitants of the seats Mediaş and Şeica Mare should join the royal army, according to their possibilities, as other Transylvanian-Saxon

19 *Urkundenbuch* VI, 479.

20 *Urkudenbuch* VI, 269–70; *Urkundenbuch* VII, 24; *Urkundenbuch* VIIII, no. 5234 (available on-line, on following link: http://siebenbuergenurkundenbuch.uni-trier.de/catalog/5284), 5451 A (available on-line, on following link: http://siebenbuergenurkundenbuch.uni-trier.de/catalog/5291).

21 Georgius Krauss, *Ausführliche Verzeichnung des Elendes und der Noth, welche von Anno 1599 bis Anno 1606 Schässburg und andere umliegende Örter, ja ein grosser Theil Siebenbürgen erduldet und erlitten, aus denen unverwerfligen Urkunden der Stadt Schässburg zusammen getragen von* –, Dr. Fritz Mildt (ed.), *Aus den Zeiten tiefster Not. Zwei chronistische Berichte aus der Fürstenzeit Siebenbürgens, von Georgius Krauss, Juratus notarius der Stadt Schaessburg* (Sighişoara: Editura Friedr. J. Horeth, 1926), 59–60.

22 *Urkundenbuch* VI, 528–29.

23 *Urkundenbuch* I, 315–16; See the context in Cîmpeanu, "Obligaţii militare," 126.

24 *Urkundenbuch* I, 331–32.

seats do: *quod iidem ad exercitus regios duntxat ad partes orientales pro tempore emergentes et non alias iuxta posse ipsorum eo modo ire teneatur, prout iidem Saxones nostro de Cibinyensi et aliis sedibus transire ab antiquoe sunt soliti.*[25] This royal charter was repeatedly confirmed by the Hungarian kingship and by the Church Chapter of Transylvania during the fourteenth and fifteenth centuries, and even if the same authorities confirmed several times the original charter issued by Charles Robert in 1318, through which the inhabitants of Mediaş and Şeica Mare were initialy exempted from service in the royal host, the military obligations of the Two Seats established in 1369 remained valid, as demonstrated by repeated orders of mobilization received by them from the kings and their military deputies, during the fifteenth century.[26] The Transylvanian Saxons of the seats Mediaş and Şeica Mare were expected to take up arms by their (probably modest!) possibilities, which also speak for the existence of a local militia. Two orders of mobilization *per singula capita*, received by the Two Seats from Matthias Corvinus, *via* the authorities of Sibiu, on 6 September 1461 and 18 May 1467,[27] clearly reveal that the Hungarian king expected all their valid men to take up arms and join the royal army. This is a clear sign that by the second half of the fifteenth century the armed forces of the Two Seats still consisted of conscripted commoners and not professional mercenaries. The contingent of the Two Seats is attested on campaing in the spring of 1467.[28]

The early military obligations of the Transylvanian-Saxon inhabitants of Braşov are unknown, but it is certain that they had their own military organization. On 28 March 1353, King Louis I of Hungary decreed that all his valid male subjects in the county and city of Braşov should join the royal campaigns in the eastern parts of the realm, on horse or on foot, according to their possibilities. If the royal army would undertake a campaign to the west, the Transylvanian-Saxons of Braşov should send under his banners "only" 500 agile and well armed horsemen.[29] This charter was confirmed by King Louis (1364), Sigismund of Luxembourg (1387, 1388) and Matthias Corvinus (1467),[30] which means that the military obligations of the Transylvanian-Saxons of Braşov remained unchanged up to the second half of the fifteenth century. Only on 27 March 1488, Matthias Corvinus orderd to István Báthory, voivode of Transylvania, not

25 *Urkundenbuch* II, 327.
26 Cîmpeanu, "Obligaţii militare," 127.
27 *Urkundenbuch* VI, 108, 283–84.
28 *Urkundenbuch* VI, 287–88, 288–89.
29 *Urkundenbuch* II, 95.
30 Cîmpeanu, "Obligaţii militare," 127.

to bother the inhabitants of the county and city of Braşov with a mobilization for a western campaign, since they were obliged to take up arms in the anti-Ottoman campaigns at the eastern border of the realm.[31]

The administrative structure of the county, later the district of Braşov, was less complex than that of the Seven Seats. Thus, its militia consisted of the citizens of Braşov and of the market towns of Prejmer, Hărman, Codlea and Râşnov, as well as out of the peasents of the other nine villages of the county/district.[32] On 27 July 1428, Sigismund of Luxembourg attests for the first time the "army" (*exercitus*) of the city and county of Braşov, under the authority of it's free elected captain, whom he grants the right to judge over his armed men.[33]

The military organization of Bistriţa and the afferent county, later district, is even less known. Only in a charter from 22 July 1453, issued by John Hunyadi as perpetual count of Bistriţa, we read that King Sigismund established that the Transylvanian-Saxon inhabitants of the city and of the district should join the royal host under its own banner.[34] This charter was confirmed by Matthias Corvinus on 20 July 1461, but there are no further details about this matter.[35] Shortly after, the militia of Bistriţa is attested for the first time: on 25 April 1468, János Pongrác of Dengeleg, voivode of Transylvania, issued an order to the town magistrate of Bistriţa to mobilize all its valid men (*per singula capita vestra* [...] *insurgere*) and to send all its horsemen and infantrymen to Orăştie, in order to prevent an Ottoman attack.[36] The Transylvanian-Saxons of Bistriţa received a similar order of mobilization *per singula capita* from the vicevoivode Domokos Bethlen, on 29 June 1469, in order to attack with the voivode's men some Moldavians, who raided Borşa (Borsa, Borscha), in Dăbâca (Doboka) county.[37] The two sources clearly state that the military authorities of Transylvania

31 *Urkundenbuch zur Geschichte der Deutschen in Siebenbürgen* VIII, no. 4772 (available on-line: http://siebenbuergenurkundenbuch.uni-trier.de/catalog/3425)

32 Liviu Cîmpeanu, "Organizarea militară a Braşovului până la sfârşitul secolului al XV-lea," in *Studii de istorie a oraşelor. In honorem Paul Niedermaier*, ed. Vasile Ciobanu and Dan-Dumitru Iacob (Bucureşti-Brăila: Editura Academiei Române – Editura Istros a Muzeului Brăilei „Carol I", 2017), 346–49.

33 *Urkundenbuch zur Geschichte der Deutschen in Siebenbürgen*, IV, 1416–1437, ed. Gustav Gündisch (Hermannstadt: Kraft & Drotleff Verlag, 1937), 366.

34 *Urkundenbuch* V, 413.

35 *Urkundenbuch* VI, 106.

36 *Urkundenbuch* VI, 335.

37 *Urkundenbuch* VI, 409–10.

expected under their banners all valid men of the city and district of Bistrița, in other words the latter's militiamen.

Orders of Mobilization and Conscriptions of the Transylvanian-Saxon Militiamen

During the fifteenth century, up to the battle of Mohács (1526), the militias of the Transylvanian-Saxon towns, seats and districts are repeatedly attested in the orders of mobilizations issued by the kings of Hungary or by the Transylvanian voivodes and other royal captains. According to circumstances and needs, the military authorities of the Hungarian kingdom could call to arms all Transylvanian-Saxons, or just separate towns, seats or districts, located in the proximity of the war threatend area. In a comprehensiv study on the subject, I could determine that the Transylvanian Saxon authorities gatherd their militias only when the mobilization order came directly from the king. It seems that they often ignored such orders if they were issued by the Transylvanian voivodes or other military deputies of the king. They didn't fear any juridical consequences because of their privileges, neither did they fear retaliation, since they had their own military forces.[38] Since I have revealed all this aspects in a separate study, I will focus here on the actual conscription of the militiamen from the Transylvanian-Saxon towns, seats and districts.

Like the other towns of the Hungarian realm, the Transylvanian-Saxon towns were expected to support the royal host with armed men and war materials.[39] However, it seems that the Transylvanian-Saxon militias were mobilized only if the armed forces of the other two „military" Estates, the nobles and the Szeklers, were insufficient for a campaign. At least this seems the logical explanation for a royal charter from 29 June 1508, through which King Wladislas II forbade the Transylvanian voivode Péter of St. Györgyi and Bazin to call the Transylvanian-Saxons to arms, before the mobilization of the nobles and Szeklers.[40]

---

38 Cîmpeanu, "Obligații militare," 130–44.

39 András Kubinyi, "Probleme bei der Mobilisierung und Logistik unter Matthias," in András Kubinyi, *Matthias Corvinus. Die Regierung eines Königreichs im Ostmitteleuropa 1458–1490* (Herne: Tibor Schäfer Verlag, 1999), 162–71; András Kubinyi, "Kriegslasten der Städte unter Matthias Corvinus," in Kubinyi, *Matthias Corvinus*, 171–87.

40 Albert Berger, *Urkunden-Regesten aus dem Archiv der Stadt Bistriz in Siebenbürgen 1203–1570*, I, ed. Ernst Wagner (Köln-Wien: Böhlau Verlag, 1986), 140 (available online on the following link:

Usually, the military authorities of the Hungarian kingdom adressed the orders of mobilization directly to the judge royal and the magistrate (town council) of Sibiu. According to the received orders, the authorities of Sibiu could call to arms only the Seven Seats under their direct authority, but also the Two Seats, respectively the districts of Braşov and Bistriţa. In their turn, the local authorities (seat or district) called to arms the communities under their direct jurisdiction. For example, in the first days of the year 1471, the authorites of Sibiu received a mobilization order from Domoks Bethlen, vicevoivode of Transylvania, as news spread about an Ottoman attack. Thus, on 7 January 1471, the mayor and magistrate of Sibiu asked the judge and councillors of the seat Cincu *statim et sine mora equites simulque pedites per singula capita exercitualiter ipsis Thurcis occurendis paratis esse debeatis.*[41] It is likely that on the same occasion similar mobilization orders were issued for the other six seats, too. This case clearly reveals a system in which the king of Hungary, respectively his military deputies, usualy addressed the orders of mobilization to the central authorites of the Transylvanian Saxons in Sibiu, who transmitted them further to the local authorities of the Seven Seats. The latter, on their turn, seem to have trasmitted the orders of mobilization to all the communities under their jurisdiction. It is true that no such written order is preserved, if there were any issued, but there is evidence for the mobilization of several communities under the jurisdiction of different seats, and it is clear that the authorites of Sibiu did not send orders of mobilization to every single market town or village separately. The latter must have been called to arms by their immediat superiors, that are the judges and magistrates of their seats. Thus, a good exemple offers the case of the Transylvanian-Saxon Seat of Cincu, where several market towns were partly exempted from the mobilization, in order to defend the newly built fortifications around their parish churches. The latter aspects will be discussed at lenghts further below, for the moment I will just focus on the moblization of the Transylvanian-Saxon cummunities. On 19 November 1466, Matthias Corvinus exempted half of the inhabitants of the market town Agnita from taking up arms in case of a general mobilization, in order to remain at home for the defence of the newly built fortifications.[42] An identical exemption received the burghers of the market town Cincu from the same king, on 7 January 1471,[43] through a charter which was confirmed by King

https://archives.hungaricana.hu/en/charters/264038/?list=eyJxdWVyeSI6ICIxNTA4LTA2LTI5In0)

41 *Urkundenbuch* VI, 479.

42 *Urkundenbuch* VI, 269–70.

43 *Urkundenbuch* VII, 24.

Wladislas II, on 18 March 1492.[44] Even the villagers of Noiştat received the same exemption fromKing Wladislas II, on 17 January 1494.[45] Athough not literally attested, it seems that the burghers of Agnita and Cincu, as well as the peasants of Noiştat were called to arms by their immediate authorites, that is the judge royal and the council of the seat.

Regarding the mobilization orders issued by the authorities of Sibiu for the other districts of Transylvania, there is scarce evidence of their existence. For instance, on 6 March 1469, in the context of another announced Ottoman raid on the south-western parts of Transylvania, János Rédei, vicevoivode of Transylvania, issued a mobilization order for the mayor and magistrate of Sibiu, asking the latter to transmit the same order to the city of Braşov.[46] On 25 May 1526, the magistrate of Sibiu issued a similar document for the magistrate of Bistriţa, urging the latter to send 1.000 well armed horsemen, according to the mobilization order issued by John Szapolyai, voivode of Transylvania, on 18 May, the same year.[47]

Of course, there are also mobilization orders issued by the military authorites of the Hungarian kingdom adressed direct to the authorities of the local seats and districts of the Transylvanian Saxons. For instance, on 21 July 1491, István Telegdi, vicevoivode of Transylvania, issued a mobilization order for the magistrate of Sebeş[48] and on 8 January 1493, the same vicevoivode issued a similar order for the seat and city of Sighişoara.[49] I already mentioned the mobilization order issued by the voivode János Pongrác of Dengeleg for the district and city

44 *Urkundenbuch* VIII, no. 5234 (available on-line, on following link: http://siebenbuergenurkundenbuch.uni-trier.de/catalog/5284).

45 *Urkundenbuch* VIII, nr. 5451 A (available on-line, on following link:http://siebenbuergenurkundenbuch.uni-trier.de/catalog/5291).

46 *Urkundenbuch,* VI, 380.

47 Berger, *Urkunden-Regesten* I, 236 (see the original charter on the following link: https://archives.hungaricana.hu/en/charters/view/308136/?pg=0&bbox=205%2C-1836%2C3744%2C-71)

48 *Urkundenbuch* VIII, no. 5124 (available as regest on the following link: http://siebenbuergenurkundenbuch.uni-trier.de/catalog/5085 see the original charter on the following link:
https://archives.hungaricana.hu/en/charters/228827/?list=eyJxdWVyeSI6ICIxNDkxLTA3LTIxIn0).

49 *Urkundenbuch* VIII, nr. 5302 (available as regest on the following link:
http://siebenbuergenurkundenbuch.uni-trier.de/catalog/4947 see the original charter on the following link: https://archives.hungaricana.hu/en/charters/231770/?list=eyJxdWVyeSI6ICIxNDkzLTAxLTA4In0).

of Bistriţa, issued on 25 April 1468.[50] For the mobilization of the district and city of Braşov the sources reveal an unique situation: on 21 October 1457, King Ladislaus the Posthumous of Hungary ordered the magistrate of Braşov to provide military support to Oswald Rozgonyi, count of the Szekler, against the rebel baron Mihály Szilágyi of Horogszeg.[51] A month and a half later, on 9 December 1457, the Szekler count confirmed to the Hungarian king that he already received the military support of the Transylvanian-Saxons of Braşov, who were still in his camp.[52] This is one of the rare cases in which the preserved sources reveal that the Transylvanian-Saxons fulfilled an order of mobilization, epsecially that the order came direct from the king.

Since the second half of the fifteenth century, several cities, market towns and villages were partially exempted from the general mobilization, in order to defend their newly build fortifications around their parish churches: in the Seven Seats, such cases are documented in the seats Cincu (the market towns Agnita - 1466 and Cincu - 1471, and the village Noiştat - 1494) and Sighişoara (the market town Saschiz [Keisd, Szászkézd] - 1470); similar cases are also documented in the Two Seats (the market towns Mediaş - 1477 and Biertan [Birthälm, Berethalom] - 1468, and the village of Aţel [Hetzeldorf, Ecel] - 1471).[53] I will discuss the problem of the defensive tasks of the Transylvanian-Saxon militias at lenght, further below, for now I want to emphasis the immediat consequences of these exemptions. According to royal chartes, a part of the militiamen could and should stay at home for defensive purposes. Since war was an expensive and risky undertaking, which could have fatal consequences, two questions arose: Who should go? Who should stay? On every conscription, quarrels broke out, and thus the mobilization was anything but simple. In order to settle this important matter, the Transylvanian-Saxon University issued later, on 17 March 1564, a regulation regarding the conscription of the seat of Sibiu. The five articles of the document reflect the problems encountered by the communities during the mobilization process: each neigborhood of a community should provide an equal number of recruits, their families should receive as a reward help from the

50 *Urkundenbuch* VI, 335.

51 *Urkundenbuch* V, 577.

52 *Urkundenbuch* V, 583.

53 *Urkundenbuch* VI, 269–270, 357, 468, 480–481; *Ukrundenbuch* VII, 27, 124–125; *Urkundenbuch* VIII, nr. 5451 A (available on-line, on following link: http://siebenbuergenurkundenbuch.uni-trier.de/catalog/5291).

community 10 days of common work, the conscripted should receieve a wage: a pikeman on foot 4, a *trabant* or harquebusier on foot 5 and a horseman 6 florins.[54]

Inner Structure of the Militias

In case of an general mobilization, the militiamen of The Seven Seats were under the personal command of the mayor of Sibiu, who was also *comes Saxonum* (count of the Transylvanian-Saxons). For instance, in a charter issued by King Sigismund of Luxemburg on 5 November 1426, we read that the militiamen of the Seven Seats of the Transylvanian Saxons under the command of Jakob, mayor of Sibiu, and Andreas, judge royal of the same city, were active in Wallachia.[55] Later on, Georg Hecht, mayor of Sibiu, commanded the entire military force of the Transylvanian-Saxons, in the battle of Câmpul Pâinii (Brotfeld, Kenyérmező), on 13 October1479.[56]

Each of the Seven Seats sent their militiamen under the command of a captain (*ductor exercitus*, *Hauptmann*). A charter from 15 June 1467, attests *Nicolaus Retheny* at the head of the contingent from the seat and city of Sighişoara, which was detached on the south-western border of Transylvania.[57]

The militias of the Transylvanian-Saxon districts of Bistriţa and Braşov were also commanded by captains. In the case of Braşov, a captain (*ductor exercitus*) was named by the city authories and by the representatives of the market towns and villages of the district, whom King Sigismund granted on 27 July 1428, the right to judge and punish the militiamen under his comand.[58] In Bistriţa, the captain of the town militia is attested only later, on 1508: in that year, the militiamen of the city were headed by a certain *dominus Josa*.[59]

According to the numerous mobilization orders, the Transylvanian-Saxon militias were composed of cavalry and infantry units. The Hungarian king and/or his military deputies requested several times to the Seven Seats under the

54 Pakucs, „*zu urkundt…*," 254–255.

55 *Urkundenbuch* IV, 258–261.

56 The participation of Georg Hecht/Csukas at the battle of Câmpul Pâinii is only attested by his charter of ennoblement, received from King Wladislas II., on 24 April 1493, see *Urkundenbuch* VIII, Nr. 5381 (available on-line on following link: http://siebenbuergenurkundenbuch.uni-trier.de/catalog/5478). However, the charter emphasis only Hecht's bravery at the head of his unit of 60 cavalrymen.

57 *Urkundenbuch* VI, 288–89.

58 *Urkundenbuch* IV, 366.

59 Berger, *Urkunden-Regesten* I, 142.

authority of the main seat of Sibiu, as well as from the Two Seats, to send their *equites* and *pedites* in the royal banner: 1438, 1461, 1466, 1468, 1470, 1481, 1493, 1497.[60] Similar orders received also individual seats and districts, threatend by internal or external enemies. Thus, the horsemen and footmen of Cincu are attested in 1471, and those of Sebeş in 1491.[61] Similar orders received the district and city of Bistriţa on: 1468, 1469, 1510.[62] Even the Rodna valley, which came under the authoriy of Bistriţa in 1475, had a militia composed of Romanian horsemen and footmen, as it appears from an moblization order received by the city from the vicevoivode of Transylvania, on 20 December 1471.[63] Since by that date Rodna was not yet under the authority of Bistriţa, the order might have ment that the Romanian militiamen were to be hired as mercenaries by the city.

Although, according to King Louis' charter from 1353, confirmed by Matthias Corvinus in 1467, the Transylvanian-Saxons of the county/district and city of Braşov were expected to join the royal army on horseback and on foot, and even sent 500 light cavalry in the king's western campaigns, there are no information about the composition of their armed forces, untill the late fifteenth century. Only on 20 December 1478, Péter Geréb, the voivode of Transylvania, requested from the authorities of Braşov 200 footmen, well armed with crossbows, handguns and pavises, as well as artillery for the siege of two rebel fortresses.[64] Two years later, on 22 December 1480, István Báthory, voivode of Transylvania asked the authorities of Braşov to hire 110 Wallachian horsemen as mercenaries and, again, on 31 March 1481, to hire 300 mercenary horsemen from Wallachia.[65] A possible conclusion might be that the Transylvanian-Saxons of the district and city of Braşov went to war mainly on foot, and that their authorites hired, if necessary, mercenary horsemen.

Unfortunately, the preserved sources do not reveal the proportion between the cavalry and infantry of the Transylvanian-Saxon militias, neither their

---

60 *Urkundenbuch* V, 1; *Urkundenbuch* VI, 108, 259–60, 340–41, 468–69; *Urkundenbuch* VII, 256–57, 257–58; *Urkundenbuch* VIII, no. 5320 (regest, available on following link: http://siebenbuergenurkundenbuch.uni-trier.de/catalog/4964), 5737 (regest, available on following link: http://siebenbuergenurkundenbuch.uni-trier.de/catalog/5163).

61 *Urkundenbuch* VI, 479; *Urkundenbuch* VIII, no. 5124 (regest, available on following link: http://siebenbuergenurkundenbuch.uni-trier.de/catalog/5085).

62 *Urkundenbuch* VI, 335, 409–410; Berger, *Urkunden-Regesten* I, 150.

63 *Urkundenbuch* VI, 518–19.

64 *Urkundenbuch* VII, 201–02.

65 *Urkundenbuch* VII, 252–53, 269.

effectives. It is true that some letters reveal cavalry effectives in the service of the seats and districts, but they rather indicate mercenary units, hired for a certain period of time, or even wages for the cavalrymen already in royal service. Thus, the central authorites of Sibiu received several times orders to hire mercenary cavalry, at their own expense: 1463 – 1.000 horsemen, 1476 – 50 horsemen, 1482 – 50 horsemen, 1493 – "all" (sic!) mercenary horsemen and infantrymen.[66] On 5 March 1510, Bistrița was expected to hire 50 mercenary cavalry, besides the district and city militia.[67] The authorities of the district and city of Brașov were also held to hire mercenary cavalry: 1480 – 110 Wallachian horsemen, 1481 – 300 Wallachian horsemen, 1492 – 60 horsemen.[68] On the eve of the Battle of Mohács, John Szapolyai, the voivode of Transylvania, requested from the Transylvanian-Saxon University to hire 1.000 cavalrymen, for the defence of the country. Later, on 27 July 1526, the Estates of Transylvania decided that the Transylvanian-Saxon University should hire 5.000 mercenary horsemen for four months. Thus, each seat and district had to hire a certain number of cavalrymen, as it cearly results from a charter from 15 August 1526, issued by the authorities of Sibiu for those of Bistrița, who were supposed to hire 1.000 of the 5.000 cavalry to send under the banners of the Transylvanian voivode.[69] It seems very clear that the effectives of 50–5.000 horsemen attested by the sources in the second half of the fifteenth century and in the first three decades of the sixteenth century are, in fact, mercenary troops, hired by the Transylvanian-Saxon central and local authorites only for the duration of several military operations. None of these sources make any refference to the horsemen conscripted from the Transylvanian-Saxon townsfolk and peasentry. There is only one refference to them, on 16 December 1480: István Báthory, voivode of Transylvania, orderd Thomas Altenberger, mayor of Sibiu, to prepare for war all the Transylvanian-Saxons who own horses, in order to prevent an Ottoman raid.[70]

---

66 *Urkundenbuch* VI, 159; *Urkundenbuch* VII, 114, 324–25; *Urkundenbuch* VIII, no. 5304 (regest, available on following link: http://siebenbuergenurkundenbuch.uni-trier.de/catalog/4949; the original on following link: https://archives.hungaricana.hu/en/charters/231770/?list=eyJmaWx0ZXJzIjogeyJEQVRBQkFTRSI6IFsiRExERiJdfSwgInF1ZXJ5IjogIjE0OTMtMDEtMDgifQ).

67 Berger, *Urkunden-Regesten* I, 150.

68 *Urkundenbuch* VII, 252–53, 269; *Urkundenbuch* VIII, no. 5245 (regest, available on following link: http://siebenbuergenurkundenbuch.uni-trier.de/catalog/5340).

69 Berger, *Urkunden-Regesten* I, 234, 240, 241.

70 *Urkundenbuch* VII, 250.

The preserved sources provide even scarcer information about the infantry of the Transylvanian-Saxon militias. Besides the simple mention in the mobilization orders listed above, there are hardly any other known details about what appears to be the bulk of the militiamen. Further information in the sources only concerns their weapons and equipment, wich will be discussed at lenght below.

One could expect to find other details about the Transylvanian-Saxon militias in the sources regarding the actual military operations in which they took part. Excepting some vague refferences about their participation the Battle of Câmpul Pâinii, 13 October 1479, the preserved sources do not record anything else but their mere participation to some offensive and defensive campaigns in and around Transylvania, during the fifteenth century.[71] Antonio Bonfini, chronicler of the Battle of Câmpul Pâinii, states that István Báthory, voivode of Transylvania, divided his army in three distinct groups, placing the Transylvanian-Saxons and the Wallachians on the right wing, the heavy cavalry in the center, and the Szeklers on the left wing. The chronicler also states that the voivode strengthend each of his flanks with two cavalry units, that might sugest that the bulk of the Transylvanian-Saxons and Wallachians were footmen.[72] This statements are somewhat confirmed by the ennoblement charter received by Georg Hecht, former mayor of Sibiu, from King Wladislas II, on 24 April 1493. This source records the deeds of arms of the former mayor of Sibiu, among wich his brave fight at the head of his unit of 60 horsemen, during the Battle of Câmpul Pâinii.[73] Georg Hecht's horsemen might be one of the two cavalry units detached by voivode István Báthory on his flanks. Yet, the Transylvanian-Saxons and Wallachians were routed at the first attack of the Ottoman cavalry, because their low effectives, according to Bonfini.[74]

This information, though strictly reffering to a particular historical event, corelated with that about the 200 footmen requested from the city of Brașov by voivode Péter Geréb, on 20 December 1478,[75] could suggest that most of the Transylvanian-Saxon militamen were infantry. Not only that going to war on foot was less expensive than on horseback (horses had to be bought, fed and

71 For the campaigns in which the Transylvanian-Saxons took part, see Cîmpeanu, "Obligații militare," 130–42.

72 Antonius de Bonfinis, *Rerum Ungaricarum Decades*, IV/1, ed. I.Fógel, B. Iványi et L. Juhász (Budapest: K. M. Egyetemi Nyomda, MCMXLI), 111.

73 *Urkundenbuch* VIII, no. 5381 (available online on following link: http://siebenbuergenurkundenbuch.uni-trier.de/catalog/5478).

74 Bonfinis, *Rerum Ungaricarum Decades* IV/1, 111–12.

75 *Urkundenbuch* VII, 201–02.

harnessed for war!), the late Middle Ages were times in which troughout Europe cavalry was replaced by large infantry units, fighting in pike and shot formation, sustained by the artillery.[76]

Weapons and Equipment of the Transylvanian-Saxon militias

The early privilegial charters received by Tranylvanian-Saxons from the Hungarian kings do not mention any specific weapons that the militiamen were expectes to bear when they were called under the royal banner. Furthermore, as shown above, the Transylvanian-Saxons of the Two Seats and those of the county/district of Braşov were conscripted, on horseback or on foot, according to their (material) possibilities. Thus, there were no regulations regarding the weapons and equipment of the Transylvanian-Saxon militiamen. Only in a charter from 13 February 1469, we read for the first time about the weapons that the inhabitants of Sibiu and of the Seven Seats were expected to bear: the Transylvanian voivode János Pongrác of Dengeleg urged them to hold their arms, horses, lances, bows and other war machines ready (*armis, equis, copiis, arcubus et aliis apparatibus bellicis dispositos tenere et appromptuare debeatis*), to intervene in case of a Turkish invasion.[77] A similar order received the town magistrate of Braşov on 20 December 1478, when voivode Péter Geréb requested 200 footmen, well armed with crossbows, handguns and pavises, as well as two great bombards and ammunition (*ducentos pedites balistis, pixidibus, scutis seu clipeis magnis thorpays dictis, ac aliis armis necessariis bene armatos, cum quibus et bombarda duo* [...], *cum lapidibus sufficientibus ac ad unumquidque bombardum quatuor centenarios seu in ideomate Hungaricali masa pulveres,* [...] *mittere*) for the siege of the rebel fortresses Bologa (Sebesvár, Cluj county) and Şoimeni (Sólyomkö, Cluj county).[78] The weapons that the town militia of Braşov were expected to bear are mentioned in a set of siege regulations, issued by the magistrate (council) of the city, in 1491. I will discuss this source at length below, for now I just want to focus on Art. II, which reads: "Each should provide good weapons, like handguns, swords, bows and other things belonging to them, pikes, spears, [hunting] spears for boars or bears, and other such [weapons], which are common up to our times or which will be used in the future". Furthermore, Art.

76 Michael Howard, "Kanoniere, Pikeniere – die Zukunft den Landsknechten," in *Streifzüge durch das Mittelalter. Ein historisches Lesebuch*, ed. Rainer Beck (München: Verlag C. H. Beck, 1995), 303–07.

77 *Urkundenbuch* VI, 375.

78 *Urkundenbuch* VII, 201–02.

V and VIII, are attesting the harquebuses (*Hacken*), handguns (*Büchsen*) and cannons (*Stücken*) in the corner-towers of the city fortifications and Art. VII mentions the gunners (*Büchsen Meister*) posted at the city gates and thus the artillery of these strategic objectives.[79]

The weapons of the militamen in Bistriţa are mentioned by the sources only in the first decades of the sixteenth century. Thus, on 28 December 1514, voivode John Szapolyai requested from the magistrate (council) of Bistriţa 16 well armed handgunners, to hunt down some highwaymen.[80] On 10 June 1526, two months before the Battle of Mohács, the same voivode requested again from the magistrate of Bistriţa 100 handgunners.[81] After the great battle, on 10 October 1526, Johann Gozthon, captain of Transylvania, wrote to the authorities of Bistriţa to send him another 25 handgunners, in order to prevent an Ottoman attack.[82]

In addition to the armed men, the Transylvanian-Saxon central authories of Sibiu received several requests for gunpowder (*pulveres bombardorum*): 1464 (twice, on 8 June, and 27 June), 1489, 1493 (twice, on 25 September, and 21 October), 1497.[83] The magistrate (council) of Braşov also received requests for gunpowder, like the one mentioned above, from 1478, as well as the authorites of Bistriţa, on 29 June 1514.[84]

Unfortunately, all this sources only reflect the expectations of the Hungarian king and his military deputies, as well as those of the Transylvanian-Saxon local authorities, and one can not be entierly shore when or if the militiamen of the cities, seats and districts really had and used the mentioned weapons and war material. In a case study about the military organization of Braşov, I have already asserted that the weapon and armour production of the city, and generaly of all Transylvanian-Saxon cities, reflects the actual status of arms and war equipment of it's/their militiamen.[85] Besides the weapon production of the

79 August Ludwig Schlötzer, *Kritische Sammlungen zur Geschichte der Deutschen in Siebenbürgen*, I *Urkunden* (Göttingen: Vanderhoek-Ruprecht Verlag, 1795), 76–77.

80 Berger, *Urkunden-Regesten*, I, 165.

81 Berger, *Urkunden-Regesten*, I, 237.

82 Berger, *Urkunden-Regesten*, I, 244.

83 *Urkundenbuch* VI, 187–88; *Urkundenbuch* VIII, no. 4823 (available on-line on following link: http://siebenbuergenurkundenbuch.uni-trier.de/catalog/4861), 5338 (regest, available on following link: http://siebenbuergenurkundenbuch.uni-trier.de/catalog/5168), 5339 (regest, available on following link: http://siebenbuergenurkundenbuch.uni-trier.de/catalog/5169), 5738 (regest, available on following link: http://siebenbuergenurkundenbuch.uni-trier.de/catalog/5164)

84 *Urkundenbuch* VII, 201–02; Berger, *Urkunden-Regesten*, I, 163.

85 Cîmpeanu, "Organizarea militară a Braşovului," 351–56.

Transylvanian-Saxon cities, which is a research theme in itself,[86] it does not provide a clear answer on the question about the weapons beared by conscripted burghers and peasants. Actually, there are very few sources on the actual use of weapons by the Transylvanian-Saxons. Yet, the few preserved historical documents reveal that the militiamen of the cities, seats and districts were quite well armed. Thus, a document from 13 December 1362, records that some craftsmen from the Transylvanian-Saxon city of Cluj, together with their companions from the neighboring villages, ransacked the Benedictine abbey of Cluj-Mănăştur, armed and equiped like real knights, with breastplates, mail hauberks, helmets, iron gloves (gauntlets), shields, lances, spears and other unnamed wapons (*loricys, pancerys, galeys, ferreis cerotecys induti, tanquam milites pylati, alii ipsorum hastis, clipeis et aliis quibuslibet armis se ipsos muniendo*).[87] Later, on 10 March 1481, one of the handgunners (*pixidarius seu bombardus*) of Sibiu, Johannes Strauws, is attested,[88] though he might have been a hired mercenary, like those attested by the town accounts already in 1468.[89]

The only preserved sources about the actual use of weapons and armour by the militiamen of Sibiu, are the inventories of the city towers, mantained and defended by the guilds. Such documents are preserved from the years 1492, 1493, 1560, 1567, second half of the sixteenth century, 1575, 1681, early eighteenth century,[90] but for our present paper I will reffer only to the first two of them.[91] Without addressing the topic of the city defence, which may constitute a separate study, I will focus here only on the cathegories and types of weapons and armour used by the militiamen of Sibiu in the late Middle Ages. The two sources are mentioning melee weapons, ranged weapons and armour. Among

86 Ioan Marian Ţiplic, *Bresle şi arme în Transilvania* (Bucureşti: Editura Militară, 2009), *passim*.

87 *Documenta Romaniae Historica*, C. *Transilvania*, XII (1361–1365), ed. Ştefan Pascu (Bucureşti: Editura Academiei, 1985), 115.

88 *Urkundenbuch* VII, 263–64: the editors of the volume wrongly consider that the term *pixidarius* reffers to a gun founder, though in that age it simple ment *handgunner*.

89 *Rechnungen aus dem Archiv der Stadt Hermannstadt und der Sächsischen Nation*, I, 1380–1516 (Hermannstadt: In Commission bei Franz Michaelis, 1880), 19.

90 See the eight documents in: Ludwig Reissenberger, "Über die ehemaligen Befestigungen von Hermannstadt, " *Archiv des Vereins für siebenbürgische Landeskunde*, XXIX, 2 (1900): 361-81

91 A more recent edition of the two documents in *Comerţ şi meşteşuguri în Sibiu şi în cele şapte scaune 1224–1579/Handel und Gewärbe in Hermannstadt und in den Sieben Stühlen 1442–1579*, ed. Monica Vlaicu (Sibiu-Heidelberg: Editura Hora-Arbeitskreis für Siebenbürgische Landeskunde, 2003), 201–10.

the melee weapons, they attest the use of short spears (*Hand Spysch*), iron flails (*Ysseren Flegel*), halberds (*Helembarden*). As ranged weapons, they list the bows and arrows (actually, only the arrows – *Bogefyl/Bogeffyl/Poge Feyl*), arbalests (*Armprost/Arnprost*) with their windlasses (*Armprost Vynden/Winden*) and bolts (*Armprostfyl/Armprost Ffyl/Arnprost Feyl*). The two inventories also attest handguns (*Hand Puxen/Hant Puxen*), harquebuses (*Hacken Puxen*), gunpowder (*Poluer*), projectiles (*Kugel*) and even mortars (*Morsser*). Finally, they list the deffensive weapons and armour, like pavises (*Seycz Tarczen*), breastplates (*Harnisch*) and mail hauberks (*Panczer*).[92] Although the two inventories list exclusively the weapons and armour used for the defence of the city, one can assume that the militiamen were armed at least in the same way when they were in offensive campaigns, as requested by the military authorities of the Hungarian Kingdom, in the the above mentioned orders of mobilization. The burghers of Sibiu were well armed up to the early seventeenth century when, in 1610, the city was occupied by the tyrant prince of Transylvania, Gabriel Báthory. At the prince's orders, on 19 December, the inhabitants were obliged to hand over not only the weapons and ammonition of the city, but also their own weapons and armour, which were immediately distributed to his foreign mercenaries.[93]

Further information about weapons and armour provides a similar inventory of the towers mantained and defended by the guilds of Brașov. Although the source was written later, in 1562, it confirms almost literaly the weapons and armour listed in the above mentioned siege regulation, issued by the city magistrate (council), in 1491. Thus, the source also attests melee weapons, ranged weapons and armour. Among the melee weapons, it mentions hunting spears for bears (*Beren Spies*) and halberds (*Hellepärth/Hellepert*). The inventory lists as ranged weapons and ammonition: handguns (*Handror*), harquebuses (*Hoken Pixen/Hocken*), barrels of gunpowder (*Fesken gut Puluer/Pulver*) and projectiles (*Kugelen/Kuglen*), as well as handguns from Prague (*Prager Pixen*), although the latter might have been acquired later, by the mid sixteenth century. Light artillery pieces were also in use, like short cannons (*kurtz Stuckle*) and falconets (*Falkenetel*). As armour, the source attests breastplates (*Harnisch*), mail hauberks (*Pantzer*) and mail collars (*Krägen*).[94] Bows and arbalests are not attested, most

92 *Comerț și meșteșuguri /Handel und Gewärbe*, 201–10.

93 Georg Kraus, *Cronica Transilvaniei 1608–1665*, ed. G. Guzinchevici and E. Reus-Mîrza (București: Editura Academiei, 1965), 9.

94 *Quellen zur Geschichte der Stadt Kronstadt*, IX, *Zunfturkunden*, ed. Gernot Nussbächer and Elisabeta Marin (Brașov-Heidelberg: Editura Aldus, 1999), 269–270.

probably because they were out of use when the inventory was written (1562), although the city accounts are recording their use up to the 1540' (for instance, in 1529 the city magistrate acquired 299 new arbalests, for 64 florins and 43, ½ aspers).[95] Of course, like in the case of Sibiu, the weapons and armours used for the defence of Brașov, were also utilized by the militiamen during offensive campaigns.

The contingent of each city, seat and district had its own banner, attested separately: the banner of Bistrița, on 22 July 1453, the banner of Sibiu, on 8 January 1493, 29 May 1494 (twice) and 19 June 1497, and the banner of Sighișoara, on 8 January 1493.[96]

Besides the individual weapons of the militiamen, (at least) some of the Transylvanian-Saxon cities had also several artillery pieces and ammunition. Thus, the Hungarian king and his military deputies requested several times artillery pieces and ammunition (gunpowder, led, stone and iron projectiles) from the city magistrate (council) of Sibiu: 1463, 1464, 1476, 1481, 1482, 1491, 1492, 1493 and 1497.[97] In this sources artillery pieces are usually designated with the general terms bombards (*bombardas*) and guns (*pixides*): 1463, 1464, 1476, 1481, 1491. In the charter from 17 December 1463, we read about great and small guns and

95 Friedrich Wilhelm Seraphin, "Kronstadt zur Zeit des Honterus," in *Aus der Zeit der Reformation. Vorträge, gehalten im Auditorium des ev. Gymnasiums A. B. in Kronstadt in den Jahren 1897 und 1898* (Kronstadt: Buchdruckerei Schlandt, 1898), 312.

96 *Urkudenbuch* V, 413; *Urkundenbuch* VIII, no. 5304 (regest, available on following link: http://siebenbuergenurkundenbuch.uni-trier.de/catalog/4949, see the original on following link: https://archives.hungaricana.hu/en/charters/231771/?list=eyJmaWx0ZXJzIjogeyJEQVRBQkFTRSI6IFsiRExERiJdfSwgInF1ZXJ5IjogIjE0OTMtMDEtMDgifQ), 5473 (available on-line, on following link: http://siebenbuergenurkundenbuch.uni-trier.de/catalog/5476), 5428 (regest, available on following link: http://siebenbuergenurkundenbuch.uni-trier.de/catalog/5112), 5738 (regest, available on following link: http://siebenbuergenurkundenbuch.uni-trier.de/catalog/5164), 5302 (regest, available on following link: http://siebenbuergenurkundenbuch.uni-trier.de/catalog/4947, see the original on following link: https://archives.hungaricana.hu/en/charters/231770/?list=eyJmaWx0ZXJzIjogeyJEQVRBQkFTRSI6IFsiRExERiJdfSwgInF1ZXJ5IjogIjE0OTMtMDEtMDgifQ).

97 *Urkundenbuch* VI, 159, 160–61, 182, 187–88; *Urkundenbuch* VII, 114, 256–57, 324–25; *Urkundenbuch* VIII, no. 5105 (regest, avaiable on following link: http://siebenbuergenurkundenbuch.uni-trier.de/catalog/4919; see the original on following link: https://archives.hungaricana.hu/en/charters/228281/?list=eyJxdWVyeSI6ICIyNDUxMzUifQ), 5225 (available on following link: http://siebenbuergenurkundenbuch.uni-trier.de/catalog/5197), 5338 (regest, avaialbe on following link: http://siebenbuergenurkundenbuch.uni-trier.de/catalog/5168), 5338 (regest, avaliable on following

bombards (*pixidibus et bombardis vestris maioribus et minoribus*)[98] and a charter from 3 September 1492, attests other artillery tipes: two howitzers (*hophniczas*) with stone projectiles, a heavy harquebus (*tharazk*) with stone projectiles, and 16 harquebuses (*zakalos*).[99]

According to the preserved sources, not all the artillery pieces in Sibiu belonged to the city. On 23 August, 1482, Voivode István Báthory requested the magistrate to send in his military camp King Matthias' bombard (*illa bombarda maiestatis regiae*). It seems that the authorites of Sibiu did not fulfilled the written order, thus the voivode repeated it on 29 August 1482.[100] Even Wladislas II requested King Matthia's bombards from the city magistrate (council) of Sibiu, on 4 February 1491.[101] Finally, the former donated the two bombards which remained in the city after the latter's death, to the magistrate of Sibiu, on 13 September 1492.[102] Thus, one can conclude that Matthias Corvinus sent (at least) two great bombards to Sibiu, in order the have them operational on the south-eastern border of the realm, sometime before 1482 (maybe even before 11 May 1464, when the king requested from the authorites of the city the great bombard on a cart, along with stone projectiles).[103] Finally, King Matthias' successor, Wladislas II., donated the two bombards to the city of Sibiu.

The sources reveal that the city of Sibiu had to support the costs for the transport of the artillery pieces and ammonition, as well as the wages for the horsemen hired for their guarding. These obligations are litteraly attested several

---

link: http://siebenbuergenurkundenbuch.uni-trier.de/catalog/5169), 5738 (regest, avaliable on following link: http://siebenbuergenurkundenbuch.uni-trier.de/catalog/5164), 5718 (regest, available on following link: http://siebenbuergenurkundenbuch.uni-trier.de/catalog?utf8=%E2%9C%93&q=5718&search_field=all_fields&commit=Suchen)

98 *Urkundenbuch* VI, 159.

99 *Urkundenbuch* VIII, no. 5225 (available on following link: http://siebenbuergenurkundenbuch.uni-trier.de/catalog/5197).

100 *Urkundenbuch* VII, 323–24, 324–25.

101 *Urkundenbuch* VIII, nr. 5105 (regest, available on following link: http://siebenbuergenurkundenbuch.uni-trier.de/catalog/4919; see the original document on following link: https://archives.hungaricana.hu/en/charters/228281/?list=eyJxdWVyeSI6ICIyNDUxMzUifQ).

102 *Urkundenbuch* VIII, no. 5209 (regest, available on following link: http://siebenbuergenurkundenbuch.uni-trier.de/catalog/4940; see the original document on following link: https://archives.hungaricana.hu/en/charters/230845/?list=eyJxdWVyeSI6ICIxNDkyKzA5LTEzIn0).

103 *Urkundenbuch* VI, 182.

times: 1463, 1464, 1476, 1491, 1497.[104] The authorities of Sibiu requested financial aid for this burden from the other cities, seats and districts of the Transylvanian Saxons. Thus, on 14 June 1485, The Seven Seats and the Two Seats, along with the districts of Bistriţa and Braşov decided to support together the costs for trasport of the artillery and war materials.[105]

In direct connection to the artillery, the Hungarian king and his military deputies also requested gunners (*magistros bombardarum*, *pixidarios*) from the authorities of Sibiu, on several occasions: 1464, 1492, 1493.[106] But the gunners received wages,[107] thus they were not militiamen, neither were they counted among the military men, being regarded as craftsmen until the mid seventeenth century.[108]

There is no similar information about the artillery of the other Transylvanian-Saxon cities, excepting one request for bombards, addresed by the Transylvanian voivode Péter Geréb to the magistrate (council) of Braşov, on 20 December 1478.[109] The later city had, instead, various artillery pieces for the defence, in its gates, towers and on its walls.[110]

Relying on the city accounts of Braşov, the scholar Friedrich Wilheln Seraphin could establish at the end of the nineteenth century, thatthe militiamen not only

104 *Urkundenbuch* VI, 160–61, 182; *Urkundenbuch* VII, 114; *Urkundenbuch* VIII, no. 5105 (regest, available on following link: http://siebenbuergenurkundenbuch.uni-trier.de/catalog/4919; see the original document on following link: https://archives.hungaricana.hu/en/charters/228281/?list=eyJxdWVyeSI6ICIyNDUxMzUifQ), 5738 (regest, available on following link: http://siebenbuergenurkundenbuch.uni-trier.de/catalog/5164; see the original on following link: https://archives.hungaricana.hu/en/charters/241207/?list=eyJxdWVyeSI6ICIxNDk3LTA2LTE5In0).

105 *Urkundenbuch* VII, 390.

106 *Urkundenbuch* VI, 182; *Urkundenbuch* VIII, no. 5225 (available on following link: http://siebenbuergenurkundenbuch.uni-trier.de/catalog/5197), 5338 (regest, available on following link: http://siebenbuergenurkundenbuch.uni-trier.de/catalog/5168; see the original on following link: https://archives.hungaricana.hu/en/charters/233576/?list=eyJxdWVyeSI6ICIxNDkzLTA5LTI1In0)

107 *Rechnungen Hermannstadt* I, 2 (first mention already in the late Fourteenth century!), 19.

108 Béla K, Király, "Society and War from Mounted Knights to the Standing Armies of Absolute Kings: Hungary and the West," in *From Hunyadi to Rákóczi. War and Society in the Late Medieval and Early Modern Hungary*, ed. János M. Bak and Béla K. Király (Brooklyn NY: Columbia University Press, 1982), 36–37.

109 *Urkundenbuch* VII, 201–02.

110 Cîmpeanu, "Organizarea militară a Braşovului," 355–56.

had several types of melee and ranged weapons, but were also trained to use them. Thus, already in 1475, they practiced arbalest shooting at a pavise (*zu der Tartschen*), later even handgun and harquebus shooting at an armoured dummy (*bewaffneter Mann*). They practiced combat on horseback with lances, in genuine knightly tournements. Even peasent horsemen, coming from the countryside of the district joined these competitions. The best shooters and lancers received prizes, consisting in cloth, jewelry and money (summs up to 5 florins).[111]

A close reading of the city accounts of Sibiu reveals that their militiamen used to train in a similar way. Thus, at least arbalest and handgun shootig at the pavise (*Tarcza*, *Tharda*, *Tharsche*) was practiced here in 1496, 1497 and 1507.[112]

The armed forces of the Transylvanian-Saxon cities, seats and districts were also regulary mustered, like the troops of the city and district of Braşov, in the year 1550.[113] Of course, the military and technological development tranformed throughout the centuries the appearence, weapons and equipment of the militiamen, but by the sixteenth century they were still townsfolk and villagers.

Militias on the Defensive

In the late fourteenth century began the fortification process of the main Transylvanian-Saxon cities and market towns. By the mid-fifteenth century, Sibiu, Sebeş, Sighişoara, Braşov and Bistriţa were already fortified with walls towers and gates, while Orăştie and Mediaş had formidable strongholds around their parish curches.[114] Of course, their defence was entrusted to the local militias, as revealed by the above mentioned example of Sebeş, desperately defended by its armed inhabitants during the Ottoman siege of 1438.[115] Nevertheless, the fortification and defence of the Transylvanian-Saxon cities is a theme that deserves a study of its own and it would far exceed the limits of the present paper. Therefore, I will focus only on the better documented case study of Braşov, which clearly reveals the active role of the militiamen in the defence of the city. The Hungarian

111 Seraphin, "Kronstadt," 317–19.

112 *Rechnungen Hermannstadt*, I, 224, 253, 472.

113 Seraphin, "Kronstadt," 319.

114 Müller, *Stühle und Distrikte*, 24–27; Reissenberger, "Befestigungen von Hermannstadt," 315–417; Radu Lupescu, "The Medieval Fortifications of Sibiu," in *"vmbringt mit starcken turnen, murn". Ortsbefestigungen im Mittelalter*, ed. Olaf Wagener (Frankfurt am Main: Peter Lang, 2010), 351–62; Cîmpeanu, "Organizarea militară a Braşovului," 337–44.

115 Georgius de Hungaria, *Tractatus*, 148–55.

Kings Sigismund of Luxemburg and Matthias Corvinus not only exempted the city and district of Braşov from several fiscal burdens in order to complete and improve the fortifications of the city, they also urged several times the burghers and even the peasents of the district to maintain and defend the newly built walls, towers and gates.[116] From the late fifteenth century, there is presrved a unique source regarding the defence of Braşov: in 1491, the magistrate (council) of the city issed the siege regulation, already mentioned above. Several articles regard the duties of the militias during a siege: according to Art. III, each gate (by that time there were 3 great gates, each fortified with a barbacan) should be under the command of a member of the city council, and Art. IV, states that each gate should be garrisoned by 50 men. In addition, Art. VII, establishes that each garrison should also have a skilled gunner. In a similar way, according to Art. V, each of the four corner towers should be guarded by 10 brave men, skilled in the firing of the artillery. Art. VI, provides that the corner towers should be under the command of a member of the city council. According to Art. IX, the rest of the towers should be defended by six men each, while Art. X writes that the walls should be defended by sufficient well armed men. Art. XI, XIV and XVIII, establish the hierarchy and organization of the militia: the supreme commander is the judge (mayor) of the city, seconded by four deputies from among the councillors, each for one of the four neighborhoods, while their inhabitants should be organized in units of 10 (*decurias*). Nevertheless, the bulk of the militiamen should wait armed, disciplined and quietly in the central square, in order to run in support of the attacked walls, towers and gates (signalized by watchmen with white flags) or to put out fires (signalized by watchmen with red flags). Art. XX, even provides that the rest of the pupulation should be steady, with buckets of water and thick blankets, in order to prevent fire.[117]

A striking aspect of this Regulation is the fact that by 1491, the city fortifications and their defence were still responsabilities of the magistrate (council) and not of the guilds. According to Art. XVI, the latter had only to pledge allegiance to the authorities of the city,[118] thus they were assimilated to the contingents of the four neighborhoods. Most likely because of the great costs of maintenance and defence of the city walls and towers, the magistrate of Braşov entrusted them to the economic prosperous guilds, around 1520.[119] A similar process might

116 Cîmpeanu, "Organizarea militară a Braşovului," 337–44.

117 Schlötzer, *Kritische Sammlungen*, 77–79.

118 Schlötzer, *Kritische Sammlungen*, 78.

119 Cîmpeanu, "Organizarea militară a Braşovului," 343–44.

have also existed in Sibiu, but earlier, since in 1492 the city towers were already maintained and defended by the guilds.[120]

The Transylvanian-Saxon historiography rightly assumed that similar regulations were also issued by the city magistrates (councils) of the other fortified towns.[121] Thus, the example of Braşov clearly reveals the defensive duties of the militias, although there are very few aditional sources on this issue.

Further information comes from the royal decrees of the second half of the fifteenth century, when several Transylvanian-Saxon communities were partially exempted from their military obligations, in order to defend their newly build fortifications around their parish churches, as a result of the Ottoman threat. The seat of Cincu provides a good example for this situation. Thus, Matthias Corvinus exempted half of the militiamen of (at least) two market towns, in order to defend their fortified churches: Agnita – 19 November 1466, and Cincu on 11 August 1474 (the latter charter was also confirmed by King Wladislas II, on 18 March 1492).[122] Wladislas II granted the same priviledge to the villagers of Noiştat, on 17 January 1494.[123] Even the market town Saschiz, in the seat of Sighişoara, received a similar exemption from the Transylvanian voivode János Ponrgác of Dengeleg, on 26 October 1470. According to the charter, half of the militiamen should stay at home in order to defend the newly built fortress, on a neighboring hill.[124]

The situation in the Two Seats is more complex. Some communities did receive such exemptions, but they were different from case to case. Thus, on 29 September 1468, Matthias Corvinus granted such an exemption to the market town of Biertan. According to the royal charter, one third of the militiamen could and should stay at home, to defend the fortifications around their cemetery (i.e. around the parish church).[125] The king exempted even a third of the villagers of Aţel from joining the royal army, in order to defend their fortified church, on 10 March 1471.[126] Instead, King Matthias granted to the market town of Mediaş

---

120 *Comerţ şi meşteşuguri /Handel und Gewärbe*, 201–05.

121 Müller, *Stühle und Distrikte*, 27–28.

122 *Urkundenbuch* VI, 269–270; *Urkundenbuch* VII, 24; *Urkundenbuch* VIII, no. 5234 (available on-line, on following link: http://siebenbuergenurkundenbuch.uni-trier.de/catalog/5284).

123 *Urkundenbuch* VIII, no. 5451 A (available on-line, on following link: http://siebenbuergenurkundenbuch.uni-trier.de/catalog/5291).

124 *Urkundenbuch* VI, 468.

125 *Urkundenbuch* VI, 357.

126 *Urkundenbuch* VI, 480–81.

the right to send under his banner only 32 militiamen, the rest remaining for the defence of the newly built fortifications of their parish church.[127]

All this sources suggest that the cities also might have received similar exemptions in the early age of their fortification process, in the late fourteenth century. Beyound any doubt, all the fortifications, large and small were guarded and defended primarly by the local militias. Of course, all this exemptions were valid only in case of general conscription of the Transylvanian-Saxons. Otherwise, the whole community participated at the defence of its fortifications, like the peasants of Prejmer (Tartlau, Prázsmár), who fought with knightly valour (*sie sich ritterlich gewehret*) during a siege imposed by the Moldavians, in 8–14 July 1552.[128]

Militias on Campaign

There is virtually nothing known about the early military activity of the Transylvanian-Saxons, up to the late fourteenth century. After the fall of Wallachia under the Ottoman strikes in 1420,[129] the southern borders of Transylvania were permanently exposed to the raids of the *gâzi* warriors. Thus, the burden of defence fell on the directly threatened Transylvanian cities, seats and districts. According to King Sigismund's charter from 24 February 1433, Sibiu, Braşov, Bistriţa and even Cluj had to support the wages of 2.000 armed men, hired to defend the southern border of Transylvania between the district of Fărgăraş in the east and the district of Haţeg (Wallenthal, Hátszeg) in the west.[130] For a more efficient defence of the southern border, King Ladislaus the Pothumous even donated the fortresses Tălmaciu (Talmesch, Nagytalmács), Lotru (Landskrone, Lotorvár) and Turnu Roşu (Rothenturm, Vöröstorony) to the city of Sibiu, on 3 February 1453.[131]

Not only the actual attacks of the Ottoman raiders, but also their mere presence in the proximity of the Transylvanian border, held the king, the voivode and other royal captains of the province in constant alert. Rumors about Ottoman attacks determined them to repeatedly urge the Transylvanian-Saxon cities, seats

127 *Urkudenbuch* VII, 124–25.

128 Hieronymus Ostermayer, "Historien," in *Quellen zur Geschichte der Stadt Brassó*, IV (Brassó: Druck von A. Gust, 1903), 514.

129 Constantin Rezachevici, *Rolul românilor în apărarea Europei de expansiunea otomană* (Bucureşti: Editura Albatros, 2001), 181–82.

130 *Urkundenbuch* IV, 493–94.

131 *Urkundenbuch* V, 374–76, 384–85.

and districts to prepare themselves for war: 1454, 1456, 1467, 1468, 1469, 1470 (twice), 1480, 1481, 1497, 1504, 1505, 1509, 1510, 1511, 1515.[132] In hindsight one can state that most of the rumored attacks of the Ottomans never took place, since Transylvania was spared from the raids of the *gâzi* warriors between 1442–1479 and 1479–1493.

Furher, the Hungarian king and his military deputies often summoned the Transylvanian-Saxon militiamen at the southern borders of the realm (or in their proximity), in order to prevent Ottoman attacks. The mobilization orders were issued for the entire community of the Transylvanian-Saxons, or separate, for each city, seat and district, according to the immediate necessities.

Sibiu and the Seven Seats received such orders, to send their armed forces, both militiamen and mercenaries, in several locations in the proximity of the Hungarian-Ottoman border, or to the royal hosts, gathered in order to march against the Turks: 1456 - Caransebeş (Karansebesch, Karánsebes) and Cuvin (Keve), 1466 - Haţeg, 1468 - Orăştie, 1481 - Agnita and Rupea, 1487 - Sebeş, 1493 - Haţeg and Luduş, 1494 - Târgu Mureş (Neumarkt, Marosvásárhely), 1497 - Ţara Bârsei (although this campaign was towards Moldavia).[133] Similar orders were also recived by each of the Seven Seats separately, like the Seat of Sebeş, in 1491, and the Seat of Sighişoara, in 1493, both called to arms by vicevoivode István Telegdi in order to prevent Ottoman attacks on the southern border of Transylvania, especially on Haţeg (named in the charter from 1493).[134]

The important role of the Transylvanian-Saxons of the city and district of Braşov in the anti-Ottoman defence of the south-eastern border of the realm is

---

132 *Urkundenbuch* V, 460, 535–36, 536–37; *Ukrundenbuch* VI, 283, 283–84, 343–44, 380, 456, 468–69; *Ukrundenbuch* VII, 250, 260, 273; *Urkundenbuch* VIII, no. 5737 (regest, available on following link: http://siebenbuergenurkundenbuch.uni-trier.de/catalog/5163); Berger, *Urkunden-Regesten* I, 125, 129–30, 144–45, 150, 154, 168.

133 *Urkundenbuch* V, 534–35, 535; *Urkudenbuch* VI, 259–60, 340–41; *Urkundenbuch* VII, 256–57, 273; *Urkundenbuch* VIII, no. 4741 (available on-line, on following link: http://siebenbuergenurkundenbuch.uni-trier.de/catalog/2563), 5304 (regest, avaiable on following link: http://siebenbuergenurkundenbuch.uni-trier.de/catalog/4949), 5320 (regest, available on following link: http://siebenbuergenurkundenbuch.uni-trier.de/catalog/4964), 5473 (available on-line, on following link: http://siebenbuergenurkundenbuch.uni-trier.de/catalog/5476), 5428 (regest, available on following link: http://siebenbuergenurkundenbuch.uni-trier.de/catalog/5112), 5738 (regest, available on following link: http://siebenbuergenurkundenbuch.uni-trier.de/catalog/5164).

134 *Urkundenbuch* VIII, no. 5124 (regest, available on following link: http://siebenbuergenurkundenbuch.uni-trier.de/catalog/5085), 5308 (regest, available on following link: http://siebenbuergenurkundenbuch.uni-trier.de/catalog/4947).

revealed by King Matthias' charter issued on 27 March 1488, through which he forbade voivode István Báthory to conscript them for capaingns in the west.[135] The authorities of Braşov also received orders to send their armed forces for the defence of the realm against Ottoman attacks, albeit on the eastern border of Transylvania: 1480 – the Land of the Szeklers, 1493 – Târgu Mureş.[136]

Even the city and district of Bistriţa, located in the remote north-eastern corner of Transylania, received orders to send their militiamen to the southern border of the province, which was under constant threat of the Ottoman raiders: 1468 – Orăştie, 1481 – Şiria, 1512 – Agnita, 1521 – Sebeş, 1526 – Haţeg.[137] The borders of Transylvania were not threatend only by the Ottomans, but also by raiding parties from the neighboring Romanian principalities. Thus, the Transylvanian voivodes and vicevoivodes often summoned the armed forces of Bistriţa, in order to repel the attacks of Moldavian raiders: 1469, 1471, and 1514 (?).[138]

Despite the great number of mobilization orders and the serious threat of *amissione capitorum* in case of disobedience, there are only a few cases when the Transylvanian Saxons actually went on campaign. For instance, after the mobilization order issued by Matthias Corvinus on 18 May 1467, the militiamen of the Seven Seats and those of the Two Seats marched into the county of Hunedoara, on the south-western border of Transylvania. Here, the armed men of Sighişoara, and those of the Two Seats ransacked the estates of some local noble families. The latter reported the case to voivode János of St. Györgyi and Bazin, who ordered the authorities of Hunedoara county to investigate the case, on 5 June 1467. The case was also prosecuted by the assembly of the Transylvanian Estates, on 16 June1467.[139] This is one of the best documented cases of actual mobilization of the Transylvanian-Saxon militiamen and it cleary reveals what most of the preserved sources seem to suggest, namely that the Transylvanian Saxons took up arms only if they received direct orders from the king or from his direct appointed deputy. In a separate study, I have already listed the offensive and defensive campaigns, in and around Transylvania, in which Transylvanian-Saxon militiamen took part: 1426 and 1427 – in Wallachia, 1442 – in Transylvania,

135 *Urkundenbuch* VIII, no. 4772 (available on-line, on following link: http://siebenbuergenurkundenbuch.uni-trier.de/catalog/3425).

136 *Urkundenbuch* VII, 248; *Urkundenbuch* VIII, no. 5357 (regest, available on following link: http://siebenbuergenurkundenbuch.uni-trier.de/catalog/5344).

137 *Urkundenbuch* VI, 335; *Urkundenbuch* VII, 280; Berger, *Urkunden-Regesten* I, 157, 198, 199, 244.

138 *Urkundenbuch* VI, 409–410, 518–519; Berger, *Urkunden-Regesten* I, 157.

139 *Urkundenbuch* VI, 283–84, 284, 287–88, 288–89.

1467 and 1476 – in Moldavia, 1479 – in Transylvania (Câmpul Pâinii), 1526 – at the southern and western borders of Transylvania.[140]

Conclusions

Protected by their priviledged status, the Transylvanian Saxons could afford to igonre some orders of mobilization received from the voivode of the province and other royal captains. Thanks to their actual military potential, represented by their militiamen and, since the second half of the fifteenth century, by hired mercenaries, they neither had to be afraid of retaliation for disobeying orders. On the other hand, the Transylvanian Saxons represented for the Hungarian kingship a steady military force, on which the latter could rely both in defensive and offensive campaigns against the ever growing Ottoman Empire. Their mere presence in the twelve – fourteen centuries and the construction of their fortified cities and churches in the fourteen –sixteen centuries assured a firm foothold for the Hungarian kingship, sustainig thus the Crown on the south-eastern border of the realm, as stated on the seal of the Seven Seats: *AD RETINENDAM. CORONAM.*

140 Cîmpeanu, "Obligații militare," 139–43.

The seats, districts and settlements of the Transylvanian Saxons, detail from *Ungaria cum finitimiis provinciis…*/Hungary and its frontier provinces, Georg Matthäus Vischer/ Matthias Greischer, 1682, cooper engraving (Landesarchiv Baden-Württemberg Abt. Generallandesarchiv Karlsruhe)

Florin Nicolae Ardelean

Frontiers and Military Organization in Transylvania: The Guardsman (*Drabant/ Darabont*) during the Second Half of the Sixteenth Century*

Abstract: The military organization of the Principality of Transylvania (1541–1691) was based, to a large extent, on semi-privileged groups which performed military duties in exchange for tax exemptions and other privileges. The guardsmen (*drabant/darabont*) were located on some of the most important fiscal estates and had an important role in the defence of frontier fortifications. However, the term guardsman, in its various forms, was also used to designate other military groups within the army of the court, the Székely military contingents, the troops provided by the Saxon University, town guards and the permanent garrison of frontier fortifications. This article is focused on some aspects of this rather complex topic like the debate regarding the origin of this military term, the use of the term guardsman (*drabant/darabont*) in contemporary sources, the social status of those who were identified as guardsmen in the Transylvanian army and their role in the defence of the borderlands.

Keywords: Frontier, Borderland, Guardsman, Transylvania, Military Organization

Introduction

The organization of late medieval and early modern confines (frontiers/borders) was, first and formost, a military matter. The transition from medieval frontiers to early modern linear borders was a complex process, marked by changes in the military organization of borderlands. The Principality of Transylvania provides and interesting case study from this point of view. A former province within the Hungarian Kingdom, Transylvania became a distinct state during the decades that followed the Ottoman conquest of Buda (1541).[1] The birth of a new state required the organization of new territorial delimitations in a region that was

---

* This work was supported by a grant of the Romanian Ministry of Education and Research, CNCS – UEFISCDI, project number PN-III-P1-1.1-TE-2019-0457, within PNCDI III; *From Medieval Frontiers to Early Modern Borders. The Military organization of the Western Parts of the Transylvanian Principality in the XVI-XVII centuries.*

1 The birth of the Transylvanian Principality was and still is an important historiographical issue for both Hungarian and Romanian scholars. The interpretation of this political change is far from being unanimous, however most recent contributions on

disputed by two major political powers, the Ottoman Empire and the Habsburgs. The survival of Transylvania was ensured through both diplomatic and military means. One of the most pressing issues was the organization of an efficient defensive system on the western edges of the principality.

A small state with limited human and material resources, the Principality of Transylvania had to rely on privileged and semi-privileged social groups, which performed military duty in exchange for tax exemptions and other benefices. The guardsmen (*drabant/darabont*), settled in the vicinity of important border fortifications, were such a semi-privileged category. They were not part of the true nobility of the country (*una eademque nobilitas*) but they were neither peasant, because they were exempted from most taxes and performed regular military service. However, the term guardsman, in its various forms (*trabant/drabant/darabont*), was also used to designate other military groups like: the permanent garrison of border fortifications, infantry troops in the army of the court, Székely military contingents and the troops provided by the Saxon University. In this article, I will analyse some aspects of this rather complex topic, like the debate regarding the origin of this military term, the use of the term guardsman in contemporary sources, the social status of those who were identified as guardsmen in the Transylvanian army and their role in the defence of the borders.

The Origins and Spread of a New Military Term

The word guardsman (*trabant/drabant/darabont*), in its various forms, was used in many regions of Central and South-East Europe, during the Late Middle Ages and the Early Modern Period, usually to designate infantry troops tasked with

---

the subject seem to agree that the formation of a distinct Transylvanian state was a long process of transition, lasting several decades, from the Ottoman conquest of Buda (1541) until the end of the sixteenth century, Cristina Feneşan, *Constituirea principatului autonom al Transilvaniei* (Bucureşti: Editura Enciclopedică, 1997); Teréz Oborni, "From province to principality: continuity and change in Transylvania in the first half of the Sixteenth century," in *Fight against the Turk in Central-Europe in the First Half of the Sixteenth Century*, ed. István Zombori (Budapest: Magyar Egyháztörténeti Enciklopédia Munkaközösség, 2004, 165–79; Edit Szegedi, "Constituirea şi evoluţia principatului Transilvaniei (1541–1690)," in *Istoria Transilvaniei*, II, eds. Ioan-Aurel Pop, Thomas Nägler, and András Magyari (Cluj-Napoca: Institutul Cultural Român, Centrul de Studii Transilvane, 2005), 107–21; László Makkai, "The first period of the Principality of Transylvania (1526–1606)," in *History of Transylvania*, I, ed. Béla Köpeczi (New York: Columbia University Press, 2001), 591–771.

defensive duties. However, opinions are still divided regarding the origins of this term.

According to one of the most common interpretations, the term derives from the German word *trabant*, meaning foot soldier or guard. It was first used during the Hussite Wars (1419–1434) to designate some of the infantry soldiers, which defended the wagon forts (*wagenburg*) of the Bohemian rebels. Since the first *trabanten* were Bohemian mercenaries it is possible that the word had Czech origins.[2] The army of the Hungarian Kingdom adopted the Hussite *wagenburg* tactics and with it a new type of infantry soldiers known as guardsmen (*drabant/darabont*).[3]

In time, the word *drabant* was used to designate various groups of soldiers in the Hungarian Kingdom. Although the contexts in which guardsmen were mentioned are different, their basic features remained the same. They were good infantry troops, armed with gunpowder weapons, which performed guard duty during peacetime. In 1439, the town of Kézsmárk (Kežmarok) was defended by a garrison of 100 guardsmen who received regular wages (*pedites stipendariorum vulgo Drabant*).[4] Another early uses of the term can be found in a letter of John Hunyadi sent to the salt chambers of Maramureş (Máramoros) county in 1448. The word guardsmen, in the form *darabones*, refered to those who were employed to guard salt trasports.[5] Later, during the Jagiellonian period (1490–1526), the term (*drabantis*) was also used to designate some of the infantry troops recruited in the baronial banderia.[6]

After the battle of Mohács (1526), in Habsburg Hungary, guardsmen are mentioned by sources in two circumstances: as local soldiers in the garrisons of border fortifications and as officer guards in German infantry regiments. During the second half of the Sixteenth century, most fortifications on the Hungarian

2 Cathal J. Nolan, *The Age of Wars of Religion 1000–1650: An Encyclopedia of Global Warfare and Civilization*, II (Westport: Greenwood Press, 2006), 868; Zoltán Péter Bagi, "Analysis of two muster registers from Krupina (Korpona)," *Acta Historica Neosoliensia* XXII, 2 (2019): 193–94.

3 Zoltán Tóth, "A huszita eredetű szekérvár," *Hadtörténelmi Közlemények*, XVII (1916): 285; Tamás Pálosfalvi, *From Nicopolis to Mohács: a history of Ottoman-Hungarian warfare, 1389–1526* (Leiden, Boston: Brill, 2018), 48, note 125.

4 Wertner Mór, "Magyar hadjáratok a XV. század első felében," *Hadtörténelmi Közlemények*, XII (1911): 552.

5 Magyar Nemzeti Levéltár Országos Levéltára (MNL OL), Budapest, Családi levéltárak, Kállay család (Q 93), DL-DF, 55383.

6 Pálosfalvi, *From Nicopolis*, 45, note 144.

frontier were defended by permanent garrisons which included both local soldiers and foreign mercenaries. Various forms of the word guardsmen are used in different documents, *drabant/trabant* in German sources, or *drabant/darabont* in Hungarian ones. In many cases the term also mentions the origin of those soldiers (*Hungerisch Trabanten*), indicating the fact that they were locally recruited soldiers who received regular wages.[7] The German infantry regiments which were dispatched on the Hungarian frontier, especially during the Long Turkish War (1591–1606), had a specific organization and a large number of officers. Some members of the leading staff like the *Obrist*, *Obristleutnant* or *Profos* were accompanied by a small number of personal guards called *trabanten.*[8]

Through diplomatic and military contacts, the guardsmen spread beyond the frontiers of the Hungarian Kingdom. This new type of infantry was adopted in neighbouring regions, maintaining their original role. In 1481, King Matthias Corvinus sent a detachment of guardsmen to duke Vlatko Hercegović Kosača with the purpose of consolidating the defense of the maritime fortress of Novi (today Herceg Novi in Montenegro). Hungarian drabants were also sent to defend the fortress of Koš (today Chos near the town of Opuzen in Croatia). With the supplies and equipment provided by the authorities of Dubrovnik (Ragusa), the garisson was able to resist until 1491 when the fortress was captured by the Ottomans.[9] Later, in the sixteenth century, the garisson of Dubrovnik included a group of foreign mercenaries, of Croatian and Hungarian origin, known as *brabanti*. Their name is considered a derivative of the Hungarian term *darabont*, which originated from the German word *Trabant.*[10]

The guardsmen also found their way into the military framework of Moldavia and Wallachia. Most Romanian historians concerned with this subject have accepted the German origin of the word. In his work *Descriptio Moldaviae* (first published in 1769), Dimitrie Cantemir stated that the word *dărăban* derives from the German word *trabant* and was adopted in the Romanian language

7 Géza Pálffy, "A Magyarországi és délvidéki végvárrendszer 1576. és 1582 évi jegyzékei," *Hadtörténelmi Közlemények* 1/108 (1995): 141–78.

8 Zoltán Bagi, "The Organization of the Imperial Army in the Fifteen Years War," *Chronica: Annual of the Institute of History, University of Szeged, Hungary* (2016), 169–70.

9 Veljan Atanasovski, *Pad Hercegovine* (Beograd: Narodna knjiga, Istorijski Institut, 1979), 131, 141.

10 Domagoj Madunić, "The defensive system of the Ragusan Republic (C.1580–1620)," in *The European Tributary States of the Ottoman Empire in the Sixteenth and Seventeenth Centuries*, eds. Gábor Kármán and Lovro Kunčević (Leiden, Boston: Brill, 2013), 349.

from the Hungarian term *darabont*. In the case of Wallachia, the first guardsmen were indeed Hungarian mercenaries, sent by the Transylvanian voivode as aid to Radu de la Afumaţi in 1523.[11] In Moldavia, narrative sources mention *dărăbani*, as infantry soldiers in the guard of the Moldavian ruler Bogdan III (1504–1517).[12] Although they were first foreigners taken into service by Moldavian and Wallachian rulers, towards the end of the Sixteenth century local guardsmen were recruited as semi-professional soldiers who performed military service in exchange for wages or, more often, tax exemptions.[13] The Wallachian and Moldavian guardsmen were not specifically employed in the defence of borders. They protected the court of the ruler, followed him on the battlefield and, during times of peace, they were used to maintain order and stability inside the country.[14]

In a recent study about the military organization of the Székely in the Principality of Transylvania, János B. Szabó claimed that the Hungarian word *drabant/darabont* might have Persian/Turkish origins, referencing an article written by Belgian byzantiniste Henri Grégoire, in 1938.[15] Grégoire argued that the Slavic word *drabant*, the German *trabant* and the French *traban*, derived from the Persian word *darband*, which was later adopted by the Ottomans as *derbend*.[16] The Persian term can be translated as closed or barred gate (*dar* "gate" + *band* "bar"). Initially, *Darband* was the name given to the defensive system built by the Sassanid Empire to protect the natural pass between the Caucasus Mountains and the Caspian Sea, during the Fifth century.[17] In the Ottoman Empire, the *derbendcis* were military support groups, whose main purpose was

11 Nicolae Stoicescu, *Curteni şi slujitori: contribuţii la istoria Armatei Române* (Bucureşti: Editura Militară, 1968), 116.

12 Axinte Uricariul, *Cronica paralelă a Ţării Româneşti şi a Moldovei*, I, ed. Gabriel Ştrempel (Bucureşti: Editura Minerva, 1993), 106.

13 Stoicescu, *Curteni*, 119; Alexandru D. Xenopol, *Istoria românilor din Dacia Traiană* (Bucureşti: Editura "Cartea Românească", 1927), 149–50.

14 Stoicescu, *Curteni*, 131.

15 János B. Szabó, "A székelyek katonai szerpe Erdélyben a mohácsi csatától a Habsburg uralom megszilárdulásáig (1526–1709)," in *A Határvédelem évszázadai Székelyföldön: Csíkszék és a Gyimesek vidéke. Szerkesztette és a jegyzékeket összeállította*, ed. József Nagy (Szépvíz: 2018), 105.

16 Henri Grégoire, "Aux confins militaires de l'orient byzantine. Hussards, Trabans, Tasnaks," *Byzantion*, 13 (1938), 279–82.

17 Erich Kettenhofen, "Darband," in *Encyclopaedia Iranica*, VII, 1, ed. Ehsan Yarshater (New York: 1994), 13–19; Kaveh Farrokh, Gholamreza Karamian, Katarzyna Maksymiuk, *A Synopsis of Sasanian Military Organization and Combat Units* (Siedlce-Teheran: Siedlce University of Natural Sciences and Humanities, 2018), 24.

to guard mountain passes, fords and other sensible transit points. They acted as an internal police force, armed with light weapons and firearms. They are considered a legacy of the Seljukid and Ilkhanid periods.[18] The *derbendcis* were similar to other auxiliary groups from the Ottoman army such as *martolos, filurici,* and *musellems*. They were entrusted with guard duty in exchange for tax exemptions. The *derbend* system was implemented in the European provinces of the empire beginning with the Fifteenth century, with a high concentration along the Danube frontier.[19] The *derbendcis* played an important role in the defence of the Ottoman frontier in the Balkans. They maintained stability in the borderlands and represented a factor of demographic growth, especially during the first half of the Sixteenth century.[20]

There are many similarities between the Ottoman *derbendcis* and the guardsmen (*trabant/drabant/darabont/dărăban*) of the Christian armies in Central and South-East Europe. However, it is unclear if this was the result of a transfer of military knowledge from one cultural area to the other. It is quite possible that the two institutions developed independently and were similar solutions to the same problem, the necessity to defend frontiers and to enforce internal order.

Guardsmen in Transylvanian Frontier Fortifications

Although Transylvania became a distinct state in the second half of the Sixteenth century, it inherited the political, social and military framework established during previous centuries. Most institutions were maintained, but underwent a slow process of adaptation. Guardsmen are mentioned frequently among the armed forces of Transylvanian rulers during this period. Giovanni Andrea Gromo, an Italian courtier of John Sigismund Szapolyai (1540–1571), provides an interesting description of such soldiers, emphasizing their role and functions.

18 Mesut Uyar, Edward J, Erickson, *A Military History of the Ottomans: From Osman to Atatürk* (Santa Barbara: Praeger Security International, 2009), 62–63.

19 Ayşe Kayapinar, Levent Kayapinar, "Application of Derbend Organization in the Balkans: An Example of Continuity of Balkan Institutions in the Ottoman System," in *State and Society in the Balkans Before and After the Establishment of Ottoman Rule*, eds. Srđan Rudić and Selim Aslantaş (Belgrade: The Institute of History Belgrade, 2017), 205–10.

20 Nikolay Antov, *The Ottoman "Wild West": The Balkan Frontier in the Fifteenth and Sixteenth Centuries* (Cambridge, New York: Cambridge University Press, 2017), 134, 153–54.

According to Gromo, there were two types of infantry soldiers in the army of the Transylvanian prince: guardsmen (*drabanti*) and hajdú (*edoni o educchi*). The guardsmen were equipped with harquebuses, spears and sabres and their main role was to guard the gates of fortifications (*questi fanno le sentinelle et guardano le porte delle fortezze, ne sono molto valorosi in battaglie*).[21] The Italian author was well acquainted with the situation in Transylvania but, nevertheless, he often makes generalizations when describing the composition of the army. In this particular case he emphasis one of the main role of the guardsmen as defenders of fortifications, but he fails to identify the various situations in which this term was used to designate Transylvanian soldiers.

Some of the largest estates in Transylvania were organized around important fortifications. The income generated by those settlements was used to support the administrative and military needs of the fortresses (construction, maintenance, provisions, wages etc.). Some of the inhabitants of these estates, usually those situated in the proximity of the fortress, were exempted from paying taxes in exchange for various services like fishing, hunting, blacksmithing, brickmaking, etc. The guardsmen were exempted in exchange for military service.[22]

In the second half of the Sixteenth century, guardsmen are mentioned in documents on the estates of important fortresses like Alba Iulia (Gyulafehérvár),[23] Gherla (Szamósujvár)[24] and Șimleu (Szilágysomlyó).[25] They were appointed by the ruling prince himself and were placed under the command of the captain

21 Andrei Veress, ed., *Documente privitoare la istoria Ardealului, Moldovei și Țării Românești, Acte și scrisori,* I (București: Cartea Românească, 1929), 255.

22 Florin Nicolae Ardelean, *Organizarea militară în Principatul Transilvaniei (1541–1691): Comitate și domenii fiscale* (Cluj-Napoca: Academia Română. Centrul de Studii Transilvane, 2019), 225–30.

23 On 28 November 1579, the Polish-Lithuanian King Stephen Báthory asked his brother Cristofor, voivode of Transylvania, to settle a dispute between the *drabant* András Nehéz and his relatives. According to this letter the *drabant* had been previously rewarded with a property on the estate of Alba Iulia, Endre Veress, ed., *Báthory István erdélyi fejedelem és lengyel király levelezése*, II (1576–1586) (Koloszvár: Erdélyi Tudományos Intézet, 1944), 137.

24 A letter sent by Stephen Báthory to the administrator of the Gherla fortress estate, Gábor Ébeni, in 1583 mentions a certain Szásznyiresi Orosz Mihály who was acknowledged as a free guardsmen (*szabad drabant*) of the fortress. He was given land on the estate of the fortress so he could fulfil his military duty, Veress, ed., *Báthory István*, II, 234.

25 David Prodan, *Iobăgia în Transilvania în secolul al XVI-lea*, II (București: Editura Academiei Republicii Socialiste Romania, 1968), 596.

of the fortress. These were the so-called free guardsmen (*szabados drabantok*), which resided in their villages, performed temporary service in the fortress and were fully mobilized in case of necessity. Documents also mention another group of guardsmen, who performed military service in exchange for regular wages, and were part of the permanent garrison of the fortification, the so-called ordinary guardsmen (*közdrabantok*). This complex situation is best illustrated by the case of Şimleu fortress according to a conscription made in 1594. The permanent garrison of the fortress consisted of 10 ordinary guardsmen who were aided in case of necessity by 113 free guardsmen and 19 free horsemen who lived in various villages of the estate.[26]

The status of guardsmen, their privileges and obligations, were sometimes discussed during the meetings of the Transylvanian Diet (Estates Assembly). In September 1593, when the prince and the representatives of the estates met in Alba Iulia, the guardsmen were recognized among those who were exempted from paying the tithe (*dézsma/decima*). However, in that particular context, they were required to pay a money contribution according to their grain harvest. Those who failed to comply or declared smaller quantities of grain were punished in the same manner as peasants.[27] This brief legal provision reveals some of the fundamental features of the guardsmen as a distinct social group. First of all, it shows that they were only partially exempted from paying taxes. They worked the fields and gathered their harvest, same as the other peasants and performed military service only occasionally. From a juridical point of view they were closer to peasants (serfs) and suffered similar consequences in case they broke the law.

As Transylvania was preparing to join the major confrontation between the Ottomans and the Habsburgs known as the Long War, or Long Turkish War (1593–1606), the situation of the guardsmen was once again debated during Diet sessions. In May 1594, the Diet agreed upon the organization of a mercenary army. Infantry soldiers were referred to as ordinary guardsmen (*közdrabantok*) and received wages of 3 florins each month. In order to gather money for these wages the population had to pay a tax of 50 denars per household. This extraordinary tax was also collected from groups, which were usually exempted, including the free guardsmen (*szabados drabantok*) who lived on the fiscal estate.[28] Several

---

26 András Kovács, "Szilágysomlyó vára a 16. Században," *Dolgozatok az Erdélyi Múzeum Érem- és Régiségtárából*, 8 (2013): 95–106.

27 *Monumenta Comitialia Regni Transylvaniae* (*MCRT*), Sándor Szilágyi, ed., III (Budapest: Magyar Tudományos Akad. Könyvkiadó Hivatala, 1877), 421–23.

28 *MCRT*, III, 440–41.

months later, in August 1594, Transylvanian authorities changed their mind and the free guardsmen were once again, exempted from paying this extraordinary war contribution.[29]

The anti-ottoman campaigns of Prince Sigismund Báthory and the presence of numerous foreign troops on Transylvanian territory had a negative impact on economic activities and social stability. Peasants abandoned their villages and sought refuge in safer areas. Many chose to settle in the vicinity of major fortifications and swelled the ranks of the free guardsmen. Tax exemptions and the security offered by defensive walls were a strong incentive for those who lived under the constant threat of war. However, the Diet was interested in maintaining the number of tax payers and took drastic measures against fugitives and those who offered them shelter. According to a legal provision adopted in February 1601, the fortress captains who accepted runaway serfs among their guardsmen had to pay a fine of 200 florins.[30] Being recognised as a free guardsman was a good opportunity for those looking to increase their social standing during peace time. The war had made this social status even more desirable for those looking for security or material gain.

The Blue Guardsmen (kék darabontok) in the Court Army of the Transylvanian Prince

Transylvanian rulers maintained a significant contingent of professional soldiers which were designated in contemporary sources as the army of the court (*aulae exercitus*), divided into two branches, the infantry (*peditatus aulae*) and the cavalry (*equitatus aulae*).[31] The term blue guardsman was used to distinguish an elite group of soldiers among the court infantry. They were first organized during the early years of the reign of Stephen Báthory (1571–1576) and were able to prove their efficiency in the battle of Sânpaul (Kerelőszentpál) against the pretender Gaspar Bekes, in 1575. The blue guardsmen were positioned in the vanguard of the Transylvanian army and performed the first assault on the enemy army during this battle. They played a decisive role in securing the victory for Báthory.[32]

---

29 *MCRT*, III, 448.

30 *MCRT*, IV, 584.

31 Attila Sunkó, "Az erdélyi fejedelmek udvari hadai a 16. Században", *Levéltári Közlemények*, 69:1–2 (1998): 99–131.

32 Wolffgangi de Bethlen, *Historia de rebus Transsylvanicis*, II (Cibinii: Typis et sumptibus Martinii Hochmeister, 1782), 309–316; Veress, *Documente*, II, 67–69; Sándor Szilágyi,

The officers of the court infantry were nobles or representatives of the Székely elite (*priomores/primipili*). The higest position in the hierarchy was held by the captain of the court infantry and was usualy entrusted to important members of the court. Among those who held this office in the second half of the Sixteenth century were: Johannes Sasa, Mihály Vadás, Lázár István and Matthew Perušić, a Transylvanian noble of Croatian origin, who led 600 'blue guardsmen' in the battle of Şelimbăr (28 October 1599).[33]

Although their main role was to defend the court and protect the ruler and his family, blue guardsmen were occasionally dispatched to enforce the garrisons of frontier fortifications. For example, in February 1575, Stephen Báthory sent 25 blue guardsmen to help the defenders of Hust (Huszt/Хуст), led by Stephen Kornis, who were threatened by the Habsburg garrison of Satu Mare (Szatmár) fortress.[34]

The blue guardsmen received regular wages and some of them enjoyed a semi-privileged status and tax exemptions, like the other free guardsmen from the fiscal estate. Narrative sources describe them as an elite infantry force which played an important role in most pitched battles during this period. Service at court as a blue guardsman was a good opportunity to gain land and a title of nobility.

The Red Guardsmen (veres/vörös darabontok) of the Székely Seats

In the Middle Ages, the Székely (*Siculi*) benefited from privileges and tax exemptions, as a community, in exchange for military service. Their main role was to defend the south eastern frontier along the Carpathians. In the second half of the Sixteenth century, as Transylvania was becoming a distinct state, the Székely gradually lost their traditional freedom and their military role and organization were redefined.[35] After 1562, the social elite of the Székely community had the

"Békes Gáspár versengése Báthori Istvánnal (1571–1575)," *Erdélyi Múzeum-Egyesület Évkönyve*, I (1859–1861), 107–15.

33 Attila Sunkó, "Az erdélyi fejedelmi testőrség archontológiája a XVI. Században," *Fons*, no. 2 (1994): 201–06.

34 Veress, *Báthory István*, II, 313–14.

35 Károly Vekov, *Structuri juridico-militare și sociale la secui în evul mediu* (Cluj-Napoca: Editura Studium, 2003), 40–50; Nathalie Kálnoky, "L'organization militaire de la nation sicule à la fin du Moyen Âge," in *La pensée militaire hongroise à travers les siècles*, eds. Hervé Coutau-Bégarie, Ferenc Tóth (Paris: Economica, 2011), 29–41.

same status as the county nobility, and continued to perform military service as cavalry units. A larger proportion was able to maintain a semi-privileged status, based on tax exemptions, and performed military service as guardsmen, most commonly known as red guardsmen because of their distinctive red cloths.[36]

In terms of social status, the red guardsmen were similar to the free guardsmen from the fiscal estate. The rulers of Transylvania held the right to appoint new guardsmen among the Székely. Letters of appointment were brief and offered little details about the privileges and obligations of those who were raised to this position. For example, on 13 October 1579, King Stephen Báthory wrote to his brother Christopher, voivode of Transylvania, to acknowledge Boldizsár Mihály from Tuşnad (Tusnád) as red guardsman. Boldizsár was rewarded thus for his loyal service and we can only assume that he had previously served as a common soldier.[37] Székel Antal and Székel Balás were similarly rewarded two days later. In this case, the letter of appointment mentions that both of them had served at court for a long time.[38]

The red guardsmen continued to play an important role in the defence of the south-eastern borderlands of Transylvania. They were also mobilized for external campaigns, especially when neighbouring regions were targeted. In September 1592, Sigismund Báthory sent military aid to his Moldavian ally, Aron Vodă. Gaspar Sibrik, the commander of this small expedition, was instructed to draft 200 black guardsmen from the town of Braşov (Kronstadt/Brassó) and 800 free red guardsmen (*szabados veres drabont*) from the neighbouring Székely Seats.[39]

The guardsmen were not the only members of the Székely community who had military obligations. Besides those who became serfs after the rebellion of 1562, some groups maintained a privileged or semi-privileged status based on military service. In 1602, General Giorgio Basta, who was governing Transylvania on behalf of the Habsburgs, ordered a conscription among the population of the Székely Seats. In Odorhei Seat (Székelyudvarhely), for example, the register mentions: 27 nobles, 566 *lófő* (so called leaders), 166 guardsmen, 1.723 free Székely and 389 serfs.[40] The guardsmen were one of the smallest groups

36 Most of these radical changes were adopted during the Diet of Sighişoara (Schäßburg) held in June 1562, after a failed rebellion of the Székely, MCRT, II, 202–08.

37 Veress, *Báthory István*, II, 134.

38 Veress, *Báthory István*, II, 134–35.

39 *MCRT*, III, 413.

40 Lajos Demény, ed., *Székely Oklevéltár (új sorozat)*, IV (Kolozsvár: Erdélyi Múzeum-Egyesület Kiadása, 1997), 116–17.

within the community. Together with the nobles and the *lófő,* they represented the social and military elite of this Transylvanian estate.

The Guardsmen of the Saxon Towns, Seats and Districts

The Saxon communities of Transylvania, like the Székely, had a traditional role in defending the frontier along the Carpathians. Unlike the Székely, they were able to maintain their privileged status, as a community, throughout the age of the Principality. However, their military obligations were adapted to the needs of the new state. The Saxons had to provide troops or financial aid for military campaigns, beyond their territorial limits.

Sources from the Sixteenth century mention Saxon guardsmen (*drabanten/ trabanten*) in two contexts: as members of the town garrison and as soldiers drafted for the military campaigns of Transylvanian rulers.

During the Middle Ages, some of the Saxon communities of Transylvania were granted the privilege to build stone walls around their settlements. Initially, local militias were conscripted for the defence of these fortified towns.[41] From the first half of the Sixteenth century, these soldiers were sometimes called guardsmen. One of the earliest mentions of the term guardsman in Saxon sources comes from the accounts of Braşov in 1528.[42] In the town of Sibiu (Hermannstdt/ Nagyszeben), the guardsmen became a permanent military force after the year 1556.[43] According to the magistrate's accounts, the guardsmen received regular wages and their main role was to defend the town gates. In April 1561, for example, the gates of Sibiu were protected by 14 guardsmen (*darabantis*). Town authorities paid 35 florins and 50 denars each month for their wages.[44]

Occasionally, the term guardsman was used for the infantry troops sent by the Saxon University in the Transylvanian army. However, in this particular context, the most common term was *pedites* or *pedites pixidarios*. As one of the

---

41 Liviu Cîmpeanu, "Organizarea militară a Braşovului până la sfârşitul secolului al XV-lea," in *Studii de istorie a oraşelor: in honorem Paul Niedermaier*, eds. Vasile Ciobanu, Dan Dumitru Iacob (Bucureşti: Editura Academiei Române; Brăila: Editura Istros a Muzeului Brăilei "Carol I", 2017), 337–43.

42 *Quellen zur Geschichte der Stadt Kronstadt in Siebenbürgen* (Kronstadt: Druck von Albrecht & Zillich, 1889), 111, 121.

43 Maria Pakucs-Willcocks, *Sibiul veacului al XVI-lea: Rânduirea unui oraş transilvănean* (Bucureşti: Humanitas, 2018), 86.

44 Serviciul Judeţean al Arhivelor Naţionale Sibiu (SJAN Sibiu), România, Primăria oraşului Sibu, Socoteli consulare, 77(1561), f.72v.

three political estates of the country, the Saxons provided soldiers, artillery and other contributions (money or provisions) for the Transylvanian army. Between 1540 and 1567, the size of their military detachments varied between 500 and 3.000 men.[45] Each Saxon town could mobilize its soldiers for various reasons. For example, in March 1551, the town judge of Brașov was accompanied by 200 guardsmen at the Diet of Aiud (Nagyenyed).[46]

The Saxons of Transylvania established their internal military regulations as they were responsible for recruiting, mobilizing and paying their own soldiers. In such a regulation, issued for the town and district of Sibiu in 1564, authorities made a clear distinction between three types of soldiers recruited for military campaigns: common footmen armed with a spear (*fusgenger mit einen spiess*), guardsmen armed with a gunpowder weapon (*trabanten oder pyxenschücz*) and mounted soldiers (*czu ross*).[47] Guardsmen were considered a superior type of infantry, armed with gunpowder weapons, and thus received higher wages than common infantry. During the war between John Sigismund Szapolyai and the Habsburgs (1556–1571), the Transylvanian Saxons had to mobilize their troops almost yearly. Both official and narrative sources indicate the fact that most, if not all, Saxon soldiers were guardsmen, armed with harquebuses. The Diet of Cluj-Mănăștur, held in October 1565, specificly asked the Saxons to send 1.000 guardsmen in the Transylvanian army (*A szászok pedig adnak ezer drabantra*).[48] Most descriptions of the battle of Hodod (Hadad) (4 March 1562), mention the fact that Saxon soldiers carried gunpowder weapons and were positioned in the centre of the Transylvanian battle line. Without the support of defensive pike formations, the Saxon infantry was routed by a swift cavalry charge of the enemy.[49]

---

45 Florin Nicolae Ardelean, "Pecunia nervus belli. The Saxon University in Transylvania and its Contribution to the Military Campaign of 1566–1567," in *Politics and Society in the Central and South-Eastern Europe (13th–16th centuries)*, ed. Zoltan Iusztin (Cluj-Napoca: Mega, 2019), 215–22.

46 *Quellen zur Geschichte der Stadt Brasso*, IV (Brasso: Heinrich Zeidner, 1903), 511.

47 Maria Pakucs-Willcocks, *„zu urkundt in das Stadtbuch lassen einschreiben". Die ältesten Protokolle von Hermannstadt und der Sächsischen Nationsuniversität (1522–1565)* (Bonn: Schiller Verlag Hermannstadt, 2016), 255.

48 *MCRT*, II, 295.

49 Endre Veress, *A történetíró Báthory István király* (Cluj-Kolozsvár: Minerva, 1933), 32–33; Ödön Hegyi, "Székely Antal tudósítása a Hadadi csatáról," *Történelmi Tár* (1990), 142–44; Mathias Miles, *Siebenbürgischer Würg-Engel* (Hermannstadt, 1670), 83–85.

The difference between common infantry and guardsmen is also underlined in a document referring to the siege of Lipova fortress from 1595. In this particular context the troops dispatched by the Saxon University consisted of black guardsmen (*schwartzen Trabanten*) and conscripted infantry (*tzendt Leutten*), recruited on a proportion of 1 soldier for every 10 men.[50]

In the second half of the Sixteenth century, Saxon guardsmen were considered good infantry troops armed with gunpowder weapons. They were proficient in the defence of fortified settlements but they were also mobilized for offensive military campaigns. Unlike the free guardsmen of the fiscal estates or the Székely guardsmen, the Saxon guardsmen didn't develop into a semi-privileged group. They were regular soldiers who received wages for the duration of their service.

Guardsmen in the County Militias

The Transylvanian Principality inherited a system of proportional recruitment, usually applied in the counties. Nobles had to mobilize armed servants according to the size of their estates. In many cases these soldiers were simple peasants without proper military equipment or combat experience.[51]

During the Long Turkish War (1591–1606), Transylvanian authorities attempted to improve this obsolete element of the army. In September 1593, the Diet of Alba Iulia decided that the soldiers drafted in the county militia should be guardsmen armed with harquebuses. Those who couldn't afford a gunpowder weapon were required to bring sabres and spears. The conscription rate was one soldier for every 10 serfs.[52] One year later, in 1594, the situation of the conscripted guardsmen was once again discussed during a Diet session. These soldiers were referred to as common guardsmen (*közdrabant*), to differentiate them from the free guardsmen of the fiscal estates and the Székely seats, and were entitled to a monthly wage of 3 florins.[53] In 1600 the conscription rate was decreased to one guardsman for every 20 households.[54]

---

50 Liviu Cîmpeanu, "„Domnul fie lăudat […] turcii au predat cetatea": Cucerirea Lipovei Otomane de către transilvăneni în august 1595," *Historia Urbana*, XXVI (2018), 97–111.

51 Ardelean, *Organizarea militară*, 83–115.

52 *az nemesség az ő jószágában meghagyja és elrendelje, hogy minden tíz jobbágyról egy-egy kész drabantja legyen, az kitől lehet, puskával, az ki semmiképen szerét nem teheti, szablyával, dárdával, jó szerrel legyen*, *MCRT*, III, 426.

53 *MCRT*, III, 426.

54 *MCRT*, IV, 579.

In the county militia, what sets guardsmen apart from the other soldiers is the use of gunpowder weapons. Their presence in this traditional structure of the Transylvanian army was an attempt of improvement and modernization, made in the specific context of a long military conflict.

Conclusions

It still remains unclear if the term guardsmen (*trabant/drabant/darabont*) has German or Oriental (Persian/Turkish) origins but, nevertheless, available sources indicated that this new type of infantry was widely spread throughout Central and South-East Europe.

In Transylvania, during the second half of the Sixteenth century, the term guardsmen was used in many circumstances and designated a large variety of soldiers. It is tempting to think it became synonymous with infantry soldier. However, such a generalization would be inaccurate. The evolution of guardsmen within the Transylvanian military framework is a surprisingly complex issue. Their presence among the armed forces of this emerging state is a sign of military innovation based on the wide spread of gunpowder weapons during the late medieval and early modern period.

Some Transylvanian guardsmen, like the free guardsmen from the fiscal estates and the Székely red guardsmen, developed into distinct social groups, which benefited from tax exemptions in exchange for military service, being thus similar to the Ottoman *derbendcis*. Others, like the ordinary guardsmen form fortress garrisons, the Saxon black guards or the county militia guardsmen were mercenaries who received regular wages. Most guardsmen were mobilized during campaigns and joined the field army as detachments of elite infantry, but they also had various duties during peacetime like protecting salt transports, catching criminals, guarding the frontiers and the court of the prince. Regardless of their social status, all guardsmen shared two main similarities: the use of gunpowder weapons and defensive duties connected to fortifications or borderland areas.

The significant development of this type of infantry soldier is also connected to the gradual transformation of confines, from vague frontiers into linear borders. The edges of the Transylvanian Principality were far from being stable and well defined. The borderlands, especially the western ones, remained extensive areas marked by strategic strong points (fortifications) and zones of influence (the estates surrounding those fortifications). Guardsmen were the best solution for the defence of the various types of fortifications built along the confines of early modern Transylvania.

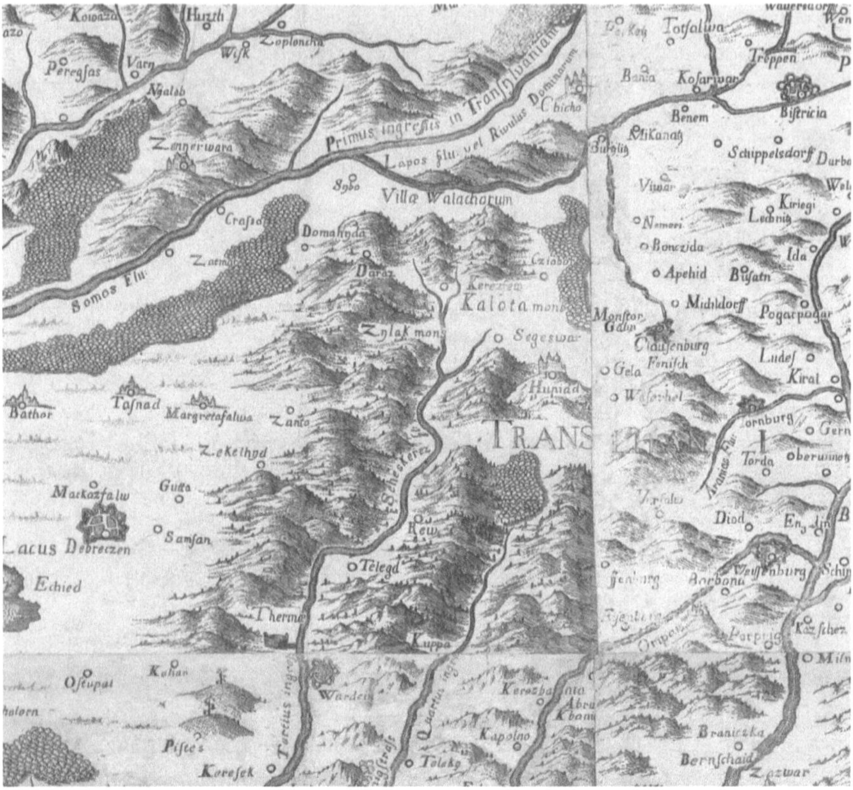

The Western borderlands of Transylvania, detail from *Ungaria cum finitimiis provinciis…*/Hungary and its frontier provinces, Georg Matthäus Vischer/Matthias Greischer, 1682, cooper engraving (Landesarchiv Baden-Württemberg Abt. Generallandesarchiv Karlsruhe)

Izsán Csaba

Between Soldier and Guard: The Roles of the Town Mercenaries in the Late Sixteenth- Early Seventeenth Century Cluj (Klausenburg/ Kolozsvár), Sighişoara (Schässburg/ Segesvár) and Braşov (Kronstadt/ Brassó)*

Abstract: The period starting with the last decade of the sixteenth century and ending with the rule of Gabriel Bethlen was eventful and harsh for the Principality of Transylvania due to the instability caused by the Long Turkish War (1591–1606), and the consequences of Bocskai's uprising. This study intends to present the everyday life and roles of town mercenaries (called *darabont/drabant/Trabant* or *Fussoldat* in primary sources) of Cluj, Sighişoara and Braşov from this period, which were also recruited in the armies of the Principality, but lost this type of role during the years of Giorgio Basta's administration. The primary sources of the study consist of the accounting books of the mentioned towns, the accountings written by the commanders of the mercenaries, and the military correspondence of the Magistrate of Sighişoara and the Magistrate of Braşov dating from three different periods of the war and also from the early years of the second decade of the seventeenth century.

Keywords: Principality of Transylvania, Long Turkish War, Sighişoara, Cluj-Napoca, Braşov, Armies of the Principality, Town Mercenaries, Military Correspondence, Accounting Books

Introduction and the Primary Sources of the Research

The period starting with the last decade of the sixteenth century and ending with the rule of Gabriel Bethlen was eventful and harsh for the Principality of Transylvania due to the instability caused by the Long Turkish War (1591–1606),[1] and the consequences of Bocskai's uprising. From a different perspective

* This work was supported by the Collegium Talentum Programme of Hungary.

1 In my opinion the form Long Turkish War is the most suitable for describing the 1591–1606 period in Transylvania, and also to clear the confusion caused by different years being counted as the start of the war in English and Hungarian historiography. The Hungarian historiography counts the 1591–92 Turkish campaign in modern day Western Bosnia as the start of the war, thus using the term Fifteen Years War. However the western/English historiography usually sets the start of the war to the spring of 1593, thus using the term of the Thirteen Years War.

though we can consider the four decades mentioned above as a period rich in sources for those who are researching military history.

My future PhD dissertation concentrates on the organization of defences of four Transylvanian Saxon towns: Brașov, Sighișoara, Sibiu (Hermannstadt/Nagyszeben) and Cluj in times of war, starting from the late sixteenth century until the seventh decade of the seventeenth century. A major part of my research intends to present the everyday life and different roles and duties of the town mercenaries (called *darabont/drabant/Trabant* or *Fussoldat* in primary sources) hired by the local authorities. In this study I would like to summarise the results of my research based on the different roles of the mercenaries from three of the above mentioned towns (Brașov, Sighișoara and Cluj), presenting each role separately in a sub-chapter. Also the study is not trying to compare the mercenaries of the three towns, but is aiming to highlight the most interesting and useful details from the different sources.

The primary sources of the research are the accounting books of the towns, the accountings written by the commanders of the mercenaries, and the military correspondence of the magistrates of Sighișoara and Brașov dating from three different periods of the Long Turkish War and from the first half of the seventeenth century. The original documents are stored in two branches of the National Archives of Romania. The sixteenth-seventeenth centuries accounting books of Cluj containing the accountings of the mercenaries are stored at the Cluj County Branch of the National Archives in Cluj-Napoca, and all the other used documents, including the letters from the military correspondence of the magistrate of Sighișoara are stored at the Brașov County Branch of the National Archives in Brașov. The documents from Sighișoara were originally stored at the archives of the town until the mid- twentieth century. During the communist period, the original funds were transported to the Mureș and Brașov County Branches of the National Archives, with the documents of the magistrate heading to archives of Brașov. There the original funds and collections were kept integrally and even the original inventory numbers from Sighișoara are used to this day, as we can read from the inventory books of the National Archives of Brașov written by the former archivist and historian Gernot Nussbächer.

The Different Roles of the Mercenaries

Before presenting the roles and duties of the mercenaries in detail, discussing the right terminology is necessary. In the original sources of the research the term *darabont* is the most commonly used one to describe the mercenaries. The term *darabont* (*Drabant* or *Trabant* in German) is a Hungarian expression taken from the German language, meaning infantryman.[2] The term is also present in Romanian language and specialized literature in the forms of *dărăban/darabant/dorobanț* etc.[3] As their primary role was to guard the city walls and gate towers, some of the mercenaries can be called guardsmen in English. However when those guardsmen were recruited in the armies of the Principality, they were accompanied by other mercenaries hired for a shorter period by each town's magistrate, thus making it hard for the author to separate the guardsmen (*darabont/drabant*) from other mercenaries.[4] Hungarian PhD student László Szokola who specialises on the fifteenth-sixteenth century town defences and Hungarian armies has a theory about the differences between guardsmen and mercenaries which can be applied in Transylvania until the middle of the sixteenth century. Szokola believes that the guardsmen were recruited from the population who had mandatory military obligations, living either in the town or in villages/other *dominiums* belonging to the town, and the mercenaries were soldiers paid from tax incomes and recruited from all over the kingdom or principality.[5] Based on the realities and details of the sources Szokola is researching, the writers of the original documents were able to differentiate the guardsmen from other mercenaries in Hungary and Transylvania in the majority of the Sixteenth century. Sadly we cannot apply this theory to our seventeenth century sources, in which often the people who wrote the documents were unable to tell the *zsoldos* (meaning mercenary) and *darabont* words apart, and were usually combining the two, creating the expression of *zsoldos darabont*.[6]

In the Latin sources of the period the terms of *pixidarius* is often used to describe the guardsmen and mercenaries, meaning firearm using infantryman or gunman. Usually both the mercenaries and guardsmen were equipped with

---

2 *Erdélyi Magyar Szótörténeti Tár*. II. ed. Szabó T. Attila et alii. (Bukarest: Kriterion Könyvkiadó, 1978), 262.

3 Florin-Nicolae Ardelean uses the form darabant. From his past works I would like to highlight the book: *Organizarea militară în Principatul Transilvaniei (1541–1691)* (Cluj-Napoca:Centrul de Studii Transilvane, 2019) as being one of the most useful volumes of specialized literature in the topic of early modern armies of Transylvania from the more recent Romianian historiography.

4 Often all the mercenaries were called either *darabont* or *mercenary* in the sources after the middle of the sixteenth century, making the separation of guardsmen from ordinary mercenaries almost impossible.

5 László Szokola, "Brassó város katonasága a késő középkorban," *Hadtörténeti Közlemények* 134, no. 3 (2021): 532–33.

6 Term which can be translated as mercenary infrantrymen or mercenary guardsmen, giving hard times for the researcher to assign a good definition to the expression.

harquebuses as their primary weapon,[7] with their equipment and gunpowder being provided or paid by the local authorities who also hired them.[8]

Guarding the Walls and Gate Towers of the Towns

As we have already mentioned in the introduction of the study, the primary role of the mercenaries called *darabont* was to guard the walls and gate towers of the town they were hired by. Thus we can call those mercenaries guardsmen. Although we have to differentiate the "ordinary guardsmen" hired by bigger towns and the elite guardsmen units called red and blue *darabont,* who served in the court and army of the prince of Transylvania. Both military units were named after the colour of the uniform they were wearing, as the blue guardsmen were the elite infantry of the prince's army, and the red guardsmen started their life living in serfdom in Szeklerland and slowly rose through military ranks becoming guardsmen of the court and residence of the prince in Alba Iulia (Gyulafehérvár).[9] János B. Szabó believes that the process began after the June 1562 Sighişoara Diet, when smaller changes were made to the military obligations of the ordinary Szekler people, directly assigning them to the armed forces of the prince.[10] The regular guardsmen of smaller towns in Transylvania where usually recruited in groups by the local authorities, this was also a practice in Western and Upper Hungarian cities.[11]

---

7 Harquebuses were hand-guns with a hook-like projection on the under surface for steadying the gun against battlements, walls or other objects when firing. The Hungarian term used in the sources for the arquebus is *szakállas puska*, which has the meaning of bearded gun, the "beard" being the hook like projection of the firearm, Károly Kozák, "A magyarországi szakállas puskák fejlődéstörténetéről," *Archaeologiai Értesítő* 101, no. 1 (1974): 290–91.

8 Csaba Izsán, "A zsoldos darabontok számadásai és a város védműveinek javítási költségei Kolozsvár 17. Századi számadáskönyveiben," in *Ezerarcú Erdély- Politika, társadalom, kultúra.* (*Studia Historica Tralsylvaniensia 2.*) ed. Áron Tőtős (Nagyvárad: Erdélyi Múzeum Egyesület, 2019), 339.

9 János B. Szabó, "A székelyek katonai szerepe Erdélyben a mohácsi csatától a Habsburg uralom megszilárdulásáig (1526–1711)," in *Határvédelem évszázadai Székelyföldön,* ed. Nagy József (Szépvíz: Alutus Nyomda, 2018), 108–09.

10 János B. Szabó, "A Szapolyaiak hadserege Szapolyai János és II. János korában," in *Egy elfeledett magyar királyi dinasztia: a Szapolyaiak,* ed. Pál Fodor and Szabolcs Varga (Budapest, ELTE Bölcsésztudományi Kutatóközpont, 2020), 234–35.

11 László Szokola, "Magyarországi városok zsoldos-állítása a Mátyás és Jagelló-korban," in *Magister Historiae II. Válogatott tanulmányok a 2014-ben és 2015-ben megrendezett középkorral foglalkozó, mesterszakos hallgatói konferenciák előadásaiból,* ed. Csaba

There were two significant differences between the ordinary guardsmen and the red and blue guardsmen. The ordinary guardsmen received a monthly military payment for their services, but usually did not have citizen rights or properties in the town they were serving, on the other hand the elite guardsmen of Alba Iulia often owned more than one estate or property (including cultivable lands) inside or outside the walls of the city which they were able to buy or sell at any time they wanted.[12] The other significant difference between the two types of guardsmen existed during their recruitment into the armies of the Principality. The regular guardsmen usually fought during conflicts inside the borders of Transylvania, the red and blue guardsmen on the other hand joined the prince in military operations outside the borders of the Principality too. As an example, after the coronation of Stephen Báthory as king of Poland and Lithuania in 1576, 500 blue guardsmen left Transylvania with Báthory, and in July 1579 the same infantry numbered a total of 828 guardsmen, the additional infantrymen being recruited also from Transylvania.[13]

Speaking of the guardsmen serving in Cluj, Sighişoara and Braşov, we have to consider a small amount of soldiers (20–30) who were constantly stationing on the gate towers and walls of the towns. This was their major role in the three towns in this period, except for a few years during Giorgio Basta's administration of Transylvania during the Long Turkish War in Sighişoara, when Walloon mercenaries were deployed in the town and caused a lot of conflict between the local authorities and the Habsburg general Basta. The presence of foreign mercenaries in the town also meant that the guardsmen lost their role completely starting with the summer of 1602 until Basta's armies left Transylvania in 1604.[14]

Returning to a more peaceful period and leaving Sighişoara behind in favour of Cluj, the sources tell us that in September 1614 a total of 22 guardsmen were paid in the city for guarding duties. On each gate tower of the city 5 infantrymen and a corporal was stationed constantly and one more infantryman was stationed

---

Farkas et. alii (Budapest: ELTE BTK Történelemtudományi Doktori Iskola, 2016), 124–25.

12 Emőke Gálfi, "The Society of the Residence of the Transylvanian Princes in the Second Half of the Sixteenth Century," *Hungarian Historical Review* 7, no. 4 (2018): 755.

13 Attila Sunkó, "Az erdélyi fejedelmek udvari hadai a 16. században," *Levéltártörténeti Közlemények* 69, no. 1–2 (1998): 102.

14 Csaba Izsán, "Hadi költségek és darabontok a segesvári városi tanács 1601. és 1604. közötti levelezésében," in *Várak, erődök, kastélyok az erdélyi régiségben. (Erdélyi Évszázadok, a Kolozsvári Magyar Történeti Intézet Évkönyve V.)* ed. Enikő Rüsz-Fogarasi (Kolozsvár: Egyetemi Műhely Kiadó, 2020), 181–85.

on each small gate tower.[15] All of the 22 guardsmen had names which suggest Hungarian ethnicity. This detail will be an important factor in an upcoming part of study.[16] The monthly payment of the regular infantrymen was 2 florins, with the corporals earning 3 florins, making a total of 47 florins in September 1614.[17] From the accounting book of 1614 we can realize that the same number of guardsmen was stationed on the gate towers each month, receiving also the same sum of money for payment in each month. This makes a total of 514 florins spent on guardsmen by the city in 1614, a sum which can be considered as average for the decade and this amount of money was around a tenth of the yearly income of Cluj in the period.[18] During the second and third decade of the seventeenth century the payment of the guardsman in Cluj was raised considerably, with both the regular infantrymen and corporals receiving 50 denars more each month.[19] The raise meant that the city's total expenditure on the same number of guardsmen was 707 florins and 29 denars for the year of 1634, and even if we discount the monthly payment of 4 florins and 17 denars of captain István Szarka (which was a total of 50 florins and 8 denars for the whole year), the total expenditures were still almost 150 florins higher compared to those of 20 years before.[20] Besides the ranks of ordinary infantrymen, corporals and captain, the sources reveal guardsmen called "*új legén*" (new boys) in Cluj, who most probably were young boys on probation time, receiving a monthly payment of 50 denars in 1616, with the ordinary infantrymen receiving two florins at the same time, for the same duties.[21]

---

15 The city had a total of three gate towers (Mănăştur gate, Bridge Street gate and Middle Street gate) and four small gate towers (Magyar Street gate, Torda Street gate, the gate of the old fortress, and Coal Street gate), Radu Lupescu, "Kolozsvár korai történetének buktatói," *Erdélyi Múzeum* LXVII, no 3–4 (2005): 56–68.

16 The primary sources suggest that by the late sixteenth- early seventeenth century Cluj's population had a Hungarian majority with still a considerably high number of Saxon citizens, on the other hand Braşov and Sighişoara having a population of Saxon majority.

17 Serviciul Judeţean al Arhivelor Naţionale Cluj (SJAN Cluj), The Accounting Books of Cluj, 13a/XVIII 1614, microfilm roll no. 20, Fund no. 584.

18 Izsán, "A zsoldos darabontok," 342.

19 Usually the conversion rate of the denar into florin was 100/1 in the period, with some special cases also present in the accounting books of Cluj when 120 denars were converted into 1 florin. Nevertheless 50 denars was a substantial raise of payment in the seventeenth century, even if we take into consideration the possible inflation rate.

20 SJAN Cluj, The Accounting Books of Cluj 19/XIII 1634, microfilm roll 43, 385–91.

21 SJAN Cluj, The Accounting Books of Cluj 14 a/IV 1616, microfilm roll 23.

The number of paid guardsmen in Cluj is comparable to the number of guards hired in Sibiu in the same period. The research of Júlia Derzsi reveals similar numbers, as until the 1580s 16–18 guardsmen were paid in the seat town of the Transylvanian Saxon University (although additional guards, not called *drabant/ darabont* were also paid in Sibiu) with the number being raised to 20–22 in the last two decades of the sixteenth century.[22] 1592 was the first year when the magistrate of Sibiu hired a captain as the military leader of the guardsmen, with a monthly payment of 3 florins.[23] The monthly payment of three florins/mercenary also correspond with the results of Florin-Nicolae Ardelean's research concentrating on the armies of Transylvania in the period of the Principality.[24]

Where did the Guardsmen Come From?

An important question, we can ask is: where did the guardsmen who were hired in Saxon towns come from? János B. Szabó argues that a considerable number of mercenaries and guardsmen who served in the Transylvanian Saxon towns (and mainly Braşov) originated from the Southern Transylvanian region of Ţara Făgăraşului, and came from a mixed social group consisting of former castle servants and those boyars whose allodial lands were not inheritable.[25] Also there is consensus in recent Hungarian historiography which considers the majority of regular town guardsmen having Hungarian of Szekler origin like the elite blue and red *darabonts* had.[26] However, we have to take into consideration the fact that the names in the primary sources could differ depending on the native language of its writer. The perfect examples are two mercenary captains from Sighişoara from the years of 1644–1645. During those two years the captain of the mercenaries from Sighişoara and Sighişoara Seat(Schässburger Stuhl) was Márton Fülöp, and his assistant was Márton Szőcs. Both names are written following the Hungarian orthography, but in other documents we can read their

22 The additional guards being paid by the *villicus* and not the magistrate of Sibiu, Júlia Derzsi, "Nagyszeben város háztartása a 16. szásad második felében," in *Veretek, utak, katonák. Gazdaságtörténeti tanulmányok a magyar középkorról*, ed. Kádas István et alii (Budapest: MTA BTK TTI, 2018), 423–24.

23 Derzsi, "Nagyszeben város háztartása," 424.

24 Florin-Nicolae Ardelean, "Oastea portală în Transilvania princiară (1542–1653)," *Banatica* 20, no. 2 (2010): 164.

25 Szabó, "A Szapolyaiak hadserege," 231.

26 Izsán, "A zsoldos darabontok," 343.

names as *Martinus Filep* and *Martinus Mebringer/Mehbringer*[27] making it harder for us to decide if they were of Hungarian/Szekler or Saxon ethnicity. In the case of Mebringer the Saxon ethnicity can be more realistic if his surname was a toponymical name, literally meaning someone from Mebrich (current day Beia, Braşov County), a village with Saxon population in the researched period.

The case of town Sighişoara is interesting from this point of view, as the sources suggest that the guardsmen and mercenaries hired in the town (and their commanders) were of Hungarian/Szekler ethnicity, on the other hand the mercenaries hired alongside the guardsmen to fulfil the military obligations of the town and seat were locals from villages belonging to Sighişoara Seat, which I want to present with two appropriate examples. At the beginning of Giorgio Basta's administration of Transylvania during the Long Turkish War, the mercenary captains of Sighişoara were called Mihály Imecsi and Demeter Nyújtódi. Both are toponymical surnames derived from the villages of Imecsfalva (Imeni) and Nyújtód (Lunga) which were part of Szeklerland (Orbai and Kézdi Seats respectively- current day Covasna County).[28] During George I Rákóczi's Upper Hungarian military expedition in the spring of 1644, the mercenaries coming from the village of Segesd (Şaeş, part of historical Sighişoara Seat, current Mureş County) were called *Hannes Beeren, Hannes Keiseren* and *Hannes Connerd* having Saxon ethnicity.[29] However, we have to mention that adjusting ethnicity to toponymical surnames can be often misleading and other sources are needed to certainly confirm those types of arguments.

Speaking of the guardsmen and mercenaries from Cluj, we have already mentioned that all of the guardsmen present in the 1614 accountings had Hungarian names. In the 1634 accountings which were also mentioned above, we can find five names which indicate German/Saxon origin, but were partially Magyarized (*Senekerssy Matias, Teribossy Matias, Tepegiöcz Marthon, Kissgoryssy Matias, Brotter Mihali*). The five guardsmen made up a total of 23 % of the whole number of infantrymen paid by the city in 1634, with the remaining persons having Hungarian names.[30]

---

27 Serviciul Judeţean al Arhivelor Naţionale Braşov (SJAN Braşov), Documents of the magistrate of Sighişoara: A.O.S. 255, attachment no. 1–2; A.O.S 1436, attachment no. 3. Fund no. 10.

28 SJAN Braşov, Documents of the magistrate of Sighişoara, A.O.S. 101, 1603.

29 From the context of a letter we can be certain that the 3 mercenaries were local villagers and not hired by the village to replace their labour force, SJAN Braşov, Documents of the magistrate of Sighişoara, A.O.S. 255, attachment no. 8, 1603.

30 SJAN Cluj, The Accounting Books of Cluj 19/XIII 1634, microfilm roll 43, 385–391.

Finally, speaking of the origin of the guardsmen and mercenaries from Brașov, using earlier sources from the first half of the sixteenth century, presented in the articles of László Szokola show very interesting results. Szokola found two lists of soldiers from 1539 and 1540 respectively, and he has considered the first one as a mercenary list and the later one a list of guardsmen. The second list can be a very important source for military historians as it is rich in details, describing the place of origin of every soldier and in the case of infantrymen, who were living in Brașov, denotes the exact city quarter they came from. The 1539 list contains a total of 67 names, from which 64 were ordinary infantrymen and 50 had Saxon/German names, thus the list having a proportion of ¾ mercenaries with possible Saxon origins and ¼ with possibly Hungarian/Szekler origins.[31] The results make the list to stand out from other sources which have totally different proportions. For example a list dating from the first decade of the sixteenth century (also examined by Szokola) has exactly different proportions, with the majority of the mercenaries seeming to have Hungarian/Szekler name and origins.[32] Returning to the list from 1540, it contains a total of 208 names, 64 of whom are mentioned as people living in Brașov, with 55 soldiers having Hungarian names and the majority noted as coming from the Hungarian/Szekler outskirts of the city called Blumena (Bolonya/Blumăna). The majority of the infantrymen from the list (142 names) were mentioned as coming from other localities of the region Burzenland (Țara Bârsei), having German names in majority.[33]

Civilian Roles in the City

Beside their guardsmen role, the mercenaries were often used by the local authorities as labour force when the situation required it. In the accounting book of Cluj from 1634 we have a registry which states that the guardsmen were paid 68 denars for "...*ezen a napon ölik meg az 34 ebeket*" (killing 34 ownerless stray dogs on that day).[34] After the great fire of 1655 which destroyed all but 6 gate towers of Cluj, the rebuilding process lasted almost five years. Beside the members of each guild, day-wage men and the guardsmen helped in rebuilding the towers and walls. A registry from the 1658 accounting book tells us that on the 14th of

31 Szokola, *Brassó város katonasága*, 526–30.
32 Szokola, *Brassó város katonasága*, 530–31.
33 Szokola, *Brassó város katonasága*, 526–30.
34 SJAN Cluj, The Accounting Books of Cluj 19/XIII 1634, microfilm roll 43, 402–404.

August, the guardsmen helped in taking down the unusable roof shingle from the Middle-gate tower of the city.[35]

The Mercenaries in the Armies of the Principality

It was established in the 1224 *Diploma Andreanum* that the Transylvanian Saxon cities and seats had to provide military contribution to the royal Hungarian armies in case of attack from abroad. The Transylvanian Saxon University had to prepare and equip a total of 500 soldiers in those cases. The soldiers from each locality marched under the flag of the count of the respective Saxon seat, with the army being led by the Count of Sibiu/Comes Saxonum/Graf der Sachsen.[36] This practice remained unchanged after the disintegration of Hungary and the formation of the Principality of Transylvania.[37] As an example, under the flag of the Count of Sighişoara were recruited the mercenaries from the following market towns and villages: Saeş (Segesd/Schaas), Saschiz (Szászkézd/Kisd), Apold/Trappold (also called Apold currently in Romanian), Brădeni (Hégen/Handerf or Henndorf), Netuş (Netus/Neithausen), Daia (Szászdálya or Dolmány/Thalheim), Buneşti (Szászbuda/Bondorf), Roadeş (Rádos/Radenthal), Beia (Szászbene/Mebrich), Archita (Erked/Arkeden), Laslea (Szászszentlászló/Grosslassein) and Hoghilag (Holdvilág/Holwelagen).[38]

The guardsmen and mercenaries of the Saxon towns were often recruited in the armies of the prince, making a good proportion of the required 500 soldiers. A good example of the practice was the general mobilization order of Prince George I. Rákóczi on the 14 January 1644, when he commanded the University to prepare 500 infantrymen equipped with guns and 200 bullets each and to be sent with their supply wagons to Alba Iulia until January 26.[39] Although the practice

35 SJAN Cluj,The Accounting Books of Cluj 30/XXVIII 1658, microfilm roll 68, 22.

36 Zsuzsanna Cziráki: *„Senkinek pénzen vött rabjai nem voltunk sem nem vagyunk". Brassó és a fejedelmi hatalom viszonya a város fejedelmi szolgáltatásai tükrében Bethlen Gábor uralkodása idején*, PhD dissertation (Szegedi Tudományegyetem: Szeged, 2010), 260.

37 With the exception of a period of instability during the disputed rule of Ferdinand I and John Szapolyai, when Georg Reicherstorffer turned the Saxon cities against Szapolyai, Emőke Gálfi, "Szapolyai János és az erdélyi városok," in *Egy elfeledett magyar királyi dinasztia: a Szapolyaiak*, ed. Pál Fodor and Szabolcs Varga (Budapest, ELTE Bölcsésztudományi Kutatóközpont, 2020), 202–06.

38 Izsán, "Hadi költségek és darabontok,"188.

39 The original document is not part of the fund, which contains two translations of it, one in Hungarian, and the other in Latin language, SJAN Braşov, Documents of the magistrate of Sighişoara, A.O.S. 261–262, 1644.

of military contribution was not changed with the formation of the Principality, there were attempts to raise the number of required soldiers to 1.000 or even 2.000. In the Schnell Collection of the National Archives of Braşov we have a dispatch written on the 8 June 1562 at the military camp near Torda (Turda). On the document we can read the confirmation made by Peter Haller, Count of Sibiu about 603 florins and 73 denars he received from Ferenc Schonkabuck, senator from Braşov, sum of money which was the military payment of the mercenaries from Braşov and the Burzenland region who were recruited among the 1.000 soldiers sent for the armies of King John II.[40] The major problem of the research is that the number of soldiers sent by the Saxon University varies in almost every second document starting with the mid- 1560s, thus making it quite hard for us to determine the exact increase of numbers from the original claim for the 500 soldiers first mentioned in the *Andreanum*. The research of Florin Nicolae Ardelean on the same topic clarifies the problem for the 1540–1567 period. In the *"Pecunia nervus belli." The Saxon University in Transylvania and its contribution to the Military campaign of 1566–1567* article he presents the increased and diversified military obligations of the Saxon University. For the 1540–1565 period the sources confirm that the University had to prepare 500–2.000 infantryman yearly, number which was increased by King John II to 2.500 and 3.000 for the years of 1566 and 1567 respectively, for his final western military efforts against the Habsburgs.[41]

There is another document in the Schnell Collection, which attests a bizarre situation from the year of 1564. During the Diet of Cluj the representatives of the Union of the Three Nations decided that the Saxon University had to prepare an additional 2.000 guardsmen (the world *drabant* was used in the original document) for the royal army beside the already sent 1.000, with a total monthly payment of 6.000 florins.[42] We do not have sources to clarify if the

40 We do not know exactly how many soldiers did the magistrate of Braşov send for the armies of King John II., but if we count a monthly payment of 2–3 florins for each infantryman, a maximum number of 200 could be realistic, SJAN Braşov, Documents from the Schnell Collection part 1/3/2 no. 165.

41 Florin Nicolae Ardelean: "*Pecunia nervus belli.*" The Saxon University in Transylvania and its contribution to the Military campaign of 1566–1567," in *Politics and Society in the Central and South-Eastern Europe (13th–16th centuries)*, ed. Zoltan Iusztin (Cluj-Napoca: Editura Mega, 2019), 220.

42 The document also describes that the representatives of the Saxons (the counts of Sibiu/Hermannstadt, Mediaş/Mediasch and Bistriţa/Nösen) tried to ask for the reduction of the numbers, but were unsuccessful in the end, SJAN Braşov, Schnell Collection part 1/3/2, no. 173.

additional 2.000 guardsmen were ever prepared by the University, but the irregularly changing numbers are also present on the documents dating from the first half of the seventeenth century. We have a list dating to the beginning of the 1630s with the title of: "...az *Universitasra repartizált gyalogok regestruma*" (the register of infantrymen assigned for the University) numbering a total of 800 infantrymen. The proportions are the following: 57 from Segesvár, 80 from Medgyes(Mediaş/Mediasch), 128 from Beszterce(Bistriţa/Nösen), 19 from Szászsebes(Sebeş/Mühlbach), 59 from Nagysink(Cincu/Großschenk), 46 from Kőhalom(Rupea/Reps), 32 from Újegyház(Nochrich/Neukirsch), 36 from Szerdahely(Miercurea Sibiului/Reussmarkt), 21 from Szászváros(Orăştie/Broos), 163 from Brassó(Braşov/Kronstadt) and 164 from Nagyszeben(Sibiu/Hermannstadt).[43]

During the 1618 military operation of prince Gabriel Bethlen, a total of 80 guardsmen (8 units with 10 soldiers in each) and mercenaries were sent from Cluj to Lippa (Lipova). Each unit had a corporal leading them, with the captain of the city's guardsmen called Gergely Vásárhelyi also having corporal duties in his unit. There was a military drummer and a flag-bearer present in the commander's unit, who's payment were equal to the payment of the corporals (4 florins), which was 1 florin higher than the money paid to the regular infantrymen. The 8 units received a total of 193 florins in the month of May 1618.[44] Sixteen years later a total of 40 guardsmen and mercenaries were sent from Cluj to the armies of the prince, led by Captain István Kőházy. The source gives us interesting details about the morals of the soldiers, as we find out that three infantrymen from the unit of corporal András Beder fled, and two others were punished for not fulfilling their duties (one of the two mercenaries was not paid, and the other person was sent into a mill for compulsory work).[45]

The Real Military Potential of the Town Mercenaries

This last part of the study lands us on insecure territory. As we have presented above, the morals of the mercenaries outside their town was apparently low. In the case of Cluj, we are not aware of any mercenaries who have fallen on the battlefield or were lost due to consequences of war. Speaking of the mercenaries from Sighişoara or Sighişoara Seat, the single person who is described in

43 Although if we add the numbers together, the sum will be 805 and not 800 as it appears on the bottom of the list.

44 SJAN Cluj, The Accounting Books of Cluj 14 b/XVIII 1618, microfilm roll 25–26.

45 SJAN Cluj, The Accounting Books of Cluj 19/XIII 1634, microfilm roll 43, 402–404.

the sources as a casualty of war was Andreas Gassner, who had fallen at Kassa (Košice) before the 1 September 1644.[46]

Before making any conclusions on the real military potential of the town mercenaries, the accountings of gunpowder from Cluj also offer us important details. The gunpowder needed for firing the harquebuses of the mercenaries was supplied by the *perceptor*s of the city, whose duty was to monitor the gunpowder production of the gunpowder mill of Cluj and to supply the powder to all of those who needed it for either military or personal use.[47] The accountings of the gunpowder reveal that mercenaries who left Cluj for the military expeditions of the princes were supplied with very small amounts of gunpowder. For example, the units sent into the army of Gabriel Bethlen in November 1616 received a total of 75 pounds.[48] As a comparison, also in the year of 1616 two of Cluj's delegates sent to the court of the prince in Alba Iulia received a total of 1 pound of gunpowder for their journey.[49] We have to highlight the fact that the pounds used in the early modern period Transylvania differ from current English pounds, with a pound from the seventeenth century Cluj weighing just 0.39 kilograms.[50] Converting the 75 pounds into current measuring units would mean that the mercenaries received a total of 29.25 kilograms of gunpowder for a period of six months, which is a considerably low quantity in the case they had to fight in an open battlefield. All of the gunpowder accountings from Cluj mention such low, or even lower quantities of gunpowder received by the mercenaries from the *perceptor*s when leaving the city for military expeditions, which questions their military potential, and with no casualties recorded during longer periods of war, and with the same names appearing on the accountings of guardsmen and mercenaries for decades, we have to question if they were even used in open battlefields?

---

46 As we find out from the report of mercenary commander Márton Fülöp sent to Stephan Mann, the mayor of Sighişoara, SJAN Braşov, Documents of the magistrate of Sighişoara, A.O.S. 255, attachment no. 1, 1644.

47 Csaba Izsán, "A portörők számadásai Kolozsvár kora újkori számadáskönyveiben," in *Interdiszciplinaritás a Kárpát-medencében. Külhoni magyar doktorandusz hallgatók konferencia-előadásaiból. Condordia Regionum I,* ed. Boda Attila (Budapest, ELTE, Márton Áron Szakkollégium, 2019), 456–60.

48 SJAN Cluj, The Accounting Books of Cluj 14 a/XI 1616, microfilm roll 23, 15.

49 SJAN Cluj, The Accounting Books of Cluj 14 a/XI 1616, microfilm roll 23, 9.

50 István Bogdán, *Magyarországi űr-, térfogat-, súly- és darabmértékek 1874-ig* (Budapest, Akadémiai Kiadó, 1991), 446, 457.

It is also worth mentioning that the monthly payments of the blue guardsmen (who are known to have fought in many battles) during military operations were 3–4 times higher than the payments of the regular guardsmen. The infantrymen from the blue guardsmen units were payed 4 Hungarian florins, the corporals 5, and the captains 20 each month during military operations.[51] The sources from Sighişoara also reveal the fact, that the payment of the wagoners who were responsible for transporting the equipment of the mercenaries was also considerably higher than the payment of the infantrymen. From a dispatch dating from 25 April 1644, written by the commander of mercenaries from Sighişoara, Márton Szőcs, we can find out that the payment of the mercenaries for a month was a total of 162 florins, and the payment of the wagoners was 118 florins.[52] Taking in consideration the fact that we are talking about (we don't know the exact number) 4–6 units of mercenaries and just a few wagoners, either the payment of the wagoners was really high, or the payment of the mercenaries was low, highlighting their low military potential.

Conclusions

As it was highlighted in the introduction, the goal of the study was not to compare the mercenaries of the three towns, but to try to highlight the most interesting and useful details from the different types of sources (the accountings of the mercenaries/guardsmen and the accountings of gunpowder from Cluj, different accountings written by the commanders of the mercenaries and finally the military correspondence of the magistrates of Sighişoara and Braşov). It seems like the clear differentiation of the terms mercenary and guardsmen is not possible in the researched towns after the second half of the sixteenth century, but we need to differentiate the ordinary guardsmen from the elite red and blue *darabont*s of the princes court in Alba Iulia. The ordinary guardsmen were hired by the local authorities for a longer period of time, and were paid monthly in this period. Besides their guarding roles, they were often used as labour force when the situation required it. Their hierarchy included new boys, ordinary infantrymen, corporals and the captain, and usually 20–30 guardsmen stationed on the gate towers of the towns. During times of war the guardsmen were also recruited in the armies of the Principality (which was their second major role), being joined by other mercenaries forming units of 10 soldiers. From Cluj and Sighişoara

51 Sunkó, "Az erdélyi fejedelmek udvari hadai," 102–03.

52 SJAN Braşov, Documents of the magistrate of Sighişoara, A.O.S. 1436, attachment no. 3, 1644.

usually 4–8 units were recruited for the army, this number being often 150 plus guardsmen and mercenaries in the case of Brașov. During those duties, military drummers and flag-bearers also appeared in their units. The primary weapon of the guardsmen was the harquebus, with the equipment and gunpowder being supplied by the gunpowder *perceptors* of the towns. The small quantities of gunpowder supplied to the mercenaries, their low payments during military operations and the absence of war casualties questions their real military potential, but further research is required for us to be able to certainly determine this assumption.

The city of Cluj in Transylvania, detail from *Principauté de Transilvanie divissée en Cinq Nations*.../The Principality of Transylvania divided in Five Nations, Nicolas de Fer, Herman van Loon, 1704, cooper engraving (Institut für donauschwäbische Geschichte und Landeskunde, Tübingen)

Jelena Ilić Mandić

Making the Border and Frontiersmen. Militarisation in *Temeswarer Banat*, 1764–1775

Abstract: This paper presents an overview of the early development of the Banat Military Border, starting with the year 1764. It focuses on the process of militarisation in three areas of the Habsburg province *Temeswarer Banat*, affected by various problems. The area around Pančevo was militarised in 1764, the main consequence of which was the resettlement of the local population and colonisation of veterans (as part of a broader state intervention in terms of spatial organisation). The area around Bela Crkva was militarised in 1764, where the main events were the transformation of the former *Miliz* into frontiersmen, and the later exchange of territory between civil and military jurisdictions. The area between Orşova and Marga was militarised after 1769. It was characterised by resistance to militarisation and emigration, and was affected by the consequences of war and bandit incursions from Wallachia. Finally, the paper shows that the change of administration (shift from civil to military) brought crucial changes to the demographics, economy and spatial history of southern parts of this Habsburg province.

Keywords: Temeswarer Banat, Habsburg Monarchy, Military Border, German Banat Regiment, Wallachian Illyrian Regiment

During the 1760s, the territorial development of the entire Habsburg Military Border was almost completed. This institution was in many ways a unique defence system of the Habsburg Monarchy, in the form of a land strip that stretched from the Adriatic Sea to the Carpathian Mountains. Indeed, it was below and on the Carpathian mountain range, in the territory of the Habsburg province of Transylvania (conquered in the late seventeenth century) and Banat of Temeswar (Timişoara/Temesvár), (conquered in 1716–1718), that the final Border regiments were established in the 1760s.[1] The decision to expand the Border to the eastern part of the Monarchy materialised only towards the end

1 The so-called "old" Military Border was established considerably earlier, from the sixteenth to eighteenth centuries, in the area of contemporary Croatia and Serbia. It encompassed the Karlovac Generalate and Varaždin Generalate, and the Banal, Slavonia and Syrmia Border, which were regulated in the first half of the eighteenth century, Gunther E. Rothenberg, *The Austrian Military Border in Croatia*, 1522–1747 (Urbana: University of Illinois Press, 1960).

of the taxing Seven Years' War – starting from 1761 in Transylvania and 1764 in Banat of Temeswar.[2]

Until 1780, the province Banat of Temeswar (*Temeswarer Banat*) was governed by the central institutions in Vienna – the Aulic Chamber (*Hofkammer*) or related financial institutions, while its administration was consistently carried out by *Landesadministration* in Timişoara.[3] In 1741, the Empress granted the request of the Hungarian Diet and estates to cede *Temeswarer Banat* to the Hungarian Crown i.e. incorporate it in the system of the counties. The central authorities therefore strove to define and regulate the Military Border in Banat before fulfilling this promise. The annexation of *cameral* Banat to Hungary was approved in 1778/79, with its militarised parts left out of this scheme.[4] These were the southern parts of the province, already under the administration of the Aulic War Council (*Hofkriegsrath*) in Vienna. It was there that the Banat Military Border (*Banater Militärgrenze*) was gradually formed after 1764. The creation of a unified Border territory was finalised with the formal establishment of two regiments in 1775/1776: the German-Banat Border Regiment (*Deutsch-Banater Grenz Regiment*) with its seat in Pančevo (Panciova/Pancsova), and the Wallachian-Illyrian Border Regiment (*Wallachisch-Illyrisches Grenz Regiment*) headquartered in Caransebeş (Karánsebes/Karansebesch). It should be pointed out that in the following decades of the eighteenth century, the territories of the two Banat regiments continued to expand, albeit at a slower pace.[5]

We will now present the course of the militarisation and the results achieved in the first decade after the establishment of military administration in southern *Temeswarer Banat*. Over a relatively short period, between 1764 and 1775, groups of settlements were one by one subsumed by the regiments. At the end of that period, the Banat Military Border included c. 140 settlements. The establishment of military administration meant that the inhabitants of these settlements assumed the obligations of frontiersmen by swearing an oath to the Empress

2 Franz Vaniček, *Specialgeschichte der Militärgrenze*, II (Wien: Kaiserl.-Königl. Hof- und Staatsdruck, 1875), 76–111, 181–236; Srećko Mileker, *Istorija Banatske vojničke granice (1764.–1873.)* (Pančevo: Štamparija "Napredak", 1926); Carl Göllner, *Die Siebenbürgische Militärgrenze* (München: Oldenbourg, 1974).

3 Sonja Jordan, *Die kaiserliche Wirtschaftspolitik im Banat im 18. Jahrhundert* (München: Oldenbourg, 1967), 75–76.

4 Johann H. Schwicker, *Geschichte des Temeser Banats* (Pest: Ludwig Aigner, 1872), 424.

5 For more information about the Banat Military Border in the second half of the eighteenth century, see the monograph, Jelena Ilić Mandić, *Banatska vojna krajina (1764–1800)* (Beograd: Istorijski institut, 2020).

and recognising the authority of the *Hofkriegsrat*. As always, frontiersmen had a dual role: on the one hand, they maintained the security in the border area itself, and on the other, they served as potential auxiliary units for the Habsburg line troops on European battlefields. The Military Border in Banat absorbed territories from three directions at once: Kanjiža (Canija/Kanizsa) – Perlez (Perlas/Perlasz) on the rivers Tisza and (Lower) Timiş from 1753 to 1764; Pančevo – Perlez – Nova Palanka (Bácspalánka) on the Danube starting from 1764; and Jupalnic – Mehadia (Mehádia) – Caransebeş – Marga on the rivers Cerna and (Upper) Timiş after 1769.[6]

In those three directions, three temporary territorial and administrative military formations – regiments – were established in southern *Temeswarer Banat*. At the beginning, they were named as single border areas: the Illyrian Military Border, the German Military Border and the Wallachian Military Border. Their names, territories and scope of administration changed in the mid-1770s, as mentioned above. The course and circumstances of the militarisation differed from one area to the next. In some areas, the military administration encountered specific tasks and difficulties, depending on the local conditions. We will discuss this below.

Illyrische Militärgrenze: The Heritage of Old Military Structures and Regulation

The first Military Border area established as a regulated regiment in southern *Temeswarer Banat* was the Illyrian Border Regiment (*Illyirsche Grenz Regiment*). Its establishment in 1764 was the result of dealing with a key strategic issue – securing the Habsburg border on the Danube, between Pančevo and Orşova. Before the regulation of the Banat Military Border started, military stations had been maintained along the Danube, in order to supervise the Ottoman and Habsburg banks. Prior to 1752, these stations had been manned by members of *National Miliz*, and from 1753 – by members of *Land Miliz*. Though they were not among the regulated frontier troops organised into regiments, these units were essentially modelled after lower-level tactical units – companies.[7]

However, it was soon recognised that the Land Militia was not suitable for manning the Danube stations. Early plans to change the status of the militia

6 Ilić Mandić, *Banatska vojna krajina*.

7 Mileker, *Istorija Banatske vojničke granice*, 15–21; Ilić Mandić, *Banatska vojna krajina*, 33–40.

to that of regular frontiersmen were developed for both financial and strategic reasons. First of all, the main motive for the development of the Military Border was financial: it entailed the principle of *autarky*, reflected in the fact that frontiersmen were a self-sufficient military force living in their own village households and granted estates. For this reason, the frontiersmen were given an advantage over the line troops, which were stationed in garrisons at the government's expense.[8] Further, it was widely known that the main fortress in Banat – Timişoara (*Haupt-und Graniz-Vestung Temeswar*) – was the only "militarily sustainable" place in Banat. This meant that regulation was supposed to create more military strongholds; although the provisions of the Belgrade Peace Treaty of 1739 prescribed they had to be unfortified.

Finally, the most important factor was the fact that the settlements of the Land Militia were too distant from the stations that had to be manned on the Danube – the true border of the Monarchy. These settlements were not only located far on the left bank of the Tisza, but their territories were also not connected. A total of eight Land Militia companies were grouped into the so-called Upper (*Oberen*) and Lower (*Unteren*) Companies based on their position and the distance between them. The Upper Companies absorbed 15 settlements from the Csanád (Cenad) and Bečkerek (Becicherecu) Districts in western Banat, while the Lower Companies included 6 settlements from the Nova Palanka District in southern Banat.[9]

In November 1763, Empress Maria Theresa approved a proposal by the *Hofkriegsrat* to classify the Banat Land Militia as regular frontiersmen "in service". This abolished the institution of the Land Militia, though only formally. Essentially, the status of its members was changed from militia to frontiersmen when they were made fully subject to the *Hofkriegsrat* on 1 May 1764. The transfer of settlements and manpower of the *Land Miliz* to the newly created Illyrian Border Regiment was the inception of the regulated Military Border in Banat. The regulation itself required the proclamation of the "act of transfer [of

8 Rothenberg, *The Austrian Military Border in Croatia*, 115–116. Similarly, in the plan for the regulation of the Transylvanian Military Border of 1761, General Buccow assessed that financing seven Transylvanian regiments from border taxes would cost 8.5 times less than maintaining the same number of standing army units, Göllner, *Die Siebenbürgische Militärgrenze*, 24; Vlad Popovici, "Establishment of the Austrian Military Border in Transylvania and Its Short- and Medium-term Effects," *Povjesni prilozi* 54 (2018): 296.

9 Mileker, *Istorija Banatske vojničke granice*, 21–28; Ilić Mandić, *Banatska vojna krajina*, 41–46.

jurisdiction]" (*Übergaab-Actus*) from cameral to military authorities, by its being read throughout the settlements. It was noted that "no discontent was observed among the military communities". Moreover, the Land Militia embraced this transfer as a clear confirmation of their frontiersman status, which they had continuously called upon since the times of their resettlement from the "old borders on the Tisza and Moriš". Frontiersman status was regarded as privileged, unlike the status of "villagers" (*paori*). In April 1764, the order was given to organise the Illyrian Military Border according to the "Slavonian border system". The former Land Militia was then for the first time conscripted among the "regular" frontiersmen (*Regulirt-Bannat-Illyrisches Gränitz-Corps*).[10]

Apart from the settlements of Upper and Lower Companies and inclusion of some *predios* or *pustare* (uninhabited areas, ceded to the frontiersmen in 1768), no territorial changes were made to the Illyrian Military Border until 1770. It appears that the territorial consolidation of the Military Border in Banat as a single unified area began only then, with the aim of making an "uninterrupted belt" (*ohnunterbrochenen Granizkette*) from Perlez and Pančevo on the Timiş to Orşova on the Danube. The first border settlements not belonging to the Upper and Lower Companies annexed were four settlements in 1770, followed by another 21 settlements in 1773. These were located on the river (Lower) Timiş, along the Deliblato Sands, and on the rivers Caraş, Nera and Danube (Upper Clisura). In this way, the unified territorial and administrative area of the Illyrian Border Regiment was formed in 1773/1774, from the Lower Timiş to the Danube Clisura. It contained a total of 56 settlements on the eve of the 1775 reorganisation.[11]

In parallel to the expansion of the Illyrian Military Border, the conditions were met to demilitarise the areas too distant from the Danube. Consequently, the final stage of territorial organisation was marked by the restoration of civilian status, i.e. cameral jurisdiction in the settlements of the former Land Militia – Lower Companies (1771) and Upper Companies (1773). Most settlements of the Lower Companies permanently lost the frontier status in 1771, being on the left bank of the Nera, which became the boundary between the Military Border and the cameral territory in Banat. Just two years later, 11 out of 15 settlements of the Upper Companies were demilitarised as well. The reason was the same, since

10 Vaniček, *Specialgeschichte der Militärgrenze*, II, 182–86; Ilić Mandić, *Banatska vojna krajina*, 30, 45 47. The *System* meant the "Verfassung oder Organisation", Vaniček, *Specialgeschichte der Militärgrenze*, III, 3, note 1.

11 Ilić Mandić, *Banatska vojna krajina*, 47–50.

they were located even farther north, on the Tisza. In both cases, the frontier inhabitants were given the opportunity to declare whether they wanted to remain in those settlements as civilians or to move to newly militarised neighbouring settlements. Despite the frontier tradition they cherished during the preceding decade, most frontiersmen of the Upper Companies opted to remain on their land as civilians, undoubtedly out of a desire to retain their large estates. Around 700 families decided to keep their frontier status and were resettled to the nearby border territory. After demilitarising the Upper Companies, the headquarters of the Illyrian Military Border was moved from Velika Kikinda (Chichinda Mare) near the Tisza to Bela Crkva (Biserica Albă) on the Nera.[12]

The Illyrian Military Border was a temporary territorial and administrative military formation in Banat. Before its abolition, it included 56 settlements. Their fate was decided in 1775 when they were allocated to the newly formed units – the German Banat Regiment and Wallachian Illyrian Regiment. The former received 16 and the latter 40 settlements of what used to be the Illyrian Military Border, and the headquarters in Bela Crkva was disestablished.[13] To preserve the urban potential of Bela Crkva, the settlement was given the "privileged" status of a city municipality – the first *Militärcommunität* in the Banat Military Border. This status was only held by a few settlements in the territory of the Slavonian and Croatian Military Border, and also by Pančevo from 1794.[14]

Deutsch Militärgrenze: The Colonisation of Veterans and Planned Construction of Settlements

As the Illyrian Military Border was being regulated, in 1764 the process of militarisation began in south-western Banat of Temeswar, in its Pančevo District (*Panczowa District*). The main characteristic of the militarisation there was the planned settlement of veteran colonists in the area around Pančevo, and the planned construction and regulation of settlements driven both by the colonists' needs and cadastral reform. The idea that German colonists would protect the border was new, unlike the distrust of "Wallachen-schizmatici" as frontiersmen, which was commonplace. One of the arguments used by *Hofkammer* officials to support the claim that the first line of defence of Banat should be the task of the line army rather than local frontiersmen was the criticism that the local

12 Ilić Mandić, *Banatska vojna krajina*, 45–46, 50.
13 Ilić Mandić, *Banatska vojna krajina*, 50–51.
14 Vaniček, *Specialgeschichte der Militärgrenze*, II, 295–98.

population retained their "liberties and [poor] habits from Turkish times".[15] The initial idea that veterans should populate the cameral territories across the Habsburg Monarchy emerged toward the end of the Seven Years' War, which was no coincidence.[16]

Besides, the plans to colonise the regimental territory were just part of the plans for colonisation throughout Hungary, Transylvania and Banat of Temeswar, which was incited by the invitation the Empress made in 1763.[17] We will not be dealing with the complicated dispute that immediately ensued in Banat between advocates for the preservation of *predios* and those in favour of the colonisation, not least of all because it did not directly concern the Military Border territory.[18] Unlike the territory of the civil Banat of Temeswar, the militarised part was colonised separately and smoothly. First, on 31 January 1764, it was decided that the recruitment of candidates for settlement would be carried out at veteran homes (*Invalidenhäuser*) in Vienna, Pest, Prague and Pettau (Ptuj), and among the veterans and capitulants in line regiments. Not long after, on 4 March

15 Ilić Mandić, *Banatska vojna krajina*, 39; The situation was similar in the Transylvanian Military Border, so General Buccow's draft plan for the regulation of regiments of 1761 foresaw that frontiersmen should mainly be Romanian Greek Catholics "because Orthodox Christians were too close to the population on the other side of the mountain", Popovici, "Establishment of the Austrian Military Border in Transylvania," 298.

16 For more information about the establishment of the German Banat Regiment and colonisation of veterans, see, Vaniček, *Specialgeschichte der Militärgrenze*, II, 198–214, 220; Erik Roth, "„...*und überhaupt durch diesen Bau, Ordnung einzuführen*". Planung der Lebensund Siedlungsform in der südwestlichen Banater Militärgrenze," *Danubiana Carpathica* 3/4 (50/51), (2009/2010): 45–76; Jelena Ilić Mandić, "Plansko naseljavanje u Vojnoj krajini: kolonisti–veterani u Nemačko-banatskoj regimenti (1764–1788)," in *Država i politike upravljanja (18.–20. vek)*, ed. Petar V. Krestić (Beograd: Istorijski institut, 2017), 37–56; Ilić Mandić, *Banatska vojna krajina*, 65–68, 109–22.

17 In late February 1763, Empress Maria Theresa issued the *Kolonisationspatent*, by which veterans and redundant soldiers who had been released from service after the Seven Years' War were invited to settle the *Erblande*, Schwicker, *Geschichte des Temeser Banats*, 369; Erik Roth, *Die planmäsigangelegten Siedlungen im Deutsch-Banater Militärgrenzbezirk 1765–1821* (München: Oldenbourg, 1988), 38–39.

18 At first, these plans encountered difficulties, since the *Landesadministration* headed by Count Perlas opposed the use of *predios* for the establishment of new settlements, as this would jeopardise the fund of highly profitable land for grazing which was leased to *Predio Societa* and its livestock merchants. However, in the end the supporters of colonisation prevailed, Ernst Schimscha, *Technik und Methoden der Theresianischen Besiedlung des Banats* (Baden bei Wien: Rhor 1939), 57–58, 156–66; Jordan, *Die kaiserliche Wirtschaftspolitik im Banat*, 88–98.

1764 the *Hofkriegsrat* announced the proposal to establish veteran companies that would settle the border districts in *Temeswarer Banat*. The territories foreseen for their settlement were the Pančevo, Nova Palanka and Orşova Districts.[19] However, it turned out that the initial plans for the settlement of veterans (*Halb-Invaliden*) in southern *Temeswarer Banat* were too ambitious and were only partially realised. This is best attested by the fact that the colonisation of veterans in the Banat Military Border was ultimately limited to just 12 settlements in the immediate vicinity of Pančevo.[20]

The direct result of the veterans' colonisation was the creation of the regiment, which was called *Ansiedlungsregiment* from 1764 and *Deutsch Grenzregiment* from 1770. Though the colonists were called *Deutsche*, they were not ethnically homogeneous. Nearly half of the immigrants had other origins (Slavs, Hungarians). Still, they all shared at least two common traits – being Roman Catholic and coming from veteran homes. It should also be pointed out that the colonisation of veterans from veteran homes (rather than civilians from overcrowded villages and towns in *Erbländer*) in southern Banat, in the 1760s and 1770s, was an unprecedented endeavour. This model of recruitment of the frontier population was not used in any other regiment in the entire Military Border. Either way, the territorial expansion of the regiment soon followed. It annexed a number of nearby native settlements, which were not colonised by foreigners. According to the 1781 Census, the German Banat Regiment contained a total of 32 settlements with 45.733 inhabitants. Of those, only 12 were populated by colonists – 7.233 of them, of both genders and all age groups.[21]

The initial plan was for colonists to use existing houses and settlements, rather than build new ones. The idea of population exchange, i.e. resettling native civilians and settling colonists who would take on the obligations of frontiersmen, was not entirely new and was already applied in the organisation of

---

19 Schwicker, *Geschichte des Temeser Banats*, 370; Vaniček, *Specialgeschichte der Militärgrenze*, II, 199.

20 It should be underlined that data on the colonisation of veterans in the Pančevo District are not stated anywhere in the discussion of the second Theresian colonisation. The data in the literature pertain only to the civil territory of Banat, where around 25.000 people, mostly Germans, moved between 1763 and 1780, Schwicker, *Geschichte des Temeser Banats*, 397–402.

21 Mileker, *Istorija Banatske vojničke granice*, 32; Ilić Mandić, "Plansko naseljavanje u Vojnoj krajini," 49–50, 119. Incidentally, the colonists made up the majority in only four of the 12 settlements. The total number of settlements in the German Banat Regiment rose to 43 by 1793.

the Transylvanian Military Border.[22] Those interested in frontiersman status could keep their homes, while the people desiring to remain civilians – cameral subjects (*Unterthanen*) – would give theirs to the colonists. As early as 1764, the Serbian inhabitants (*Raitzen*) present in 10 settlements of the Pančevo District were surveyed for their choice of status – civilian or frontiersman (*Cameralisten/Militaristen*). To receive the population which was resettled due to having declined frontier obligations, in 1765/66 the cameral authorities founded new settlements: Novo Selo (Satu Nou), Bavanište (Bavanişte) and Dolovo (Doloave). These three settlements were the first planned settlements in southern Banat. However, they were themselves absorbed by the German Regiment, which had grown in the meantime. The territory of the regiment gradually expanded at the expense of the cameral settlements, until the entire Pančevo District came under military administration in 1775.[23]

In 1770 the territorial unification of the border as an "uninterrupted belt" became a priority. Consequently, *predios* (previously excluded from cameral jurisdiction) were also gradually militarised, as was a group of settlements on the (Lower) Timiş and the edges of the Deliblato Sands, which were populated by natives – mostly Serbs and, to a lesser extent, Romanians. Military administration soon also incorporated the group of settlements whose agricultural area was regulated and increased owing to cameral investments in the construction of the canal built for draining the Ilandža and Alibunar swamps along the Brzava River (*Bersavaer-Canal*, based on the project by the engineer *Fremaut*, 1767–1769).[24] This group of 16 Serbian and Romanian settlements between Perlez and Dubovac was first included in the territory of the Illyrian Military Border in 1773. Once the Illyrian Military Border was abolished, in 1776 the settlements were for the first time conscripted as part of the newly formed German Banat Border Regiment.[25]

As the German Regiment expanded to incorporate the entire Pančevo District, the idea of replacing the native populace with colonist frontiersmen was abandoned. The division of the inhabitants into taxpayer Serbs (*Illyren*) and frontiersmen colonists (*Deutsche Militare*) became unnecessary, given that frontier obligations were imposed on all households in the regiment.[26] In this way,

---

22 Göllner, *Die Siebenbürgische Militärgrenze*, 51–53.

23 Mileker, *Istorija Banatske vojničke granice*, 32; Roth, *Die planmäsigangelegten Siedlungen*, 47–49; Ilić Mandić, *Banatska vojna krajina*, 66–67.

24 Schwiker, *Geschichte des Temeser Banats*, 380–81; Ilić Mandić, *Banatska vojna krajina*, 190–92.

25 Ilić Mandić, *Banatska vojna krajina*, 66–67.

26 Ilić Mandić, *Banatska vojna krajina*, 66.

another significant characteristic of the early development of the German Border gained importance – the planned construction and regulation of settlements. Even though this was initiated by a decree which prescribed that, along with their houses, every colonised family would also get a yard, accompanying arable land, livestock and tools,[27] the tasks related to settlement regulation were soon transferred to the native population as well.

On the ground, military administration was faced with the poor quality of the existing houses, and the fact that the settlements were not regulated (*reguliert*). Without exception, every settlement required the construction of new houses, together with urban cores and a street network based on urban plans. Thus, besides building new quarters for colonists, old residential quarters were regulated, dividing settlements into sections "by language and faith". Schematised plans prepared from 1770 to 1776 envisaged Serbian parts of settlements in addition to the German ones.[28] Since the colonists settled in villages with native populations, they could be assigned a proportionately smaller area of arable land.[29] This and the fact that colonist households were made up of single families (on average 2–4 members), as opposed to native households which had more members (on average 4–6, or more), makes it clear that native households ensured the demographic and economic stability of frontier order.[30]

Regulation also entailed that agricultural areas in settlements (*Hottars*) should be standardised, in addition to urban cores. In practice, this meant the implementation of the primary elements of cadastral reform (*Conscription, Mappirung, Individualvertheilung des Gründe* and made of *Grundbücher*).[31] The

27 The allocation of land and goods to colonists in civilian territory was prescribed in *Impopulations-Haupt-Instruction* in 1769. Its provisions were also observed in military territory, though the conditions in terms of allocated land were less favourable, Schwiker, *Geschichte des Temeser Banats*, 393–94; Schimscha, *Tehnik und Methoden der Theresianischen Besiedlung*, 181–83, 184–98.

28 Roth, "*„…und überhaupt durch diesen Bau, Ordnung einzuführen*", 56–58.

29 Unlike a peasant land unit (*Session*), prescribed to equal 36 acres (24 acres of arable land, 6 acres of meadows, 6 acres of pastures), a colonist estate in the German Border was smaller. For example, in Kovin it measured 25 acres (15 acres of arable land and 10 acres of meadows), and in Jabuka – 20 acres (10 acres of arable land and 10 acres of meadows), Ilić Mandić, *Banatska vojna krajina*, 273–75.

30 Ilić Mandić, *Banatska vojna krajina*, 116–17, 121–22, 143.

31 The first results of cadastral and tax reform were seen in *Temeswarer Banat* around 1770, where the first *Landesmappierung* was performed, and the first cadastral tax books were made (*Steuerkataster*) for the purpose of controlling annual tax revenues of the state collected from owners of arable land, Schwiker, *Geschichte des Temeswer*

German Banat Regiment was the leader in terms of cadastral reform in the entire Military Border. By 1782, its commander, Major General Geneyn established a model that was to be applied in other areas of the Military Border in the years that followed, in the form of a *Cantonal System*.[32]

Wallachische Militärgrenze: Militarisation in Spite of Resistance, Emigration and War

Although the official creation of the Banat Military Border began in 1764 with the establishment of Illyrian and German Border Regiments, the intense militarisation in Banat of Temeswar started in 1769/1770, with the focus on the settlements on the Danube and in the direction of the Principality of Wallachia. In 1766 it was decided that the area "from Orşova to Transylvania, towards Wallachia" should be regulated as a Military Border. The implementation of the plan started three years later. The final decision made by Empress Maria Theresa to include the Wallachian villages in the border area was signed on 17 March 1769. That June saw the first (preliminary) census of 33 villages designated for militarisation in the territory of Caransebeş and Orşova Districts, in the strip of land including the settlements Jupalnic, Mehadia, Caransebeş and Marga.[33]

However, the inhabitants of these villages soon put up resistance to military administration, expressing their unwillingness to assume frontiersman status. But in the case of the Wallachian Military Border, military authorities were not inclined to resettle the population, while militarisation was postponed until the conditions conducive to changing the will of the inhabitants were met. We assume that the high degree of autonomy of Wallachian villages up until then resulted from the loose control of district officials, and from its geographic location. Both factors were crucial in allowing those communities to fiercely resist militarisation until mid-1772.[34]

Banats, 392; Benjamin Landais, "Land-Plot Mapping and the Construction of an Ethnic Patchwork in the Banat (1773–1848)," *Catastrum*, 6, 4 (2019): 3–16.

32 Vaniček, *Specialgeschichte der Militärgrenze*, III, 4–5.

33 Vaniček, *Specialgeschichte der Militärgrenze*, II, 195–98; Ilić Mandić, *Banatska vojna krajina*, 60.

34 The Transylvanian population strongly resisted militarisation, which is why two Székely and two Romanian regiments were formed in the period 1762–1764/1766. The resistance was mostly caused by pressures on Romanians to accept Greek Catholicism and the socio-economic changes in the status of Székelys, as well as by other factors, Popovici, "Establishment of the Austrian Military Border in Transylvania," 298–99, 300.

Militarised settlements in eastern Banat were located along the rivers Cerna (and its tributary the Bela Reka) and Upper Timiş (and its tributaries the Feneş, Sebeş and Bistra). The impassable wooded mountaintops made a natural border between Banat and Wallachia, while the settlements were dispersed along the narrow river valleys. The route leading from Orşova through Mehadia to Caransebeş was also the only road, which was traversed by passengers and caravans, as well as by brigands. It was this road that the Ottoman troops took on the way to Lugoj and Timişoara in all Austrian-Ottoman wars in the eighteenth century. The advantage of the defending army in this terrain was in fact that the gorge could be protected by a small force, while the benefit for the Ottomans was the point of entry into the Cerna – Timiş valley from the vassal Principality of Wallachia. The construction of military barracks in Caransebeş in mid-eighteenth century was the first step towards reinforcing military positions in that part of the Border, particularly after the Ottoman fort in Mehadia was torn down in accordance with the 1739 Belgrade Treaty. Before and during the process of establishing the Military Border towards the Principality of Wallachia in the 1770s, the security there was entrusted to line troops and *Playaschen*, a Wallachian people's militia, which was active both in Transylvania and the mountainous parts of Banat.[35]

The regulation of the Wallachian Military Border from Jupalnic to Marga and the acquisition of villages from the jurisdiction of *Landesadministration* was the task of *Obristlieutenant Pavle Dimić von Papilla*, whose headquarters were situated in Caransebeş. In military terms, 33 (soon 35) settlements exempt from Caransebeş and Orşova Districts were to provide enough frontiersmen for a battalion (*Wallachische Battalion*).[36] However, the militarisation of the Wallachian Military Border was no easy feat, lasting up until mid-1772. A disruptive factor was the turmoil caused by the Russo-Ottoman War (1768–1774), which brought Russian (and Wallachian volunteer) troops to the neighbouring Wallachia, and Ottoman troops to the nearby Danube area. In these circumstances, some Wallachian communities were considered rebellious due to "a tendency to emigrate to Wallachia in large numbers". Some would join the Russian military or bandits, but most migrants from Banat emigrated as entire families. We are not aware of their fate in Wallachia under Russian occupation, and it is confirmed that a number of them did come back to Banat. From May 1771 to July

35 Ilić Mandić, *Banatska vojna krajina*, 59–60.
36 Ilić Mandić, *Banatska vojna krajina*, 61.

1772, a total of 601 families emigrated to Wallachia from villages in the Banat Wallachian Border.[37]

The main reason for the prolonged militarisation in this part of the Border was the resistance offered by the local Wallachian population to military obligations and military administration. It is indisputable that the local populace was loath to take part in far-off wars, and moreover, it appears they were afraid they might have to change their religion due to pressures by the military administration. This was an important factor, even though it was deliberately ignored by the authorities bent on conducting the militarisation. However, it is a fact that in 1762 in Transylvania, General Buccow encountered resistance to taking the oath precisely for this reason.[38] The sentiment in mountainous Banat was practically identical. During the first declaration of local leaders, *knezovi*, regarding the future status of their villages (civil or frontier), in May 1770 in Caransebeş, officials noted that the majority of people were reluctant to take on the frontier obligations, being afraid of "dying or losing their faith on the march to the battlefield". Though the fear of "losing faith" was not justified in Banat, it was probably a reflection of the situation in Transylvania, where pressure in the form of imposing a religious union (*griechisch-unierten ritus*) was part of the state agenda. Most of *knezovi* formulated their decision as: *Wollen in das Camerali überziehen, und den Militair Stand nicht annehmen*. Consequently, it may be concluded that the local population was hesitant to substitute its "fluid" status in the borderlands with frontier obligations and swap the loose control of civilian district officials for the firm supervision of military officers.[39]

The census of people and property took longer than planned and was only concluded in mid-1772. The Wallachian Military Border then consisted of 35 settlements with 2.823 households, divided into four companies. The 20 settlements of the former Caransebeş District formed two companies, headquartered in Ilova and Ohaba Bistra, and the 15 settlements of the Orşova District made up another two companies, headquartered in Globurău and Mehadia. The strengthening of the Mehadia Company took precedence since a

37 For more information about the resistance to militarisation in the form of mass emigration and desertion, and the impact of war and outlaws in the period 1769–1772, see J. Ilić Mandić, "Forging the Wallachian Military Border1769–1772," *Banatica* 31/2 (2021): 251–73 .

38 Sabine Jesner, "Privileges and duties. Reflections on the circumstances of life of the Năsăud border regiment during the 18th century," *Astra Salvensis* III, no. 5 (2015): 20–30.

39 Ilić Mandić, "Forging the Wallachian Military Border," : 267–70.

road connecting the entire area passed through the town. It was also home to a few German and Wallachian craftsmen and Greek merchants, who paid a fee to the Border Treasury instead of serving in the military. Due to the unrest caused by the militarisation and the vicinity of a foreign army, some line troops were also located in the area. The evacuation of line troops and disbandment of the *Playaschen* took place only after the Russo-Ottoman War was formally ended in 1774. The last list of salaries paid to the *Playaschen* dates back to 1774, and their service was formally terminated by July 1775, when the watchtowers from Marga to Mehadia were taken over by frontiersmen.[40] According to Vaniček, the entire Wallachian Border contained 50 cordon watchtowers, manning up to 244 guardsmen. The first line of defence numbered 1.034 frontiersmen, while the total number of recruits was three times that: 2.383 *Dienst-taugliche* and 756 *Halb-Invalide*.[41]

To link the Wallachian Military Border to the Illyrian Military Border, both of them had to be expanded, which occurred in 1773. As it was already mentioned, that year the Illyrian Border subsumed around 20 more settlements in the area of Deliblato Sands, on the Nera and in the Upper Klisura on the Danube. The jurisdiction of the Wallachian Military Border in the vicinity of those areas was established in 1773, by its expansion to the villages in the areas Almăj, Craina and (Lower) Clisura. In August 1774 another five villages were taken over from the Caransebeş District, finally completing the Wallachian Military Border. Given the different time of militarisation, a distinction was made between the *Old* Wallachian Military Border with 35 settlements from Jupalnic to Marga and the "new" one, containing 31 recently militarised settlements in the areas Almăj, Craina and (Lower) Clisura.

In 1775 they were joined by another 40 settlements from the defunct Illyrian Military Border, creating the cumbersome formation of the Wallachian-Illyrian Border Regiment, with its 110 settlements, headquartered in Caransebeş. Regardless of the regulation, which was successfully completed in eastern Banat Military Border, some economic and social idiosyncrasies, such as *transhumance*, made the population of those areas more prone to migration than elsewhere.[42]

40 Ilić Mandić, *Banatska vojna krajina*, 62–64.

41 Vaniček, *Specialgeschichte der Militärgrenze*, II, 198.

42 F. Vaniček, *Specialgeschichte der Militärgrenze*, II, 221–226; J. Ilić Mandić, *Banatska vojna krajina*, 63.

Table: Territorial development of the Military Border in *Temeswarer Banat* 1764–1775.[43]

Military Border	Area	Year of militarisation	Company	Settlements
Land Militia (1753–1764) / Illyrian Military Border (1764–1775)		1753/1764	Botoš	Botoš, Marino Selo (Tomaševac), Sige (Perlez)
		1753/1764	Vranjevo	Vranjevo (Novi Bečej), Karlovo (Novi Bečej), Kumane
		1753/1764	Melenci	Melenci, Taraš
	"Upper" Companies	1753/1764	Mokrin	Mokrin, Jozefovo (Novo Miloševo), Krstur
		1753/1764	Idvor	Idvor, Leopoldovo (Čenta)
		1753/1764	Velika Kikinda	Velika Kikinda, Mala Kikinda (Bašaid)
		1753/1764	Potoc	Potoc, Makovişte, Petrilova
	"Lower" Companies	1753/1764	Okruglica	Okruglica, Sokolovac (Socol), Langenfeld (Lugovet, Câmpia)
		1770	Lescoviţa	Gaj, Dubovac, Zlatiţa, Kusić, Rebenberg (Kaluđerovo), Lescoviţa

43 Table taken from: J. Ilić Mandić, *Banatska vojna krajina*, 69–71. (*) settlement flooded; (**) settlement disappeared.

Military Border	Area	Year of militarisation	Company	Settlements
	Around Nova Palanka	1773–1775	*Uj* Palanka	Malo Kakovo (Nikolinci), Izbište, Zagajica, Uljma, Deliblato, Kajtasovo, Grebenac, Omor, Dupljaja, Jasenovo, Lagerdorf (Straža), Orešac, Parta, Naidăş, *Uj* Palanka, Vračev Gaj, Crvena Crkva, Kruščica, Bela Crkva
	Upper Klisura	1773–1775	Militarily organised after 1775	Divici, Belobreşca, Şuşca, Radimna, *Ratzische* Pojejena (de Sus), *Wallachische* Pojejena (de Jos), Măceşti, Moldova (Veche), Sicheviţa, *Gornia* Liubcova (de Sus), *Donia* Liubcova (de Jos), Berzasca
	Deliblato Plateau	1773–1775		Alibunar, Sent Mihalj, Seleuš, Ilandža, Dobrica, Margitica, Jarkovac, Marinovo, Tomaševac, Uzdin, Orlovat, Farkaždin, Perlez
		1769–1772	Mehadia	Mehadia, Pecinişca, Bârza, Topleţ, Coramnic, Tufari, New and Old Jupalnic

Military Border	Area	Year of militarisation	Company	Settlements
Wallachian Military Border (1769–1775)	"Old" Wallachian Border	1769–1772	Globurău	Cornereva, Bogâltin, Globurău, Plugova, Bolvaşniţa, Domaşnea, Cănicea
		1769–1772	Ilova	Ilova, Sadova, Armeniş, Rusca, Feneş, Ruieni, Crâjma
		1769–1772	Ohaba Bistra	Var, Ohaba Bistra, Valeamare, Mal, Marga, Măru, Dalci, Turnul, Zerveşti, Borlova, Bolvaşniţa, Cicleni, Vârciorova
	Lower Clisura	1773	Militarily organised after 1775	Sviniţa, Tişoviţa*, Plavişeviţa*, Ogradena*, Dubova, Eşelniţa, Criviţa**
	Craina	1773		Iablaniţa, Petnic, Lăpuşnicel, Cruşovăţ, Globu Craiovei, Cuptoare, Pârvova, Mehadica, Verendin, Luncaviţa, Cornea
	Almăj	1773		Borlovenii (Vechi), Pătaş, Prilipeţ, Bozovici, Lăpuşnicu (Mare), Moceriş, Dalboşeţ, Şopotu (Vechi), Gârbovăţ, Bănia, Rudăria (Eftimie Murgu), Prigor, Putna
	District of Caransebeş	1774		Teregova, Slatina, Vălişoara, Cârpa (Valea Timişului), Slagna

Ansiedlungs/ German Military Border (1764–1775)	District of Pančevo	1764	Sefkerin, Jabuka, Srpsko Pančevo, Nemačko Pančevo
		1768	Starčevo, Omoljica, Brestovac, Pločica, Kovin, Opovo
		1772	Ostrovo, Sakule
		1773	Bavanište, Novo Selo, Dolovo, Crepaja
	Area from Perlez to Alibunar	1775	Alibunar, Sent Mihalj, Seleuš, Ilandža, Dobrica, Margitica, Jarkovac, Marinovo, Tomaševac, Uzdin, Orlovat, Farkaždin, Leopoldovo (Čenta), Perlez, Sige, Idvor

Epilogue

Unlike the Transylvanian Military Border, which was never successfully regulated in territorial and administrative terms, the Banat Military Border was founded and regulated much more easily. First of all, its establishment should be seen in the context of the intent to complete and round off the Military Border belt, secure the southeast border of the Monarchy with the Ottoman Empire, and prevent potential illegal cross-border activities. In contrast to the Transylvanian feudal system, *Landesadministration* had for decades already successfully governed *Temeswarer Banat* on behalf of central state institutions. Thus, the aim of establishing military administration was not to ensure efficient state control or suppress the aspirations of local political entities.[44] Regardless, militarisation in the entire area neighbouring the Ottoman Empire must also be seen as a reflection of political and centralist objectives, rather than merely a result of military

44 Meanwhile, the military administration came into conflict with various political and social, religious and ethnic groups in Transylvania. The resistance of the local nobility and population to the militarisation lasted from 1762 to 1766, and stable structures of military administration were solidified only after two decades of experimenting. Vienna saw the establishment of the Military Border in Transylvania, among other things, as an opportunity to relax social relations, in particular against the "presumptions of the nobility", Göllner, *Die Siebenbürgische Militärgrenze*, 9–33, 34–35; Popovici, "Establishment of the Austrian Military Border in Transylvania," 298–99, 300.

and security objectives. The utilisation of the Military Border for internal policy needs is attested by the fact that, as time passed, the main function of that institution was reduced to the maintenance of *Cordon Sanitaire* and combat against the illegal movement of persons and goods.[45]

Although the Banat Military Border was for the most part delimited by rivers: the (Lower) Timiş - Danube - Cerna - (Upper) Timiş, the organisation of its defence was no easier for it. On the one hand, the Danube was far too wide and expansive, and its numerous distributaries, swamps and islands made proper observation impossible, despite the numerous watchtowers, which left crossing points for outlaws and emigrants. Precisely for this reason, as early as mid-eighteenth century, Banat was seen as the "weak spot" of the Habsburg border in terms of security. On the other hand, the border with Wallachia was practically open, seeing as the bordering river Cerna and its tributaries were not a considerable obstacle either, while the wooded areas in the surroundings served as a refuge for bandits and a crossing point for people migrating from and to Wallachia. Another significant drawback in terms of oversight of the Danube and the Wallachian border was the fact that, between 1739 and 1791, the confluence of the Cerna was held by the Ottomans rather than the Habsburgs. The settlement Old Orşova and island New Orşova (Ada Kale in Turkish), along with the confluence of the Cerna and Danube were Ottoman lands, and the Habsburg border started at the settlement Jupalnic, where the quarantine area was located (*Vor-Contumaz*).[46]

In the early 1780s, a new reorganisation of the entire Military Border was considered and, as a result, in 1786 the *Cantonal System* was introduced. By that time, the Banat Military Border was, together with the Slavonian-Syrmian Military Border, among the best organised segments of the entire border system.[47] This was due to the considerable accumulated experience in military and administrative affairs, but probably also to the geographic features of the terrain along the Sava and Danube rivers. The settlements along the river plains were rich in arable land and had sufficient resources for animal husbandry – pastures (in Banat) and forests (in Slavonia). This made it possible to implement the cadastral reform, at least partially, as early as around 1770. Such reform was

45 Göllner, *Die Siebenbürgische Militärgrenze*, 20–21; Xenia Havadi, "Die Österreichische Militärgrenze: Staatliche Kontrolle der Grenze im Absolutischen Zeitalter," *Geographia Napocensis* III, no. 2 (2009): 69–82.

46 Ilić Mandić, *Banatska vojna krajina*, 60.

47 Vaniček, *Specialgeschichte der Militärgrenze*, III, 2–6.

considered a precondition for improving the economic position of frontiersmen. In addition, settlements were successfully regulated in accordance with the plans for establishing nucleated settlements furbished with suitable infrastructure for both administrative and military purposes.[48] Reform measures in terms of *mercantilism* and *cameralism* policies, the main aim of which was *centralisation* in all aspects of state administration, had for decades already been applied *experimentally* in Banat of Temeswar. They paved the way for far-reaching *modernisation* processes and enabled the overall trend of development of Banat into the nineteenth century, primarily in the form of state efforts to populate and utilise land as best as possible by suppressing animal husbandry for the benefit of agriculture.[49]

Finally, we should mention another interesting fact regarding the establishment of the Military Border in Banat of Temeswar. Like in the Transylvanian Military Border, the regiments here were named after the ethnicity of frontiersmen, rather than after the location of their headquarters. The latter principle had until then been consistently applied in the naming of all military borders and their regiments – from "old" military borders of Croatia, entitled the Karlovac Generalate and Varaždin Generalate after their headquarters, to the Banal Military Border and Slavonian Military Border.[50] The regiments in the Transylvanian and Banat military borders were named after the peoples to whom they pertained, at least originally. In the somewhat older Transylvanian Military Border, whose project of regulation had been drafted in 1761, the regiments were called: the 1st and 2nd Romanian and 1st and 2nd Székely regiments. Starting from 1764, the regiments in the Banat Military Border were also named after the ethnicity of their frontiersmen – Illyrian (Serbian), German and Wallachian (Romanian).

The question arises what the regiments in Transylvania and Banat had in common that led to the use of the new "ethnic" principle in their naming. First of all, the Illyrian Border was created through regulation, i.e. change of status

48 Karl Kaser, *Slobodan seljak i vojnik. Povojačeno društvo (1754–1881)*, 1 (Zagreb: Naprijed, 1997), 238–39; Kinga Xenia Havadi-Nagy, *Die Slawonische und Banater Militärgrenze. Kriegserfahrungen und Räumliche Mobilität* (Cluj-Napoca / Klausenburg: Rumänische Akademie – Zentrum für Siebenbürgische Studien, 2010).

49 Jordan, *Die kaiserliche Wirtschaftspolitik im Banat*, 201–04.

50 The regiments there were named after (local) headquarters, specifically Otočac, Ogulin, Slunj and Lika regiments (in the Croatian Border/Generalate), Križevci and Sent Georg regiments (in the Varaždin Generalate), Gradiška, Brod and Petrovaradin regiments (in the Slavonian Border), or after the area, like the 1st Banal and 2nd Banal regiments.

of Serbian Land Militia to that of frontiersmen. This was similar to the position of Székelys, who enjoyed personal freedoms and had been engaged in the military earlier. In Banat, the name *Illyren* was used only for Serbs, whose interests were under the jurisdiction of *Hofdeputation in Illiricis*.[51] Further, the territory the Illyrian Border inherited from the Land Militia was not concentrated – it was made up of individual settlements with frontier status, surrounded by the civilian territory of the *districts*. The situation was the same with "select" villages of Romanian and Székely frontiersmen, which extended into the civilian territories of various counties, seats and districts (*Comitats*, *Stuhl* and *Districts*).[52]

The same principle was used when establishing the *German* Border Regiment. The plan was for the majority of its frontiersmen to be German colonist veterans. The settlement of veterans in a military border area had been unprecedented in the history of the Military Border. Far less important is the fact that the results of this state endeavour did not meet expectations, so the frontiersman status was assigned to other inhabitants as well.[53] Finally, later practice affirmed the "ethnic" naming of military units. Based on a model dating to its origins, in 1838, the Wallachian Illyrian Border Regiment was divided in two formations: *Wallachisch-Banater Grenz Regiment* and *Illyrisch-Banater Grenz Bataillon*. As times changed, in 1848 the name of the first formation was changed to *Romanen-Banater Grenz Infanterie Regiment*. After the second formation was renamed *Serbisch-Banater*

---

51 Schwiker, *Geschichte des Temeser Banats*, 368. The institution *Hofdeputation in Banaticis, Transsylvanicis et Illyricis* was founded in 1745, from which some responsibilities were gradually separated, first for Transylvania in 1751 and then for Banat in 1755.

52 There is a possibility that these similarities led to the new principle in "naming" the regiments in eastern parts of the Military Border. Given the initial resistance to militarisation by estates, the nobility and the diets, who were not in favour of arming their subjects (Romanians) and losing their land, the establishment of the border in Transylvania was proclaimed in the form of an (adapted) principle: frontier regiments would recruit only Romanian Greek Catholics and Székely Catholics. In 1764, the territory of the Transylvanian Military Border was reduced to certain settlements, rather than entire areas, Göllner, *Die Siebenbürgische Militärgrenze*, 22–23, 32–33.

53 Among the frontier population of the German Banat Regiment, colonists of German origin were not the majority compared to the dominant Serb and Romanian population, neither in late eighteenth nor in the nineteenth century. Among other things, this was due to the fact that from late eighteenth century, other peoples, such as Hungarians and Slovaks, also settled the regiment, Ilić Mandić, "Plansko naseljavanje u Vojnoj krajini," 49–50, 160; Nino Delić, "Popis Banatske vojne granice 1819. godine," *Mešovita građa – Miscellanea* XXXVII (2014): 76.

Grenz Infanterie Regiment in 1860, the anachronous policy of using the names *Illyren* and *Wallachen*, instead of Serbs and Romanians, was finally abolished.[54]

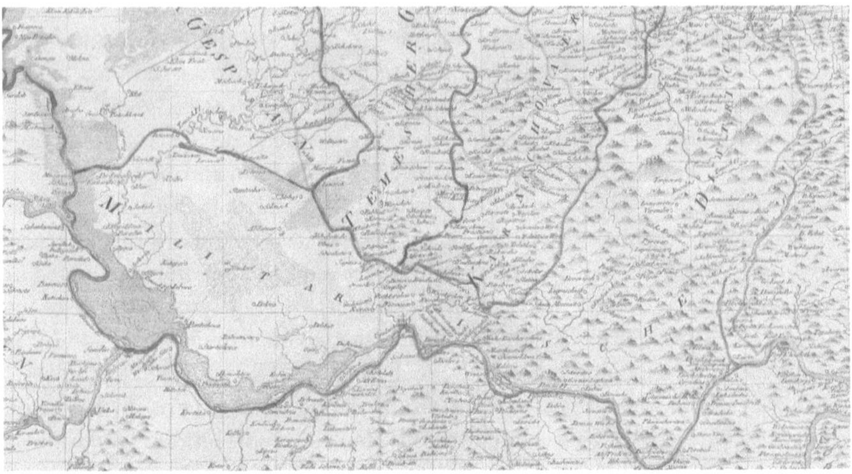

The Military District in the Banat of Timişoara, detail from *Temeschwarer Banat/* The Banat of Timişoara, Jakob Barzelini, 1788, cooper engraving, (Institut für donauschwäbische Geschichte und Landeskunde, Tübingen)

54 Irina Marin, *The Formation and Allegiance of the Romanian Military Elite Originating from the Banat Military Border* (Ph. D. Thesis, University College London, 2009), 95, 118–19, 123.

Csaba Horváth

Defending the Eastern Confines of the Habsburg Monarchy: A Forgotten Border Guard Regiment in Eighteenth-Century Transylvania

Abstract: The 45th Wallachian Border Guard dragoon regiment was established as part of the Transylvanian Military Border (*Siebenbürgische Militärgrenze*). The regiment was a military unit that lasted nine years and it wasn't involved in any armed conflicts. The following paper aims to present the history of this partly forgotten military unit and it also makes an attempt to reconstruct the composition of the staff of the above-mentioned regiment. The paper was written to shed light on this unit and to foster future research regarding it and its officers.

Keywords: Transylvania, Border Guard, Wallachian, Dragoon, Cavalry, Habsburg

The Foundation and the History of the Unit

Between 1762 and 1764, during the reign of Austrian Archduchess, Queen of Hungary and princess of Transylvania[1] Maria Theresa, the eastern border of the Habsburg Empire was militarized and thus the Transylvanian Military Border came into existence. Among its most important purposes was to counter the threat of possible attacks coming from both the diminishing but still menacing Ottoman Empire and the nascent Eastern power, the Russian Tsardom, to combat smugglery, respectively to create a military force capable of defending the border but at the same time, could be deployed both domestically (in suppression of an internal revolt) and internationally (fighting in external wars and campaigns).[2]

Initially, there were six border guard units: three Szekler (or Székely) and three Wallachian[3] regiments. The former included the 1st and 2nd

1 The province of Transylvania became Grand Principality in 1765, after the foundation of the Transylvanian Border Guard regiments.

2 Lajos Szádeczky, *A székely határőrség szervezése 1762–64-ben*. (Budapest: Magyar Tudományos Akadémia Történeti Bizottsága, 1908), 9; Liviu Maior, *Românii în armata habsburgică* (București: Editura Enciclopedică, 2004), 53.

3 The official name of these units was "*Wallachen*" which is an old ethnonym for Romanians. The term became increasingly pejorative during the nineteenth century, and during the Hungarian revolution of 1848–1849 the two infantry units

Székely[4] Border Guard infantry regiment and the Border Guard Hussar regiment, while the latter was composed by the 1st Wallachian and 2nd Border Guard infantry regiment, respectively the Wallachian Border Guard Dragoon regiment.

The dragoon units were a branch of the cavalry organized inside the imperial army from 1602, and consisted of mounted infantrymen equipped with firearms. According to military historian István Nagy-Luttenberger, the regiments structure was slightly changed in the middle of the eighteenth century to "semi-heavy", and it was used for both aiding the vanguard of the army and cavalry charges during battles. In 1758 a new branch was created, the *chevaux legers*, organized as a lighter offshoot of the dragoons.[5] The two branches co-existed for the most part of their history with the exception of a short period (1798–1802) when the two merged.[6]

Unfortunately, there are no archive sources about the regiment. The reconstruction of its history relies mostly on indirect archive sources and the relatively reduced amount of literature that mentions it. The unit is relatively unknown in both the Hungarian and Romanian historiography, although there were some notable exceptions.[7]

---

were renamed as *Romanen-Regimenten* (Romanian regiments), Alphons vonWrede, *Geschichte der k. und k. Wehrmacht* (Wien: L. W. Seidel & Sohn, 1898), 438, 465. In this paper, I am using the term strictly in its eighteenthcentury, non-pejorative meaning.

4 The Székelys/Szeklers are a Hungarian-speaking population located in the Curvature Carpathians, on the historical eastern border of the medieval Hungarian Kingdom (modern-day Romania) who have a long history as border guardsmen and soldiers.

5 István Nagy-Luttenberger, *A császári-királyi 1765–1815. Szervezettörténet és létszámviszonyok* (Pápa: Gróf Esterházy Károly Múzeum, 2013), 158–60.

6 After the defeat of the Habsburg Monarchy in the War of the First Coalition, the cavalry was reorganized and one of the most important changes that occurred was the merging of the seven chevaux legers, the six dragoon regiments along with some other smaller units into 15 light-dragoon regiments. During the War of the Second Coalition, this system failed to live up to the expectations and was disestablished afterwards, Nagy-Luttenberger, *A császári-királyi*, 183, 188.

7 Joseph HeinrichBenigni von Mildenberg, *Statistische Skizze der Siebenbürgischen Militär-Grenze* (Hermannstadt, 1834), X-XI; Gustav Amon von Treuenfest, *Geschichte des k. k. 11.Huszaren-Regiments Herzog Alexander v. Württemberg. 1762 bis 1850 Székler Grenz-Huszaren* (Wien: Verlag des Regiments), 1878; Carl Göllner, *Die Siebenbürgische Militärgrenze. Ein Beitrag zur Sozial- und Wirtschaftsgeschichte 1762–1851* (München: R. Oldenbourg Verlag, 1974); Tamás Csikány, "A csíkszéki határőrvidék története. 1764–1851," in *Határvédelem évszázadai Székelyföldön. Csíkszék és Gyimesek védelme*, ed. József Nagy (Szépvíz, 2018), 163, 165.

The unit was, along with the Karlovac, Varaždin, Banal, Slavonian and Székely border guard Hussar units, one of the original six border guard cavalry regiments of the Military Border, and it was the only non-Hussar regiment among these.

The headquarters of the Wallachian dragoon regiment was located in the southern Transylvanian settlement of Vajdarécse (Recea/Waywodretschen).

According to Nagy-Luttenberger, in 1764 a dragoon regiment of the Habsburg army consisted of the regiment's staff (*Regiment-Staab*, 10 persons including a colonel, a lieutenant colonel, a major, a military chaplain and auxiliary personnel), 13 companies (*Companies*), out of which one was an elite grenadier company (consisting of 100 persons) and the other 12 were rifled companies organized in six squadrons (*Schwadron* or *Escadron*). This meant an 830-strong dragoon regiment. Three years later the size of the regiments was modified, in the specific case of the dragoons being reduced to 818.[8]

There is no evidence that the 45th Wallachian Border Guard dragoon regiment had exactly the same structure. Being a border guard unit, it most probably wasn't fully uniform with its regular army counterparts which in fact may have included a somewhat different number of personnel. This is clearly visible from the example of the other Transylvanian border guard cavalry unit, the Székely Hussar regiment, which throughout its existence had its own effective and form of organization that was different from those of the other Hussar units.[9]

According to Romanian historian Liviu Maior, the regiment had in 1773 a total number of 1.738 soldiers[10] which seems unlikely because the unit was disestablished before the indicated year.

From a financial standpoint, the Wallachian Dragoon regiment, at first sight, wasn't too profitable for the state. According to Carl Göllner, it had the lowest amount of tax collected from any unit of the Transylvanian *Grenze*: 7.506 out of 85.387 golden florins in 1767 and 4.628 out of 53.614 Guldens in 1770.[11] The Hussars had the second-lowest amount of collected tax (10.834, respectively 5.120). It's interesting how the Transylvanian border guard cavalry regiments paid considerably lower amounts of tax compared to their infantry counterparts. There is no direct evidence regarding this situation, most probably it was due to the fact that horses were regarded as an asset of the state that had to be taken care

8 Nagy-Luttenberger, *A császári-királyi*, 162–63.

9 Nagy-Luttenberger, *A császári-királyi*, 207.

10 Maior, *Românii în armata*, 53.

11 Göllner, *Die Siebenbürgiche Militärgrenze*, 48, 50.

of and there could have been different tax policies regarding them. The low tax amount can also be determined by the financial situation of the local population.

The disbanding appears in the monthly tables[12] of the other regiments with the influx of officers, non-commissioned officers, auxiliary personnel and the soldiers of the disbanded military unit. In the monthly table from September 1770 of the 1st Wallachian infantry regiment it is recorded that the chaplain, one *Profoss,*[13] a drummer, two sergeants and 13 corporals were transferred from the dragoons to the mentioned unit.[14] They were followed by the commanding officer, one captain, the aide-de-camp, one Fourier, respectively 348 soldiers.[15] These changes occurred between mid-August and mid-September 1770.

The dissolution of the Wallachian Border Guard dragoon regiment can be observed in the 2nd Wallachian infantry regiment's August table of the month. In this month the regiment saw the transfer of 1 captain, 1 medical staff member, 1 standard-bearer, 1 sergeant, 9 corporals, 6 drummers and a total number of 315 footsoldiers.[16]

Those transferred to the 2nd Wallachian infantry were from the following villages: Rebra Mare (Rebra), Ilva Mică, Földra (Feldru), Pauren (unidentified settlement), Szalva (Salva), Runck (Runcu Salvei), Hordó (Coşbuc), Rebrisora (Rebrişoara), Verara (unidentified settlement), Mittide (Mititei) and Zagra.[17]

Regarding the information of this document, one can observe an interesting situation. There are two ways in which the Wallachian dragoon regiment is referred to: "*reducirten Chevaux Legers Regiment*" (lit. "disbanded Chevauxleger regiment"), respectively "*reducirten Wall. leichten Dragoner Regimnt*" (lit. "disbanded Wallachian light Dragoon regiment").

The recruiting area of the Wallachian dragoons was transferred partly to the Székely hussars[18] and partly to the 1st Wallachian Border Guard infantry

12 *Monat Tabella* (table of the month) was a document used to keep a monthly evidence of the personnel serving in a Habsburg military unit.

13 The regiment's member in charge of keeping the order and cleanliness in the military unit, Nagy-Luttenberger, *A császári-királyi*, 42.

14 Österreichisches Staatsarchiv (ÖStA), Kriegsarchiv (KA), Personalunterlagen (Pers), Musterlisten und Standestabellen (MLST) I Grenzinfanterieregiment Nr. 16 (GIR), 16 6140.

15 ÖStA, KA Pers, MLST I, GIR, 16 6140.

16 ÖStA, KA Pers, MLST I, GIR, 17 6177.

17 ÖStA, KA Pers, MLST I, Greninfanteriereigment Nr. 17 (Border Guard infantry regiment, Nr. 17, GIR 17) 6177.

18 Tövis (Teiuş), Dobra.

regiment. The reason for this decision has to do with the fact that the recruiting areas of the two units were geographically closer to the district of the Wallachian dragoons.

Commander of the Regiment: Johann Do(a)mbrowka

During its brief existence, this unit had only one commander: lieutenant colonel baron Johann Dambrowka or Dombrowka. It wasn't uncommon for a cavalry regiment to have a lieutenant colonel as its commander. The Székely Hussars also had a lieutenant colonel, Joseph von Ernst, as commanding officer until 1769.

On 1 October 1770, Do(a)mbrowka was transferred to the 1st Wallachian infantry regiment as a colonel. This transfer is mentioned by Gustav Amon von Treuenfest in his monograph about the Infantry Regiment No. 46 (the successor unit of the 1st Wallachian Infantry Regiment) and by the October *Monat Tabella* of the mentioned unit of that year.[19]

Holy Roman Emperor Joseph II visited the district during Do(a)mbrowka's tenure as commander. He remained commander of the unit until 1778, when according to Amon von Treuenfest, because of his serious illness, he had to hand over the leadership of the Transylvanian Wallachian Border Guard infantry field battalion to his deputy, lieutenant general (and future major general) Hannibal Sburlatti.[20] The change in office was quite urgent because the unit had been mobilized to participate in the Bavarian War of Succession. The battalion would go on and fight in the war, while Sburlatti would go on to become colonel of the unit.

Do(a)mbrowka retired on 21 July 1779[21] and was promoted to the rank of honorary major general. He died in 1787.

Conclusion

The Wallachian Border Guard dragoon regiment remains an obscure military unit because of its short existence, the lack of direct archival sources and the fact that it didn't enter the collective memory of the communities whose members served in it. The main reason for the dissolution of this border guard unit was most probably an economic one. According to Göllner, out of the six Transylvanian border guard units, the Wallachian border guard dragoon regiment paid the lowest amount of tax in both 1767 and the year of its dissolution.

---

19 Amon, *Geschichte des Nr. 46*, 41; ÖStA, KA, Pers, MLST I, GIR, 16 6140.

20 Amon, *Geschichte des Nr. 46*, 41-44.

21 ÖStA, KA,Pers, MLST I, GIR, 16 6142.

The proximity of the recruiting area of a cavalry unit and that of a border guard infantry regiment may have also played a considerable reason in the disbanding of the regiment.

Annex I. Reconstruction of the Officer Staff Who Served in the Wallachian Border Guard Dragoon regiment

The regiment's staff (Regiment-Stab):

Lieutenant colonel and commanding officer: John Da(o)mbrowka (†February 18, 1787)[22]

Regiment chaplain: Paulinus Stewanek OFM Conv. (†August 31, 1790)[23]
Transferred to the 1st Wallachian Border Guard infantry regiment on June 1, 1770.[24] He remained the spiritual leader of the unit until his death.

Fourier: Michael Gierald
He began his career in the 2nd Székely Border Guard infantry regiment was transferred from the 2nd Székely Border Guard infantry regiment in 1767 to the border guard dragoons and stayed there until 1769, when was transferred to the Székely Border Guard Hussar regiment. He reached the rank of first lieutenant and was a member of the unit until 1793, when he left for Blakenstein Hussar regiment.[25]

Regiment's drummer: Conrad Schreder
Transferred on August 16, 1770 to the 1st Wallachian Border Guard infantry regiment.[26]

Profoss: Francis Grubhoffer
Transferred on August 16, 1770 to the 1st Wallachian Border Guard infantry regiment.[27]

---

22 Antonio Schmidt-Brentano, *Kaiserliche und k. k. Generale (1618–1815)*. Österreichisches Staatsarchiv, 2006. 23.
23 ÖStA, KA, Pers, MLST I, GIR,16 6147.
24 ÖStA, KA, Pers, MLST I, GIR,16 6140.
25 ÖStA, KA, Pers, MLST I, Szekler Grenzhusarrenregiment Nr. 11 (Székely Border Guard Hussar regiment, Hus) 11 7782.
26 ÖStA, KA, Pers, MLST I, GIR, 16 6140.
27 ÖStA, KA, Pers, MLST I, GIR, 16 6140.

Captains:
N. Fux
Transferred on August 1, 1770 to the 2nd Wallachian Border Guard infantry regiment.[28]

First lieutenants:
Anton Rohr von Rohrau[29]

Second lieutenants:
Johann Márton[fy]
Transferred from the Székely Hussars to the Wallachian dragoon regiment in May 1767.[30]

28 ÖStA, KA, Pers, MLST I, GIR, 17 6177.
29 ÖStA, KA, Pers, MLST I, GIR, 11 7780.
30 Amon von Treuenfest, *Geschichte des k. k. 11*, 9.

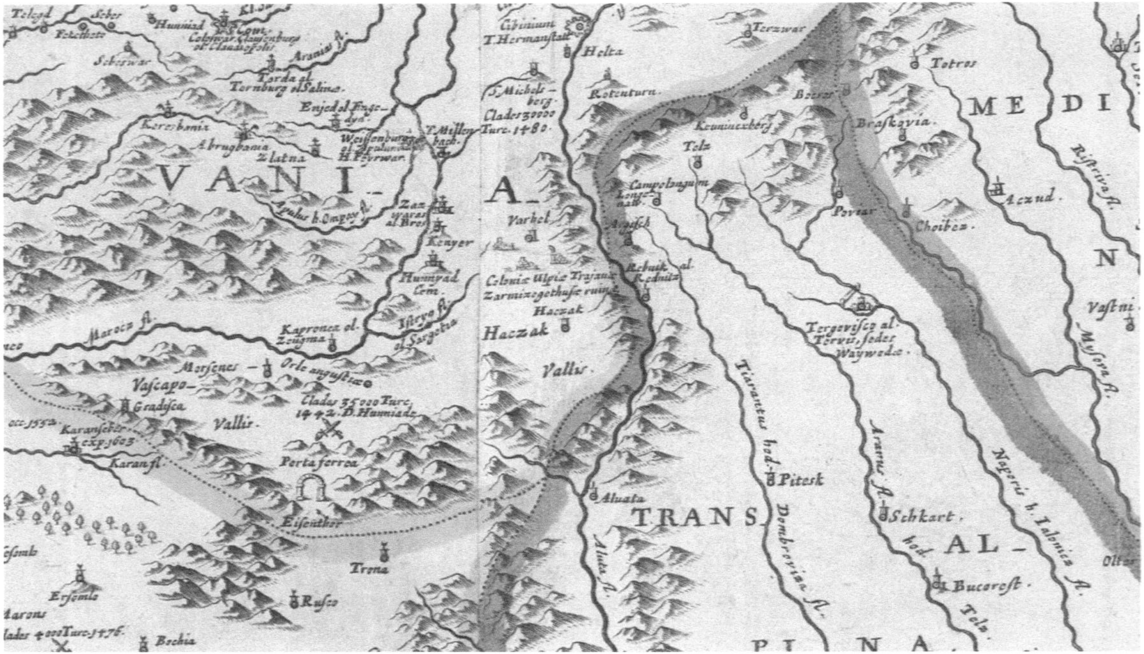

The Eastern and Southern borders of Transylvania, detail from *Danubius Fluviorum Europae Princeps…*/The Danube, Monarch of European Rivers, Sigmund von Birken/Jacob von Sandrart, 1683, cooper engraving, (Badische Landesbibliothek, Karlsruhe)

Fortrtifications, Sieges and Changing Borders

Julia Derzsi

The Border Fort and its Servants.
Turnu Roşu in the Sixteenth Century

Abstract: The road passing through the Southern Carpathians and the fortress at its feet was transferred from the intendancy of the voivode of Transylvania to the Saxons in the middle of the fifteenth century, in order to sustain and control the access through the Pass. The tower itself, which is right next to the main road connecting the southern part of Transylvania with Wallachia, was under the control of a burgrave appointed by the authorities of Sibiu, the administrative centre of the Transylvanian Saxon Seats and Districts, and the town recruited some armed men to guard it. In our paper we attempt to identify the material and human resources needed to maintain the border fort, using data from city accounts of Sibiu. We will try to show the structure of the guard, the recruitment of the burgrave and the guard, in correlation with the town's defensive system.

Keywords: Border Fort, Turnu Roşu, Tălmaciu, Sibiu, City Accounts

"Not far from here [Sibiu], further south, stands *Rubea Turris* [Turnu Roşu], a very strong castle up in the hills, near the river which flows down here, where a narrow entrance to Transylvania opens between the mountains, and serves as a sort of bulwark for the whole territory, as no one can enter from the south if the commander of the castle blocks the way." – writes the German cartographer Sebastian Münster in his work *Cosmographia*, which dedicates a special chapter to the description of Transylvania.[1] The tower, which still stands in its modified form, was part of the defensive system of the Olt River valley on the southern border of Transylvania, from the Middle Ages up to the nineteenth century. The

1 After the first edition was published in Basel in 1544, the text was corrected, the illustrations were enlarged, and the book was reprinted several times until 1628. In the editions of the *Cosmographia*, the description of Transylvania is found in *Liber* IV, and the passage about the tower of Turnu Roşu Red is found under the title *Civitates Transylvaniae*, Sebastian Münster, *Cosmopgraphey: oder Beschreibung aller Länder, Herrschaften und fürnemesten Stetten des gantzen Erdbodens* (Basel: 1588), 919. (online availability: https://www.e-rara.ch/bes_1/content/zoom/13635601; last download: 07.12.2021). For a presentation of the part relating to Transylvania, with translations of the text in Hungarian and Romanian, see Măriuca Radu, Sándor Tamás, "Erdély Sebastian Münster műveiben," *Acta Siculica* (2016–2017): 101–124.

pass itself is named after the castle. We do not know all the details of the history of this strategically important fort and its role in the border defence system, as we cannot always clearly link written sources to the actual sites.[2] However, we can explore some aspects of the administration of the castle, the evolution of its defensive functions, the personnel who defended the border and the role they played in the management of the estate destined for the maintenance of the fortifications.

Medieval sources mention four fortifications from the late fourteenth century to the early sixteenth century, which defended the borders of the Kingdom of Hungary in the southern part of Transylvania, overlooking the Cibin Depression. The sources firstly attest the castle of Tălmaciu, which stood opposite the entrance to the pass.[3] The castle, called *Landskrone* ("Crown of the Country"), was built in 1370 by King Louis I to protect the southern Transylvanian frontier, and to control the river valley road.[4] The castle was under the jurisdiction of the Transylvanian voivode and was considered an administrative centre, as the king attached seven villages to it, which later formed the territory of the *Talmescher Filialstuhl*.[5] The revenues of these villages were used to maintain the defences.[6] The Saxons from Sibiu helped build the castle and were granted trade privileges in return for their services. Other two fortifications, the tower of Turnu Roşu (Vöröstorony/Rothenturm) and the castle of Lotrioara (Latorvár/Lauterburg), first mentioned in 1396, also played a strategic key role.[7] The tower of Turnu

---

2 Based on historical and archaeological sources, Andárs Sófalvi gives a brief overview of the history and chronology of the medieval castles in the Turnu Roşu Strait, Andárs Sófalvi, "Vöröstorony várai," *Várak, kastélyok, templomok*, yearbook (2016): 22–26.

3 Sófalvi, "Vöröstorony várai," 23. Tălmaciu was originally the property of the Talmácsy clan, and in the early fourteenth century a fortified monastery was built here in honour of St. Nicholas. In 1322, during a rebellion against Charles I (King of Hungary and Croatia, 1308–1342), it was reconquered by the voievod of Transylvanian, Thomas Szécsényi (1321–1342). In 1369, Vladislav I (Voievod of Wallachia, 1325–1377), had it burnt, Balássy Ferencz, "Szelistye és Talmács várának és területének jogtörténeti nyomozása," *Századok* 6, 2 (February – 1872): 90.

4 Petre Beşliu Munteanu, "Consideraţii generale asupra securităţii frontierei central-sudice a Transilvaniei (secolele XII–XVI)," *Transilvania*, 3 (2009): 75–84 (77).

5 Tălmaciu (Talmus major, Gross-Tallmesch), Boiţa (Ochsendorf, Boitze), Tălmăcel (Talmus minor, Klein-Tallmesch), the village of Turnul Roşu (Porsesdinum, Portschescht), Sebeşul de Sus (Sebes superior, Ober-Sebesch), Sebeşul de Jos (Sebessinum, Unter-Schebesch), and Plopi (that no longer exists today), Balássy, "Szelistye és Talmács," 86.

6 Balássy, "Szelistye és Talmács," 90.

7 Sófalvi, "Vöröstorony várai," 23.

Roşu was built on a high platform directly at the entrance to the gorge, below the village of Boiţa, and the castle of Lotrioara was a border defence post about 10 kilometres to the south, both used to watch the enemy advancing across the Olt Strait and to relay news.[8] In addition to border protection, the castles also controlled commercial traffic, with Turnu Roşu being one of Transylvania's customs posts from the Middle Ages onwards.[9] The fortresses therefore served a dual purpose, on the one hand to control through traffic, and on the other to protect the territory. The castles were guarded and served under the authority of the burgrave.

The defensive organisation of these fortifications was reorganised under King Ladislaus V.[10] In his decree of 3 February 1453, the king granted the castles to the Seven Seats, along with their villages and appurtenances.[11] The integration of the settlements originally belonging to the Alba (Fehér) County into the administration of the Seven Seats also meant an increase in the power of the Transylvanian Saxons, and especially of Sibiu, as it created the opportunity to get rid of the officials appointed by the ruler who did not act according to the former's law.[12]

---

8 The castle of Lotrioara was a small fortress built on a ridge between the River Lotrioara and the Olt floodplain. The name of the fortress derives from the Latin *latro, latronis*, meaning robber, from which the names Lotru/Latoriţa/Lotrişor were derived, referring to the mountainous borderland covered with forests used by robbers and homeless people. The remains of the castle were the victim of stone quarrying in the 1970s-1980s. Sófalvi, "Vöröstorony várai," 23.

9 The markets of Sibiu also attracted traders. More about the trade of the Transylvanian Saxons, with a summary of the literature, see Mária Pakucs-Willcocks, *Sibiu – Hermannstadt. Oriental trade in the sixteenth century Transylvania* (Köln, Weimar, Wien: Böhlau Verlag, 2007), 6–10.

10 Sófalvi, "Vöröstorony várai," 23.

11 The Seven Seats were a common representation of the Saxon jurisdictions (seats) of the former province of Sibiu, under the leadership of the town of Sibiu. On its establishment, organisation and jurisdiction, see Georg Eduard Müller, *Stühle und Distrikte als Unterteilungen der Siebenbürgische-Deutschen Nationsuniversität, 1141–1876* (Köln, Weimar, Wien: Böhlau Verlag, 1985), 181–195, 199, 244.

12 Braşov, another important Saxon town on the border of South Transylvania, received a similar donation when it received de castle of Bran and its villages from the ruler in 1498, Zsuzsanna Cziráki, "Durante beneplacito nostro. Brassó és a szász rendi érdekérvényesítés Bethlen Gábor uralkodása idején a Törcsvári birtokok tükrében," in *Bethlen Erdélye, Erdély Bethlene. A Bethlen Gábor trónra lépésének 400. évfordulóján rendezett konferencia tanulmányai*, eds. Vernka Dáné, Ildikó Horn, Mária Lupescu Makó, Teréz Oborni, Enikő Rüsz-Fogarasi, Gábor Sipos (Kolozsvár: Erdélyi Múzeum-Egyesület, 2014), 610.

However, as a property of the Crown, the corpus of the estate was not alienable, the donation was not hereditary, and its incorporation into the Transylvanian Saxon Seats meant only the administration of the castles and the domains were assigned to them, and the free use of their revenues.[13] The royal charter contained the stipulation that the Transylvanian Saxons should demolish the castle of Tălmaciu, which was already in a damaged state at the time, and fortify the tower of Turnu Roşu (*turris Weresthoron*) and the castle of Lotrioara (*Lothorwar*).[14] Increasingly intense Turkish attacks seem to have been prevented by directly blocking the valley. The fortification of Turnu Roşu forced the invading armies to march on more difficult roads, for example, at the Battle of Câmpul Pâinii (Kenyérmező/Brodfeld) in 1479, the Ottoman troops marched not through the strait but along the valley of the Lotru River crossing thus the mountains into the Transylvanian Basin.[15] To reinforce their position, the Saxons, with the support of King Matthias, built another tower, which was completed by 1487–1488 – as András Sófalvi indicates: at that time the documents refer to two red towers (*duae turres rubeas*).[16] The *Landskrone* may have been standing at this time, as King Matthias ordered the fortress to be demolished afterwards.[17]

Despite the existence of the fortifications, the Ottoman armies managed to invade and ravage the Olt Valley in February 1493.[18] The Saxons then invested large sums in the defence system, as attested by the account books kept by the mayor of Sibiu. In 1503, new building costs were accounted for, and to cover the expenses the King waived the traditional Saxon tax on St. Martin's Day for three years.[19] Between 1520 and 1526, building work continued,[20] repairing the

---

13 Balássy, "Szelistye és Talmács," 88–89.

14 For similar reasons and in a similar way, King Matthias linked the land of Amnaş and the castle and territory of Sălişte to the Seven Seats in 1468 and 1485, Balássy, "Szelistye és Talmács," 88–89.

15 Sófalvi, "Vöröstorony várai," 24.

16 Sófalvi, "Vöröstorony várai," 23.

17 *Urkundenbuch zur Geschichte der Deutschen in Siebenbuergen*, 8, no. 4813 (14.02.1489).

18 Jenő Rónai Horváth, *Magyar hadi krónika. Első rész. A Honfoglalástól a Mohácsi vészig* (Budapest: Magyar Tudományos Akadémia Hadtudományi Bizottsága, 1895), 335.

19 According to Sófalvi, another tower was built, probably as part of the fortress of Split Tower, Sófalvi, "Vöröstorony várai," 23.

20 In 1520, the Seven Seats *super provisione Rubearum Turrim* paid 250 florins, after having accounted for the damage previously caused to the fortress, Serviciul Judeţean al Arhivelor Naţionale Sibiu (SJAN Sibiu), Fondul Magistratul oraşului şi scaunului Sibiu. Socoteli consulare. Inventarul 107, no. 30 (1520), f. 24v. The accounts register between 1520 and 1528 were published by Toma-Cosmin Roman, *Sibiul între diplomaţie şi*

tiled roof, spending on building materials, transporting workers,[21] repairing the drawbridge, and the valley barrier,[22] equipping the towers with war materials, and building a hearth and furnace in the castle rooms.[23] In late spring and early summer 1525, the mayor and the royal judge (*judex regius*) of Sibiu travelled twice to Turnu Roşu to inspect the works.[24] The parish priest of Tălmaciu celebrated the mass for the workers and the garrison.[25]

However, the written sources, containing mostly sporadic information, do not clearly indicate which fortress is meant, the one on the high terrace at the entrance to the gorge, or the so-called Split or Half Tower, which stands about 6 km to the south, directly on the banks of the Olt.[26] The latter building is also referred to as the tower of Turnu Roşu on old maps, it could only have been given its present name after it was destroyed by flooding or explosion in the late fifteenth or early sixteenth century.[27] The archaeological excavations also uncovered the remains of the roadblock wall next to the tower, as well as the outer wall surrounding the tower in a 0.9 m wide perimeter. This proves that the main defensive strategy at the time was to close the valley road to the Turkish threat.[28] The fortification of Turnu Roşu also left its mark on the way in which the

---

război (Sibiu: Honterus Verlag, 2017), *passim*. In 1521 the account books record maintenance expenses of 220 florins, in 1525, 200 florins. Because of the high expenditure, the king waived the St. Martin's Day tax for three years. In 1526, building work was still going on, and the account books recorded 274 florins for various masonry works and the transport of materials, Roman, *Sibiul*, 262, 263, 326.

21 Roman, *Sibiul*, 253, 258. For the wall supporting the stairs, stone supports (*pro lapidus vulgo kragschtein*) were used from the previously renovated building of the town church. Ibid., 323.

22 Roman, *Sibiul*, 194.

23 Roman, *Sibiul*, 158, 149. 222, 248, 261.

24 Roman, *Sibiul*, 247, 249.

25 Roman, *Sibiul*, 93, 327.

26 Sófalvi, "Vöröstorony várai," 24, 26.

27 Sófalvi, "Vöröstorony várai," 25; András Sófalvi does not rule out the possibility that the remains of a tower are hidden under the present highway, next to which a second tower was built in the second half of the fifteenth century, the ruins of which can still be seen today (the Split Tower).

28 Sófalvi, "Vöröstorony várai," 25, 26; This paper does not provide a detailed historical analysis of the events, but only highlights the most important aspects. For more information, see Pál Fodor, Teréz Oborni, "Between Two Great Powers: The Hungarian Kingdom of the Szapolyai Family," in *A Forgotten Hungarian Royal Dynasty: the Szapolyais*, eds. Pál Fodor, Szabolcs Varga (Budapest: Research Centre for the Humanities, 2020), 127–61.

chancellery of the town referred to the Tălmaciu estate: the contributions of the villages belonging to it, for example, are recorded in the account books of 1524 under the heading *Pertinenciae Turrim Rubearum*.[29] However, the designations of the office were not consequent; the permanent staff of the border guards was still referred to as servants of the castle of Tălmaciu in the payrolls of the account books until the mid-1550s.

The fortification at Turnu Roşu was certainly also linked to the fact that the customs were administered by the Transylvanian Saxons of Sibiu. From the late fifteenth century, the town leased the right to collect the customs toll more or less regularly, on an annual basis, and took over the administration of the custom station.[30] Even the earliest documentary references link the tower to customs, both as a location and as a use of revenues.[31] In 1468 King Matthias ordered that part of the customs income be given to the town of Sibiu for maintenance of the castle.[32] However, this did not mean, or not always, that those who held the castle could collect the customs duties. The customs station came under the administration of Sibiu only from 1484 onwards, and not until they received the lease from the rulers.[33] Neither then nor afterwards, when the revenues of the customs were administered by Sibiu, the costs of maintaining the castle were not charged to the town, but to the account of the Seven Seats.[34] The situation was different at the castle of Bran (Törzburg/Törcsvár), another custom station at the border of Transylvania. The property of Bran, originally divided into two parts – the estate and the customs –, were in practice merged in the hands of town officials of Braşov, who, according to the account registers, managed all the revenues of the castle of Bran together.[35]

---

29 Roman, *Sibiul*, 181.

30 On the customs administration and the sixteenth century customs registers, see Pakucs-Willcocks, *Sibiu – Hermannstadt*, 24–29, 34–40.

31 SJAN Sibiu, Colecţia de documente medievale, U II, no. 280.

32 Pakucs-Willcocks, *Sibiu – Hermannstadt*, 24.

33 Under Habsburg rule, and occasionally at other times customs duties were administered by officers appointed by the king, Pakucs-Willcocks, *Sibiu – Hermannstadt*, 21, 26.

34 The account register of the town shows that the income of the customs of Turnu Roşu, which was paid into the town treasury, was essentially (mostly directly) used for the construction and maintenance of the town defence works, the purchase of military materials and the construction and repair of defences, Júlia Derzsi, "Nagyszeben város háztartása a 16. század második felében," in *Veretek, utak, katonák. Gazdaságtörténeti tanulmányok a magyar középkorról*, eds. István Kádas, Renáta Skorka, Boglárka Weisz (Budapest: MTA BTK Történettudományi Intézet, 2018), 433, 429.

35 Cziráki, "Durante beneplacito nostro," 611.

Customs could be paid both in money and in goods, with suppliers paying money for exports and goods for imports.[36] The revenue from the customs lease proved to be a significant item. According to the calculations of Mária Pakucs-Willcocks, in the sixteenth century the annual turnover of the customs duty averaged around 20.000 gold florins (the highest value, 50.000 florins, was recorded in 1553, and in times of war, too, in 1594, 8.000 florins). Most of the trade were oriental goods, mainly textiles, cotton, silk, spices, dried fruits, leather goods, alum and dyestuffs.[37] The customs registers, made by the town's officials, also recorded the names of the merchants from the second half of the sixteenth century, who came from Wallachia. Customs was thus not only a means of monitoring the volume of goods, but also a means of controlling the traders entering the country.[38] The administration was handled by customs officers appointed by the town council. In addition to these, the town employed two clerks (one at the customs office in Turnu Roşu and the other at the customs house in the town) who kept the records and two servants who worked alongside the customs officer and undertook various tasks, travelling to the fairs. The town also employed two other servants (*trabanten*) at the customs post at Turnu Roşu, whose duties probably consisted of guarding the station.[39]

The maintenance of the fortifications was covered by the income of the Tălmaciu estate. The mayor of Sibiu, who was also the chairman of the Seven Seats, accounted for the estate's assets. Various taxes were levied on the estates, the amount of which varied from year to year, as did the revenues from the Tălmaciu milling rights and fines. In the absence of concrete and clear data, it is difficult to estimate the overall value of these revenues, while the maintenance costs of the mills and fortifications were also constant. The items of the accounts were recorded in separate registers for the Seven Seats and the town.[40] There we also find data on the payrolls and other wages of the burgrave and servants.

The castle's defence was organised by the burgrave. He had to give an oath when he took up the office. The text of the oath taken by the burgrave of Turnu

36 Pakucs-Willcocks, *Sibiu – Hermannstadt*, 17.

37 Mária Pakucs Willcocks, "Economy and trade. Making a profit in Sibiu in the sisteenth century: oriental goods, commercial capitals and betrayed friendhips," *Historical Yearbook* III (2006): 99.

38 Pakucs Willcocks, "Economy and trade," 100.

39 Pakucs-Willcocks, *Sibiu – Hermannstadt*, 18.

40 In the second half of the sixteenth century they were bound together in the same book, the first part containing the accounts of the Seven Seats, the second the accounts of the town of Sibiu.

Roşu (*Jurament des burggrawens oder porkolabens bey dem rothen thurn*) around 1600 gives the best indication of the nature of his activities (see **Annex II**).[41] The existence of an oath implies a regular procedure whereby the persons appointed to command the castle held the office of *Porkolaben Ampt*, in direct subordination to the mayor and royal judge of Sibiu as superior authorities. The exact terms or duration of the mandate are not known, but the tasks were to be executed according to the more or less precise duties prescribed in the instructions mentioned in the oath.[42] Half of the articles in the oath deal with border and military matters, the other half with the administration of the estate. The oath to keep and uphold the law was also an affirmation of legal obligations. Breaking the rules, however, would have given rise to legal liability even if the oath had not been taken. The tasks of guarding the border fort included forwarding mail, preventing illegal border crossings and maintaining an adequate staff at the post. The tasks related to the administration of the estate of Tălmaciu included taxation, the judiciary (with civil and criminal competences) and the administration of the village's revenues.

The first point mentioned in the oath refers explicitly to the activity of the outpost: the duty to deliver the mail. The responsibility of the burgrave and the castle defence in this respect complements our knowledge of the Transylvanian princely postal service.[43] The postal services covered a wide range of activities and tasks, transporting letters, goods and people, providing the escort and catering for the princely envoys, equipping them with horses and carts. Although the organisation was managed by the prince's chancellery, the actual tasks were delegated to the municipalities, which bore the costs of maintaining the service. It was a permanent and costly obligation for the communes. The oath of the burgrave shows that the frontier castle was an important station of the postal service. The oath required the burgrave to deliver the mail and news promptly,[44] but also to refrain from conspiracy and treason against the country.

---

41 SJAN Sibiu, Colecția de documente medievale, U IV, no. 1703.

42 Müller, *Stühle und Distrikte*, 272.

43 For information on the organisation of the postal service in Sibiu, see Julia Derzsi, "Servicii poştale la Sibiu în a doua jumătate a secolului al XVI-lea," in *Studii de istorie a oraşelor. In honorem Paul Niedermaier*, eds. Vasile Ciobanu, Dan Dumitru Iacob (Bucureşti, Brăila: Editura Academiei Române, Editura Istors a Muzeului Brăilei "Carol I", 2017), 360–374.

44 "From Wallachia, the mail, be it bad or good, I will at once give to my highest authority, so that I may also be able to tempestuously give understanding of them to Royal Grace." (see below, **Annex II**).

Border guard duties also included the control of roads and crossings. From the Olt Gorge, there were several possibilities to reach the Transylvanian villages under the mountains: on the Lotru Valley and on the plain road with several exit options: Sadului Valley, Orlatului Valley, Tilişca River Valley, Sebeş Valley, Lotrioarei Valley. In all cases it was possible to bypass the customs house of Turnu Roşu.[45] Legally, however, the only way to enter the country was at Turnu Roşu.[46] In his mid-sixteenth-century writing about the *oppidum* of Tălmaciu, the *pfarrer* (parish priest) Johann Lebelius calls Turnu Roşu "the fortified gate of the kingdom,"[47] where only with a letter of safe conduct (*salvus conductus*) one was allowed to enter the country.[48] In addition to securing the crossing, efforts were made to prevent clandestine trade. The repair of the barrier (*Schrancken*) belonging to the guard post is recorded in 1524.[49] Guarding the passes and mountain roads was a difficult task, as they were used by horse thieves, serfs fleeing to Wallachia and smugglers. In the extensive mountainous area, the insecurity was exacerbated by conflicts between shepherds over pastureland.[50] The burgrave's oath also tells us how the tasks were organised: the illegal crossing points were guarded by the *Plajaschen* (mountain rangers, hill people), inhabitants of the border villages,[51] who were mandated either by the burgrave of Turnu Roşu or directly by the town council of Sibiu. Colomanus Schneyder's letter to the mayor of Sibiu (1532) reveals that, as commander of the castle of Turnu Roşu, he sometimes communicated with the *Plajaschen* through their priest.[52] The area was then secured by exploratory patrols, organised for reconnaissance, to

45 Beşliu, "Consideraţii generale," 78.
46 SJAN Sibiu, Colecţia de documente medievale, U IV, no. 1209.
47 Beşliu, "Consideraţii generale," 78; The text was published in Johannes Seivert, *Nachrichten von Siebenbürgischen Gelehrten und ihren Schriften* (Preßburg: Weber und Korabinstischen Verlag, 1785), 266–274.
48 Derzsi, "Servicii poştale," 364.
49 Roman, *Sibiul*, 194.
50 Beşliu, "Consideraţii generale," 77.
51 Beşliu mentions the report of General Adolf Bukow to the Aulic War Council, the central military authority of the Habsburg Monarchy, in 1761, which took into account the military realities of the South Transylvanian territory. The military commander proposed the dissolving of the *plajaschen*, the old garrison of the territory, and the creating of the border police service. According to the statutes of the organised regiments, the new institution would be entrusted with the same tasks as the old guard, namely the pursuit of thieves, the prevention of imports and the clandestine export of goods, see Beşliu, "Consideraţii generale," 76.
52 SJAN Sibiu, Colecţia de documente medievale, U V, no. 1957.

detect enemies or bands of robbers.[53] We also learn from the letter of Colomanus Schneyder, castellan of Turnu Roşu, that the securing of the area was sometimes solved by robbing the transalpine regions in an attempt to prevent the enemy troops from advancing and providing logistical support.[54] The burgrave Emerich Klausenburger reported in a letter to the mayor (in 1531 or 1532) that he had left the castle, leaving the *trabants* sent from the town for reinforcements hidden in Boiţa. Having learned from a Romanian villager near Lotiroara that a large number of the enemy were approaching (500 cavalry and 100 foot soldiers), they retreated to the tower and tried to defend the position from there. The burgrave asked the mayor for reinforcements and food, as they were running out of food in the castle, because the mill in Tălmaciu had been raided by the enemy. The letter also reveals that he offered the informant money in exchange for the news, but the man asked for more.[55]

A crucial point in the fulfilment of garrison duties was the keeping of the guards (*Thurknechte*). It was the responsibility of the burgrave to ensure that the castle servants were kept at full strength. One of the points of the oath concerned the payment of the wages in cash. Information on the identity and number of the burgraves and servants is given in the account books (see table in **Annex I**). The most important person in the castle guard was undoubtedly the burgrave. In the sources, the names *castellan*, *provisor*, *prefectus*, *burgrab*, *porkolab* were initially used to describe the position of the head of the castle of Tălmaciu and the associated fortified towers. In the first half of the sixteenth century, two *Porkolaben* are sometimes simultaneously mentioned by the sources. In 1528, for example, Benedict was paid a full salary alongside Nicolaus (*Porkolab de Talmach*, attested in 1525 and 1526).[56] The appointment of the two burgraves was not without precedent, as already King Sigismund, in 1419, addressed his letter ordering the free crossing of the frontiers of the merchants from Sibiu, along

---

53 The burgrave was sometimes personally entrusted by the ruler to organize exploring incursions, Roman, *Sibiul*, 294; SJAN Sibiu, Socoteli consulare, no. 68 (1555), f. 23v., and at other times, one of the castle's servants was on patrol in the mountains, Roman, *Sibiul*, 259, 262.. In 1524, as a member of a troop sent on a reconnaissance expedition to the Wallachian lowlands, Jancko, a servant from Turnu Roşu, was wounded during a skirmish. For his medical treatment, the mayor of Sibiu charged 3 florins to the account of the Seven Seats, Roman, *Sibiul*, 188.

54 SJAN Sibiu, Colecţia de documente medievale, U V, no. 1957.

55 SJAN Sibiu, Colecţia de acte fasciculate, O. Armata, no. 54, f. 6. The date of the letter is unknown, but it was probably written in 1531 or in 1532.

56 Roman, *Sibiul*, 382, 395, 259, 294.

with the Transylvanian voivode and vice-voivode, to the castellans of Tălmaciu and Turnu Roşu.[57] In 1531 Emericus and Kolman Schneyder signed a letter to the mayor of Sibiu, Stephan Klesser, as *Burgraben in dem rotten turren*, in which they informed the mayor of the news brought by their scouting servant Mihal Kisch from Wallachia about the movements of the Turkish troops and asked for gunpowder, lead and food for the garrison.[58] Two burgraves served at the same time in 1555, and according to the annual accounting of the mayor of Sibiu *ad turrim Tholmacz et familiam*, Boltisar was paid a full salary of 16 florins, and Nicolaus was also given the same amount.[59] After this time, we no longer see cases where two burgraves are appointed at the same time.[60] An analogy to this may be drawn from the castle of Bran, which was also under the command of two castellans. Their position, however, was more prestigious than that of the paid employees of the burgraves (*Törzburger Porkolab*),[61] and were held by the highest-ranking councillors of Braşov, usually the outgoing judge and the first senator.[62] The other frontier territory belonging to the Seven Seats, the estate of Sălişte, was also administered by two town councilors from Sibiu.[63] It is not clear from the sources what circumstances led to the doubling of the command of Tălmaciu estate and the tower castles. It cannot be said that in the first third of the sixteenth century Turnu Roşu and Tălmaciu were protected by separate garrisons (as in 1419, for example), but it cannot be ruled out either. The use of words in the sources is not helpful either, as the town notaries did not always make a clear distinction between the two castles. For example, the taxes collected

57 SJAN Sibiu, Colecţia de documente medievale, U IV, no. 1210.

58 SJAN Sibiu, Colecţia de documente medievale, U V, no. 1278.

59 SJAN, Socoteli consulare, no 68 (1555), f. 24r.

60 In 1568, there were two burgraves, but they did not serve at the same time. Thomas Wayda, who died during his term of office, was replaced in April by Nicolaus/Miklós Nagy, SJAN Sibiu, Socoteli consulare, no. 88 (1568), f. 54v.

61 For more information on the burgrave of Bran, see András Bándi, András Péter Szabó, "Hajdú István törcsvári porkoláb kéziratos kötete. Két ismeretlen magyar vers Báthori Gábor fejedelem korából," *Magyar Könyvszemle* 2 (2017): 129–154.

62 On the appointment of officials in Braşov, see "Chronik von Marcus Schunckabunk 1597–1603," *Quellen zur Geschichte der Stadt Brassó (Kronstadt). VI. Chroniken und Tagebücher. III. (1549–1827)*, ed. Julius Fross (Brassó: In Kommission bei H. Zeidner, 1915), 2–7.

63 Júlia Derzsi, "Párhuzamos életrajzok: Thomas Bomelius és Matthias Fronius. Éretelmiségi pályák a közösség szolgálatában," in *Hivatalnok értelmiségi a kora újkori Erdélyben*, eds. Zsolt Bogdándi, Tamás Fejér (Kolozsvár: Erdélyi Múzeum-Egyesület, 2016), 50.

from the Tălmaciu estate are recorded in 1524 under the entry: *Pertinencie Turrim Rubearum*.[64] However, from the mid-sixteenth century, the position of the burgrave of Turnu Roşu seems to have lost its former importance – perhaps because of the devaluation of its role as a border defender, since the southern mountain range of the Carpathians was no longer the frontier of the Ottoman Empire. The coexistence of two burgraves can only be identified in 1528, 1531 and 1555, when Sibiu was under Habsburg rule. As evidenced by the oath text analysed, the burgrave of Turnu Roşu was, by the end of the sixteenth century, a paid official, remunerated for his services at a fixed annual amount, measured on the salary scale of the Seven Seats.

The account books from the mid-sixteenth century also record the wages of servants (*servitores, famulus, Knechten*,[65] from 1585 *Trabanten*[66]) working at the side of the burgrave. Unfortunately, the scarce information available does not allow us to determine if all of these personnel were armed soldiers. The payroll of 1572 mentions one hand gunner besides the four servants of the tower (*Michaele Dick servitor pixidarii*), each of them receiving 8 florins a year.[67] In a letter addressed to the mayor of Sibiu in 1531 (or 1532), the burgrave Emrich Klausembriger called his servant Toma, with whom he sent mail to the town, *trabant*.[68] Nevertheless, there may have been a difference between the two statuses, servant and *trabant*, as can be seen in other enterprises of the Seven Seats. The posse sent out at the expense of the Seven Seats to the county (*Gespanschaft*) to catch and punish evildoers, led by town councillor Blasius Rhaw, consisted of 15 servants and 2 town soldiers (*trabanten*), with a fairly substantial pay differential in favour of the servants.[69] We can suppose a similar composition in the

64 Roman, *Sibiul*, 181; In 1568, on the other hand, we find payments under the following title: *Stipendiariorum ad rubeam turrim iuxta Talmacii executias agentium annua solutio*, SJAN Sibiu, Socoteli consulare, no. 88 (1568), f. 54v.

65 SJAN Sibiu, Socoteli consulare, no. 67 (1554), f. 32r; no. 72 (1558), f. 58r

66 SJAN Sibiu, Socoteli consulare, no. 102 (1585), f. 19r.

67 SJAN Sibiu, Socoteli consulare, no. 92 (1572), 39v.

68 SJAN Sibiu, Colecția de acte fasciculate, O. Armata, no. 54, f. 6.

69 *25 tag Aprilis hatt ein ersam weiß radt für gutt angesehen, das man einen radtherrenauff die spansag die übelthetter zu fahen und zu straffen ausschicken sollt, da hatt man den weißen herrn Blasium Rhaw angeschickt sampt 15 knechten und 2 stadt söldnern, da hatt man den herrn auff sein person geben fl. 8, den knechten einem jeden fl. 3, und den stadt söldnern iden pro fl. 2. Facit tota summa fl. 57*, SJAN Sibiu, Socoteli consulare, no. 82 (1565), f. 39v; On 10 June 1570, the mayor of Sibiu sent Miklós Nagy and Matthias Bolog to Alămor (Alamor, Mildenburg) to enforce the law against an arsonist who had been killed by the people of Topârcea (Taporcsa, Tsapertsch). They were

case of the garrison contingent in Turnu Roşu: in addition to the servants who permanently guarded the tower, the town sent a special detachment for unexpected tasks, and the help of the population was also called upon. The custom station was watched over by a second guard, paid by the customs officer.[70] The staffing of the guard was of course determined by necessity, and in the event of military danger, the service was extended. From the above-quoted letter of the burgrave Emrich Klausembriger, we know that in 1531 (or 1532), fearing an attack by enemy troops, he asked the mayor of Sibiu for 30 more men to defend the castle, along with the food and ammunition they were to receive, in addition to the 34 he already had.[71] This number is not far from the number of armed men recruited to invade villages in enemy territory.[72] For the period when we can observe this – broadly from the fifties to the mid-seventies – payroll records show four to five men on permanent posts until the late sixties, six from 1568, and eight from 1592 onwards. The same is confirmed by the decree of Stephen Báthory in 1583, which ordered the keeping of 32 *trabants* in wartime and 8 in peacetime.[73] This number is also broadly in line with the number of *trabants* who were permanently employed in the castles and fiscal estates of the time.[74]

No accurate records of the military equipment of the castle have been made or survived. However, occasional payments show that a skilled man or equipment was sent from the town to the castle, when needed.[75] After the major construction works of the first third of the century, there is only scattered information about the repairs and provisioning of the castle. This suggests that the castle's maintenance was not entirely paid for from the mayor's budget, or that no records of the costs have survived. At the same time, repairs were also paid by the customs

---

accompanied by 6 *trabanten* and 12 *walachen*, paying 1.73 florins each, SJAN Sibiu, Socoteli consulare, no. 90 (1570), f. 29.

70 Pakucs-Willcocks, *Sibiu – Hermannstadt*: Appendix IV. The Customs Account Books of Sibiu 1537–1597, 120, etc.

71 SJAN Sibiu, Colecția de acte fasciculate, O. Armata, no. 54, f. 6.

72 In 1532, Colomanus Schneyder informed the mayor of Sibiu that the bishop of Transylvania had provided 50 handgunners and 50 soldiers to plunder the mountain dwellers in Wallachia, SJAN Sibiu, Colecția de documente medievale, U V, no. 1957.

73 https://varak.hu/latnivalo/index/2753-Bojca-Vorostorony/ (08.12.2021).

74 Florin Nicolae Ardelean, *Organizarea militară în Principatul Transilvaniei* (Cluj-Napoca: Academia Română, Centrul de Studii Transilvane, 2019), 227–229.

75 Roman, *Sibiul*, 261, 265, etc.

officer.[76] As was the case in other areas of the city's budget at the time, the handling of money was not rigorous.[77]

According to the payroll records, the castle servants received 8 florins in cash payments per year. Their salaries were supplemented by grain, bread, wine, salt, blankets, tuckers and clothing. The mill of Tălmaciu, which was assigned to maintain the castle, provided the most significant supplement to the wages, but the incomes of mills of the two settlements Sebeş and Racovia also counted. Several times a year, wheat was distributed to the soldiers; according to records from 1592, the castle's *trabantas* received wheat to the value of 35.91 florins.[78] The rations to be distributed were probably determined by the burgrave, who also had control over the income allocated to the castle: he sometimes paid for repairs at the castle with wheat.[79] The lack of food could also erode the loyalty of the guards. The above-mentioned letter from Emrich Klausembriger reveals that, because the mills had been destroyed by the enemy and were not receiving their wheat, the soldiers had deserted.[80] A woman cooked for the staff of the castle, her annual wages are recorded in the accounts from 1585 onwards, and in 1583 a *Bäkerin* was also paid.[81] During the fasting period, the provisions were supplemented, the servants receiving peas, onions and oil from the mayor.[82] There was also a stable in the castle, as the rapid delivery of the mail required mounted service.

From the account registers we can identify the names of 12 burgraves during the century. Between 1554 and 1573 we also know the names of the servants in permanent service. By comparing their names with the names of people on the payrolls of the Seven Seats or the town, we can also identify the career paths of those who have worked for Turnu Roşu. Antonius Ballogh (elsewhere Bollog), who held the office of burgrave in 1569, had previously served as a *servitor civitatis* (*Stadtdiener*) in Sibiu in 1559 and worked as a postal servant in the service of the Seven Seats from 1551 to 1558. He was later appointed town captain

76 Pakucs-Willcocks, *Sibiu – Hermannstadt:* Appendix IV. The Customs Account Books of Sibiu 1537–1597, 134.

77 Derzsi, "Nagyszeben," 418.

78 SJAN Sibiu, Socoteli consulare, no. 104 (1592), f. 9r.

79 In 1582, for example, a Romanian was given half a measure of wheat for repairing the stable, SJAN Sibiu, Socoteli consulare, no. 99 (1582), f. 13; The rest of the income from the mills was held by the Seven Seats.

80 SJAN Sibiu, Colecția de acte fasciculate, O. Armata, no. 54, f. 6.

81 SJAN Sibiu, Socoteli consulare, no. 102 (1585), f. 19r; no. 101 (1583), f. 32v.

82 SJAN Sibiu, Socoteli consulare, no. 97 (1581), f. 6v.

(commander of the town militia), a post he held from 1570 to 1574.[83] Thomas Wayda is found at the head of the guard post at Turnu Roşu in 1567 and 1568, and before that, between 1555–1558 and 1561–1562, he served as postal servant to the Seven Seats.[84] He died in April 1568, and was succeeded in the *Porkolaben Amt* by Nicolaus (Miklós) Nagy, who before that, and after this, also worked as a postal servant in the service of the Seven Seats.[85] Another burgrave, Georg Leitscher (Leotschei, de Lőcse, Leutschau, Levoča, today in Slovakia), started his career in the same way, as a servant. He worked for the town in 1570, 1572, 1573, then was employed by the Seven Seats in 1578 and 1582, then became burgrave of Turnu Roşu (attested in 1583, 1585, 1588, 1592). In 1596 he was designated captain of Sibiu.[86] Johann Pokai, who worked as a servant in Turnu Roşu in 1569, 1570, 1572 and 1573 (no data for 1571), was probably related to Gregor Pokai, who served as a post servant of the Seven Seats in 1572 and 1573. Gregor later became town captain in Sibiu (his activities in this office are documented between 1581 and 1592), a position which seems to have helped Johann's career: between 1581 and 1585 Johann is also found in the sources as a postman in the employ of the Seven Seats. A document issued on 21 December 1577 for the repayment of a debt refers to János (Johann) Pokai as a burgrave of Hunedoara (Vajdahunyad, Eisenmarkt).[87] If it is the same person, the former servant of the Turnu Roşu could have had an impressive career. The captaincy of Gregor Pokai may have been a good connection for Ambrus Pokai, who is mentioned in 1582 and in 1597 as postal servant.[88] The kinship between the servants of Turnu Roşu can also be shown: at the same time, two persons named Lossardy appear in 1572 on the payrolls.[89] For those who started their careers in Turnu Roşu, working as a servant in the service of the town and the Seven Seats was a big step forward. First of all, they received a higher salary (30 florins a year), and then they probably also had the advantage of being in this position, carrying out important political tasks, diplomatic missions, being close to influential people, Transylvanian and Wallachian court dignitaries and foreign ambassadors (Ottoman, Polish,

83 Derzsi, "Servicii poştale," 369.
84 Derzsi, "Servicii poştale," 369.
85 SJAN Sibiu, Socoteli consulare, no. 97 (1581), f. 88 (1568), f. 54.
86 Derzsi, "Servicii poştale," 369.
87 Serviciul Judeţean al Arhivelor Naţionale Cluj, Fond Familial Bánffy, seria 1, Documente medievale, no. 72.
88 Derzsi, "Servicii poştale," 368–369.
89 SJAN Sibiu, Socoteli consulare, no. 92 (1572), f. 39v.

French).[90] The task required loyal, tried and experienced people with an excellent knowledge of the roads and the local population. For these men, who aspired to be in the service of castles or towns, with various missions, including military service, the highest aim was to achieve the rank of captain, the office of burgrave being an intermediate station. Socially, these people belonged to the middle echelons of the circles of officials, and were not prominent in their personal standing. The oath of the burgrave reveals that the social perception of the castle servants or *trabants* was not very favourable: if he had to consent to pay the men their wages in money, as honest persons. Their names suggest that the servants were of mixed ethnic origin, Hungarian, German, Romanian (*wallach*) and Gypsy origin to (Thoma Zygan). Most of them probably had their surnames from their place of provenance: *Szakadát* (Săcădate), *Midwesch* (Mediaş), *Brassai* (from Braşov), *Halmagyi* (from Hălmeag), *Mihalyfalvi* (from Boarta), *Klausenburger* (from Cluj), *de Talmasch* (from Tălmaciu), *de Boicza* (from Boiţia), and to a lesser extent their occupation: *Schneyder* (Tailor), *Weber* (Weaver), *Pribék* (Henchman). Perhaps to ensure their loyalty to the town and the Saxons, the town council of Sibiu decided in 1596 that the tower of Turnu Roşu should no longer have a Hungarian burgrave.[91]

The judicial and other administration of the estate of Tălmaciu was carried out by the royal judge of Sibiu, as Saxon *comes* and the mayor of the town and of the province, representing the Seven Seats. In 1583 the prince of Transylvania confirmed the judicial and administrative powers of these highest officials of the Transylvanian Saxon Nation, as well as those of the burgraves appointed by them.[92] One of the most important roles of the burggrave was to hold court for a population of the villages belonging to the seat.[93] As stated in the oath, he was obliged to provide a public procedure accessible to all inhabitants, to convene the council of the seat at the usual place and time, to conduct the proceedings in accordance with the law, without partiality either for goods, gifts or personal involvement. The burgrave had to be sworn to pronounce sentence in accordance with the Saxon Statutes and in the presence of the Seat and the public,[94] does not

90 For example, Demeter Nagy, one of the servants of the town and the nation between 1555 and 1573, later became a captain of the prince, Derzsi, "Servicii poştale," 369.

91 SJAN Sibiu, Colecţia de documente medievale, U II, no. 2.

92 Müller, *Stühle und Distrikte*, 271.

93 Müller, *Stühle und Distrikte*, 271–273 (the chapter "Die Hermannstädter Gerichtsbarkeit in den Siebenrichterbesitzungen der Talmescher Burggrafschaft").

94 *Statuta jurium municipalium Saxonum in Transsylvania/Das Eigen-Landrecht der Siebenbürger Sachsen* (1583), the own land rights of the Transylvanian Saxons, which

stand in the way of an appeal, to keep a record of the sums received from the fines and to deliver them to the superior authority, to give an annual account of the money and to retain none for himself.[95] Furthermore, it does not introduce new habits in administration, tax management and judging, it does not burden the inhabitants of the seat with unjust or useless services, it does not allow others to do so, it is content with its usual income.[96] According to an instruction from 1701, some of the appeals went to the Transylvanian Saxon comes and others to the provincial mayor. The burgrave was to seek advice from the supreme officials of the Nation in difficult cases. In criminal cases, he was not allowed to bring a criminal court without the prior knowledge of the magistrate (town council) of Sibiu. The burgrave received only one third of the court fees, while two thirds went to the two senior officials.[97] The burgrave was assisted in his judging by the assessors of the Seat of Tălmaciu. That they acted not only as councillors but also as judges is clear from the oath reserved for them, which is found immediately after the oath of the burgrave (see **Annex III**!).[98]

The involvement of the burgrave in the judiciary could of course be traced back to the Middle Ages. The statutes of the guilds of Sibiu, Sighişoara, Sebeş and Orăştie were drawn up in 1376 by representatives of the king and the Seven Seats, in the presence of Johann de Scharpenek, castellan of *Lanzkrone*.[99] In 1561, in a lawsuit between Kristóf, the apothecary of Sibiu, and the widow of Simon Schuler over a property in the market town of Tălmaciu, the testimonies were recorded by *Burgraf*, *Honn* (judge of the market town) and the burghers of

---

was valid until the Austrian Civil Code was introduced, in 1853. For moore on this see Moldt Dirk, *Deutsche Stadtrechte im mittelalterlichen Siebenbürgen. Korporationsrechte – Sachsenspiegelrecht – Bergrecht* (Köln, Weimar, Wien: Böhlau Verlag, 2009), 227.

95 The 1701 Instruction also mentions the burgrave's obligation to keep court records, Müller, *Stühle und Distrikte*, 272.

96 No separate account of the villages administered by the burgrave has survived. However, a register from the end of the sixteenth century of the grain contributions of the settlements of the Sibiu seat (*Regestrum super gelimarim in sede Cibiniensis*) shows that the contribution of the Tălmaciu estate was supervised by the burgrave (Georg Leitscher), SJAN Sibiu, Colecţia de acte fasciculate, B. Agricultură, no. 52.

97 Müller, *Stühle und Distrikte*, 273.

98 Müller, *Stühle und Distrikte*, 273.

99 *Comerţ şi meşterşuguri în Sibiu şi în cele şapte scaune 1224–1579/Handel und Gewerbe in Hermannstadt und in den Sieben Stühlen*, ed. Monica Vlaicu (Sibiu/Hermannstadt: Hora, 2003), 64.

Tălmaciu and sent to the authorities in Sibiu.[100] In another legal transaction, in which the boundaries of the commune of Bradu and Tălmaciu were surveyed, the report dated in 12 June 1588, was signed by Georg Leytscher, burgrave of Turnu Roşu, and sent to the mayor, royal judge and chair judge (judge of the town and the Seat) of Sibiu.[101] But we do not find the burgrave among the judges who arbitrated the disputes of the inhabitants of the market town of Tălmaciu.[102] This can be explained by the fact that the local residents, as well as the Greek merchants who settled in the market town, were free to resolve their disputes (and if they did not concern real property) before their own judges (*Hann* and burghers), thereafter appeals to be lodged with the council of Sibiu.[103]

The tower of Turnu Roşu belonged to the guard castles of the border, in terms of its function. However, its strategic importance was increased by the fact that it was a customs post on the trade route through the Olt Valley, which not only controlled goods but also people entering the country. This strengthened the position of Sibiu, which administered the castle, and the Saxons, both economically and in terms of their political interests, and was also essential in maintaining direct relations with the rulers of Wallachia. Although the castle's defences showed signs of decline from the mid-sixteenth century onwards

---

100 The seven testimonies show that the house and courtyard in question were built by the late Simon Schuler in the year when Majláth (Stephen, the Transylvanian voivode) left Tălmaciu, SJAN Sibiu, Colecţia de documente medievale, U V, no. 685.

101 SJAN Sibiu, Colecţia de documente medievale, U IV, no. 1298, with valuable local historical data.

102 Dionisie Avalus, a resident of Tălmaciu, asked the town council of Sibiu to mediate his conflict with his neighbours, whom he accuses of thievery, deceit, lying and villainy. The letter reveals that the complainant was suspected of cheating at the wine tapping, measuring and selling more wine than the local rules require. He was reprimanded (fined 2 florins if he continued to sell his wine) by the local authorities for the offence and swearing in church. In his own defence, the complainant claimed that he needed more wine because he was building his house and that foreign craftsmen and workers would stop working for him if they were not properly supplied, and that in the delay the residents of Tălmaciu would steal everything from the construction site, SJAN Sibiu, Acte fasciculate, M. Administraţie, no. 169, f. 42–43; Undated document, probably written at the end of the sixteenth century.

103 Anna, Jacob's wife, testified before the own judge and burghers in the divorce trial of Mathias Raw, a councillor in Sibiu, and his wife. The letter, issued on October 11, 1590, was sent by the *Honn* Hannes Fekesch and the council of Tălmaciu to the Dean of the Chapter of Sibiu, who was judeged the divorce case, SJAN Sibiu, Fond Capitlul evanghelic CA Sibiu, seria 2, f. 337; About the disputes of the Greek merchants of Tălmaciu in 1561, see Pakucs Willcocks, "Economy and trade," 109.

(mainly the number of guards was reduced, but also the costs of development and maintenance), its strategic role remained central: in addition to defending the customs station, the castle's burgrave managed the tasks of forwarding the mail and guarding the border zone. The surviving sources do not allow us to establish the exact reason for the changes, but only to see that while in the first half of the century there were several examples of the duplication of the command of the castles forming the defence system (two burgraves were appointed at the same time), in the second half of the century there was only one person in this office. This can be probably explained by the relatively peaceful times, but it also shows that the function of the castellans was transformed into an office subordinate to the authorities of Sibiu (*Porkolaben Amt*), held by town employees who also performed military functions, received a fixed salary and belonged to the middle echelon of the official corps: they were required to carry out the duties of castle guards in accordance with instructions issued by the municipal authorities and to take an oath on their entering the service. In the second half of the century, we can identify the names of four persons who held the office of the burgrave, who, before serving in Turnu Roşu, had worked for the town and/or the Seven Seats (among other things, they delivered letters), of whom two later became captains of the town of Sibiu. The castle employed only four or five servants on a permanent basis in the mid-century, growing to six in the 1570s and eight in the 1580s, when sources refer to them as *trabant*. This number is also in line with the number of castle staff permanently employed by the castles of the fiscal estates. The burgrave managed the taxes and the jurisdiction of the villages that supplied the border forts – a role that also points towards that of the fiscal administrators.

Annex I. Burgraves and Servants Employed by the Seven Seats at the Tower of Turnu Roșu in the sixteenth century

	Burgrave	Servant					
1525	Nicolaus (Porkolab de Thalmach)						
1526	Nicolaus						
1528	Nicolaus / Benedict						
1531	Emerich Klausenburger / Colomanus Schneyder						
1532	Colomanus Schneyder	Toma Trabant					
1554	Nicolaus		Fabian	Opra walach	Benedict Todt		
1555	Boltisar / Nicolaus	Christoffor	Opra walach	Kinda walach	Peter	Mon	
1556	Boltisar	Christophor	Opra walach	Thoma Zakadathy			
1557	Boltisar	Peter	Jakob	Christophor	Mahn		
1558	Nicolaus	Jacob	Mon	Peter Ham	Kinda		

	Burgrave	**Servant**					
1561	Nicolaus	Opre	Mano	Valentinus Varanya	Thoma Zygan	Luca Istany	
1569	Anthon Bollog	Opre	Kinda	Antall	Moga		
1566	Paul Cursor	Peter Ham	Opre Curtan	Kinda	Colman		
1567	Thoma	Opre Tatul	Jacob Weber	Walacho Bretelin	Andreas Pribeck		
1568	Thoma Wayda/ Nicolaus Nagy	Opre Tatul	Jacob Textori	Bartholomeo	Andreas Pribeck		
1569	Anthonius Schwarcz	Johann Midwesch	Hieremie Brassay	Martin Lossardy	Georg Lossardy	Johann Pokay	Melchior Sicz
1570	Antonius Schwarz	Martin Lossardy	Georgio Lossardy	Johann Pokai	Opra Walach	Stephan Hassagu	Halmag Valach
1572	Antonius Schwarcz	Michael Dick servitor pixidari	Gerog Lossardy	Petro Bezegfalvi	Opre de Boicya	Halmagyi	Johann Pokai
1573	Antonius Schwarcz	Peter Bezegfelwy	Opre Valach	Halmag Valach	Johann Pokai	Adam Mihalfalwy	
1581	Neppendorfi Janos						
1583	Löchy Jörg						
1588	Georgius Leytscher						
1592	Leochey Georg						

Annex II. The Oath of the Burgrave of Turnu Roşu around 1600

(Serviciul Judeţean al Arhivelor Naţionale Sibiu, Colecţia de documente medievale, U IV, no. 1703)

Jurament des Burggrawens oder Porkolabens bey dem rothen Thurn
Ich N.N. schwere bey Goth dem Watern, bey Goth dem Sohn undt bey Goth dem heyligen Geist, das ich in dem porkolaben ampt, darinnen ich ietzunder nach inhalt meiner instruction statuiret werde, redlich undt aufrichtig handeln will, aus der Wallachey die posten, sie seÿen böse oder gute, will ich alsobaldt meiner höchsten obrigkeit an tag geben, damit ich königlichen gnaden auch tempestive möge können darvon verständigkeit, den freünden ein freünd, den feinden ein feind im friedlichen undt unfriedlichen zeiten will ich nebst denen die mir an die handt gegeben worden, meine schuldigkeit thun, standthäftigen, beÿ diesem ohrt verfarren bies an mein ende. In den stuel wil ich keine neue bräuche nicht gesinnet seÿe aufzubringen oder ihn mit ungewöhnlichen diensten gebürren, viel weniger unnutzliche ankasten auch andn solches zutun nicht zulaßen, sondern mit den dem content stehen, uns was bieshero alle aufrichtige und redliche porkolaben content gewesen. Die verborgene wege mit dem plajaschen wil ich fleißig laßen verwachten, den litiganten wil ich auch einer freÿen urteile geben, und den stuel zu gewöhnlicher zeit, wie bieshero im brauch gehalten, an seinem gewöhnlichen ohrt laßen convocieren, in gegenwart des stuehl der litiganten klag und antwort öffentlich abhören, Ihnen das recht nicht aus gunst, freundschaft, feindschaft oder umb geschenk, sondern laut unserer Statuten aussprechen, den rechten seiner freÿen lauff laßen, die straffen ihren öffentlichen gegenwart des ganzen stuels ankündigen, selbige auffs papier bringen, exigiren, und jährlich nach gehaltener rechenschafft meiner höchsten obrigkeit administriren, keine, sie sey groß oder klein, mir allein vendiciren. Andere einkommens von früchten, hew, wie auch aus der mühlen, sie haben ihre nahmen wie sie wollen, wil ich aufs fleißigkeit laßen cumulieren, zu recht schaffen, und bishero observirten brauch nach meiner höchsten obrigkeit zu rechten zeit lassen einschaffen, die thurnknechte wil ich allerzeit in völligen zahl halten, die besoldung nicht in meinen nutzen wenden, in summa was einem ehelichen, aufrichtigen mann zustehet, wil ich auch gesinnet lassen zustehen. So wahr helffe mir Goth und gebe mir meine seele seeligkeit.

Annex III. The Oath of the Councillors of Turnu Roşu around 1600

(Serviciul Judeţean al Arhivelor Naţionale Sibiu, Colecţia de documente medievale, U IV, no. 1703)

Juramentum Talmacensium

Wir N.N. schwere beÿ Goth dem Vater, Goth dem Sohn, undt Goth dem heiligen Geiste, daß wir wollen neben unserer höchsten obrigkeit, auch diesem unsren neuen eingeführten herren burggraffen getreu seÿn, gehorsam in allem billigen sachen, wie bieshero im brauch gehalten worden, beÿ allen aufrichtigen undt redlichen burggraffen. Was wir warden hören, böses oder gutes, wollen wir beÿ zeit an tag geben, dieses ohrt beÿ guten undt unfriedlichen zeiten nebenst den her burgraffen helffen verwachten, bies auf unsern letzten bluttroffen. Die strafen, der übelthäter nicht bergen, freündschafft, geschenk oder gunst wegen, sondan diselbigen beÿ guten gewißen zu rechter zeit an tag geben. Im gerichte nebenst dem her burggrafen den thädigt patheÿen, nicht aus gunste freunndschaftlich, feindtschaftliche, sondern nach den geschriebenen Statuten das recht helffen sprechen: nach eröffneten sentenz auf die straff verfallende fleißig helffen achtung geben, damit er bieshero gehaltenen gebrauch nach, in rechter form die straffen möge austreiben, undt unserer höchsten obrigkeit, von früchter auf dem feldt, wie auch das der mühlen, sie haben nahmen wie sie wollen, wolte schmälleren sich gutigeren oder wir dienste, unkosten undt bürfe dem stuel aufdrigen, sich heimliche straffen machen, ohne wißen undt willen des stuelsbeÿsitzen, außerhalb seiner portion, willen wir solches nicht verschweigen, sondn unserer höchsten obrigkeit alsobaldt an tag geben. Unserer höchsten obrigkeit einkommung gehörige, von früchten, mühlen, sie haben nahmen wie sie wollen, wollen wir aufs fleißigste helffen cumulieren, einschatzen, unverletzt, wie bishero im stuel brauchlich gewesen. Mit einem wort, was rechtsaffenen gefrewen unterthanen gebühret zuthun, wollen wir auch nach alle mögligkeit zuthun gesinnet seyen. So wahr helfe etc.

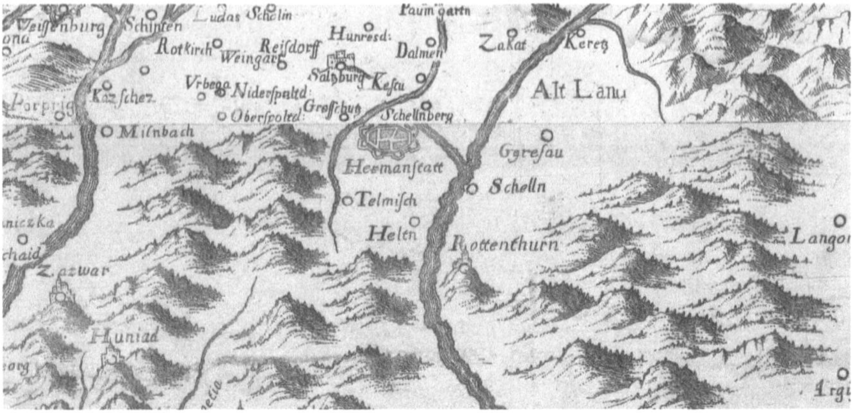

Turnu Roşu (*Rottenthurn*), detail from *Ungaria cum finitimiis provinciis…*/Hungary and its frontier provinces, Georg Matthäus Vischer/Matthias Greischer, 1682, cooper engraving (Landesarchiv Baden-Württemberg Abt. Generallandesarchiv Karlsruhe)

Gizella Nemeth and Adriano Papo

The Fortress of Eger in the Mid-Sixteenth Century, on the Border between the Kingdom of Hungary and the Ottoman Empire: the Siege of 1552

Abstract: In this paper, after a virtual reconstruction of the fortress of Eger in the mid-sixteenth century, and a brief summary of its history, we will retrace the story of the 1552 siege that the joint Ottoman armies of the second vizier Kara Ahmed Pasha, of the *beylerbeyi* of Rumelia Mehmed Soqollu, and of Buda's governor Khadım Alı, in vain tried to conquer by fighting for 38 consecutive days. After the occupation of Temesvár (Timişoara), Lippa (Lipova) and Szolnok, the Ottomans aimed to conquer also the important fortress of Eger, the key to access Upper Hungary (roughly present-day Slovakia), and its rich mining towns. The three Ottoman armies arrived in Eger between 9 and 13 September 1552. Eger was defended by about 2.000 men, mainly coming from the free royal cities, the counties of Upper Hungary, and the properties of neighbouring landowners and ecclesiastical lords. István Dobó was the commander-in-chief of the castle. The fortress was subjected to heavy bombardment; the defenders, also aided by the women, repelled all the assaults by heroically fighting with all means (throwing stones and incendiary tools, hand-to-hand combat, use of sharp poles with hot tips and so on). On the other hand, the Ottomans tried to take over the fortress by digging underground tunnels and placing mines at the base of the walls. On 17 October, Kara Ahmed pasha, worried about the arrival of winter and aware of the losses suffered by his army and the diseases that had affected the surviving soldiers, decided to withdraw. The failure of the Ottoman siege of Eger was mainly due to the determination of the defenders, their acts of heroism, the strict self-discipline, the efficiency and genius of the commander and the collegial management of the defence.

Keywords: Ottoman Empire, Hungary, Ottoman Conquests in Hungary, The Fortress of Eger, The Siege of Eger (1552)

Introduction and Objective

The murder of Friar George Martinuzzi Utyeszenics,[1] cardinal, soldier, and lieutenant of the queen of Transylvania Isabella Jagello, occurred on 17 December

---

1 About George Martinuzzi Utyeszenics we refer to the following monographs: Adriano Papo and Gizella Nemeth Papo, *Giorgio Martinuzzi. Figura e ruolo politico di un monaco-statista dalmata nella storia ungherese del Cinquecento* (Szombathely: Savaria

1551 in the castle of Alvinc (Vințu de Jos) on order of the king of the Romans and Hungary, Ferdinand of Habsburg, brought about a renewal of the Ottoman offensive in Banat and Hungary.

The purpose of the Ottoman army was to conquer the fortresses of Upper Hungary (roughly present–day Slovakia), which guaranteed the defence of the nearby mining region. The fortress of Eger was located on the important communication route between Buda and Upper Hungary: its conquest was therefore of primary importance.

In this paper, after a virtual reconstruction of the fortress of Eger in the mid–sixteenth century, and a brief summary of its history, we will retrace the story of the 1552 siege of Eger that the joint Ottoman armies of the second vizier Kara Ahmed Pasha,[2] of the *beylerbeyi* of Rumelia Mehmed Soqollu,[3] and of Buda's governor Khadım Alı,[4] in vain tried to conquer by fighting for 38 consecutive days.[5]

University Press, 2011); Adriano Papo and Gizella Nemeth Papo, *Frate Giorgio Martinuzzi. Cardinale, soldato e statista dalmata agli albori del Principato di Transilvania* (Canterano, Roma: Aracne editrice, 2017); Adriano Papo and Gizella Nemeth Papo, *Il diavolo e l'acquasanta. Frate Giorgio Martinuzzi, fondatore del Principato di Transilvania* (Oradea: Ratio & Revelatio, 2020); Adriano Papo and Gizella Nemeth Papo, *Nemăsurata ispită a puterii. Gheorghe Martinuzzi, adevăratul rege al Transilvaniei în secolul al XVI-lea*, trans. Raluca Lazarovici Vereş (Oradea: Ratio & Revelatio, 2019).

2 Kara Ahmed Pasha, of Albanian origin, was the commander in chief (*serdar*) of the Ottoman army.

3 Mehmed Soqollu [Sokolović] (1506–1579), a renegade of Serbian–Bosnian origin, recruited according to the practice of *devşirme*, became in 1565 Ottoman grand vizier, and remained in that office until his death. The *beylerbeyi* was the governor of an Ottoman province called *beylerbeyilik* or *eyalet*.

4 Khadım Alı Pasha was Buda's governor from May 1551 to the end of February 1553 and, a second time, from 22 (23) February 1556 until the beginning of February 1557.

5 The bibliography on the siege of Eger is extremely vast: we limit ourselves to pointing out the monographs by Imre Soós and Imre Szántó, *Eger vár védelme 1552–ben* (Budapest: Művelt Nép Könyvkiadó, 1952) and by Imre Szántó, *Küzdelem a török terjeszkedés ellen Magyarországon* (Budapest: Akadémiai Kiadó, 1985), 153–255 as well. As for the narrative works relating to the siege of Eger we refer to: Sebestyén Tinódi, *Cronica*, ed. István Sugár (Budapest: Európa, 1984), part VI: *Eger vár viadaljáról való ének história*, 223–90 and part VII: *Egri históriának summája*, 291–309; Miklós Istvánffy, *Regni hungarici historia Libri XXXIV* (Coloniae Agrippinae: Sumptibus Henrici Rommerskirchen, 1724), 208–15; *Francisci Forgách de Ghymes de statu reipublicae hungaricae commentarii* (*Monumenta Hungariae Historica, Scriptores*, XVI) (Pest: Magyar Tudományos Akadémia, 1866), 55–73; *De' Commentarii della guerra di Transilvania del S. Ascanio Centorio de gli Hortensii. Ne quali si contengono tutte le cose, che successero nell'Ungheria dalla rotta del re Lodovico XII. sino all'anno MDLIII.*

An Outline of Eger's History

Eger, today the chief town of the county of Heves in northern Hungary, was a bishopric already in the third century; however, it had probably played an important role since the time of the so called "conquest of the homeland" performed by the Magyars in the late ninth century. In 1009, King Stephen I (1000/1001–1038), Saint Stephen, reorganized the bishop's seat by surrounding it with walls, and starting the construction of the cathedral dedicated to Saint John the Evangelist, a three-nave Romanesque-style basilica (we have been informed of this construction through a diploma of 1261 drawn up by the king of Hungary Béla IV). In 1241, the Tatars destroyed the town but not the fortress. In 1271, King Béla IV (1235–70) rebuilt a part of the town, and protected it with walls and moats. At the time of the occupation of the Taborites of Jan Giskra (1400–1469) the town was set on fire; probably, its fortifications were also destroyed, because in 1491, under the bishopric of Orbán Dóczy, Eger had neither walls nor embankments.

The reconstruction of the fortress began in 1541 on behalf of the castle captain Tamás Varkocs starting from the bastion that bears his name. The siege of 1552 reduced the fortress to a poor condition. The reconstruction work was carried out in the years 1553–55 by the new captain Gergely Bornemisza. The castle's renovation works took place in 1569 based on the design of the Italian architect Ottavio Baldigara. The fortifications were strengthened during the Ottoman domination following the conquest of 1596 and were almost completely destroyed in 1687 during the re-conquest of the fortress by the imperial army of General Antonio Carafa.[6]

In 1542 Péter Perényi obtained the territory of Eger at the time of the Hungarian civil war between the two kings of Hungary, Ferdinand I of Habsburg

---

Con le tavole delle cose degne di memoria (Vinegia/Venice: Appresso Gabriel Giolito de' Ferrari, 1566), 221–24; *Delle Historie de' svoi Tempi di Natale Conti. Parte Prima. Di Latino in Volgare nuouamente tradotta da M. Giovan Carlo Saraceni* (Venetia: Appresso Damian Zenaro, 1589), 146v–148r; János Zsámboki, "Eger ostroma. 1552," in *Magyar történelmi olvasókönyv*, ed. S. Mika (Budapest: Lampel, 1907), II, 33–47. We also refer to our paper: "L'assedio di Eger del 1552," *Studia historica adriatica ac danubiana* XI, no. 1–2 (2018): 38–116.

6 About the fortress of Eger and its history, cf. János Kárpáti, *Az egri vár "titkos" föld alatti világa* (Eger: Motívum, 2004); the book is provided with a copious bibliography. About the St. John the Evangelist church cf. István Sugár, *Az egri főszékesegyház* (Eger: Heves megyei Idegenforgalmi Hivatal, 1967), as well as the paper by Gergely Buzás, "Az egri székesegyház XIII–XIV. századi gótikus épülete," *Az Egri Vár Híradója* 38 (2006): 24–65.

(1526–1564) and John I Szapolyai (1526–1540). According to a project drawn up by the Italian architect Alessandro da Vedano, at this time the fortification was divided into two parts, the inner and outer fortress, connected only by a bridge and a door. Péter Perényi, who was the brother of Bishop Ferenc and the son of the Hungarian palatine Imre, held many important dignities: voivode of Transylvania (1526–1529), governor (*főispán*) of the county of Temes (Timiş), captain of Temesvár (Timişoara), keeper of the crown of St. Stephen and protector of the Protestant preachers. After taking part in the battle of Mohács in 1526, he pledged loyalty to King John I Szapolyai. In the following year, he passed to the service of Ferdinand of Habsburg, who rewarded him with the donation of the castle of Sárospatak. In 1529 he returned to serve King John I Szapolyai and later, in 1540, he returned once again to the service of the Habsburgs as chancellor of the kingdom. Between 1540 and 1542 he held the position of commander-in-chief of the Hungarian army. In 1541 he participated together with General Johann von Roggendorff in the offensive conducted against Buda. In 1542 he was suspected of participating in a plot against the sovereign; therefore, he was accused of aspiring to the Hungarian crown and consequently imprisoned.[7]

The Description of the Fortress as Existing in 1552

The fortress – as described by Miklós Istvánffy[8] – was located on a hill, rocky on one side, covered with vineyards and fruit trees sloping down to the valley on the other. The town extended under the castle to the south-west. It was surrounded by a wood and earth rampart (*palanka*) and crossed by a small river, the Eger, which collects various tributaries before flowing out in the Tisza River. Not far away, to the south, "boiling" thermal waters gushed out; they were suitable for milling, as well as for bathing even in winter.

According to the description given by Ferenc Forgách, the town of Eger was surrounded from the east to the west by vineyards and fertile fields. A fortress was erected in the uncultivated areas and extended over a vast space. During the Hungarian civil war, King Ferdinand sent a Spanish garrison to defend the fortification, but the Habsburg mercenaries soon abandoned their post. Péter Perényi occupied the deserted fortress and ordered the construction of stone walls and very high embankments. Then, he divided the fortress into two parts separated by a moat and a very thick wall. The king of the Romans regained possession of

---

7 About Péter Perényi's biography cf. the voice *Perényi, Péter*, in *Új Magyar Életrajzi Lexikon*, ed. László Markó (Budapest: Balassi Kiadó, 2004), V, 255.

8 Cf. Istvánffy, *Regni hungarici historia*, 209.

the fortress after Perényi was taken captive to Vienna, and reinforced it by means of new bastions and embankments. The Royal Seat was situated on a small hill, about 300 steps to the north, right in front of the fortress. It was a place where, according to tradition, King Stephen oversaw the architects and blacksmiths involved in the construction of the church dedicated to St. John the Evangelist. Considerable tithes (*decimae*) were donated to the Church thanks to the abundant production of wine.[9]

Ascanio Centorio degli Ortensi and Natale Conti emphasize the proximity of the eastern hills overlooking the fortress. The hills were a stone's throw away from the walls according to Centorio,[10] or the shooting of a harquebus, according to Conti.[11]

The most detailed description, however, is undoubtedly that given by Sebestyén Tinódi.[12]

The fortress of Eger was and is nowadays positioned on a hill in a wonderful place. It had the typical shape of a turtle, stretching from the west to the east for just under 400 meters, from the south to the north for about 250 meters. A stone wall (i.e. that built in 1542 on the project drawn up by Alessandro da Vedano), which in some points was 4 meters thick, divided the fortress – as said above – into two parts: a) the inner fortress, about 210 meters long and wide; b) the outer fortress, approximately 180 meters long and 260 meters wide from the south-west to the north-east. The southern side of the fortress – i.e. that facing the town – was dominated by an imposing bastion with a gate built by Tamás Varkocs, still existing nowadays 60 meters far from the Ippolito gate, which was walled up in the Middle Ages (reference is made here to Ippolito d'Este, who was Bishop of Eger from 1497 to 1498). Above the Ippolito gate there was a bell tower with a clock, remembered in the eighteenth century by the Turkish traveller Evlia Çelebi; above the door ran a 4 meters thick curtain wall with a covered walkway. To the west, the Dobó bastion overlooked the underlying town; a large circular tower stood on the bastion. From the north-west end protruded the so-called earthen bastion, a truncated pyramid embankment, 10–12 meters high, wrapped in a wooden pile filled with earth; close to it, there was the Tömlöc bastion, so called because it served as a prison until the end of the sixteenth century; the

9 Szántó, *Küzdelem a török terjeszkedés ellen*, 155.
10 Centorio, *Commentarii*, 221.
11 Conti, *Delle Historie de' svoi Tempi*, 146–47.
12 Cfr. Tinódi, *Cronica*, VI, 226–30.

bastion had been built in stone between 1542 and 1548 on a square medieval core, whose ruins are still evident today.

From the Tömlöc bastion – according to Centorio[13] and Ortelius[14] – the women of Eger fought like lionesses, pouring hot water and pitch on the unfortunate attackers. The earthen bastion was often the object of attack by the Turks, because, once the wooden poles of the *palanka* were set on fire – even if externally protected by mud – the whole embankment would have been more easily knocked down by cannon shots. Between the Dobó bastion and the earthen one there were various buildings, such as kitchens, ovens and houses, leaning against the inner curtain wall, which was 95 meters long, 12–15 meters high and 1,7 meters wide. To the north, a not very high wall running from the Tömlöc to the Sándor[15] bastion protected elegant buildings, including the Bishop's palace, which was constructed in 1470, nowadays known as the Gothic Palace. Within the inner fortress on the east side of the square, there are the ruins of the former cathedral, which was enclosed by two towers; its sacristy was used in 1552 as a casemate. After it had been destroyed by the Tatars, the St. John the Evangelist's church was rebuilt in the thirteenth century with three naves; in the fourteenth century, a large sanctuary was erected behind the main apse of the church. In 1542, when the fortress was divided into two parts, the sanctuary was transformed into a bastion. The temporary seat of the bishop and the homes of the Chapter priests were situated in front of the church.

A strong *palanka* (still existing in 1568) extended from the Varkocs gate to the Dobó bastion; near the Varkocs gate there was, still visible today, the so called "guns hill", a high embankment where the guns were positioned. These guns could fire in two different directions: to the west and to the south. An embankment with similar functions and surrounded by a wooden pile, known today as "the Calvary Hill", rose to the south–east, near the walls that separated the inner fortress from the outer one. It was not visible from the Almagyar hill, where the Janissaries would later camp. After the construction of the wall separating the two fortresses, the sanctuary behind the cathedral was transformed into a bastion filled with earth, the Sanctuary (in Hungarian "Szentély") bastion. This

---

13 Centorio, *Commentarii*, 223–24.

14 Hyeronimus Ortelius, *Redivivus et Continuatus, oder Der Ungarischen Kriegs–Empörungen historische Beschreibung* (Frankfurt a. M., D. Fievet für P. Fürst in Nürnberg, 1665), 87.

15 The bastion took its name from the aforementioned architect Alessandro (Sándor in Hungarian) from Vedano, who worked in Eger between 1542 and 1548 in the service of Péter Perényi.

bastion was connected by means of an embankment to the Sándor bastion. The eastern end of the bastion was demolished in the seventies of the sixteenth century, during the reconstruction works directed by Ottavio Baldigara. From the Sanctuary bastion, it was possible to shoot both to the north and to the east. The outer fortress was accessed through the "middle door", also known as the "dark door", and an underground passage connected to an elevated bridge. Between the two fortresses, from the Sándor bastion to the "ancient gate", there was a deep moat (now crossed by the railway). A thin wall branched off from the Sándor bastion to the fortress corner, where a round tower (Bolyky tower, originally Bebek tower, also known as the "corner tower") once stood.[16]

At the south-eastern end of the outer fortress Imre Bebek (his brother Ferenc, together with Gáspár Serédy, had taken the castle from King John Szapolyai in November 1529) had built another bastion (the Bebek bastion), which was connected by means of a thin wall to the "ancient gate", dominated by a not very strong tower. Externally, a narrow moat ran along the walls. Within the inner fortress there was a *palanka* reinforced by a series of seven multiple earthen bastions. The *palanka* was defended by the Csabi bastion, which had taken its name from the former captain of Eger István Csabi, who already in 1531 had anticipated Perényi's idea of dividing the fortress into two parts and had thought of opening near that bastion an exit door to the north. North of the Csabi bastion there was a ledge forming the external stone wall of a building (in Hungarian "Szeglet Palota"). Stables had been built near the "ancient gate".[17]

In 1552, the commander of the fortress was István Dobó de Ruszka (ca. 1502–1572), a member of the Hungarian aristocracy of northern Hungary. He had been in the service of Bálint Török in Belgrade, before passing, after the death of his lord in the prisons of the Seven Towers of Constantinople, to that of the king of the Romans. In 1548, after the acquisition of the Eger fortress by King Ferdinand (20 July), István Dobó was appointed captain of the fortress. Immediately after his appointment, the lord of Ruszka secured the buildings and provided for the strengthening of the fortress with the purchase of cannons, weapons and gunpowder.

16 Tinódi, *Cronica*, VI, 226–28.
17 Tinódi, *Cronica*, VI, 228–30.

The Defenders of Eger

After the Ottoman occupation of Temesvár,[18] Lippa (Lipova),[19] and Szolnok,[20] the troops of the second vizier Kara Ahmed Pasha, despite the approach of the autumn season and the losses suffered in previous campaigns, headed towards Eger on the basis of a plan previously elaborated with the governor of Buda, Khadım Alı Pasha, who considered the conquest of Eger a feasible undertaking. Kara Ahmed was also convinced that the defenders would either surrender immediately or abandon the fortress without fighting. However, the second vizier, satisfied with the results achieved in the military campaign that ended with the conquest of Szolnok (4 September 1552), had deemed it more appropriate to return to Constantinople, having already complied with the sultan's orders. However, Khadım Alı warned him not to miss such a good opportunity.[21]

The defenders of Eger, who had been informed about the Turks arrival through dispatches of their spies, discouraged after receiving the news of the fall of Szolnok, were all convinced that they could keep the fortress for no more than a couple of weeks. On the other hand, the king and his advisers, despite being aware of the arrival in Eger of the Ottoman armies, took care to strengthen the fortifications of Kassa (Košice), since this town was located at the intersection of important roads of communication between Poland, to the north, and Transylvania to the east. Shortly, once Eger was conquered, the Ottomans would have the way free to Upper Hungary and therefore to Poland and to Transylvania as well.[22]

In view of the presumed Ottomans arrival, the first objective of the commander of the fortress was the reinforcement of its garrison, which was then made up of just under 400 units (about 200 infantrymen and 200 cavalrymen, whose number rose to 278 in the month of September). According to Dobó and his officers, this number could increase not only thanks to the contribution of

---

18 Cf. Gizella Nemeth and Adriano Papo, "La conquista ottomana di Temesvár. 1552," *Studia historica adriatica ac danubiana* 6, no. 1–2 (2013): 7–79.

19 Cf. Gizella Nemeth and Adriano Papo, "Il caso 'Bernardo de Aldana': l'abbandono di Lippa/Lipova e le sue conseguenze. 1552–1556," *Crisia* 43 (2013): 85–99.

20 Cf. "L'occupazione ottomana di Szolnok. 1552," *Studia historica adriatica ac danubiana* 7, no. 1–2 (2014): 13–35, and "L'offensiva ottomana contro Szolnok ed Eger nel racconto del milanese Francesco degli Streppati. 1552," in *Quaestiones Romanicae* (Szeged: Jate Press, 2015), vol. III/2, 758–63; this latter paper also reports a brief summary of the siege of Eger written by Francesco degli Streppati.

21 Cf. Szántó, *Küzdelem a török terjeszkedés ellen*, 184.

22 Cf. Tinódi, *Cronica*, VI, 231; Szántó, *Küzdelem a török terjeszkedés ellen*, 185–86.

the troops gathered by neighbouring lords or through the conscription of mercenaries and the employment of the inhabitants of the surrounding villages inside the fortress, but also, and above all, through the intervention of the royal army. Dobó was aware that Eger's eventual fall could be attributed not to his lack of merit but to lack of an adequate number of defenders. However, the reinforcements were not very consistent.[23]

With the treaty of 20 December 1548, the bishop of Eger and grand chancellor of the kingdom Miklós Oláh had discharged on the sovereign the obligation to financially provide for the defence of Eger. For his part – as Sebestyén Tinódi recalls – the bishop would instead contribute to the defence of the castle only with prayers and through the celebration of propitiatory masses. Eger was teeming with priests of all orders and ranks. However, after receiving the news of the Turks arrival, only very few of them remained in the town,[24] even if a resolution of the Diet of Besztercebánya (Banská Bystrica) of 1542 obliged each convent to provide two monks for the accomplishment of religious practices. On the other hand, the contribution of the Eger Chapter to the fortress defence was scarce. The Chapter supplied Dobó with only 27 infantrymen out of the 100 promised, 17 of which deserted at the first sign of danger. On the other hand, infantrymen (*trabants*) were sent to Eger by the provost of Jászó (Jasov) of the Premonstratensian Order and by the Cartusian monks of Felsőtárkány. Not even one soldier was recruited by the landowners of the Heves County, the administrative unit in which Eger was situated.

István Dobó was very careful and foresighted in procuring everything needed for the defence of the castle. For this purpose, various surgeons (barbers who also acted as doctors and nurses), blacksmiths, carpenters, millers, butchers, cooks, peasants and also two priests were gathered in Eger. Everyone had to work following orders without discussion. No one had to come to terms with the enemy or even listen to the announcements of the Turkish heralds under penalty of death. Everyone swore to defend the fortress, procure provisions and everything else necessary for a long siege. According to Miklós Istvánffy, Dobó took into his own hands, in addition to the command of artillery, also the direction of workers. István Mekcsey, his deputy, was responsible for the organization of the guard. Both commanders supervised the arrangement of militias in their defence posts. The captain led other four officers who controlled as many areas of the fortress.

23 Cf. Tinódi, *Cronica*, VI, 231; Szántó, *Küzdelem a török terjeszkedés ellen*, 186.

24 Cf. Forgách, *Commentarii*, 57.

Below, a synoptic picture of the number and origin of Eger's reinforcements (the sources are listed in brackets):

Local garrison:

200 infantrymen (according to Tinódi); 278 fixed + 7 occasional infantrymen
200 cavalrymen (Tinódi) + 2 commanders
11 gunners (Sugár)[25]

From neighboring villages:

88 trabants (Tinódi; Forgách)
46 cavalrymen (*officiales*) (Tinódi; Forgách); 56 cavalrymen (Sugár)
110 fusilier peasants (Tinódi; Forgách)

From the king:

40 + 40 cavalrymen (Tinódi); 100 (Istvánffy); 41 + 41 (Sugár), under the command of Gáspár Pethő and István Zoltai;

150 infantrymen (Tinódi); 250 (Istvánffy; Forgách); 251 (Sugár), under the command of Gergely Bornemisza;

230 infantrymen (Tinódi; Istvánffy); 213 (Sugár), under the command of Antal Blaskó and Ambrus Zádornik from Kassa:

From ecclesiastical seats:

- from the Chapter of Eger: 27 infantrymen (Tinódi), under the command of János Figedy
- from the Provost of Jászó: 41 infantrymen (Tinódi), under the command of Márton Jászói
- from the Cartusian monks of Felsőtárkány: 4 trabants (Tinódi); 5 (according to other not specified sources)

From counties:

- from Borsod: 50 infantrymen (Tinódi), under the command of Tamás Bolyky
- from Abaúj: 50 infantrymen (Tinódi), under the command of Farkas Choron or Kózon
- from Sáros: 76 infantrymen (Tinódi), under the command of Mihály Bór
- from Szepes (Spiš): 40 trabants (Tinódi), under the command of Márton Szenci
- from Ung: 18 infantrymen (Tinódi), under the command of György Szalacskay and Imre Nagy

25 Cf. István Sugár, *Az egri vár és viadala* (Budapest: Zrínyi Katonai Könyv– és Lapkiadó, 1971), 51–56.

- from Gömör: 50 infantrymen (Tinódi), under the command of Antal Péter Kis

From the free royal cities:

- from Bártfa (Bardejov), Eperjes (Prešov), Késmárk (Kezmarok) Lőcse (Levoča), Kisszeben (Sabinov): 100 infantrymen (Tinódi); 101 (Sugár), under the command of Mihály Lökös

From great landowners:

- from the land ownership of Gábor Perényi: 25 rifle infantrymen (Tinódi; other not specified sources)
- from the land ownership of György Serédy: 50 trabants + 50 infantrymen (Tinódi; Istvánffy), under the command of Bálint Kendy
- from the land ownership of György Báthori: 30 rifle infantrymen (Tinódi); 31 infantrymen (other not specified sources), under the command of Pál Nagy
- from the land ownership of Gabriella, the wife of György Drugeth Homonnai: 24 infantrymen (Tinódi); 26 infantrymen (other not specified sources), under the command of Ferenc Somogyi and Tamás Nagy
- from the land ownership of Gáspár Serédy of Regéc: 14 infantrymen (Tinódi)

Auxiliaries:

workers: 88; barbers (surgeons and nurses): 13; cooks: 14; women, children, priests: 47

Eger's defenders were almost exclusively Hungarians, except for the presence of six German and Austrian artillerymen, six Italian masons and two Italian stonemasons, some Slovak, Southern Slavic and Polish infantrymen.

In summary, Istvánffy and Centorio hypothesize a number close to 2.000 defenders. Similarly Conti speaks of 2.000 men. According to Tinódi there was a number of defenders just under 2.000 men (more exactly: 1.935), but elsewhere (as can be seen from the data reported in the table above) he speaks of 1.753 or 1.858 armed defenders; Szederkényi mentions a total number of 2.600 soldiers, workers, officials and women.[26] According to Gusztáv Gömöry, there were about 1.800[27] armed defenders. According to István Sugár, at the beginning of the siege there were 2.098 people in Eger, of which 1.714 or 1.799 were armed. According

26 Cf. Nándor Szederkényi, *Heves vármegye története* (Eger: Heves Vármegye Közönsége, 1890), II, 145.

27 Cf. Gusztáv Gömöry, "Eger ostroma 1552-ben," *Hadtörténelmi Közlemények* (1890): 613–35: here 623.

to Ferenc Salamon, out of 2.000 people 824 were armed peasants (the so called *portalis militia*), and 560 royal soldiers,[28] if we add the servants paid by the bishopric, this number rises to 1.358. The royal soldiers were totally 546 according to Sugár, 1.935 according to Gyárfás (1.500 infantrymen, 300 cavalrymen and 9 gunners, the remainder being doctors, workers, women and children.[29] It should be noted that the number of armed men in Eger was overall small in relation to the size of the fortress. On the other hand, according to László Kerecsényi, the country's response to Eger's defence was not negligible.[30] Most of the defenders – this was a peculiarity of the sixteenth century armies – were made up of peasants, people who in combat transformed the anger deriving from their humble condition into boldness and courage.

The initial tasks of the captain of Eger were: (1) the provision of foodstuffs, in order to avoid the conquest of the castle by starvation; (2) the soldiers positioning, which was conditioned by the size of the fortress.

As for the provisioning, 4.000 lambs, 456 cattle ready to be slaughtered and smoked, were catered in part directly from Dobó, in part acquired from the neighbouring villages. One hundred and twelve hectolitres of wheat were procured; large quantities of hay, straw and other fodder for the animals were stocked, but also wine, vinegar, various vegetables, salt, eggs, bacon, salted and smoked fish. Wine was mixed with water because there were insufficient reserves (grapes had not yet been harvested). The mercenaries had to pay for all food, including wine, only meat was provided to them for free.[31]

The fortress had 4 large siege guns (bombards), 14 field guns (11 falcons – small field guns of about 1,5–3 tons, firing balls of about 6–8 lbs. – and 3 mortars), 345 culverins, which could easily be moved from one position to another, and 287 rifles, not to count the firearms carried by the reinforcements. There was a large amount of gunpowder and cannonballs, including 17.000 bullets for culverins. The largest gun could fire 14 kg iron balls, the second largest cannon 6,2 kg balls,

28 Cf. Ferenc Salamon, *Magyarország a török hódítás korában* (Budapest: Heckenast Gusztáv, 1864), 143–44.

29 Cf. István Gyárfás, *Dobó István Egerben* (Budapest: Magyar Tudományos Akadémia, 1879), 66–67.

30 L. Kerecsényi to T. Nádasdy, Szíget, 26 September 1555, "Kerecsényi László levelei Nádasdy Tamáshoz. 1553–1562," ed. A. Komáromy, *Történelmi Tár* 1 (1906): 103–38: here no. 37, 131–32. On the armed peasants cf. Soós – Szántó, *Eger vár védelme*, 35.

31 Szántó, *Küzdelem a török terjeszkedés ellen*, 194.

the third one 2,25 kg balls, the fourth one was slightly bigger than a falcon. The barrels of the guns were made of iron or copper.[32]

Dobó, as mentioned above, directed the artillery; however, also Bornemisza was an expert in firearms. The fortress's captain placed the peasants at the service of master gunners and they quickly mastered the shooting techniques. The blacksmiths were very busy not only to fix the weapons, but also to modify them as needed. In conclusion, 963–986 men were stationed in the inner fortress, 694–894 men in the outer fortress. Only culverins were placed in the outer fortress. The cannons (each station was occupied by 2–4 cannons) were protected by baskets of intertwined branches filled with earth, 1–2 meters high, 1 meter large (the baskets were sometimes filled also with the ruins produced by bombing), or they were more simply protected by sandbags, which had the function to cushion the enemy's cannon fire thus preventing the cannons themselves from being damaged. Dobó placed the most important cannons on the Sanctuary bastion and on the nearby embankment in order to keep under control the outer fortress, the moat between the two sections of the fortress and its western part.[33]

The Ottoman Forces

By summarizing and mediating the positions of the various authors of the mentioned narrative sources, we can assume that the Ottoman armies arrived at Eger between 9 and 15 September 1552. However, there are no specific dates on this matter. The number of Ottoman troops is also very uncertain and controversial. According to Istvánffy, Khadım Alı Pasha first appeared in front of Eger with 25.000 men, number also confirmed by Forgách. On the other hand, the armies of Kara Ahmed and Mehmed Soqollu were far more numerous: 125.000 soldiers, even if, as already mentioned, the Turks themselves exaggerated in stating the number of their troops. Forgách even attributes 180.000 men to both Ottoman armies. On the contrary, the number proposed by Tamás Varkocs is limited to 100.000. Finally, more realistically, both Centorio and Conti set the number of soldiers of the joint army of Kara Ahmed and Mehmed Soqollu at 60.000 men. Considering the fact that János Zsámboki sets the size of Khadım Alı's army at 35.000 men, it can be realistically assumed that his army could not have exceeded a total number of 40–50.000 armed men.[34]

---

32 Szántó, *Küzdelem a török terjeszkedés ellen*, 195.

33 Szántó, *Küzdelem a török terjeszkedés ellen*, 197–98.

34 Cf. Tinódi, *Cronica*, VII, 300; Forgách, *Commentarii*, 61; Centorio, *Commentarii*, 221; Conti, *Historie de' svoi Tempi*, 146v.; Zsámboky, *Eger ostroma*, 34.

The troops of the sanjaks of Belgrade, Pécs, Székesfehérvár, Szendrő (Smederevo), Hatvan, Bosnia and Illyria were part of the army led by the governor of Buda, Khadım Alı Pasha. The troops of Kara Ahmed Pasha and those of Mehmed Soqollu arrived, along with 125–150,000 fighters and with the artillery pulled by camels and other pack animals, five days after the arrival of Buda's pasha. The Ottomans also included in these numbers, prisoners, serfs, peasants, workers, as well as the so called *martalosi* (irregular infantrymen recruited in the Balkan area). They deliberately spread exaggerated rumours about the size of their army with the aim of frightening the defenders of Eger. The main forces of the Ottoman army were the Janissaries and the cavalrymen (*sipahi*). A part of the joint army of Kara Ahmed and Mehmed Soqollu, which even came from Temesvár, was dispersed along the way, partly decimated by disease (plague) and starvation.[35]

Khadım Alı Pasha's troops camped near the Royal See to Felnémet, a village four kilometres north–west of Eger. Khadım Alı placed the bulk of his troops and artillery on the high ground of the Royal See. Arslan *bey*, who led the vanguard, had stopped with 25.000 men outside the town, near the sanctuary of the Blessed Virgin, and placed 4 guns without erecting embankments or other defences. The cannons were aimed at the earthen bastion and the Tömlöc bastion. Kara Ahmed's army camped south of the town, across the river (the camp stretched for about 10 kilometres), Mehmed Soqollu occupied the foot of the Almagyar hill while the Janissaries settled on the hill itself. The hill was 298 meters high, offering thus an excellent vantage point over the nearby area. The town and the fortress were thus completely surrounded in a death grip. The Ottomans had placed a long line of tents on the hills and in the valleys. On the same day of his arrival in Eger (11 September) Khadım Alı had placed three old siege guns of unusual size and without protection on a hill in front of the fortress.[36]

The Turkish batteries were installed: (a) in the garden of the provost's house, 100 meters west of the castle (Kara Ahmed Pasha's troops), right in front of the western walls: they were aimed at the earthen and the Dobó bastions; (b) near the church of the Blessed Virgin (Arslan *bey*'s troops) at an altitude of 162 meters, north–west of the castle: they too were directed against the earthen bastion and the western walls; (c) at the Royal See (Khadım Alı Pasha's troops) at an altitude of 188 meters, north of the castle: they were facing the northern walls that ran from the earthen bastion to the Sándor one; (d) on the slopes (altitude 200–210)

35 Szántó, *Küzdelem a török terjeszkedés ellen*, 199–200.

36 Szántó, *Küzdelem a török terjeszkedés ellen*, 205–07.

of the Almagyar hill (Janissaries): they were aimed at the northern curtain wall between the Sándor Bastion and the Bolyky one; (e) at the top of the Almagyar hill (Janissaries) at an altitude of about 240 meters: they were directed against the north-eastern walls, from the Bolyky bastion to the Bebek one; (f) about 200 meters on the Almagyar hill (Mehmed Soqollu's troops): they were facing the south-eastern walls, from the Bebek bastion to the ancient gate; (g) near the Eger river (troops of Kara Ahmed Pasha), in front of the southern walls: they were aimed in particular at the keep of the Varkocs gate. The assaults of the Ottoman infantry damaged the earthen ramparts, the Tömlöc bastion, the wall curtain behind the Gothic Palace, the Bolyky and Bebek bastions and the keep of the ancient gate.[37]

The Siege

For 38 days and nights, the Turks bombarded and dug mines beneath the walls, but also the towers, the palaces and every castle defence. Digging large trenches, they approached the walls with cruel and terrible assaults, one of which lasted almost three continuous days. However, despite the shortage of gunpowder and provisions, the Hungarian defenders resisted, often fighting hand-to-hand even with sticks and stones for lack of harquebuses and swords and filling the graves with the corpses of the attackers. Not only the men, but also the women of Eger played their part in the battle.

Both the attackers and the defenders often used very ingenious tricks. For example, Kara Ahmed Pasha had filled the moat between the Bolyky and Bebek ramparts with debris transported with a large number of wagons, camels and mules (for this work they also used local peasants they had captured as prisoners). In some places the filling of the moat even exceeded the height of the fortress walls. The Turks advanced on the embankment sheltering themselves with wooden boards covered with animal fat and wet skins, which the defenders tried to harpoon and destroy. By leaning the stairs on the embankment, the attackers attempted to climb the walls by throwing wooden boards into the slits, which they then tried to block with sacks full of clods of earth. At this point, in order to destroy the wood bastion raised by the attackers, Bornemisza, who the Orientalist historian Joseph von Hammer has defined the "Archimedes of Eger", had a brilliant idea: he filled small barrels with shingles, guns loaded with gunpowder, lard and tallow, mixed with straw and other incendiary materials. At

37 Szántó, *Küzdelem a török terjeszkedés ellen*, 206–07.

night the barrels, to which a fuse was applied, were thrown into the ditch. When the Turks approached to put out the fire, the guns started firing on their own, and the unfortunate soldiers were thus injured or killed. On the other hand, the defenders, aided by the glow of fire, were able to aim precisely at the attackers with arrows and rifles.

Moreover, if the attackers came too close to the moat next to the Bebek bastion passing through tunnels and on sinuous embankments, the defenders could easily reach them with spears and very long poles with hot spikes through small breaches opened in the walls. The Turks, trying to pull the poles and spears far from themselves, ended up burning their hands.

In the meantime, the Turks continued the excavation of tunnels and trenches, reaching the ancient gate. The Hungarians closely followed the excavation of tunnels by the enemy: in the most suspicious points they placed plates full of water or beans on drums, so that a minimum shaking of the floor corresponded to a minimum oscillation of the water surface or the movement of the beans. Thanks to the excavation of underground tunnels, the Turks could approach unnoticed the walls, under which they deposited mines, the explosion of which caused a large breach.

Ascanio Centorio degli Ortensi points out some examples of valiant and courageous behaviour of women during the battles of Eger.

The last assault took place on 12 October. Already after midnight, the Turkish soldiers began to gather with great noise and shouting. The Ottoman couriers (*çavuş*) scolded the slowest and most fearful soldiers, encouraging them not only with words but also with an iron mace. Meanwhile, Kara Ahmed, Khadım Alı, Arslan *bey* and other officers got on horseback, leading the Janissaries, the *azabı*,[38] the *akıncı*,[39] and the *sipahi* to attack.[40] The battle broke out with shouts, trumpets and drums, but the defenders resisted.

38 Irregular infantrymen armed with spades.

39 The *akinci* were irregular Ottoman soldiers.

40 About Ottoman military organization cf. Pál Fodor, "Ottoman warfare, 1300–1453," in *The Cambridge History of Turkey*, ed. Kate Fleet (Cambridge: Cambridge University Press, 2009) I, 192–226, and Gábor Ágoston, "Ottoman Warfare in Europe 1453–1826," in *European Warfare 1453–1815*, ed. J. Black (London: Palgrave Macmillan, 1999): 118–44.

The Withdrawal of the Turks

By mid-October the Eger fortress was practically reduced to rubble. Kara Ahmed decided to abandon the siege, being irritated as well as worried in learning the unfavourable news giving for certain the arrival of the reinforcements of Prince Maurice of Saxony and of the Transylvanian troops of Giovanni Battista Castaldo and Stephen Báthori of Ecsed. However, the second vizier was also worried about the arrival of winter. Certainly, he had lost every hope of taking Eger, and, at the same time, he was aware of the numerous losses suffered by his army and the weariness of the surviving soldiers. Kara Ahmed and Mehmed Soqollu began their return trip on 17 October, heading towards Belgrade. Khadım Alı left the following day for Buda. Before leaving, the Turks devastated the hill of Almagyar, robbed and burned 48 villages in the Heves County, made a large booty around Eger, and captured a lot of prisoners. The losses were not large in absolute value among the defenders (300 dead and 200 wounded people according to Tinódi), but they were remarkable among the attackers (5–11.000). Once the siege was over, Dobó rewarded the wounded people, the widows, the orphans, the peasants and all the workers who had done their duty with fervour. For six years the local peasants were exempted from paying taxes. On the other hand, the fighters of Eger obtained tax exemption for life.[41]

According to Turkish historians the failure of Eger's conquest was due to the arrival of winter as well as to lack of provisions. Gelalzade also justifies the Turkish failure with the magnitude and impregnability of the fortress. According to Sándor Takáts,[42] the fortifications of Eger were not exceptionally strong. However, the *palanka* defensive system was very effective in the outer fortress. Moreover, the autumn season did not favour the besiegers, generally unaccustomed to the cold climate. Even according to non-contemporary "western" historians, as for example Leopold von Ranke, the Turks withdrawal was due to the arrival of the cold season. Von Ranke also underlines the proximity of the fresh troops of Prince Maurice of Saxony as a reason for the Ottoman withdrawal.[43] László

41 Szántó, *Küzdelem a török terjeszkedés ellen*, 252; "Eger 1552-iki ostromához," ed. Samu Barabás, *Történelmi Tár* (1888): 388–94.

42 Cf. Sándor Takáts, "Oroszlán basa," *Történeti Szemle* 4 (1915): 51–70: here 23–25. On defence systems in Hungary through the *palanka* cf. László Gerő, *Magyar várak* (Budapest: Műszaki Könyvkiadó, 1968), 29.

43 Cf. Leopold von Ranke, *Deutsche Geschichte im Zeitalterder Reformation*, vol. V, Leipzig 1868, 210.

Gorove[44] attributes the departure of the Turks to fear for the expected arrival of the armies of Prince Maurice of Saxony, Giovanni Battista Castaldo and András Báthori. Franz Bernhard von Buchholtz indicates also the fall of a cold rain and an incipient snowfall.[45] As for Ignác Acsády, the fortress was saved by the heroic behaviour of its defenders and by the divine Providence as well. The early arrival of the cold weather accelerated the Turks departure.[46] Undoubtedly, according to Szántó,[47] the main factors that urged the Turks departure were the tenacious resistance and determination of the besieged people, their courage, cohesion, the collegial management of the defence. István Dobó set a good example by fighting himself in the front row, instilling courage into all his subordinates. The commander-in-chief was also capable of imposing strict rules of behaviour and discipline, by organizing the defence in a brilliant way.

Moreover, shortage of food deprived the Turkish soldiers of strength and will to fight. Their food was also not diversified, and they suffered from lack of vitamins as well. In addition, the plague and other epidemics (dysentery, typhus) had spread through the Turkish army since the end of the siege of Temesvár.

We should also take into account the defeat suffered by the Turkish army of Iskender Pasha by the Persian troops at Lake Van, which prompted Suleiman to call back Kara Ahmed Pasha and his soldiers. In fact, between the end of September and the beginning of October, the second vizier had received the sultan's order to return as soon as possible to the Bosphorus in order to replace Rüstem Pasha in the command of the Ottoman army for the Persian expedition. However, some sources indicate that Kara Ahmed Pasha was ordered to spend the winter in Temesvár and Mehmed Soqollu in Buda, before renewing hostilities in the coming spring.

The Aftermath

According to Sebestyén Tinódi, Kara Ahmed Pasha praised the defenders of Eger: "I travelled a lot all over the world, I fought in many castles and in many countries, but I never found better heroes than in Eger, wrongly considered an

44 Cf. László Gorove, "Egernek esetei várának első ostromáig," in *Eger városa történetei, Tudományos Gyűjtemény* 4 (1826): 48.

45 Cf. Franz-Bernhard Buchholtz, *Geschichte der Regierung Ferdinand des Ersten* (Wien, Schaumburg, 1836) VII, 317.

46 Cf. Ignác Acsády, "Az ország három részre oszlása. 1541–1547," in *A magyar nemzet története*, IX, ed. Sándor Szilágyi (Budapest, Kassák Kiadó, 1997).

47 Cf. Szántó, *Küzdelem a török terjeszkedés ellen*, 246.

ugly sheepfold". On the other hand, Kara Ahmed Pasha was angry with the governor of Buda who had involved him in that enterprise, and who had called Eger an "ugly sheepfold" by comparing its castellans, hussars and infantrymen to animals. He lost a lot of money, he lost many excellent fighters, he gained only shame and dishonour and was expecting the wrath of the sultan.[48]

Dobó was awarded the title of baron and obtained from Bishop Miklós Oláh the right to collect the tithe of wine for four years in the territories of Zemplén and Bars (Tekov). The other officers received land holdings. In addition, Dobó was elected by Sopron's Diet together with Ferenc Kendy voivode of Transylvania in place of András Báthori, who had in the meantime passed away. However, since he was accused in 1568 of treason, he spent several years in prison in Pozsony/Presburg (Bratislava). Dobo's deputy István Mekcsey would have received the same honours and benefits but he died in a fight between the soldiers of his escort and the inhabitants of a village. Gergely Bornemisza, who succeeded Dobó as Eger's captain, was captured and handed over to Kara Ahmed Pasha. Bornemisza was hanged after being held as a prisoner in the Seven Towers castle. However, not long after, on order of sultan Süleyman and, above all, on incitement of his wife Roxelana and his son-in-law Rüstem, candidate for the assignment of grand vizier, Kara Ahmed Pasha suffered the same fate as the victim he had executed: he was strangled on 28 September 1555.[49] On 10 May 1553, Miklós Oláh was elected archbishop of Esztergom. The Turks defeat at Eger had enormous resonance throughout Europe and was considered an insult to the sultan: the enterprise of Dobó and his men helped demolish the myth of Ottomans invincibility. Ottoman advance in Hungary was held for 40 years. They eventually conquered the fortress of Eger just in 1596, and held it until the liberation by the Habsburg army in 1687.

48 Cf. Tinódi, *Cronica*, VI, 281.
49 Cf. Tinódi, *Cronica*, VI, 287–88; Istvánffy, *Regni hungarici historia*, 215; Forgách, *Commentarii*, 73.

Eger (*Erla*) and its neighbouring settlements, detail from *Ungaria cum finitimiis provinciis*…/Hungary and its frontier provinces, Georg Matthäus Vischer/Matthias Greischer, 1682, cooper engraving (Landesarchiv Baden-Württemberg Abt. Generallandesarchiv Karlsruhe)

Zoltán Péter Bagi

Raids and Sieges along the Habsburg-Ottoman Frontier in Hungary: The Siege of Hegyesd: 31 March–9 April, 1562*

Abstract: Hamza, the bey of Székesfehérvár attacked and captured the stronghold of Hegyesd on the Northern shore of Lake Balaton, on 17 April 1561. This opened the way for Ottoman raiders to Vas and Zala counties, thus it is no surprise that Józsa Ormányi, the prefect of Sümeg, Veszprém episcopate, demanded and suggested sending troops to retake Hegyesd right after it was captured. The campaign was launched only in the Spring of the following year. The palatine, Tamás Nádasdi decided to start the siege of Hegyesd with an army of about 2.300 men, on 31 March. The Christian units occupied the stronghold of Hegyesd on 9 April.

Keywords: Hegyesd, Hamza, Bey of Székesfehérvár, Tamás Nádasdi, Eck Graf zu Salm, *Generalobrist* of Upper Hungary

Having captured Buda on 29 August 1541, the military command of the Ottoman Empire considered the conquest of Vienna to be a major strategic goal. On the one hand, this would open up the path to the heartland of the Holy Roman Empire, on the other hand, it would make the occupation of the Hungarian Kingdom complete.[1] Süleyman considered besieging Vienna during the 1543 campaign, but due to the short time available, the Ottoman forces decided on Esztergom and Székesfehérvár, both being strategically important in the defence of Buda. During the war for controlling Transylvania (1550–1552), Ali Khadim, beglerbey of Buda took Veszprém on 1 June 1552, which opened up a path across the Bakony hills and the northern banks of Balaton until the Rába River, and to the regions of Zala, Vas and beyond. Even in times of peace, raiders of the Ottoman army in Hungary kept trying to subjugate more and more villages in these regions. For their excursions, they needed such bases as the small but strategically important Hegyesd castle.[2]

---

* This paper was supported by the János Bolyai Research Scholarship of the Hungarian Academy of Sciences.

1 Pál Fodor, *Magyarország és a török hódítás* (Budapest: Argumentum Kiadó, 1991).

2 Zoltán Péter Bagi, "Mohácstól Zsitvatorokig (1526–1606)," in *Magyarország hadtörténete. Az oszmán hódítás kora 1526–1718*, ed. Kálmán Mészáros (Budapest: Zrínyi Kiadó, 2020), 13–106; 22–55.

So this was a time of peace in theory, nevertheless in the spring of 1561, the beglerbey of Buda arrived at Veszprém in person to supervise the operations – Farkas Perneszi reported this in a letter, written on 10 April, from Babócsa: "Pasha Kászon is gathering his forces very much, though we do not know for what purpose; should he intend to go on raids, he cannot pass without us being informed"[3] Perneszi feared that the Pasha would attack the Southern Dunántúl region (Babócsa and Sziget).[4] The next information about the supposed direction of the campaign was sent from Szenyér six days later, on 16 April by Péter Orosztónyi to Ákos Csányi. Based on a witness report, the prefect in Szenyér informed that three siege cannons and some wagonloads of cannonballs were transferred from Buda to Pécs. In addition, a Turk captured during a raid near Kaposvár disclosed that Pasha Kászon was preparing to lead forces towards Kanizsa and Csurgó.[5]

The Hungarian officers correctly assessed the preparations and the long-term purpose of the beglerbey's attack, but they did not know its exact direction. This may have been the reason for their surprise when on the night of 16–17 April in 1560, Hamza, bey of Székesfehérvár attacked and captured the castle of Hegyesd, on the northern coast of the lake Balaton.[6] Józsa Ormányi, prefect of Sümeg wrote to Csányi on 19 April and stated the cause of the fall of Hegyesd: "Hegyesd was lost by the new burgrave (*porkoláb*) appointed by the lords Czobor, his name being András Kalozy, and he is a drunkard – I had wondered much when he was made burgrave, many good men here in Symeg had heard me say that now this one drinks even more than the earlier one [burgrave Gergely], who is also a bad drinker himself. This I can surely relate to you, the day on whose eve the Turks had won Hegyesd, András Kalozy and the other burgrave had been drinking all day at a wine cellar on the hill and had returned to the castle very drunk; they

3 Magyar Nemzeti Levéltár Országos Levéltár (MNL OL), Magyar Kamara Archivuma (MKA), E 185 Archives of the Nádasdi family, Missiles 28. d., Farkas Perneszi to Bálint Magyar nr. 2.

4 MNL OL, MKA, E 185 Archives of the Nádasdi family, Missiles 28. d., Farkas Perneszi to Bálint Magyar nr. 2.

5 *Kászon bassa ű maga el jű rablani Kanizsa és Csorgó felé. Szándoka ez, hogy adig fűre nem bocsát. Ezt is mongya, hogy ímár az begler bék kihajája elől kű jüt et Pécset vagyon*, MNL OL, MKA, E 185 Archives of the Nádasdi family, Missiles 26. d., Péter Orosztonyi to Bálint Magyar nr. 2; András Komáromy, "Magyar Levelek a XVI. Századból," *Magyar Történelmi Tár*. Új évfolyam X (1909): 219.

6 MNL OL, MKA, E 185 Archives of the Nádasdi family, Missiles 26, Józsa Ormányi to Tamás Nádasdi nr 15.

were so intoxicated that Kalozy could only be wakened from his very bed and would not rise otherwise, and the other burgrave, though had managed to gain his senses when the Turks were inside, still escaped from the castle and is on the run now; but Kalozy is guarded better now than how he had stood guard for his lords' stronghold."[7]

The same letter also relates that after the capture of Hegyesd, voivode Bajazed went to subjugate the nearby villages right away. The Sümeg prefect also deduced that the Turks were planning to erect further fortifications around Hegyesd, also to "make a stronghold of the Hatos mill in Taplocza, for many riders". Based on information from his men, Antal Molnár and János Molnár, Ormányi also reported on 27 April that 20 wagons of food, escorted by 500 riders, were brought to Hegyesd, and that: "Hegyesd has a great number of Turks and is being built at a great pace. The voivode requested one hundred beams to be taken up to the castle, he is having beams and tinder prepared every day and also wood for the stockade."[8] Ormányi deduced from the supplies and constructions that "the whole Zala province would be lost to them".[9] In other words, the cavalry sent to the Hegyesd stronghold and perhaps to Tapolca would use the two sites as launch points to conduct further raids in the mentioned province and in the Szigliget lands of Bálint Magyar – turning a region of relative peace into a frontline area. In the cited letter, the Sümeg prefect also informed (based on Antal Molnár's report) that the beglerbey had mobilized the forces of two additional Sanjaks, sending them to Veszprém.[10] Another source confirmed this possibility, as the judge in Városlő learned from the Hungarian wife of the Veszprém dizdár[11] that "[the Turks] won't stand down until they pillaged the Zalaság greatly, and only the day of their start is unknown yet, as they are otherwise ready."[12]

Ormányi's fears about the construction works and raids were not without cause. His letter from 20 August informs that the voivode had been at Tapolca the preceding day, to have a "field inspection", beating the judge there with a mace. Then he took cover into the woods around Sümeg to ambush the unwary. In addition, the prefect of Sümeg also informed that one of the Hegyesd Turks

7 András Komáromy, "Magyar Levelek a XVI. századból," *Magyar Történelmi Tár*. Új évfolyam VIII (1907): 132; Csaba D. Veress, *Várak a Bakonyban* (Budapest: Zrínyi Kiadó, 1983), 79–80.
8 Komáromy, "Magyar Levelek," 134.
9 Komáromy, "Magyar Levelek," 131.
10 Komáromy, "Magyar Levelek," 134.
11 Komáromy, "Magyar Levelek," 134–35.
12 Komáromy, "Magyar Levelek," 135.

went from Tapolca "through Hegymagas and proceeded toward Zegliget with drawn sabre. When he was spotted by burgrave Balás Trombitás, this had the gate drawn up and put the lock through the lockhead and fastened it. This is something significant – but the Ederics people do not reckon it a good thing, as those Ederics folks are everyday in Zegliget but also enter Hegyesd daily."[13]

All this explain that, following the capture of Hegyesd, Ormányi requested and proposed that a force should be sent swiftly to recapture the place. In his 19 April letter he wrote the following to Csányi, an attack should be launched by the troops of four counties, along with units from private lords and from Győr.[14]

He also mentioned in the same letter that the loss of Hegyesd was the most dangerous to László Gyulaffi as the Csobánc castle, his estate, was now completely surrounded by the Ottomans.[15] Thus the Sümeg prefect expressed his bewilderment in his 26 May letter as to why Gyulaffi had moved around Veszprém with his 400 infantrymen, suffering a bitter defeat, instead of "if lord Gyulaffi had marched to Hegyesd with the same force and destroyed the beam tinder there, it would have been better, or taking a cannon he could have ruined the Hegyesd turret, as it is said with certainty that this bastion is in such a poor shape that merely three shots would ruin it. Even the Turks are afraid within and put timber under the turret in windy weather."[16]

However, the Christian forces made no attempt to retake Hegyesd in the same year, only the next, in the spring of 1562. On 24 March, Ormányi claimed (based on the report of a spy sent to Buda) that the beglerbey moved toward Transylvania with the bigger portion of his force, some five and a half thousand riders and a huge number of wagons and cannons.[17] Bajazed voivode stayed to

13 Komáromy, "Magyar Levelek," 148.

14 "Csak fejenként négy vármegyét vennének ezennel föl és az mellett az győri had és ahol mi népet az urak tehetnének, ellene álhatnának, hogy nem csinálhatná meg, sőt fejenként kellene az vármegyéket föl venni, és ugy reá menni." Komáromy, "Magyar Levelek," 131.

15 Komáromy, "Magyar Levelek," 132.

16 Komáromy, "Magyar Levelek," 135–36.

17 As Hungarian captain Menyhért Balassi defected and thus the lords of Upper Hungary joined the Habsburg monarch at the end of 1561, the Gyulafehérvár (Alba Iulia/Weißenburg) court retained its rule only in Transylvania, Bihar (Bihor), and Máramaros (Maramureş) provinces. Early in the next year, Balassi attempted to rally the Székelys who were discontent with John II's rule. The elected Hungarian king responded by commanding István Báthori, captain of Várad (Oradea/Großwardein) and Ferenc Németi to pillage Balassa's estates in Transylvania. Then in February 1562 the Transylvanian army besieged and captured Hadad (Hodod), dominating the valleys

defend Veszprém and Hegyesd. So the prefect recommended that: "Christians should also be fast to move, if they have any intention." In addition, he knew that the voivode moved empty barrels to Hegyesd and was transporting water in these up to the stronghold, and strove to store large amounts of food. He was also fortifying the walls with earthworks and timber.[18] We also know of another letter of Ormányi from the same day, sent to Tamás Nádasdi, informing about the same developments.[19]

However, apart from the Sümeg prefect, the palatine could be informed by Magyar as well, who related that Bajazed was filling up the walls with earth from the inside while digging a ditch on the outside. He was forcefully driving village folk to the construction site, handling them cruelly. No one was released without being replaced by another. Those who did not comply were nailed to wooden planks by their ears and held there from morning until dusk.[20]

With the Beglerbey of Buda and most of his troops moving to Transylvania, the palatine, Tamás Nádasdi decided to start the siege of Hegyesd on 31 March.[21] The army, consisting of 2.300 men, included: 1294 men from Győr, 464 soldiers from Pápa – led by Ferenc Török of Enying, 444 brought by János Csoron from Devecser, and László Gyulaffi's 240-strong units coming from Csobánc.

---

of Kraszna and Szamos rivers, whose lord György Sulyok also joined King Ferdinand I. Soon enough, however, a 5000-strong army of Balassi and Ferenc Zay, *Generalobrist* of Upper Hungary, also arrived. The battle near Hadad took place on 4 March – the Transylvanian army had twice the numbers but the disputes of its leaders and its low combat value caused them to lose. The next day the castle was taken by the Habsburgs again. But Balassi and Zay did not continue the campaign, as Archduke Maximillian (the later Maximillian II Holy Roman Emperor and Hungarian king) forbade them to do so. Thanks to this, John II could turn his attention to the rebelling Szekelys, subduing them in the May of 1562. To keep them in check, he had two strongholds built: Székelytámad and Székelybánja. Following the defeat at Hada, the elected king asked for military help from the beglerbey in Buda, who besieged Szatmár (Satu Mare/ Sathmar) with his gathered armies – but was not successful, *Istvánffy Miklós magyarok dolgairól írt históriája Tállyai Pál XVII. századi fordításában*, II (Budapest: Balassi Kiadó, 2003), 320.

18 Komáromy, "Magyar Levelek," 156.

19 Komáromy, "Magyar Levelek," 159.

20 MNL OL, MKA, E 185 Archives of the Nádasdi family, Missiles 18. d., Bálint Magyar to Tamás Nádasdi nr. 64; Excerpt published by András Komáromy, "Magyar Bálint kapitány életéből," *Hadtörténelmi Közlemények* 13 (1912): 271.

21 MNL OL, MKA, E 185 Archives of the Nádasdi family, Missiles 18. d., Magyar Bálint Nádasdy Tamásnak nr. 65; Komáromy, "Magyar Bálint," 271; Komáromy, "Magyar Levelek," 432.

Additionally, Ferenc Batthány sent 81 men, the bishop of Veszprém sent a force of 88 from Sümeg, led by Józsa Ormányi, 47 came from Zala county,[22] and 44 from Vas county. Palatine Tamás Nádasdi ordered 42 men-at-arms from Sopron County, while Bálint Magyar also joined the force with some of his own troops, as did the Horváths of Vázsonykő with their own infantry.[23] Eck Graf zu Salm, the Obrist in Győr had been commanded on 11 March by Archduke and Czech King Maximillian to follow Nádasdi's orders to full extent. This also meant that the 1.758-strong contingent appointed to the borderlands were also subject to the palatine's command. The situation was further complicated by the fact that Nádasdi was not directly present on the field due to sickness, thus his representative Magyar was responsible for controlling at least the troops of private landlords and the counties; he was also ordered to send daily reports back to him.[24] It must be noted that Bálint Magyar was not at best health either. His letter from 17 February to Fonyód states that he had competed at lance with one called Törpendi, and he suffered a bad fall.[25] It is almost certain that Salm did not permit much intervention in the control of his own contingent[26] while in turn the units of the country's nobility did not accept his lead.[27] But the issue of the leaders' jurisdiction posed no problem yet, as Salm and the men from Győr arrived to the siege as late as 8 April.[28]

The siege of Hegyesd started on the last day of March. By then only the armies of Batthány, the bishop of Veszprém, Török and Gyulaffi had arrived to storm the castle, the last bringing two field howitzers along with his 80 men. Csoron was expected to bring a third howitzer from Devecser. Accorsing to Török's report, the two howitzers dealt significant damage to the walls already on the first day. In addition, a Christian who escaped the castle brought information on

---

22 Komáromy, "Magyar Levelek," 432.

23 Österreichisches Staatsarchiv (ÖstA), Kriegsarchiv (KA), Alte Feldakten (AFA), 1562-4-ad, 5a; MNL OL, MKA, E 185 Archives of the Nádasdi family, Missiles 18. d., Magyar Bálint Nádasdi Tamásnak nr. 65; Komáromy, "Magyar Levelek,"432; Komáromy, "Magyar Bálint," 271.

24 MNL OL, MKA, E 185 Archives of the Nádasdi family, Missiles 18. d., Magyar Bálint Nádasdi Tamásnak nr. 68; Komáromy, "Magyar Bálint," 272.

25 MNL OL, MKA, E 185 Archives of the Nádasdi family, Missiles 18. d., Magyar Bálint Nádasdi Tamásnak nr. 62.

26 ÖstA, KA, AFA, 1562-4-5; ÖstA, KA, AFA, 1562-4-ad5a.

27 MNL OL, MKA, E 185 Archives of the Nádasdi family Missiles, 18. d., Magyar Bálint Nádasdi Tamásnak nr. 70. Komáromy, "Magyar Bálint," 273; ÖStA KA AFA 1562-4-5.

28 MNL OL, MKA, E 185 Archives of the Nádasdi family Missiles 18. d., Magyar Bálint Nádasdi Tamásnak nr. 69.

the conditions inside: voivode Bayazed had a 100 Turkish men and another 100 villagers who had been driven in from the countryside. They did not have much water or food, one barrel of water and without the cattle they had intended to drive up the castle but lost due to the siege. Intimidated by the siege, the voivode started having the gate reinforced with earth.

Török had asked the palatine to send his troops as soon as possible, especially footmen. This is why he suggested calling all cis-Sava counties to arms, sending word to Győr and urging them to join the siege. He also requested that the palatine sent two guns capable of breaking walls while waiting for the troops.[29]

Magyar himself first wrote to the palatine from the camp under Hegyesd on 3 April, reporting that he had arrived with the footmen only one day earlier. He explained that if the palatine should order him to summon his cavalry too, he would need to send the infantry back home so that his estates would not lay unguarded. However, he believed that the besiegers could make better use the infantry. Magyar also mentions that János Csoron's company was already present, while the troops from the counties were still en route.[30]

On the next day, 4 April, Bálint was able to report that the howitzers requested by Török had arrived by eight in the morning. Magyar and the artillery master measured the castle around. The artillerist judged that firing positions would be set up by noon, where the wall breaking work could commence.

Magyar was also informed that captain of Palota, György Túri, had defeated the Ottomans at Veszprém. Nevertheless, there was a chance for a relieving force showing up, as there was word about many infantrymen arriving to Veszprém, with Hamza bey being expected back at Székesfehérvár with his 800-strong cavalry.[31]

The artillerist operating the palatine's cannons showed quick results, as already stated by Magyar's report on 5 April. Artillery fire damaged the turret over the gate to the extent that an assault could be launched. However, Magyar asked for more gunpowder and cannonballs from Nádasdi, as they were running very low on them. In turn, the defenders kept reinforcing the walls from the inside with earthworks.[32] Magyar also asked for ladders so that they could climb the walls,

29 Komáromy, "Magyar Levelek," 432.

30 MNL OL, MKA, E 185 Archives of the Nádasdi family, Missiles 18. d. Magyar Bálint Nádasdi Tamásnak nr. 65; Komáromy, "Magyar Bálint," 271.

31 MNL OL, MKA, E 185 Archives of the Nádasdi family, Missiles 18. d., Magyar Bálint Nádasdi Tamásnak nr. 66; Komáromy, "Magyar Bálint," 271–72.

32 „Az tornyot, az kapu felet igen jűjük, jó móldon. Jó móldon meg is töröt, hiszem ma alkolmasson meg törük, hogy talám ostromot is tehetünk. De nagyságod külgyön port, golyóbist, mert ma ha meg érjük vele, ha penig tágyétjuk eggyüld belől épéjtik." MNL

and that the workhorses hauling the artillery should not be returned, but kept and fed, beast and driver alike.[33]

At the same time, Ormányi also wrote to the palatine about the disorder perceptible in the camp, asking for regulating the camp and its nobles. Though Ormányi had the field camp surrounded with wagons and left only two gates, troops still left to raid and plunder. Thus he asked the palatine that he should command both the noblemen and Magyar to keep strict discipline among their subordinates.[34]

In a letter sent to Kristóf Nádasdi on 6 April, Magyar mentions that more reinforcements had arrived: the infantry led by Gáspár and János Horváth of Vázsonykő.[35] Thus the army was growing, with Bálint complaining about the lack of gunpowder and ammunition. Without these, Bayazed could keep repairing destroyed walls. The letter of 6 April reports Hungarian casualties for the first time: János Keleti and others were shot dead.[36]

Magyar reported the next day, 7 April, that the artillery expected from Győr and Sopron had not arrived and he had only the palatine's "wall breaking cannons", each with 37 shots left, while the two howitzers from the start of the siege had run out. According to him, the artillery worked well given the circumstances, having destroyed the turret above the gate and continuing to break the walls beside. He also expressed his hope that the palatine will arrive in person at the siege camp.[37]

OL MKA E 185 Archives of the Nádasdi family, Missiles 18. d. Magyar Bálint Nádasdi Tamásnak nr. 67; Komáromy, "Magyar Bálint," 272.

33 MNL OL, MKA, E 185 Archives of the Nádasdi family, Missiles 18. d. Magyar Bálint Nádasdi Tamásnak nr. 67; Komáromy, "Magyar Bálint," 272.

34 „Jóllehet az uraktúl ün magoktúl semi vétek nincsen, de hogy az táborbeli népnek erőssen nem parancsolnak, csak az az vétek, mert az minémű tábort jártatonk, kinek én az urak akaratyából csak két kaput csináltam vala és mógya szerént amint én tuttam, az szekereket egymáshoz vertem vala, abban nem marada, hanem immár vagyon tíz kapuja és szertelen nagy sákmánlás és kobollás vagyon az táborból, kit az úristen nem szeret. Te nagyságod parancsolyon keményen az uraknak és Magyar Bálint uramnak, ki nagy emberségel szolgál mast it, hogy legyen minden dologban jó szertartás, jó vigyázás, egyenesség, szeretet és isten ellen ne legyen semi, mert ha isten velönk lészen, senki nem lészen ellenönk." Komáromy, "Magyar Levelek," 160.

35 MNL OL, MKA, E 185 Archives of the Nádasdi family, Missiles 18. d., Magyar Bálint Nádasdi Kristófnak nr. 1.

36 MNL OL, MKA, E 185 Archives of the Nádasdi family, Missiles 18. d., Magyar Bálint Nádasdi Kristófnak nr. 1.

37 MNL OL, MKA, E 185 Archives of the Nádasdi family, Missiles 18. d., Magyar Bálint Nádasdi Tamásnak nr. 68; Komáromy, "Magyar Bálint," 272.

Although the palatine did not come on 8 April, the Sopron cannons and Salm and the Győr army did. Magyar actually rode out to Tapolca to meet the new artillery, soon bringing them to position and laying waste to the walls. This, and probably the strength of the army from Győr, did have an effect: it was not long before soldiers from the trenches came running to Bálint, reporting that the besieged were calling out his name. Thus he went under the walls and asked why. They promised to give up the stronghold on the condition that they would not be slain by the infantry outside. These words did not convince Magyar, who demanded that two of the defenders should come out and speak their intentions in front of the noblemen. However, Salm did not like the prospect that the besieged would surrender to Magyar and resumed firing on the castle, killing several Turks including one negotiator. Then the Obrist sent Vince Tolmácsi to negotiate; the defenders asked that two officers be sent in from the Christians for token, but the mutual disrespect of the parties derailed any agreements. Thereafter, although word had it in the camp that the castle surrendered, Magyar's report informs that Salm was still firing on the walls from various positions, and the besieged were standing their ground.[38]

The Turks must have made up their minds soon enough. A letter from 9 April to the palatine already mentions the distribution of the looted goods and the destruction of the walls, the conditions being assessed already on Salm's orders.[39] Magyar reported to Nádasdi the next day that Csoron's and Török's troops had already marched back home, as had most of the county armies. He made efforts to stop the latter, but did not succeed. Magyar stayed at camp with Gyulaffi and Ormányi, their remaining troops amounting to a couple hundreds of *darabont* infantry and a 100 horsemen. Even before Nádasdi issued the order, Magyar had sent off the artillery with an escort led by György Horváth. Cannonballs and captured firearms were claimed and taken by Salm.[40]

The recapture of Hegyesd is interesting for more than one reason. On one hand, although the castle itself was not large, contemporaries assessed its great strategic significance. By taking it, the Ottomans established good routes for their trans-Rába raids on Vas and Zala Counties. This affected the palatine's

38 MNL OL, MKA, E 185 Archives of the Nádasdi family, Missiles 18. d., Magyar Bálint Nádasdi Tamásnak nr. 69.; Komáromy, „Magyar Bálint," 272–73.

39 MNL OL, MKA, E 185 Archives of the Nádasdi family Missiles 18. d., Magyar Bálint Nádasdi Tamásnak nr. 70; MNL OL, MKA, E 185 Archives of the Nádasdi family Missiles 18. d., Magyar Bálint Nádasdi Tamásnak nr. 70; Komáromy, "Magyar Bálint," 273.

40 Komáromy, "Magyar Bálint," 273–74.

income as well, as he had large properties there. On the other hand, though the Christian campaign was successful, it also highlighted the problems of authority and jurisdiction that were prevalent in Habsburg Hungary during the sixteenth and seventeenth centuries.

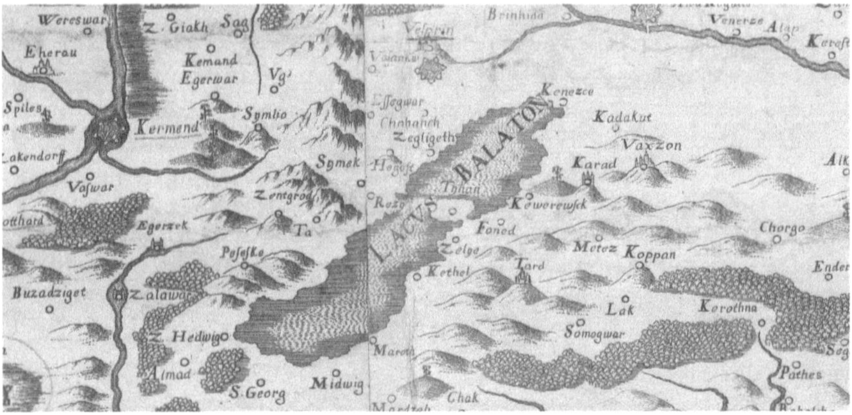

Lake Balaton and the fortress of Hegyesd (*Hegest*), detail from *Ungaria cum finitimiis provinciis…*/Hungary and its frontier provinces, Georg Matthäus Vischer/ Matthias Greischer, 1682, cooper engraving (Landesarchiv Baden-Württemberg Abt. Generallandesarchiv Karlsruhe)

Ovidiu Cristea

Castello Di Varadino Passo Principale Della Transilvania: Giovanni Marco Isolano's Relation On the Siege of Oradea (1598)

Abstract: The "Long Turkish War" (1593–1606) determined a permanent reconfiguration of the frontiers between the main actors involved in the conflict. Year after year the military campaigns as well as the diplomatic contacts had serious repercussions on the map of the region and, as a result, on the strategy adopted by the Ottoman Empire and their enemies. The siege of Oradea (Nagyvárad/Grosswardein) in 1598 by an Ottoman army led by Satirgi Mehmed pasha may be considered as a key event due to the fluid political situation in the region at that moment. More specifically, the return of the Prince of Transylvania, Sigismund Báthory from his self-imposed exile was followed by an attempt of the prince and Transylvanian elite to abandon the anti-Ottoman war and to conclude a peace with the sultan. In a very complicated context the citizens of Oradea decided to swear allegiance to the Habsburgs and to open the gates to a Habsburg army led by Melchior von Redern. While the episode is already known in historiography, the present paper will focus on a new testimony written by an Italian officer, Giovanni Marco Isolano. *Relatione del Assedio del Castello di Varadino* written sometime after the Ottoman siege points to interesting insights concerning the Habsburgs' camp, on the strategic value of Oradea as a border fortress between Transylvania, the Habsburg territories and the Ottoman Empire, and on the measures undertaken by the Archduke Maximilian to preserve the fortress at any costs. Not in the least the strategic importance of Oradea is underlined by the fact that the Prince of Wallachia, Michael the Brave, decided to stop his expedition in the Ottoman territory when he received news of the Ottoman siege of Oradea.

Keywords: Long Turkish War, Oradea, Siege, Relation, Narrative Source

.....Castello di Varadino passo principale della
Trans[ilvani]a
piazza se non fortissima almeno tale che sarebbe stata
insuperabile
a i Transilvani et che senza molta fatica
et con perdita d'una stagione intiera
non si savia potuto espugnar da Turchi

Ferrante Rossi's advice to Archduke Maximilian[1]

A Text without Context

The starting point of the following pages is a text – *Relatione del Assedio del Castello di Varadino*[2] – written by an Italian officer, Giovanni Marco Isolano, involved between 1594 and 1602, in the "Long Turkish War" (1593–1606). It is a peculiar document for more than one reason. We ignore when it was written, for what reason and to whom it was sent. The precision of the details, the lack of any information about what happened after the Ottoman retreat (for instance the fact that before leaving for the imperial camp, the commander Melchior von Redern entrusted the captaincy of the fortress to Pál Nyáry)[3] and the absence of any comment concerning the outcome of the Ottoman campaign seems to suggest that *Relatione* was written soon after the end of the siege but there is no clue for a better approximation.

The author himself is an intriguing character. He was a nobleman from Bologna and his family's name seems to derive from its place of origin, the island of Cyprus. According to a seventeenth century source, a member of the Lusignan family attended the University of Padua and after he settled in Italy, took a new name related to his fatherland.[4] His descendant, Giovanni

1 Magyar Nemzeti Országos Leveltar (MNL OL), microfilm 19047, f. 180v; I express my gratitude to Nagy Levente and Ovidiu Olar for their support in obtaining a copy of the document. The original manuscript is preserved in Ambrosiana Library, Milan, Bibl. Cod. S103 SUP. F. 182–204. The text was recently published by Tamas Kruppa, "Várad ostromának emlékezete. Giovanni Marco Isolano gróf jelentése a vár és a város 1598. évi ostromáról," *Lymbus. Magyarságtudományi Forrásközlemenyek*, Budapest, 2018 who used the copy preserved in Budapest.

2 MNL OL, microfilm 19047, f. 180r-204r. (*Relatione*).

3 Beda Dudik, "Rödern Menyhért Császári Tábornagy Tudósítasa. Nagy-Várad 1598-iki Ostromoltatásáról," *Magyar Történelmi Tár* 25 (1878): 115.

4 Pompeo Scipione Dolfi, *Cronologia delle famiglie nobili di Bologna con le loro insegne e nel fine i cimieri* (Bologna: Presso Gio. Battista Ferroni, 1670), 429.

Marco Isolano, was born probably around 1575 an estimation based on a Venetian report. According to the *Serenissima's ambassador* in Prague, Pietro Duodo, Isolano had in 1602 between of 25–28 years of age, which means that he was very young when he entered in Habsburgs' service, in 1594.[5] The same Duodo described him as a literate man, excellent designer and mathematician.[6]

Isolano's career in Hungary is difficult to follow until 1598. One may assume that he took part in the battle of Mezőkeresztes (24–26 October 1596) as he gave a detailed account on the battle in another work *Guerre descritte della felice memoria del signor conte Giovanni Marco Isolano governatore et colonello in Alba Reale per sua Maesta Cesarea.*[7] In 1598 he was one of the defenders of Oradea against the Ottomans and became quite famous due to his deeds during the siege.[8] In 1600 he was appointed to inspect the fortifications of Vienna, and to propose measures for strengthening the defences.[9] In 1601 he was involved in the fights around Székesfehérvár[10] while in the next year he was appointed as

---

5 See the document published by Tamás Kruppa, "Egy epizód a tizenöt éves háborúból. Adatok Giovanni Marco Isolano grófmagyarországi pályafutásához," *Hadtörténelmi Közlemények* 131, no. 3 (2018): 719–33 (726): *È gentilhomo Bolognese giovine di 25 in 28 anni, sano, prosperoso, valoroso di sua persona, pratico et intelligente. A lui s'attribuisce in particolare la difesa di Varadino et la sua virtù l'ha anco condotto al governo d'Alabaregale, che vuol dir molto tra tedeschi.*

6 Kruppa, "Egy epizód," 719–33; a similar virtuosity in mathematics is mentioned by Ciro Spontoni, *Historia della Transilvania* (Venetia: Apresso Giacomo Sarzina, 1638), 69.

7 Bayerische Staats-Bibliothek, München Cod. Ital. 35 fol. 1–72. A Hungarian translation was published by Kálmán Benda, "Giovanni Marco Isolano grof ezredes feljegyzesei a magyarorszagi török haborurol, 1594–1602," *Hadtortenelmi Közlemenyek* 96 (1983): 651–681.

8 Spontoni, *Historia della Transilvania*, 77; Also see *supra* n. 5 for Pietro Duodo's testimony or Melchior von Redern's opinion see Dudik, "Rödern Menyhért Császári," 113: *ein ehrlicher, tapferer, redlicher, verständiger Mann*. Giorgio Basta also mentioned that *il conte Isolano ci ha aquistato molta riputatione nell' haver fatto molte retirate et contramine* see Endre Veress *Basta György havdezér levelezése és iratai*, I (Budapest: Kiadja a Magyar Tudományos Akadémia, 1909), 141, no. 133.

9 Archivio di Stato Venezia, Senato. Dispacci Germania, 29, f. 605v: *E' venuto qui il conte Giovanni Marco Isolani (sic) bolognese, famoso per le cose di Varadino, chiamato da maestà per la fortificatione di Vienna, la quale ha intentione di fornire dalla parte del Danubio.*

10 He is silent about his deeds during the campaign (see *Guerre descritte della felice memoria…, passim*). Fortunattely other sources mention his actions; see for instance the testimony of another Italian officer, Girolamo Dentice in the volume *San Lorenzo*

governor of the same city. Unfortunately, he was taken captive after the recapture of Székesfehérvár by an Ottoman army led by the Grand Vizier, *Yemisci* Hassan Pasha in 1602 and ended his life as a prisoner of war. In 1603 the Grand Vizier used him as an ambassador *ad hoc* in a new attempt to conclude peace with the Habsburgs. The letter sent on the occasion by Isolano to Emperor Rudolph II shares some interesting details on his captivity.[11] Unfortunately, the negotiations failed once again, and it seems that the Ottomans judged Isolano to be responsible for the failure. They refused his ransom several times[12] and, eventually, Isolano ended his life, according to Ciro Spontoni, in the prison of Edi Kule.[13]

If the author of *Relatione del Assedio del Castello di Varadino* is barely known, the receiver of the text could be only guessed. Tamas Kruppa argued that *Relatione* was sent to Cesare Speciano, bishop of Cremona and former papal nuncio at the Court of Rudolf II.[14] The hypothesis seems to be supported by the fact that both *Relatione* and Speciano's papers were preserved in the Ambrosiana Library in Milan. However, the text includes many details about the siege techniques and a thorough account concerning the fortress' artillery, the number of cannons destroyed, and also the number of shots and barrels of powder used during the siege,[15] information which suggests that the receiver was, more probably, a military. It is known, for instance, that just before the siege, Isolano sent a letter and a sketch of the fortress to an Italian superior, Ferrante Rossi,[16] and one may wonder if *Relatione* was not directed to the same officer. It is only an assumption

da Brindisi. Dottore de la Chiesa universale (1559–1619), IV/1. *Documenti*, (Venezia-Mestre: Curia Provinciale dei FF. MM. Cappuccini, 1960), 174, no. 202: *Et in questo venne ad offerirsi il colonello Prainer et il conte Isolano che volevan' andar a mantener quel posto nell'eminenza del monte che si confidava con il suo reggimento il Prainer mantener quello luoco.* It seems that Isolano's suggestion generated a serious dispute among Archduke Matthias's staff: *Ci fu gran disputa. Il cont 'Isolano* ***si pigliò gran colera et parlo fuora di denti*** (my emphasis) *perch' alcuni offitiali supremi contradicevano. Questo fu in publico.*

11 The document is preserved at Bibliothèque Nationale de France, ancien fonds mss. fr. 3460, no. 59, f. 110–111. I am preparing an edition of the document along with a commentary.

12 See the instructions sent by the Cardinal Scipione Borghese to the papal nuncio in Prague, Stefano Ferreri in Kruppa, "Egy epizód," doc. 2–3, 729–30.

13 Spontoni, *Historia della Transilvania*, 69:…*havendoli il suo riscatto mai conceduto, fini la vita in quella miserabile servitù dentro la Torre del Mare negro.*

14 Kruppa, "Várad ostromának emlékezete," 155–91 (156).

15 *Relatione*, 203v.

16 Andrei Veress, *Documente privitoare la istoria Ardealului, Moldovei și Țării Românești*, V. *Acte și scrisori (1596–1599)* (București: Cartea Românească, 1932), 193–94; a

and, in lack of any other information, the only certain thing is that the text was written for a non-Hungarian speaker (Isolano translated in Italian the names of the rivers and of the fortress' bastions)[17] unfamiliar with *Varadino* (Oradea/Nagy-Varad) and its surroundings. The frequent use of expressions *come ho detto* ("as I said [before]"),[18] or *per le caggioni dette di sopra* ("the aforementioned reasons")[19] suggest that Isolano had someone in mind when he wrote the text. The Italian nobleman even states, before starting his story of the siege, that "to better understand the rest of my narration it would be appropriate to describe the city and the land around it".[20] Such specification would have been pointless if Isolano would have written the text only for himself. As Tamás Kruppa already pointed out, the topographic details indicate that the addressee was unfamiliar with the fortress and the surrounding region.[21] Such recipient could also have been Ciro Spontoni, a Bolognese by origin, who took part as a secretary in the "Long Turkish War" and wrote a "History of Transylvania" published posthumously in 1638. Spontoni's "History" includes a detailed account of the siege of *Varadino* who has some remarkable similitudes with Isolano's text. Although there is no certainty that Isolano addressed his *Relatione del Assedio del Castello di Varadino* to Spontoni, it is highly probable that the latter saw the text.

The lack of the details related to the purpose of the text makes difficult any attempt of categorization. It may be seen as a report, similar to the one sent by the commander of Habsburg's troops, Melchior von Redern, to the archduke Maximilian after the end of the siege.[22] It also may be considered a journal as, after several pages, Isolano organized the events day by day. Even better, the text may be seen as belonging to a particular genre, "the memoirs on war". These types of narratives have been under the scrutiny of historians in the last years. Some scholars considered them as mirroring the revolt of the authors against history; others, on

---

Romanian translation of the letter was published in *Călători străini despre Țările Române*, IV, eds. Maria Holban, Maria Matilda Alexandrescu-Dersca Bulgaru and Paul Cernovodeanu (București: Editura Științifică și Enciclopedică, 1972), 108–10.

17 *Relatione*, 186v; cf. Kruppa, "Várad ostromának emlékezete," 171.

18 *Relatione*, 183v., 188r.; Kruppa, "Várad ostromának emlékezete," 170, 173.

19 *Relatione*, 184v., 189r.; 185r with a slight difference *per le ambiguita dette di sopra*; Kruppa, "Várad ostromának emlékezete," 169.

20 *Relatione*, 186r-v.: *Ma perche meglio se intenda il resto sara bene che io descrivi brevemente il sito del Paese a torno della Citta et della fortezza*; with slight differences of transcription Kruppa, "Várad ostromának emlékezete," 171.

21 Kruppa, "Várad ostromának emlékezete," 155

22 Dudik, "Rödern Menyhért Császári," 106–16.

the contrary, look at them as a "natural evolution of history".[23] The formers underline the place of the "self" in a greater story while the latter stress the role "of the memoirist as an eyewitness, using his lifestory to guarantee historical truth".[24]

However, despite some of these elements could be found in Isolano's text, his narration hardly fits in the aforementioned typology. There is no clear delimitation between history and "self-story" as Isolano seldom mentions himself. Even when he does, his presence is ephemeral or allusive. We may assume that he was already in the entourage of Archduke Maximilian when he offered his services for the defence of Oradea. One may guess that his expertise in fortifications and artillery was considered valuable for a fortress which expected an Ottoman siege. As a result, Isolano was appointed by the Archduke *luogotenente general dell'artigliaria* and was sent with a small escort and six artificers (*bombardieri*) towards Oradea.[25] He added that he arrived on 23 September at 8 o'clock in the morning just before the Tatars appeared in the vicinity of the city.[26] Once he reached the fortress, Isolano became almost unnoticeable in his own testimony. The main characters of the text are Melchior von Redern, the commander of the garrison, along with another imperial commander, Pál Nyáry[27] and of the governor of the city, György Király, who was killed during the fights. Even these are scarcely mentioned as Isolano emphasises the role of the defenders as a whole.

Isolano presents himself as a member of the crowd, not as a distinctive figure. The exceptions are few and, even then, brief (for instance when he mentions that he was asked by Redern to follow him everywhere on October 12[28]or when he said that, due to the death of György Király, he was appointed at the defence of the wooden bastion and, later on, at the bastion Kyralfia[29]). Sometimes we may presume that he played a certain role in the defensive measures undertaken during the siege. For instance, one can guess that Isolano was behind the decisions aimed

23 See the discussion in Yuval Noah Harari, *Renaissance Military Memoirs. War, History and Identity*, (New York: The Boydell Press, 2004), 10.

24 Harari, *Renaissance Military Memoirs*, 10.

25 In Tokaj, Isolano added another two artificers to his group *Relatione*, 182v.; Kruppa, "Várad ostromának emlékezete," 167.

26 *Relatione*, 182v.; Kruppa, "Várad ostromának emlékezete," 167.

27 He was the governor of Eger when the city fell into Ottoman hands in 1596, see the testimony of captain Cogonara published by Henrik Marczali, "Közlemények a párisi nemzeti könyvtárból," *Magyar Törtenelmi Tár* 23 (1877): 113–122. Cogonara blamed Nyáry for the surrender.

28 *Relatione*, 194v.: *et a me comando che sempre le tenessi compagnia*; Kruppa, "Várad ostromának emlékezete," 180.

29 *Relatione*, 198v and 200v.; Kruppa, "Várad ostromának emlékezete," 184, 186.

to counter the Ottoman attempts to mine and destroy the city walls or in the construction of the *retirate*.[30] At a certain moment, he explains thoroughly how the defenders tried to counter the Ottomans' mining works and how the *retirate* protected efficiently the imperial garrison after the Ottomans managed to make a breach in the wall. Another time, he expresses his displeasure concerning how the cannons and the ammunition were preserved in the fortress before the siege.[31] It may be assumed that he changed the situation but we ignore how he decided to proceed. Finally, a last occurrence concerns an incident. The Italian officer mentions that during an Ottoman assault on the walls a bag of gunpowder caught fire and burned a number of defenders, Isolano among them.[32]

Apart from these short notices, Isolano is invisible in his story of the siege. He seems to be a simple man of the troop but a very perceptive one. There are striking differences between his relation and other two similar relations written by Melchior von Redern[33] and a certain captain Schels.[34] His text is more elaborate and mixes eyewitness information with history,[35] geography[36] and a detailed description of the fortress of Oradea. He insists on the works of fortification during the sixteenth century, praising the Italian architect Francesco (sic!) Baldigara.[37] By contrast, he criticized the "mason" who built the wooden bastion

30 For this type of defensive work, see Cristopher Duffy, *Siege Warfare. The Fortress in the Early Modern World 1494–1660,* (London: Routledge & Kegan Paul, 1979), 15.

31 *Relatione*, 184v: *S[igno]r Redern mi fece consignare in mano dal Governator della Piazza tutte gli artiglierie et monitioni che v'erano dentro, le quali erano tutte sossopra et in mal essere di sorte che quei che prima le havevano in cura non sapevano che cosa s'havessero ne in che luogo, ne in che quantita*; Kruppa, "Várad ostromának emlékezete," 169.

32 *Relatione*, 200v-201r.: *s'accese una fiama grandissima dalla quale furono bruggiati molti fra i quali oltre il sergente maggior delli Alemanni, Mon [signo]r di Ussi //201r. et alcuni gentilhuomini Ungheri ivi io ancora*; with minor differences Kruppa, "Várad ostromának emlékezete," 187. The face and the left hand of Isolano seem to be affected by the fire see Spontoni, *Historia della Transilvania*, 77: *e degl'Italiani restandovi gravemente offeso nel viso, ne nella mano sinistra il conte Marco Isolano*. See also the testimony of Giorgio Basta in Veress *Basta György*, I: *Detto conte é uscito abbrusciato da i proprii fuochi artificiati, ma giá sta fuori di pericolo*.

33 Dudik, "Rödern Menyhért Császári," 106–116.

34 Karoly Kiss, "Nagy-Várad védelme. 1598. Kapitány Schels után," *Felső magyar-országi Minerva* 7 (1831): 518–531; Kruppa, "Várad ostromának," 155 assumes that Schels' testimony was written in German.

35 *Relatione* 186v. ff.; Kruppa, "Várad ostromának emlékezete," 171–172.

36 *Relatione* 186v. ff.; Kruppa, "Várad ostromának emlékezete," 171–172.

37 The correct name of the Italian architext is Ottavio Baldigara. *Relatione* 186v; Kruppa, "Várad ostromának emlékezete," 172 and note 28.

(one of the Ottoman targets). According to Isolano, the aforementioned bastion was constructed without any respect for the military architecture, a fact which complicated the defenders' task.[38]

What is more surprising is the fact that the testimony is in striking contrast with another work of Isolano, the *Guerre descritte della felice memoria* mentioned above. This latter text was written after 1602, during Isolano's captivity in Istanbul, and is based only on his memory.Thus several chronological errors may be explained, some empty spaces and other small mistakes. However it is hard to explain how the siege of Oradea was reduced to only several days: from 29 September to 3 October![39] *Relatione* mirrors a difficult and enduring experience which lasted no less than 40 days (35 of combat) while *Guerre descritte* reduced the confrontations to five days, giving the impression that it was a minor clash despite the detail that the Ottomans used all the possible means (*ogni sforzo possibile*) to conquer the fortress.[40] One may assume that *Guerre* was conceived as a "global" narration of the "Long Turkish War" in which the siege of Oradea was just an episode among many others. Maybe Isolano didn't want to insist on an event to which he already dedicated a long *Relatione* few years before. Nevertheless, it remains difficult to understand how in 1602 a siege that lasted more than a month was reduced to only five days.

All these peculiarities suggest that *Relatione del Assedio del Castello di Varadino* is an intriguing and important testimony for the understanding of the "Long Turkish War". At first glance the episode of 1598 was one of many sieges occurred during a conflict labelled by Fernand Braudel as a "monotonous war" dominated by "a series of minor actions: positions were besieged, surprised, surrendered, saved, blockaded or relieved".[41] However, the conclusion applies to many other wars of sixteenth-seventeenth centuries in territories thickly defended by networks of fortifications.[42] To be sure, the monotonous aspect from a historian's perspective was less so for those engaged in actual combat. Isolano's *Relatione* is

38 *Relatione*, 187v.: *il quinto* [bastione] *e di legno et terra fabricato da un muratore senza giudicio alcuno et che per esser molto piu in dentro che gli altri difende non col fianco ma con la parte piu in fuori delli orecchione.*

39 *Guerre* 32v.

40 *Guerre* 32v.

41 Fernand Braudel, *The Mediterranean and the Mediterranean World in the Age of Philipp II*, transl. Syân Reynolds, II (New York: Harper & Row, 1973), 1200.

42 David Parrott, "The Utility of Fortifications in Early Modern Europe: Italian Princes and their Citadels, 1540–1640," *War in History* 7, no. 2 (2000): 127–53 (130).

a vibrant description of the complex situation (bad weather,[43] lack of provisions, disease, accidents) and of multitude of actions, reactions, expectations and emotions occurred during the siege. The simple fact that the Italian nobleman put his impressions on the paper suggests that he considered the imperial victory significant, that the event deserved to be known and remembered. One of his conclusions blends his thanks to God with a touch of pride and an amount of bitterness: "…by the grace of God and by our own example," states Isolano, "we liberated ourselves not only without receiving any help from our camp but not even any kind of news".[44] The reproach underlines the overwhelming importance of information during a war and seems to strengthen the eyewitness' frustration for the lack of support from the imperial camp. Isolano seems to imply that the defenders were completely abandoned and that the final success was a miracle. In an indirect way the blame for the lack of support strengthened the garrison's merits and seems to emphasise the importance of victory.

Other contemporaries, in the first place Emperor Rudolph II and his Court, shared a similar view as the success brought prestige and promotions for the protagonists. The commander of the garrison, Melchior von Redern, had a spectacular career being, in the next years, promoted to field marshal; Pál Nyáry, the ex-commander of Eger in 1596, was appointed as captain of Oradea; last but not least Giovanni Marco Isolano, was praised for his deeds. Subsequently he was appointed to inspect Vienna's fortifications and to propose defensive measures. Later, in 1602, he was appointed as governor of Székesfehérvár an unusual decision for Rudolf II's Court. According to the Venetian ambassador in Prague, Pietro Duodo, such office was reserved usually to German nobles and it was unexpected for an Italian to receive such a position from the emperor.[45]

---

43 For on overview on the impact of bad weather on the Long Turkish War see Zoltán Peter Bagi, *Stories of the Long Turkish War*, (Beau Bassin: Globeedit, 2018), 63–65 and 102–19.

44 *Relatione*, 203v.: *noi per singolar gratia di d'Iddio et con quasi nuovo essempio ne siamo stati liberati senza haver mai non che ricevuto soccorso ma ne ancho un minimo aviso in tanto spatio di tempo da i nostri.*

45 The document was published by Tamás Kruppa, "Egy epizód a tizenöt éves háborúból," 726: *È gentilhomo Bolognese giovine di 25 in 28 anni, sano, prosperoso, valoroso di sua persona, pratico et intelligente. A lui s'attribuisce in particolare la difesa di Varadino et la sua virtù l'ha anco condotto al governo d'Alabaregale, che vuol dir molto tra tedeschi.* About the enmity of the Imperial counsellors for the Italians see the opinion of Gianfrancesco Aldobrandini in Tamás Kruppa (ed.), *Pápai csapatok Magyarországon (1595–1597, 1601)* (Budapest-Rome: MTA-PPKE Fraknói Vilmos Vatican Historical Research Group, 2020), 17, no. 8.

40 Days of Siege[46]

Isolano's works are chronologically structured. In *Guerre descritte della felice memoria* he ordered the events year after year paying attention to the events both in Hungary and Transylvania. *Relatione* follows a similar logic, day by day. The exception consists in the first pages[47] when Isolano explains how Oradea became an imperial fortress and how Melchior von Redern was able to gather necessary troops for the defence of Oradea.

Isolano's detailed relation is relevant to understand how a siege combat was waged during the "Long Turkish War". Many techniques, stratagems and actions used during the siege of Oradea are to be found in other cases. What makes the siege of 1598 special is the fortress' ability to resist the Ottoman attack without the support of a relief army.[48] Or, the latter aspect was considered essential even before the Habsburgs garrisoned their troops in Oradea. In a council summoned by Archduke Maximilian in Košice, Giorgio Basta advised against the occupation of Oradea by the imperial troops. Basta expressed the idea that the fortress needed at least 3.000 troops and a comparable relief force and that both conditions were difficult to fulfil.[49] Moreover, the general considered that an imperial garrison in Oradea could have strained the Habsburgs' relations with Transylvania and could have caused collusion between Sigismund Báthory and the Ottomans. However, other two councillors, Ferrante Rossi and Melchior von Rederen expressed a contrary opinion and strongly advised for an immediate occupation of the city. In their view, the fortress had a strategic value and could be used also as a diplomatic tool in the relations with Transylvania. Eventually, Rossi and Redern's advice prevailed and Archduke Maximilan decided to accept the submission of the city offered by Captain György Király. Almost immediately Melchior von Redern was sent to Oradea with the order to gather the necessary

46 For a detailed analysis of the siege according to archival material see Zoltán Bagi, "Várad 1598. évi ostroma – más nézőpontból," *"Őrizzük Váradot…" Nagyvárad és Bihar vármegye története a kora újkorban*, ed. Teréz Oborni (Oradea: Varadinum Kulturális Alapitvány, 2017), 12–32.

47 *Relatione*, 180v-183r.; Kruppa, "Várad ostromának emlékezete," 163–66.

48 For the conjunction between the field armies and the garrisons see David Parrott, "The Utility of Fortifications in Early Modern Europe: Italian Princes and their Citadels, 1540–1640," *War in History* 7, no. 2 (2000): 127–153.

49 *Relatione*, 181r: *La qual Piazza habia per il meno richiesso tre milla fanti per guardarla et piu un altro essercito in pronto per soccorerla de quali doi bisogni a pena s'havia potuto suplire al primo*; Kruppa, "Várad ostromának emlékezete," 165.

garrison. He accomplished his mission not long before the Ottomans appeared in front of the fortress.

In *Relatione*, Isolano speaks about the Ottoman decision to attack Oradea as an obvious one, but in his other work (*Guerre descritte della felice memoria…*) he states that that the *sandjakbeyi* of Gyula convinced the Ottoman commander, Satirgi Mehmed Pasha, that the fortress was the gate of Transylvania and that the principality could be easily invaded once Oradea was conquered.[50] As usual, the first enemy units which emerged around the city were the Tatars.[51] After several skirmishes in the surroundings of Oradea,[52] Redern decided to retreat behind the walls and to release his cavalry. The decision had a side effect as other units decided to abandon the place, despite receiving their payments.[53] Moreover 400 hajduks on imperial payroll revolted and tried to abandon the fortress. They were repulsed by the German units and accepted to stay only when Redern promised them a gift in money.[54] The event underscores how delicate and important was the ability of a commander to control his troops, an endeavour even more difficult when the army was an ethnic mixture.

Melchior von Redern tried to strengthen the soldiers' fidelity by promising gifts and by demanding an oath of loyalty. Also, he took care to separate the German from the Hungarians and to appoint commanders of same origin. In the end, the garrison swore to fight to the death, while Redern, in his turn, promised to stay along his troops regardless the outcome of the combat. Any attempt to negotiate the surrender was considered an act of treason to be punished with death. The measure seemed to be well pondered as several times during the siege the Ottomans tried to convince the defenders to capitulate.

The first attempt was made on 30 September, when Ibrahim Pasha asked Pál Nyáry, as a friend,[55] to open the gates until it was not too late. However, Nyáry submitted the letter to commander Redern who decided to put the messenger, a Christian peasant, in chains and to refuse any discussion. Next day it was the turn of the Tatar Khan, Ghāzī Girāy Bora, to send a letter to the Captain György Király with similar arguments: it was better to accept the mercy of the vizier, Satîrgi Mehmed Pasha, before it was too late. The reply was also identical. The

50 *Guerre*, 32r.: *ma il Sangiach Beg di Giulla lo essorto a pigliar Varad come che da quel luogo era piu facile entrare in quel Paese* [= Transilvania].

51 For the use of Tatars during the siege of a fortress see Duffy, *Siege Warfare*, 210–11.

52 The clashes took place on 25, 26 and 29 September see *Relatione*, 183v–185v.

53 For a general view on desertion during the Long Turkish War see Bagi, *Stories*, 62–63.

54 *Relatione*, 189r.; Kruppa, "Várad ostromának emlékezete," 171.

55 *Relatione*, 189r.: *essortandolo come amico*; Kruppa, "Várad ostromának emlékezete," 174.

defenders refuse to answer and the envoy was put in chains.[56] On 2 October, the Khan renewed his offer promising to mediate good terms of surrender for the Christians but once again his plea fell on deaf ears.[57] The last attempt to obtain a negotiate surrender was made by the pasha of Timişoara, on 23 October. This time the message was attached to an arrow and used a different diplomatic approach. The pasha expressed his admiration for the defenders' courage and added that it would have been a shame for such valuable people to die. The pasha guaranteed also that he was ready to escort the Christian garrison wherever it wanted, and that the Ottoman commander, Satîrgi Mehmed Pasha, will respect his promise.[58] Isolano makes no comment on the matter but it may be assumed that, once again, the Ottoman offer remained without reply.

Along with the diplomatic attempts, the Ottomans used the standard means to conquer the place. They concentrate their efforts on three of the five bastions of the fortress ("Wooden bastion," *Chiunca* and *Kyralfia*) while the other two ("the Venetian bastion" and *Aragnas*) suffered only a slight bombardment. The artillery didn't seem very efficient. Isolano mentions initially four canons installed in front of the *Kyralfia* bastion and another four installed on the hills against the Venetian bastion and *Aragnas* which proved inefficient. During the combats, the Ottomans redeployed several times their artillery but with minor results. The late chronicle of Naima considers the lack of heavy artillery as one of the main reasons for the failure. He also added that Satîrgi Mehmemed Pasha called the pasha of Eger, Sufi Sinan, for support but the latter claimed that he had no pack animals to transport the cannons.[59] Whether Naima's story is accurate or not it is certain that the Ottomans were aware of the inefficiency of their artillery and concentrated their efforts on other siege techniques. They began to fill the fortress' ditches and, in the same time, to dig tunnels aiming to mine and blow up the walls. In parallel, they approached the fortress by digging trenches. As usual, the Ottomans dug a main vertical trench straight towards the walls; from this central dig were dug to left and right parallel trenches at regular intervals.[60] On

56 *Relatione*, 189r.; Kruppa, "Várad ostromának emlékezete," 174.

57 *Relatione*, 189v.; Kruppa, "Várad ostromának emlékezete," 174.

58 *Relatione*, 201v.; Kruppa, "Várad ostromának emlékezete," 187–88.

59 *Annals of the Turkish Empire from 1591 to 1659 of the Christian Era*, transl. Charles Fraser, I (London: J. L. Cox and Son, 1832), 119–22.

60 Duffy, *Siege Warfare*, 211–12 (and illustration 70); for the system of entrenchments in the "Long Turkish War" see especially Tibor Szalontay, *The Art of War during the Ottoman-Habsburg Long War (1593–1606) according to Narrative Sources* (Ph. D. University of Toronto, 2004), 79–83.

6 October the trenches were already near the fortress' ditch and the Ottomans were able to install there no less than 3.000 arquebusiers who fired continuously against the defenders.[61]

Together with this progressive encirclement, the Ottomans concentrated their actions on the mining process. Isolano mentions two initial tunnels directed towards the bastions *Kyralfia* and *Chiunca* and the countermeasures undertaken by the imperials. The counter-mining was not an easy task due to the lack of sappers and the extent of the enemy's actions. The soldiers became also workers and the text suggests that shovel was a weapon as important as the musket, the arquebus, the cannon, and the spear.[62] Soon, commander Redern was forced to use for the works not only soldiers but also prisoners and also civilians who took refuge behind the walls. Isolano adds that even the women were used to carry the excavated earth.[63]

From 8 to 12 October the fights and the digging went hand in hand. Fortunately for the Christians, the Ottoman attempt to blow up the walls failed as the explosion had no effect and both bastions *Kyralfia* and *Chiunca* remained unharmed. The Christians considered the fact as a miracle and shouted three times the name of Jesus as prayer for the divine help.[64] As a following assault was also without results, the Ottomans resumed the next day the works at the tunnels. To the previous ones they added a new gallery towards the bastion *Kyralfia*. The new attempt bore some results on 17 October, when the Ottomans made a breach in the bastion *Chiunca*. Subsequently, they launched an assault but they were unable to overcome the *retirata* built by the defenders. After a long and bloody engagement, the Ottomans were repelled with heavy casualties from both sides. In parallel, the Turks also launched an assault against the wooden bastion which was also eventually repelled.

The attacks were resumed in the next days, simultaneously with the mine digging but, once again, without results. On 20 October, a new attempt to blow up the *Kyralfia* bastion failed but the fights continued with even more resolve. Isolano praises the courage shown by the warriors on both sides and even deplores that

61 *Relatione*, 191r.; Kruppa, "Várad ostromának emlékezete," 176.

62 *Relatione*, 193v.; Pieter Martens, "Siege Warfare (Early Modern)," *The Encyclopedia of War*, IV, ed. Gordon Martel (Oxford: Wiley-Blackwell, 2012), 1987–994 (1992).

63 *Relatione*, 193v.; Kruppa, "Várad ostromának emlékezete," 179. The use of women was, by no means, exceptional. For the "Long Turkish War" see Bagi, *Stories*, 80–89.

64 *Relatione*, 195r: *et noi all'incontro dentro la fortezza, cridando ad altissima voce tre volte il nome di Giesu ringratiatissimo il Dio dal benef[ici]o ricevuto*; Kruppa, "Várad ostromának emlékezete," 181.

due to excessive bravery a number of 25 imperial soldiers lost very lives in a useless way. Another stupid incident provoked a fire which burned many defenders, Isolano among them. The Italian officer describes the event without complaining or blaming his comrades but as a proof that the defenders fought with honour and that they overcome not only the enemy but also unfortunate events and bad weather.

After other unsuccessful attacks on 21 and 22 October, the Ottomans were determined to start another two tunnels directed towards the bastion *Chiunca* in parallel with continuous attacks. On the morning of 28 October, the Ottomans failed again in their plan to blow up the walls. It was a stroke of luck which helped the Christians. A bag of powder was ignited incidentally just when the Turks prepared the explosion. The following commotion destroyed the tunnel, killed the artificers and left the walls again unharmed. The incident demoralized the infidels who remained inactive for the next days and waited for the works at the two new tunnels to be finished. But once again something went wrong and the explosions barely scratched the walls, without provoking their collapse. The new failure and the news that another Christian army was besieging Buda, compelled Satîrgi Mehmed Pasha to order the retreat. "Thus" concluded Isolano "the enemy stubbornly besieged the fortress for 35 days or 40 days from the first appearance of the Tartars. We freed ourselves not only without receiving any help from our camp but not even any kind of news". The survivors were less than 1/3 of the initial garrison. The fights, the disease, the lack of food and wine took their toll.

The weapons and the ammunition were also intensively used. From the initial number of 22 cannons (8 *mezi canoni*, 5 *falconi*, 5 *falconetti* and 4 *petrieri*) five were destroyed during the fights; there were launched, according to Isolano's estimation, no less than 2.200 cannon balls and were consumed 450 powder kegs. After these impressive numbers Isolano leave the conclusions on the reader's behalf. *Relatione* ends abruptly leaving the impression that its author was too exhausted to add any further comment on the event.

Conclusions

It is hard to draw firm conclusions on a text with so many unknows. It is certain that *Relatione del Assedio del Castello di Varadino* was written by an eyewitness probably short time after the end of combat. It is a testimony which rather suggest than explicitly affirms. The author, Giovanni Marco Isolano, puts on paper his thoughts trying to draw an ideal image on how a fortress should be defended against the Ottomans. It was an exercise which maybe had something to do with the surrender of Győr (in 1594) or Eger (in 1596). Both events were seen as serious blows for the prestige and the moral of the Imperials. Ironically, one of the main figures of the fall of Eger in 1596, Pál Nyáry, was also involved in the defence of Oradea. Isolano praises the valour of the Hungarian captain, especially during the fights which took place on 20 and 21 October.[65] Isolano makes no allusion to Nyáry's previous career but, according to the Italian's testimony, Nyáry's deeds during the siege of Oradea were without reproach.

The overall conclusion is that the courage and the resolve of the officers and the soldiers as well as the divine help were the main reasons for the victory. The expected support from Archduke Maximilian never arrived and even the news received from the Imperial camp was unreliable. Far from easing the situation, the untrustworthy information affected further the troop's moral and, in the end, only the help of God, ensured the successful outcome. The last lines of Isolano's text draw a detailed account of the cannons and ammunition used during the siege and expresses the scepticism towards a joint action of imperial and Transylvanian troops against the Ottomans.

The lack of a wider perspective or any further comment about the probable impact of the success could strengthen the impression that the siege of Oradea was an episode without serious impact on the war. However, as Isolano puts it in his other work, there were several consequences. Archduke Maximilian resigned as a commander of the imperial troops[66] protesting against baron of Schwarzenberg's refusal to support Oradea.[67] More important, the occupation of Oradea by the imperial garrison tensioned further the delicate relation between the Habsburgs and Transylvania. The loss of the fortress also damaged Sigismund

---

65 *Relatione*, 200r.: *S[igno]r Niarij Paolo che guardava detto baloardo mostro valore et fermezza di animo grande.*

66 *Guerre*, 33v-34r: *Nel mese di Decembre l'Arciduca Massimigliano sdegnato che non gl'era stato osservato il promesso et che era stato abandonato dal soccorso dell'essercito d'Ungheria bassa per aiutar Varad come prima era stato convenuto di riunirsi insieme in verso quella parte alla qualle fosse andato l'inimico et vedendo tornato Sigismondo in Transilvania per la qual cagione egli era venuto se ben contra la volontà dell'Imperatore delibero di partire di Cassovia et tornare in Vienna et cosi presa licenza da Sua Maesta si transferi a Mergentol residenza sua del Gran Maestro di Ordino Theuttonico dove essendosi trattenuto non ha mai piu servito sino al presente.*

67 *Guerre*, 32v-33r: *Nell'istesso tempo che gl'Inimici combattevano Varadino ancora l'Arciduca Massimigliano che s'era fermo in Cassovia molto appresso il fratello solecitava che il Baron di Svorzemburgh andasse verso quella //<33r> parte per soccorrere ditto luogo nientedimeno Sforzemburgh (sic) posto da parte questo pensiero o pensando divertire l'Inimico ando a combatter Buda…*

Báthory's prestige and deteriorated further his position in Transylvania. Next year he abdicated once again for the benefit of his cousin, Cardinal Andrew Báthory, a decision which opened a long and tortuous struggle for Transylvania. In the end, from all the Archduke Maximilan's advisers, Giorgio Basta was the one with a correct prediction. By taking possessions of Oradea in 1598, the Habsburgs unlocked "Pandora's box". They opened a new front and tried hardly to impose their control on the principality. On a short term they succeed either through an unpredictable ally (Michael the Brave of Wallachia) or by their own means. On the long term the Transylvanian front consumed troops, money and time and, in the end, irrevocably damaged the relations with the principality's elite.

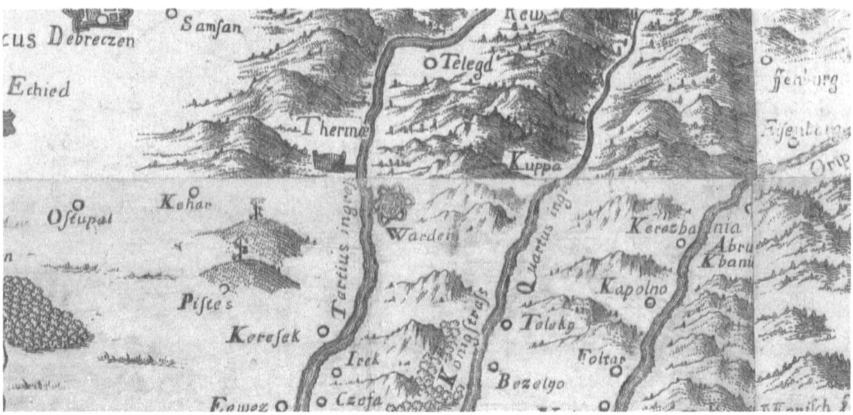

The fortress of Oradea (*Wardein*) on the western frontier of Transylvania, detail from *Ungaria cum finitimiis provinciis...*/Hungary and its frontier provinces, Georg Matthäus Vischer/Matthias Greischer, 1682, cooper engraving (Landesarchiv Baden-Württemberg Abt. Generallandesarchiv Karlsruhe)

Florina Ciure

The Conquest of Oradea by the Habsburgs in Italian Sources (1691–1692)

Abstract: This article analyses the information about the conquest of Oradea contained in *Corriere ordinario*, the oldest newspaper published in Italian language on Habsburg territory. These reports, published in Italian, in Vienna, by Johann van Ghelen and included in the 8th and 9th volume of *Avvisi italiani, ordinarii e straordinarii*, offer a detailed presentation of the operations conducted by the Imperial armies against the Ottomans in Oradea, during the years 1691 and 1692. By publishing these documents, the Habsburgs intended to popularise the victories of their armies after the failed Ottoman siege of Vienna (1683). These documents provide new evidence about a tumultuous period in the history of Oradea and the frontier area between the Habsburg and Ottoman empires. They also attest the level of knowledge on the political and military situation in these parts of Europe.

Key words: Oradea, Habsburgs, Ottomans, *avisi*, siege, armies

Introduction

This article is dedicated to the military confrontations between the Habsburgs and the Ottomans during the years 1691–1692 for the domination of the town and fortress of Oradea (Nagyvárad/Großwardein), reflected in *Il Corriere ordinario*. This was the oldest newspaper published in Italian on Habsburg territory, between 1671 and 1721, first by the Flemish printer Johann Baptist Hacque, and after his death in 1678, by his brother-in-law, Johann van Ghelen, a native of Antwerp, who often signed his editions as an "Italian printer". Two issues appeared weekly, on Wednesdays and Saturdays: *Il corriere ordinario* (the regular courier), dedicated almost entirely to international events, and *Il foglio aggiunto all'ordinario* (the added paper to the ordinary), with news about the Habsburg Empire and Vienna, along with other information from abroad. Sometimes a *foglio straordinario* (extraordinary paper) was published, which included other news or an extensive account of an important event. Each of the three components of the newspaper was printed on a single sheet, on one or two columns. *Il Corriere Ordinario* was essentially an official journal, protected by the privilege of printing and containing a selection of information, strongly controlled by censorship[1] and became a useful tool in the fight against French propaganda.[2] In Italy, *Il Corriere Ordinario*, like other non-periodic reports printed in Vienna, was an important resource for procuring news about Central and Eastern Europe, and was also used as a source for compiling other publications.[3]

The annual papers printed in a year were reunited in a volume, which received the title *Avvisi italiani, ordinarii e straordinarii*. The information we will analyse in this study is extracted from the extraordinary papers or the added papers, included in volumes eight and nine, dedicated to the events of 1691,[4] respectively 1692,[5] which culminated with the conquest of Oradea by the Habsburgs.

These newspapers are similar to other publications through which the West rediscovered Central and Eastern Europe, as the Habsburgs, after the Ottoman's siege of Vienna (1683), won resounding victories against the Sublime Porte, taking control of the former territories of the Kingdom of Hungary. The defeat of the Ottomans under the walls of the imperial city marked the breaking of balance between the two great powers and the beginning of the inexorable retreat of Ottoman presence in Central and Eastern Europe. Thus, the Habsburgs gave up their attempts of hegemony in Central and Western Europe and concentrated their forces and attention, unhindered, to the east, the imperialists conquering, one by one, Visegrád, Pest (1684), Gran (Esztergom), Neuhaüsel (Érsekújvár/Nové Zámky), Buda, Seghedin (Szeged) (1686) and Belgrad (1688).[6]

Oradea in the Context of the Habsburg Offensive in Central and South-East Europe at the End of the Seventeenth Century

On 9 May 1688, due to the pressure exerted by the Habsburg troops led by General Caraffa, the Transylvanian Diet gathered at Făgăraş (Fogaras/Fogarasch)

---

1 Rudj Gorian, "Il Corriere ordinario," In *Asburgo. Quattro secoli di governo in una contea di confine, 1500–1918*, ed. Marina Bressan (Gorizia: Edizioni della Laguna – Centro ricerche turismo e cultura di Gorizia, 2015), 111.

2 Nina Lamal, "A transnational newspaper venture. Publishing an Italian Newspaper in Habsburg Vienna (1671–1700)," *Quaerendo* 49, no. 3 (November 2019): 228.

3 Mario Infelise, *Prima dei giornali. Alle origini della pubblica informazione (secoli XVI e XVII)* (Roma-Bari: Editori Laterza, 2002), 128.

4 *Avisi italiani, ordinarii, e straordinarii, dell'anno 1691* (Vienna: Appresso Gio. Van Ghelen, 1691).

5 *Avisi italiani, ordinarii, e straordinarii, dell'anno 1692* (Vienna: Appresso Gio. Van Ghelen, 1692).

6 Géza Pálffy, *Hungary Between Two Empires 1526–1711*, trans. David Robert Evans (Bloomington: Indiana University Press, 2021), 219–28.

decided to break the ties of suzerainty with the Ottomans. On these legal bases, thanks in particular to the army, which excluded the conduct of free negotiations, Transylvania recognized the authority of the Vienna.[7]

The first attempts to liberate Oradea from Ottoman rule, which had been take in 1660 from the Principality of Transylvania, took place during the campaign of late 1685 and early 1686, when General Antonio Caraffa recaptured the fortress of Sâniob (Szentjobb) and General Heissler intended to besiege the fortress of Oradea, but in the absence of sufficient military forces he abandoned the initiative. On 16 August 1686, Lieutenant-Colonel Corbelli attacked the outskirts of Oradea, and in October, at the same time with Corbelli's attack on Olosig (Érolaszi/ Schwäbisch Wallendorf), Major Strozzi ambushed a formation of Turkish soldiers heading for Salonta (Szalonta) to collect taxes. Small skirmishes in the area were also recorded during the years 1687 and 1688.

In the spring of 1689, a Hungarian detachment, which was tasked with interrupting communications between Oradea and Gyula, conquered the fortress of Batăr (Bátor), favouring the advance of imperial troops to the south of Bihor (Bihar) County and thus the encirclement of Oradea. Beiuş (Belényes) remained the only major Ottoman possession in the area. Finding out that the Pasha of Oradea was waiting for an important transport from there, on 16 June 1689 General Corbelli attacked the settlement which surrendered on 30 July. Corbelli was later sent to southern Hungary, and the command of the imperial troops was taken over by General Leopold Schlick, who had to prepare a decisive siege of Oradea. On 3 July, the commander of the Hungarian troops, Tunyogi Sámuel, along with his subordinates began digging trenches near the fortress. Soon after, the 1.200 Turkish soldiers from the garrison attacked them by surprise. The skirmish resulted in many losses on both sides, even the Hungarian commander Tunyogi was killed in combat.[8]

In the summer of 1690, the Ottoman defenders of Oradea received news about the defeat of the Austrian troops at Zărneşti. At the head of an army of 6.000 men, Imré Thököly entered Transylvania on 21 August 1690 and with the help of Constantin Brâncoveanu, the prince of Wallachia, Ottoman and Tatar troops, defeated the imperial army and took General Donat Heissler prisoner.[9] The Diet

7 Jean Nouzille, *Transilvania. Zona di contatti e conflitti* (Roma: Edizione Columbus, 1998), 209.

8 Mihai Georgiţă, "Asediul cetăţii Oradea (1691–1692)," *Crisia*, no. 31 (2001): 73–5.

9 Constantin Rezachevici, *Constantin Brâncoveanu – Zărneşti 1690 –* (Bucureşti: Editura Andreas, 1989), 183–208.

of Transylvania, convened on 15 September 1690 at Cristian, near Sibiu, elected Thököly as prince of Transylvania, thus confirming the sultan's decision.[10] On 8 June, Süleyman II appointed Thököly to rule the Principality of Transylvania. However, Thököly's reign was short-lived and on 25 October he was defeated, forced to abandon Transylvania and take refuge in Wallachia.

Meanwhile the Turks inside the fortress of Oradea received unexpected help from Prince Galga, the son of the Tatar khan. On the Christmas Eve of 1690, at the head of 40.000 men, Galga managed to break through the imperial blockade and supply Oradea with food, so that the soldiers and the inhabitants of the town were able to continue their resistance. A decisive siege of Oradea was planned for 1691, after the situation in the war theatre of southern Hungary, where the Ottoman counter-offensive was gaining ground, had been resolved. The victory of the Ottomans at Belgrade in 1690 gave the Vizier Mustafa Köprülu confidence that he would succeed in reclaiming all the lost territories. Aware of the danger, the Court of Vienna sent most of its troops from the Rhine region to Hungary, and named Margrave Ludwig von Baden as commander. He was joined from Transylvania by General Veterani with 12.000 men and from Brandenburg by a corps of 6.000 soldiers, under the command of General Hans Albrecht von Barfus, along with other troops from the Habsburg Empire. In July 1691 Baden had at his disposal a consistent military force of 40.000 people. The victory of Salankemen (Stari Slankamen/Szalánkemén), on 19 August 1691, resulting in the death of Vizier Köprülu, paved the way for the Habsburg conquest of Oradea. Leading an army of 14.000 men, Ludwig von Baden headed for the town situated on banks of the Crişul Repede River, in September.[11]

1691 – The Beginning of the Siege

From the beginning of the year, the *Extraordinary Papers*, sent every three days, recorded the continuous engagements between the Ottomans and the Habsburgs. The report published in Vienna on 21 January states that "about 800 Turks rode out of Oradea and headed for Debrecen, to act in detriment of our people",[12] and in the one dated on 1 March about the defeat of "a party beyond the Tisza near Debrecen by the Turks and rebels", who were heading to Oradea with "40 of our

---

10 Susana Andea, "Evoluţii politice în secolul al XVII-lea. De la Ştefan Bocskai la Mihail Apafi," In *Istoria Transilvaniei*, vol. II (*de la 1541 până la 1711*), ed. Ioan-Aurel Pop, Thomas Nägler, Magyari András (Cluj-Napoca: Institutul Cultural Român, 2005), 120.

11 Georgiţă, "Asediul," 75–6.

12 *Avisi*, 8 (21 January 1691).

own, Germans and Hungarians, taken prisoner", but the latter "were reached by another party of ours…and meeting these victorious Turks he defeated and liberated not only our 40 prisoners, but he cut many barbarians to pieces, took many prisoners and captured 150 horses".[13]

The report printed on 1 April announced Thököly's move to Oradea, where "Sultan Galga had left 8.000 Tartars", and the 24 May report confirmed that "there were followers of Teckely [Thököly] in the proximity of Oradea, even though he had not yet arrived, but only Petrozzi [Petrőczy István], who threatened to intervene", while "the Turks from Oradea left the fortress with a few pieces of artillery…apparently, to attack the Lugoj castle".[14] On 31 May, it is noted "that Petrozzi (one of Thököly main followers) was in Oradea, trying to tempt and persuade Hungarians faithful to Her Majesty to deviate from their devotion to the House of Austria",[15] but he did not find too many adherents, as the 1 July issue headlined.

On 8 July, another event with repercussions on the unfolding of the hostilities is evoked: "the army being sent to Oradea, it found, half an hour away from that bridge, 16 carts full of salt and flour, which were going to Oradea, they were all captured and taken by our troops to Kalo (Nagykálló), without the Turks having any attempt to leave the fortress to prevent them".[16]

On 30 September, in the *extraordinary paper* printed in Vienna, it was recorded that on the way to Oradea "the Count of Aversperg [Otto von Auersperg] met and defeated…600 rebels, killed over 100, took 30 or 40 prisoners"[17] so that on 11 October it was announced that on 26 September Count Schlick "advanced with an army in the islands between the rivers Criş and Peţa…and at noon the count surprised the Turks, who had a large number of animals in the field, defeated the guards and captured over 900 heads", without the enemy being able to recover anything.[18] In a report published in Vienna on 14 October, the public was informed that "General Heissler, released by Thököly,[19] was in Sibiu, and

13 *Avisi*, 8 (1 March 1691).
14 *Avisi*, 8 (1 April 1691).
15 *Avisi*, 8 (21 May 1691).
16 *Avisi*, 8 (8 July 1691).
17 *Avisi*, 8 (30 September 1691).
18 *Avisi*, 8 (11 October 1691).
19 General Heissler was released in exchange for Thököly's wife, Elena Zrinyi, who heroically defended the fortress of Muncaci (Munkács/Mukacevo) from the siege of the Imperials for three years, until January 1688, when surrendered to General Caraffa, Nouzille, *Transilvania*, 208.

was expected to join the army in a short time".[20] On 18 October it was noted that "there is no fresh news about the march of the imperial army to Oradea…despite the long and difficult road, which due to frequent swamps and waters required bridges to be built in many places, the news of the arrival is expected daily, the fortress will be attacked by force, for this purpose they brought not only a large contingent of heavy artillery and mortars, but also important supplies of military fireworks of unusual invention,[21] with which (with divine help and favourable weather) in a short time that unfaithful occupants should submit to the victorious armies of His Majesty".[22]

The report published in Vienna on 21 October summarizes the military operations carried out between 10 and 14 of the same month: "On the 10th the cavalry arrived in Bihar [Biharia]", near Oradea; "on the 11th, while waiting for the infantry, which arrived at noon, the Prince of Baden with about 200 cavalry went to inspect the fortress and its surroundings", but "the enemy fired the cannon several times against ours". On the same day, in the evening "the heavy artillery, which remained at Zollnock [Szolnok]…was led on the battlefield by the Prince of Vaudemont, together with 100 carts full of ammunition and other necessary supplies, the convoy being accompanied by 1.000 horses". On the 12 arrived "the general of the cavalry, the count of Stirum [Styrumb], with 1.000 officers… followed by all the cavalry and infantry", and on the 13 at noon "12 battalions, namely one of Baden, one of old Stahremberg, one of Etting, one of de Houchin [Heuschin], one of Guido Stahremberg,[23] one of Archinto, one of Amenzaga, one of Chizzola, one of Herberstein and the three electors of Brandenburg, all under the command of Lieutenant General Barfus and Count Guido of Stahremberg", all "took up positions in a valley near the city, and in the evening the trenches occupied by 1.500 people were opened and improved a battery to the gate of the stockade, located beyond Criş and Olosig…and on the morning of the 14 he

20 *Avisi*, 8 (14 October 1691).

21 The document refers to the flammable material, which could not be extinguished, invented by the Franciscan monk Tüzes Gábriel, which was successfully used in the siege of Buda and Esztergom. The famous pyrotechnician was helped by 21 fireworkers in the arson actions of the Oradea fortress, Georgiță, "Asediul," 79.

22 *Avisi*, 8 (18 October 1691).

23 Guido von Starhemberg (1657–1737) fought under his cousin Ernst Rüdiger von Starhemberg (1638–1701) during the siege of Vienna (1683), then followed the imperial army in campaigns against the Ottoman Empire and participating in the siege of Buda (1686), at the battle of Mohács (1687), at the siege of Belgrade (1688), at the battles of Salankemen (1691) and Zenta (1697).

started firing with 6 pieces of heavy artillery towards the stockade, the enemy responded with cannons, muskets and harquebuses".[24]

On 28 October the papers published the information contained in the letters sent on the 19 from the camp near Oradea, regarding the operations carried out in the previous days: "on the 16, at 6 o'clock in the evening, the city and the stockade beyond the river Criş were attacked, an action in which the Hungarians of Colonel Mollner [Molnár] stood out…who managed to cross the fence". In addition, "other Hungarians broke the fence with axes, and thus managed to enter", along with the actions of German musketeers who attacked the gate, "which was half destroyed by our cannons, and cut the rest, and with the loss of a small number of people also took possession of the stockade, where a small mortar was found, the Turks retreating to another town, beyond the Cris". The attacks continued in order to deprive the Ottomans of any moment of rest. Thus, "on the 17 our army crossed the other side of the river", and "on the 19 they positioned the hussars behind the castle, where trenches will be dug to attack the enemy from that side as well; they will even try to empty the ditch". The report also gives an account of the situation in which Oradea was at that time: "the stockade, now in our hands, has a wooden fence with a ditch on this side, it is separated from the other city by the river Criş, which passes through the middle of both: and on the left, beyond the city is the castle, which has a regular shape, with 5 bastions, quite high, surrounded by water, which flows around the other town".[25]

The article published in Vienna on 1 November resumes the series of military operations carried out between 14 and 24 October, providing more precise details, but we reproduce only those mentioned after 20 October. Even if "nothing remarkable happened in 19 and 20, they just continued to advance with the preparations and perfect the batteries, on the same night the one in the Olosig stockade was finished, 11 large cannons were placed" on the 21 "they started to fire with them", and "on the 22 approximately 2.000 Serbs arrived in the camp, returning from Transylvania both on foot and on horseback", in the same day "having finished the other battery beyond Criş, where 11 large cannons were also placed", so "it was started from the morning of the 23 to constantly fire on the fortress with 22 cannons, and a breach was made, which allowed the launch of an attack in 24 hours; but the enemy did not wait for this to happen, around 3 o'clock in the afternoon he set fire to several places in the city, the flames spreading everywhere". However, "our people advanced and took possession of

24 *Avisi*, 8 (21 October 1691).
25 *Avisi*, 8 (28 October 1691).

that place, capturing many animals, and on this occasion 100 Serbs living there were saved, who would have risked being killed by the Turks".[26] It is also stated that "on the 23 General Heisler arrived at the camp near Oradea".[27] Thus, more decisive actions were resorted to against those in the citadel, as published in the 8 November issue: "on the 26 the fortress began to be heavily bombarded, so that the heads, arms and legs of the Turks were often seen flying in the air, with terrible screams and noises".[28] Unfortunately, "on the same night, while going to inspect the places, Sergeant Major Lebenstein [Löwenstein] was wounded by a cannonball"[29] as reported in the 11 November article. "On the 27 the besiegers fired 18 mortars at once", and another regrettable event is also mentioned: "the next night, lieutenant-colonel of the Amenzaga Regiment, Sig. Tûrck died". "On the 28 it was continued not only with the bombardment and the incessant throwing of fire, but a new battery was raised, in order to leave the enemy defenceless".[30]

On 15 November, it was announced that "many Turkish flags had arrived in Vienna from the imperial army, partly from the Battle of Salankemen, partly captured at Oradea", but also that "on Monday the Count of Aversperg will return to the army, it's believed, with instructions from the Prince of Baden regarding the winter quarters". At the same time, the news coming from the camp of Oradea "confirms that on the 29 the 2 batteries were finished, in the same morning the bombardment of the enemy's lines of defence started; and the harassment of the fortress continued, most of it being on fire, which lasted over 6 hours".[31]

The paper of 22 November presents the contents of new documents: "Letters dated on 10 November from the imperial camp at Oradea, under Prince Ludovico di Baden, confirm that, despite the cold and humid weather, the bombing of the fortress continued; but the enemy would not surrender". Therefore, "a large fort of ours raises 5–600 steps from the gate of the fortress, where during the winter 1.000 German infantry and cavalry troops will be hosted; and the Olosig stockade will be guarded by Hungarian soldiers…other German regiments, the Serbian and Hungarian militias will be stationed both in Debrecen and in other places near Oradea".[32]

---

26 *Avisi*, 8 (1 November 1691).

27 In other documents, the arrival is mentioned on 24 October, Georgiță, "Asediul," 79.

28 *Avisi*, 8 (8 November 1691).

29 Major Löwenstein was seriously wounded by a bullet fired from the fortress, Georgiță, "Asediul," 80.

30 *Avisi*, 8 (11 November 1691).

31 *Avisi*, 8 (15 November 1691).

32 *Avisi*, 8 (22 November 1691).

The harsh climatic conditions determined the Habsburgs to abandon the prospect of a decisive attack and opt for the establishment of a blockade, under the leadership of General Auersperg. Ludwig von Baden established his headquarters at Debrecen for a few days, where the bulk of the troops rested. Cavalry General Styrumb marched with his regiment to Vienna, and was replaced by the Dorische Cavalry Regiment and over 100 of knights.[33]

On 29 November, in Vienna the information received from a Turkish deserter[34] who left the fortress of Oradea was published, "who arrived here on Monday with a courier, it was found that in the fortress there were 1.400 soldiers: they lack supplies, but also wood, so they have to live in cellars and in the ruins of the walls, but still they hope to be saved, or at least to receive supplies, otherwise they will not be able to last too long".[35]

On 6 December, the document sent to the public announced the end of the campaign, so that "imperial regiments and national troops are distributed in the quarters, both in Upper Hungary and especially in the areas near Oradea". However, the "acquisition of what is necessary to continue in force the conquest of the fortress" is not interrupted.[36]

1692 – The Second Phase of the Siege

Military actions resumed in the spring of 1692, after the fortress was completely surrounded by General Auersperg's troops during winter. On 5 April, the cavalry general, Donath Heissler, baron von Heitersheim, was appointed commander of the army. Several military contingents were mobilized, both infantry and cavalry, including some of Veterani's regiments stationed in Transylvania, those of Baron Pfeffershofen operating in the Lipova (Lippa) and Sătmar (Szatmár) area, the Styrumb, Heissler, Truchsess regiments, Schlick, and those of Hungarian and Serbian hussars. The siege was resumed on 7 May 1692, as Habsburg artillery began to break through the defences. After water was evacuated from the ditches, the besiegers built a mining gallery towards one of the bastions. The operation was successful and on 30 May one of the bastions was severely damaged.

33 Georgiță, "Asediul," 85–6.

34 Turkish soldier Hussein, who was in charge of ammunition in the fortress, considered a prisoner during interrogation, taken from Oradea to Debrecen on 20 November Georgiță, "Asediul," 84.

35 *Avisi*, 8 (29 November 1691).

36 *Avisi*, 8 (6 December 1691).

A general attack on the fortress was planned for 5 June, but it did not take place, as the Ottomans decided to surrender.[37]

During the year 1692, between January and July, information regarding the military operations against the Ottomans for the capture of Oradea was published in 50 issues of the *Ordinary Courier*. In January we have seven extraordinary papers containing news about the events in Oradea. For example, on 3 January, it was announced that "a Turk was captured again, who along with 4 others, including an officer, found a way to get out of the fortress during the night and travelled on unmarked roads to Gyula, and from there to Timişoara (Temesvár/Temeschwar), from where the official went to Adrianople (Edirne), to expose the situation of the fortress and ask for help".[38] He was captured on his return, without bringing any news of any help in favour of those inside the fortress. More consistent is the information provided in the 6 January edition, when it was confirmed that "there was a revolt of janissaries and soldiers against senior officials, due to long shortages, but persisting in their decision not to surrender, 300 decided to leave the fortress on the first favourable opportunity and use force to get past our guards". The harsh living conditions led many to abandon the citadel: "men and women come out every day, all confirming that with each passing day the lack of food deepens, having already consumed all of the rations in the warehouse, there was only a small amount of wheat half burned and destroyed by bombs in another warehouse; as well as some millet residues, which being too old, rotten and mouldy, makes the bread not too good and very bitter".[39]

During February, the Ottoman response seemed to diminish, as it appears in the report sent on the third day of the month: "It is no longer heard that the Turks from Oradea try to get out of the fortress, or even shoot at us, as they did before; on the contrary, it has been found that the dissensions between the Pasha and the janissaries have increased, and instead of continuing to encourage the garrison, as imposed on him by the Porte, they advise him to think better of a good surrender, knowing that, in reality, there is little hope of receiving help".[40] According to five other extraordinary papers published during the same month, the situation of the Ottomans worsened due to the lack of food and the promised help, even if "the enemy made efforts to gather a large number of people near Timişoara to try to bring some food to Oradea",[41] as headlined on 21 February.

37 Georgiță, "Asediul," 93, 99.
38 *Avisi*, 9 (3 January 1692).
39 *Avisi*, 9 (6 January 1692).
40 *Avisi*, 9 (3 February 1692).
41 *Avisi*, 9 (21 February 1692).

Instead, the Habsburgs are the ones who received war supplies, according to the report sent on the 24: "letters were received from Debrecen on the 12 of this month, in which it was announced that from Upper Hungary, through Tokaj, 300 cannon shots were sent to our fort in Oradea".[42]

During March, eight extraordinary papers were printed, one every three days, each containing information about the evolution of the Habsburg-Ottoman confrontations for the control of Oradea. The one of 2 March presents the information contained in the letters sent on 19 February from Debrecen, regarding the Ottomans' attempt to break the blockade: "that the Turks from Oradea Mare, after making a big noise at night with many cannon shots, during the day they attacked the Hajduk guarding the fort near the bridge on the Criș, but they were immediately reinforced by Lieutenant-Colonel Bauman with German troops, each consisting of 50 people, who, after a long confrontation and loss of life on the part of the enemies, drove them back". The report continues to present the testimonies of the deserters, who reported that "the shootings during the night had no other purpose than to terrify our troops and to animate their own, and during these shootings the Pasha gathered the janissaries and other officers in a house not far from the dungeon, in the tower, for consultations; and a cannon shot fired by our soldiers dropped in their midst causing them damage and scattering them". All deserters confirmed that those in charge of the garrison decided to: "surrender within 15 days, if the help they had been waiting for would not come". But nothing is heard about the aid, the *Courier* continues, instead "the Count of Aversperg...distributed a significant amount of money to the Hungarian troops on the Olosig stockade".[43]

The 6 March issue of the newspaper contains the news received from Debrecen on 22 February regarding the actions of the Count of Aversperg, the Count of Truchses and other soldiers "who went to the fort of Oradea to accelerate military operations against the barbarian leaders". At the same time, another bridge was built over the Criș, "our guards remaining vigilant, receiving supplies for a few days, to face the possible attempts of the Ottomans to break through the blockade".[44]

On 9 March, the pages of the newspaper reproduced the information contained in the letters dated in 26 February and sent from Debrecen, confirming "the return to our fort of a soldier, the so-called *Forierschuz* of the Labatscheck

42 *Avisi*, 9 (24 February 1692).
43 *Avisi*, 9 (2 March 1692).
44 *Avisi*, 9 (6 March 1692).

Regiment, who two months ago had deserted us and had fled to the citadel of Oradea, he, as well as a Brandenburg drummer who came with him, but also others who arrived on the same day, a few hours earlier, all unanimously reported that the Turks in the citadel remained constant in their desire to expect help; at most rejoicing that they have supplies for a few more weeks, but if it is found that this is true, it will be seen shortly". Regarding the situation on the field, the public is informed that "the rivers Criş and Peţa swelled so much that you could not cross them without boats, moreover the connecting bridge between the Olosig stockade and the Great City was destroyed and carried away by the waters", and the Turks "took advantage of the opportunity"[45] to attack the Habsburg troops but were rejected. During the confrontations the Baron de Chlim, sergeant major of the Amenzaga Regiment was killed. We also find out that the Habsburgs were engaged in rebuilding the bridges in order to re-establish the connections with the observation posts, and the Ottoman help cannot be mentioned for the time being, as it was impossible for it to arrive due to the floods.

On 13 March, also through letters received from Debrecen, we learn that the Count of Aversperg, "after he began repairing the bridges over the river Criş, to ensure the connection between the Great City and the Olosig stockade, and gave other necessary provisions",[46] returned to Debrecen on 25 February, on the 28 he attended the interrogation of a Turk brought from Oradea, from whom, however, despite the torture he was subjected to, they did not manage to find out anything. In the last edition of the month, on 30 March, it was announced that General Truckses left Debrecen on the 14 for Oradea, "arriving safely, together with his men, at the Olosig stockade", so that on the 15 the Count of Aversperg was supposed to arrive in Oradea, but his arrival was delayed due to the waters that had not receded.[47]

An attempt to help the defenders of Oradea was mentioned in the 3 April issue: "about 1.000 Turks had gathered near Gyula, who had been ordered to try with all their might to get as many janissaries as possible to Oradea, to strengthen the garrison reduced (according to the deserters) to 500 soldiers", but "in order to prevent any similar attempt, General Conte Truckes was prepared with his men at the Olosig stockade".[48] On 16 April, it was announced that there would be concerted attacks by Habsburg troops, in which sense General Heissler

45 *Avisi*, 9 (9 March 1692).
46 *Avisi*, 9 (13 March 1692).
47 *Avisi*, 9 (30 March 1692).
48 *Avisi*, 9 (3 April 1692).

was sent and a general call to arms was decreed. On 24 April it was added that "those in the fortress continue to use heavy artillery, sometimes injuring some of our soldiers", but that there was no hope of help, instead "our people built another fort in Oradea, where the locals worked, being sent by an engineer from Debrecen to finish it as soon as possible, in order to stop the attempts to break the blockade by the enemy". In addition, "the imperial regiments had already been ordered to move, and General Conte de Aversperg was about to leave Debrecen for Oradea".[49] On 27 April it was confirmed that "the march of troops from Debrecen, as well as from other parts where the imperial regiments were encamped, and it is believed that the effective assault of the fortress will soon begin, with the engineers already leaving to carry out the works".[50] Meanwhile, "the Turks have shown their original intention, implying that they want to fight to the end, so they have repaired the destroyed places in their bastions, equipping them with gabions" – as the report from 4 May confirmed – and they seem to have enough gunpowder, and do not save at all, often firing up to 150 or more cannon shots in a day: it has been observed, however, that the gunpowder itself is damp and of poor quality, as it is necessary for a double charge when they want to shoot straight or far, and it is also seen that they do not have too many cannonballs available, because they are looking, with all their efforts, for the ones that ours shoot in the fortress". In the meantime, the Habsburggs "had built a new fort under the mountain known as St. Stephen, on the banks of the Criș River, not without great consternation to the Turks, as it could do them great damage. The small river had actually been cut off, and so had the Peța River; thus being manufactured the devices to remove the water from the ditch".[51] On 15 May, the *paper added to the usual* reproduces the information recorded in the letters sent from Debrecen on the third of the same month, confirming the arrival of General Heissler on 26 April: "and then together with the Count General of Aversperg and General Truchses…arrived on the 30th, entered our fort and escorted by two companies of hussars visited all the places, despite the cannon shots from the Turks, which did no harm". The information from the letters brought by a courier and dated at Oradea, 7 May, confirm the intensification of military actions: "From the 1st the trenches were opened and advanced so much that on the 7th the attack on the left flank reached up to 30 steps from the ditch of the fortress, and the one on the right to 60; work has been done on the cannon

49 *Avisi*, 9 (24 April 1692).
50 *Avisi*, 9 (27 April 1692).
51 *Avisi*, 9 (4 May 1692).

batteries and mortar, which will be probably ready on the 15th and to remove, if possible, the water from the ditch; and that in the meantime the regiments encamped beyond the Tisza and the heavy artillery, with ammunition, sent from the depots and arsenals of Upper Hungary, with great solicitude, were expected by General Marquis Nigrelli".[52] In 3 days, other news was published about the siege of Oradea: "with the arrival of the two regiments of dragons Schlick and Laport, the old fort, where the Hajduk had been staying during the winter, was occupied, then the trenches were opened on the 2nd", and from the 3rd the construction of two redoubts facing the Golden Bastion and the Ciunt Bastion began. The report continues with the development of military operations: "on the 4th the trenches continued to advance, which the enemy opposed not only by continuous cannon fire, but at 9 o'clock attempted an incursion with 200 men against our new posts, which, after several confrontations were rejected, causing deaths on both sides". The public is also informed about the events of the 5th, when "the enemy did not shoot much, neither with cannons nor muskets, and shortly after with the artillery they were mostly using stones, so it was concluded that the Turks may be missing large cannonballs".[53] On 22 May, the newspaper published in Vienna resumed the information from the letters sent from Oradea on the 10th, according to which the Turks in the fortress tried on the seventh day of the month to break through the siege, "with 200 men against our outposts, which were immediately defeated without any effect, the lines having already been perfected so well that little damage could be done by their incursions". The letters also mention the arrival, on the same day, of a miller,[54] "who promises to leave the enemy without water, turning it elsewhere".[55]

The 25 May edition summarizes what happened between day 7 and 13 of the month. Thus, "on 7 May the Ottomans fired their artillery and muskets, 30 Germans and Hajduk were wounded or killed, among the last was Captain Barts of the Schlik Regiment". On the next day, in the morning, "300 Turks left the fortress, cut some bushes and fences and took them inside, and in the afternoon they started firing with the cannon, carrying larger guns on the bastions in order to attack". The artillery fire continued on both sides until the 12 May when

52 *Avisi*, 9 (15 May 1692).

53 *Avisi*, 9 (18 May 1692).

54 Other documentary sources mention the arrival of a miller on May 20, who promised General Heissler that he would show him how to get water out of the ditch, as he had witnessed in 1660 when the drainage canal was built between the Bethlen Bastion and Peța, Georgiță, "Asediul," 98.

55 *Avisi*, 9 (22 May 1692).

"there was not much shooting with the cannon, but we worked on the batteries and removing the water from the ditch", but in the evening "the Turks fired with artillery and other weapons, some of ours being killed and wounded", also "on the 13…the Turks went out at noon with about 500 men against the Hajduk who were fighting, but they were soon rejected by our people".[56]

On 29 May, the newspaper presents the military operations for the conquest of Oradea, starting with the 13 and continuing until the 19 of the month. On 13 May "on the same evening, to the north, our people slipped close to the ditch, and the Turks threw many stones and arrows, so that many soldiers were wounded, including 3 Hungarian captains and a colonel named Thesle, who after 2 hours entrusted his soul to the Creator, and he was replaced by another named Mr. Pagoschi". After two days of calm, "on the 16 they started firing large-calibre cannons at enemy cannons, killing two good gunners and three others wounded". On the 17, "when our troops fired incessantly", was the day when "a Turkish deserter came and reported that the Ottomans were waiting for help, that a few days had passed since they had sent the so-called Hassan Saim, who in 15 days had to bring news about the aid, and they gave him rotten millet to show others the difficult conditions they were facing, millet that would have helped them for another month", moreover, "the deserter's horse was slaughtered, the meat sold for 400 Hungarian florins, also a cow was sold for 120 florins". On 18 May, "large-caliber cannons were fired all day to make a breach", but "the miller in charge of removing the water from the ditch was killed". In the same day, the arrival of the Heister regiment was announced, "Immediately a captain and 2 lieutenants went to the fortifications, where 500 people are exchanged daily". On 19 May, the offensive continued, and results were soon visible: "2 large breaches were obtained, and so much progress was made with the removal of the water that it was no deeper than half a man, so it was thought that the assault would soon be possible", especially since the Houschin and Herberstein regiments had also arrived at Oradea.[57]

The newspaper published on 1 June contains information about the continued efforts of the Habsburg troops for the conquest of the fortress. Thus, "the number of people in the fortifications was increased to 1.100…the besieged came twice on the 21 May with small boats across the ditch, and with some poles they tore down some gabions and fascines…and in these actions some of our soldiers were wounded or killed", another battery of 4 mortars was finished.[58] Four days later,

56 *Avisi*, 9 (25 May 1692).
57 *Avisi*, 9 (29 May 1692).
58 *Avisi*, 9 (1 June 1692).

the *paper added to the usual* headlined: "Oradea is hit with 16 large cannons of 36 and 24 pounds, in addition to mortars…the wall of the bastions are almost demolished".[59]

The 8 June edition of the *Ordinary Courier* first reproduced the information from the letters received from Sibiu on 24 May, according to which the long-awaited help of the besieged would be on the way, apparently, to save Oradea, but "our men continued on 23 May to make a breach in Oradea, without any notable damage from the enemy", but in the evening "several of our own were injured, including 3 engineers, a captain of the Heister regiment lost a hand and a standard-bearer a leg".[60] On 12 June, the news of the conquest of the city of Oradea was published in Vienna: "to give in to the forces of our brave attackers, they demanded and obtained the capitulation". And for the correct information of the public, the detailed presentation of the events of 27–31 May continues. Therefore, "on the 27, in order to widen the breach, they fiercely continued to fire cannons…throwing bombs and stones inside the fortress", injuring or killing the besieged, and on the 28 the casemates were targeted. On Sunday afternoon the news of the capitulation arrived in Vienna, "because of the rather large breaches, all preparations were made for the general assault, the besieged, on Thursday, 5 July, on the feast of Corpus Christi, displayed white flags and brought the keys, asking to capitulate, as it happened". The victory was celebrated with a Te Deum in the cathedral and triple cannon salvos.[61]

Although the siege was over and the Habsburgs were victorious, in the 19 June issue, additional details were published about the events from 3 to 6 of the same month: "on 3 June, 300 carts arrived with ammunition, continuing the whole day with cannon shots…and in the evening, as well as all night, the works continued in the ditch, where 15 of our people were wounded and killed". On 4 July, "at noon, 5 Turkish officials came out, 2 of whom went forward waving a white handkerchief, and even if they were fired at, they did not give up addressing us, in the end our people advanced towards them and led them to Colonel Molner's quarter, and after being heard by General Heisler and receiving a response to their proposals, they returned to the Citadel, where, after a short stay, they reappeared to negotiate the capitulation, lasting until the night of the meeting, meanwhile, all hostilities on both sides were suspended, and the works ceased". On 5 July, reaching an agreement, General Heissler and other senior officers rode

---

59 *Avisi*, 9 (5 June 1692).
60 *Avisi*, 9 (8 June 1692).
61 *Avisi*, 9 (12 June 1692).

to inspect the entire ditch, and the whole fortress, which was guarded all around by German soldiers, "and our troops worked incessantly to the construction of the bridge to take the enemy's belongings out of the fortress".[62]

New details about what happened on the occasion of the capitulation were made public on 22 June. The successive events are resumed starting with the fourth day, when "the gap was widened a lot, and the gallery under the ditch was ready, all the preparations for the assault were made. The Ottomans sent 4 soldiers with a white flag out of the city at noon to our fortifications to demand a free exit, offering along with their surrender the castles of Papmessù [Pomezeu] and Solanka [Salonta] , General Heisler agreed to their conditions".[63] The capitulation was signed by both sides on 5 July, after which the fortress was given to the Habsburgs, including the war depots and the remaining supplies. The Christian soldiers found "a large quantity of millet and a few crumbs with which the Turks could have survived for several months", and among the weapons, 71 cannons, small and large, 6 so-called howitzers, and 4 small mortars, of which one of 20 pounds was functional", and gunpowder. At the same time, "all Christian slaves were released on 6 July, about 70 in the city, and on the 7 the Turks began to come out…3.000 people together with women and children, among them over 1.000 people with weapons, oxen and only 4 horses left". Figures on the losses suffered by the Imperials are also provided to the public: "During the entire siege, from the beginning of May until June 4, 160 German soldiers were counted dead, and 239 wounded, including senior officers". On 26 June, the news arrived with the letters sent from Oradea on the 14, which announces "that all the Turks have left that garrison, a total of 4.000, and among them 2.000 soldiers, so that the information provided by all the deserters who left the fortress this winter were not confirmed, not even in terms of supplies, because a large amount of grain was found". On 12 June there was a solemn procession for the feast of Corpus Christi, celebrated on the first Thursday after the eighth day of Pentecost, which was attended by General Heisler and all the other officers. During July, sporadic news was published about the fate of the city of Oradea in the possession of the Habsburgs. On 13 July it was reported "that most of its fortifications had been rebuilt".[64]

---

62 *Avisi*, 9 (19 June 1692).

63 For surrender conditions, see *Istoria orașului Oradea*, eds. Liviu Borcea, Gheorghe Gorun (Oradea: Editura Cogito, 1995), p. 157–8; Zoltán Péter Bagi. "Asediul cetății Oradea din anul 1692", In *Studii despre istoria Țării Bihorului*, 7, ed. Teréz Oborni, (Oradea: Fundația Culturală Varadinum, 2020), 24.

64 *Avisi*, 9 (13 July 1692).

Conclusions

Throughout the early modern period Oradea was considered a major strategic point on the frontier between the Ottoman and Habsburg empires. The fortification was initially controlled by the rulers of the Transylvanian Principality but was lost to the Ottomans in 1660. In 1692, after 32 years of Turkish rule, the town and the fortress were taken by the Habsburgs as a result of their successful offensive in Central and South-East Europe.

The sources analysed in this article offer a detailed view on the complex process of conquest and the difficulties of early modern siege warfare. The authors of the Italian *avisi* have clearly identified the early military actions which prepared the actual siege of Oradea, like the conquest of the smaller fortifications in its vicinity. An important aspect revealed by these sources is the organization of the besieging army. All the important phases of a well conducted siege are presented: setting of the blockade, building artillery platforms and forts, long periods of sustained artillery, the building of mining galleries and direct assaults. The complex system of fortification that defended Oradea is presented with accuracy: the fortress (castle) with five bastions, a stockade with a wooden fence and a deep moat filled with water. The sources are also very rich in details regarding the logistic aspects of war. The authors of the reports sent to the *Il Corriere ordinario* understood that lodging, provisions, munitions and the rapid deployment of troops were essential in wining early modern wars.

There are limits to the relevance of these sources. They were, without a doubt, tools of propaganda, and offer a one sided perspective on the events they describe. However, their accuracy is confirmed by other contemporary documents. It is also important to underline the fact that these texts were intended for a large audience which followed with great interest the political and military events that were taking place on the distant frontiers of the empire.

The fortress of Oradea at the end of the seventeenth century, (Țării Crişurilor Museum, Prints and maps collection, inv. 378)

Eastern and Central European Studies

Edited by Christian Gastgeber and Alexandru Simon

Vol. 1 Iulian Mihai Damian / Ioan-Aurel Pop / Mihailo St. Popović / Alexandru Simon (eds.): Italy and Europe´s Eastern Border (1204-1669). 2012.

Vol. 2 Florin Ardelean / Christopher Nicholson / Johannes Preiser-Kapeller (eds.): Between Worlds: The Age of the Jagiellonians. 2013.

Vol. 3 Pour l'amour de Byzance. Hommage à Paolo Odorico. Edité par Christian Gastgeber, Charis Messis, Dan Ioan Mureşan et Filippo Ronconi. 2013.

Vol. 4 Ioan-Aurel Pop: "De manibus Valachorum scismaticorum...". Romanians and Power in the Mediaeval Kingdom of Hungary. The Thirteenth and Fourteenth Centuries. 2013.

Vol. 5 Miia Ijäs: *Res publica* Redefined? The Polish-Lithuanian Transition Period of the 1560s and 1570s in the Context of European State Formation Processes. 2016.

Vol. 6 Florin Nicolae Ardelean / Liviu Cîmpeanu / Romulus Gelu Fodor / Livia Magina (Eds.): From Medieval Frontiers to Early Modern Borders in Central and South-Eastern Europe. 2022.

www.peterlang.com

www.ingramcontent.com/pod-product-compliance
Ingram Content Group UK Ltd.
Pitfield, Milton Keynes, MK11 3LW, UK
UKHW041825100926
8556IPUK00002B/28

9 783631 88011